STONEHENGE

THE STORY OF AN ICON

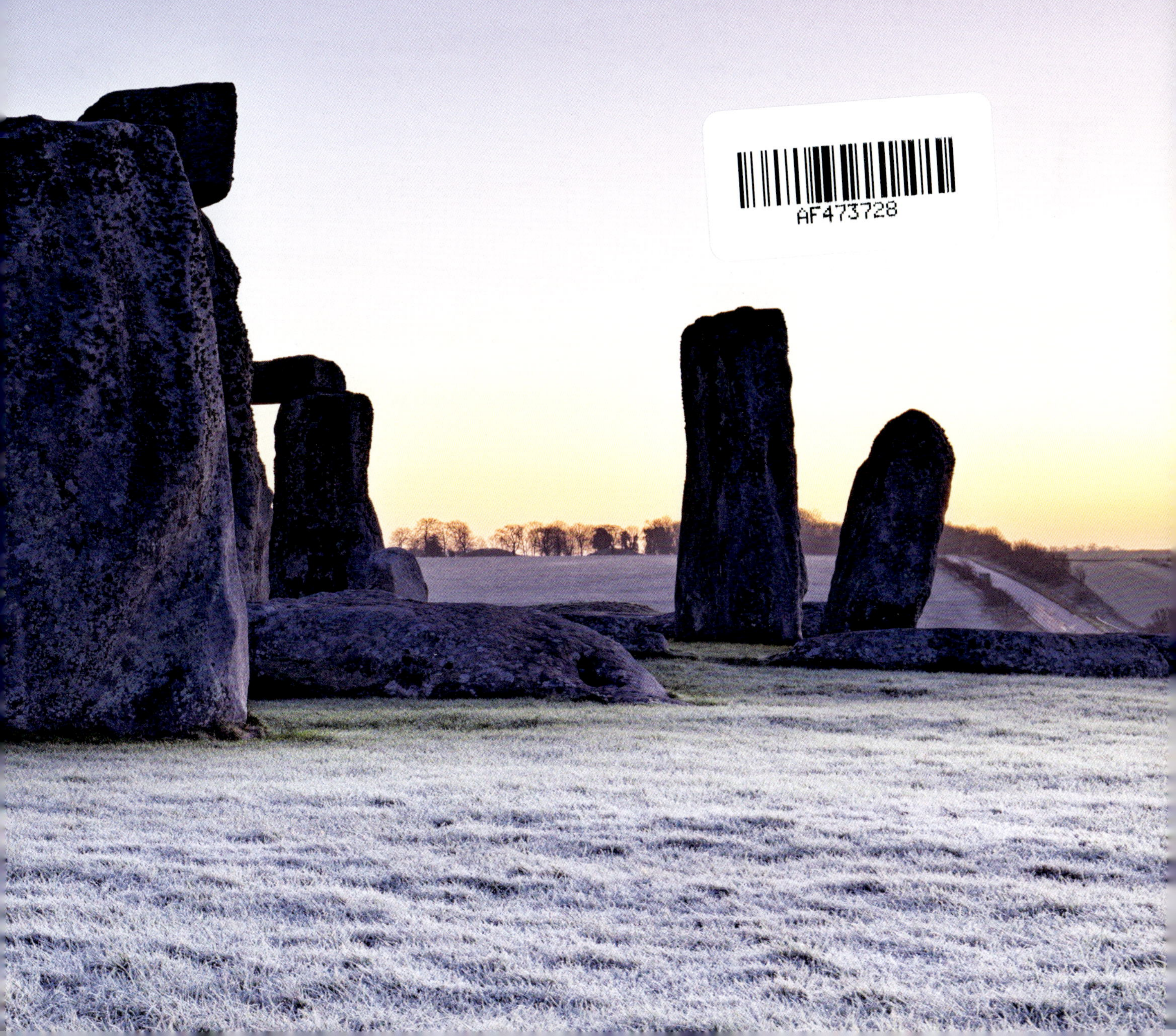

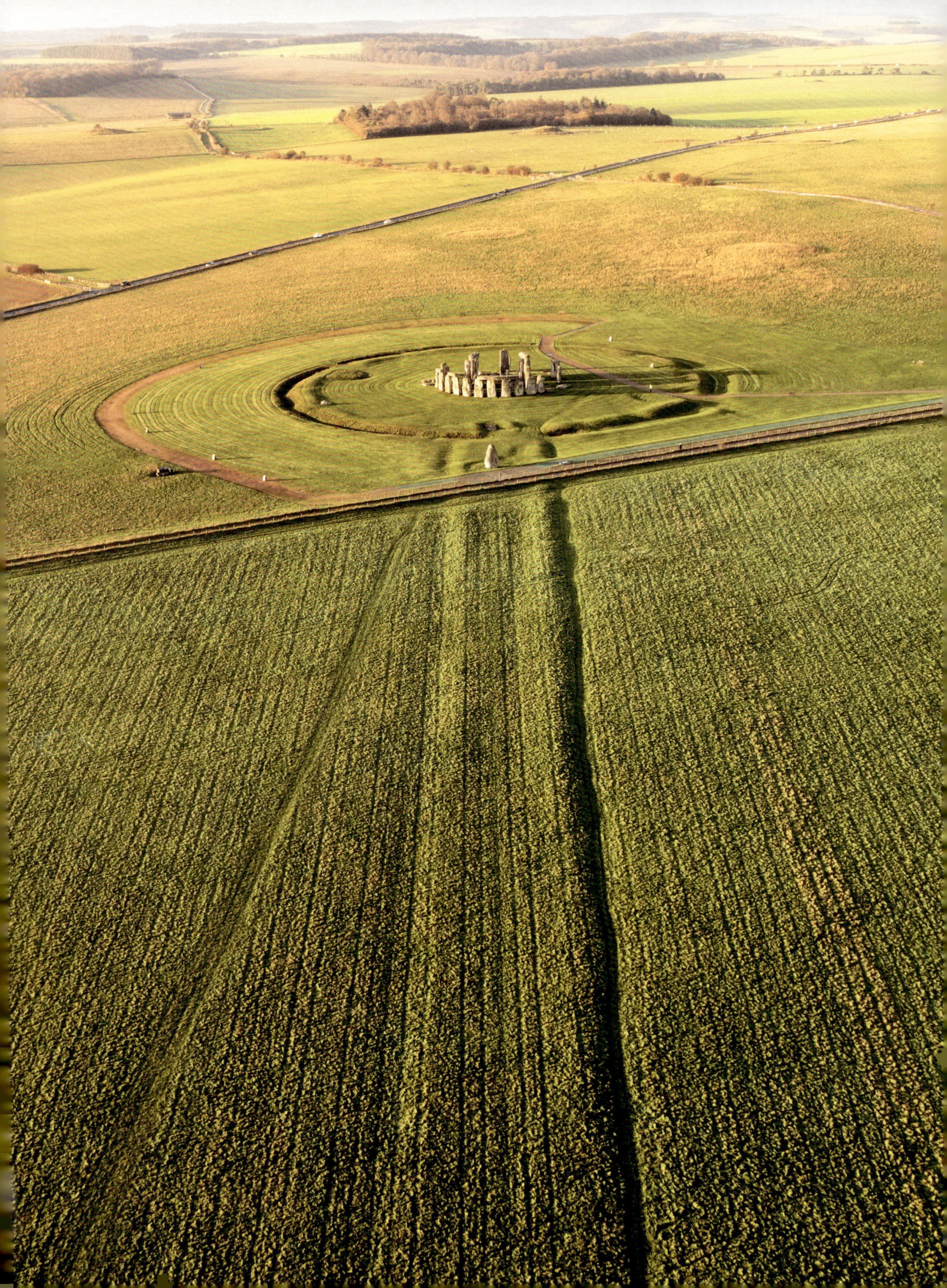

STONEHENGE

THE STORY OF AN ICON

SUSAN GREANEY

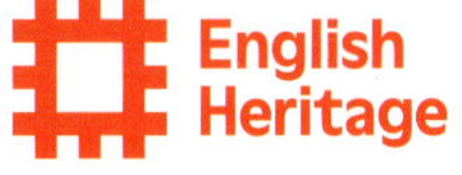

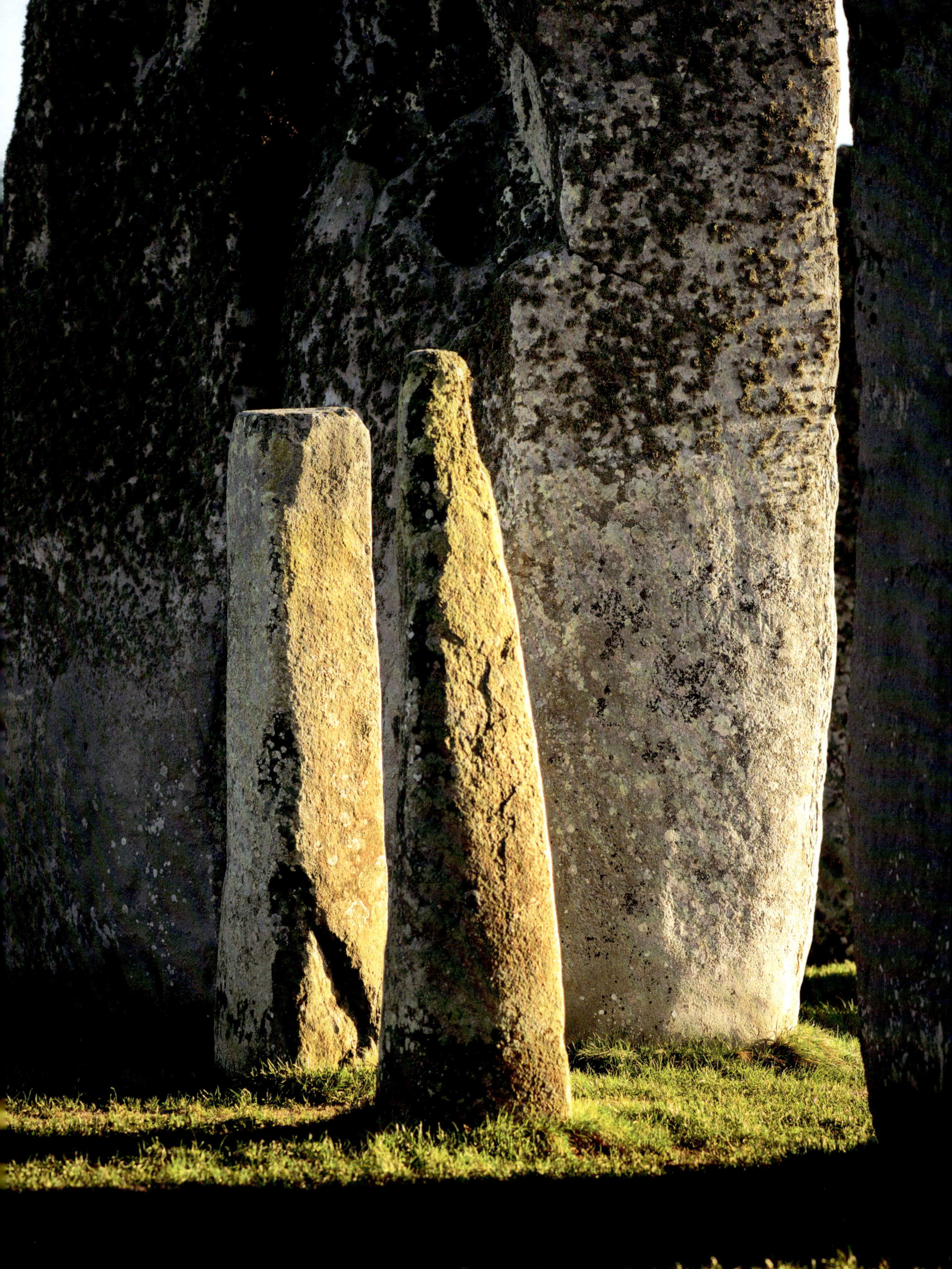

CONTENTS

OPPOSITE Two of the surviving bluestones standing alongside the much larger sarsen stones, clearly showing the size difference between the main two types of stones at Stonehenge.

PREFACE

Stonehenge is the most famous prehistoric monument in the world. The dramatic shapes formed by its enormous standing stones, topped with horizontal blocks, are instantly recognisable and so the site has become an icon of Britain and of the deep past. Standing on the green rolling downs of Salisbury Plain for over 4,500 years, these silent forms offer a dizzying perspective on the passing of time, a reminder of our own fleeting existence. We marvel at the engineering and organisational skills of those who moved and raised the stones. We try to imagine what life may have been like so long ago and wonder what motivated people to take part in such a complex and arduous endeavour.

The story of Stonehenge cannot, however, be told only through this one monument. It is a tale that unfolds across an entire landscape, encompassing traces left below ground, earthworks, artefacts and even the skies above. Our story covers thousands of years of human activity, and the lives of many different peoples who have dwelt here. Stonehenge is the key that unlocks our understanding of this place, and those people.

Our story concentrates on the period from 4000 BC to 1500 BC when all the major monuments in this landscape were built, including Stonehenge. At this time, it was a place where people gathered to feast, to exchange goods and ideas, to build monuments and conduct rituals and burial ceremonies. Activity ebbed and flowed: sometimes this was a busy, even frantic landscape, with intensive building work and throngs of people; at other periods there was quiet, with only herders and their animals occasionally passing through. The story continues in the period after Stonehenge went out of use, when it remained in the landscape, a witness to the coming of the Romans, the rise of medieval villages and towns, the first investigations of antiquarians in the 17th century, the arrival of the modern military, and, more recently, the wonder of tourists from around the world.

Sometimes our picture of Stonehenge and its landscape comes into sharper focus, allowing us to glimpse the stories of individual people: the so-called Amesbury Archer; the man buried under Bush Barrow; the early antiquaries who explored the ancient landscape. But for much of this tale we are dealing with communities of people whose lives remain shrouded from the present. We can see traces of them in the things they left behind: broken pieces of pottery, antler picks and animal bones, and in the monuments that they built. But the details of personal lives remain out of reach. Prehistory can sometimes be frustrating in this respect; we must join the sparse dots between pieces of evidence and use our imaginations to picture these distant people and what motivated them. But this is also what makes the period of Stonehenge endlessly fascinating; a time so remote from our own lives

This is a not a static story, but an ever-changing and evolving one. Over the last 25 years there have been countless excavations, surveys and research projects that have added new information and, in some cases, overturned old ideas.

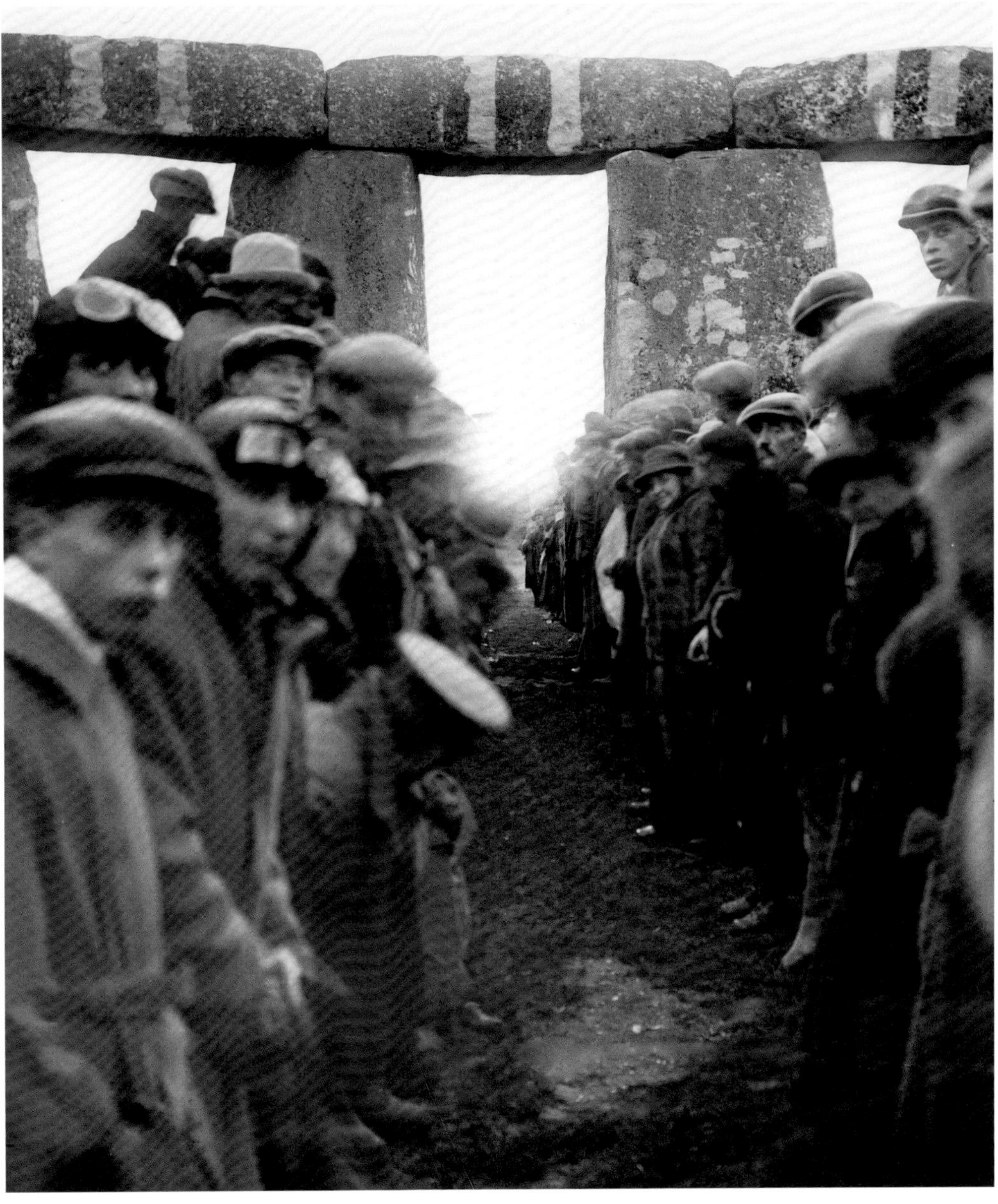

ABOVE Crowds part to allow the rising sun to shine into the centre of the stone circle, at summer solstice, early 20th century.

OVERLEAF The stones glow in the setting sunlight of an early evening, casting long shadows.

that we must set aside modern perspectives and allow the archaeology to tell the story.

This is not a static tale, however, but an ever-changing and evolving one. Over the last 25 years there have been countless excavations, surveys and research projects that have added new information and, in some cases, overturned old ideas. A bibliography of Stonehenge collated in 1901 listed 947 books and papers that had been written about the monument; this number must now be in the tens of thousands. So why add yet another book to the pile? The aim of this volume is to provide an accessible introduction for those wishing to discover Stonehenge and its surrounding landscape. It is based on the latest archaeological research, setting it within the grander sweep of prehistory, and is informed by the author's extensive experience in writing about Stonehenge. It is hoped that the story of Stonehenge, freshly told and beautifully illustrated, will provide a key to help readers unlock a deeper appreciation for the achievements of those who came before us, and a thorough understanding of this spectacular monument and the time in which it was built.

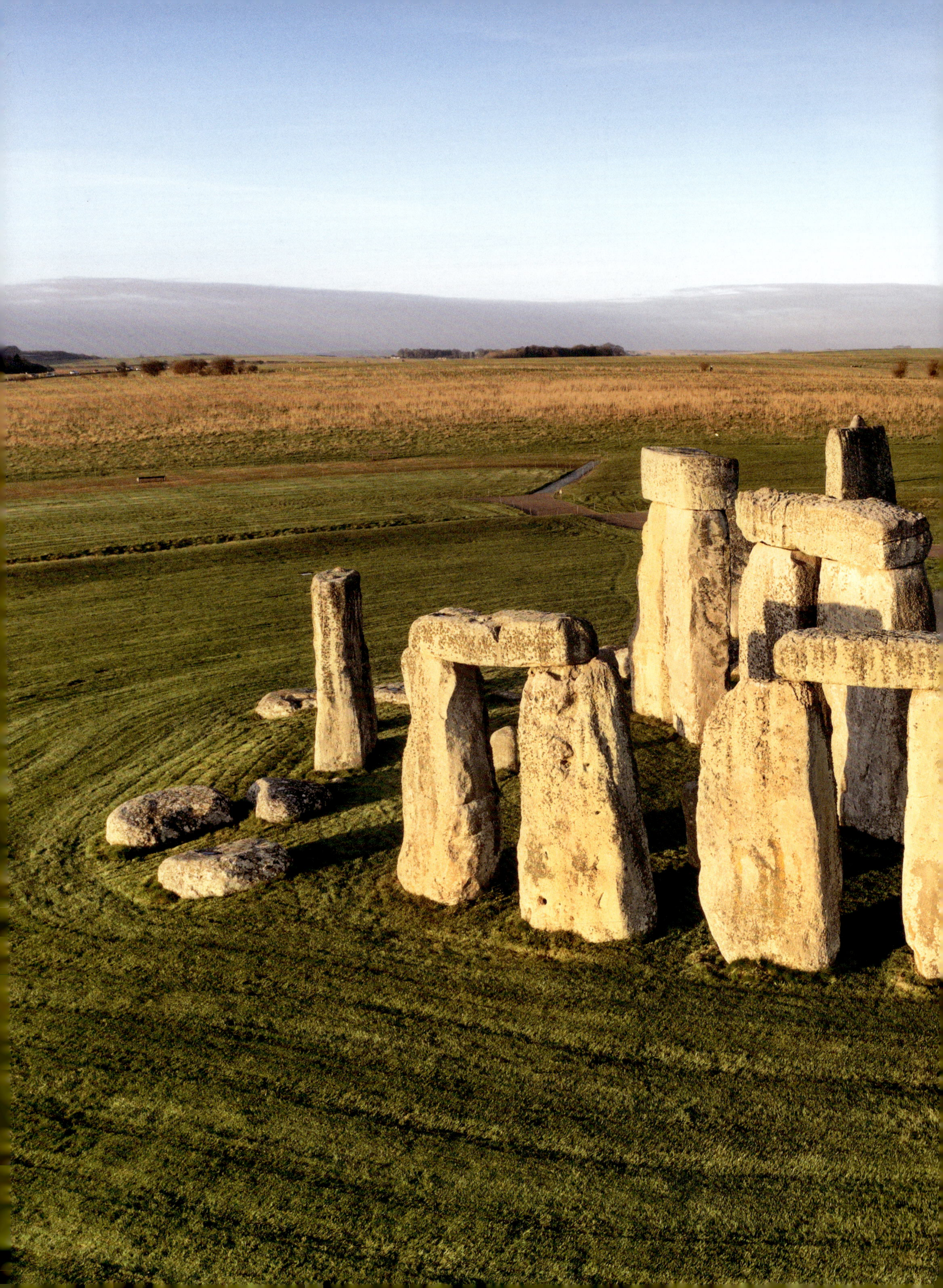

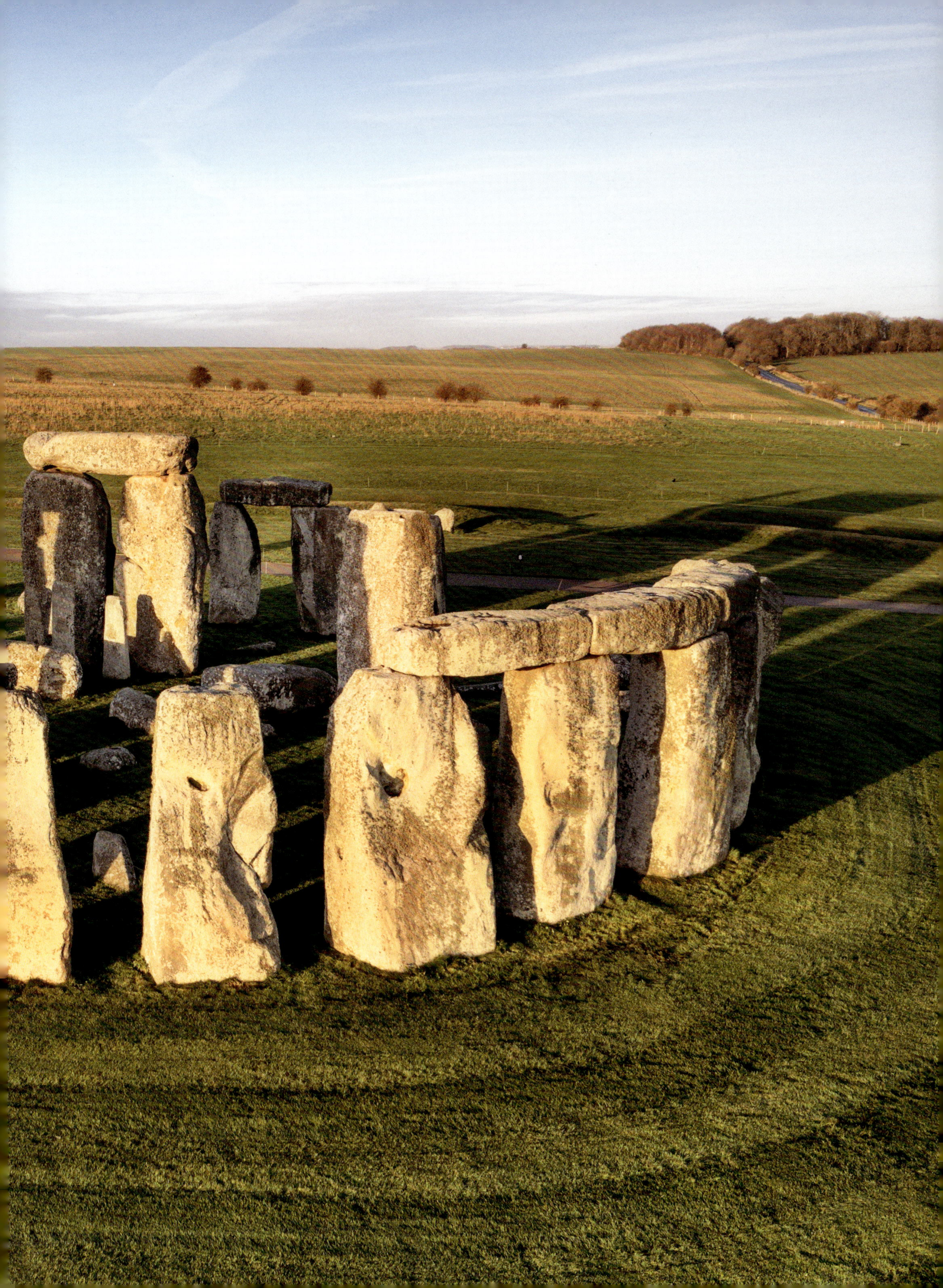

INTRODUCTION

Stonehenge was built about 4,500 years ago, before the time of written history. The prehistoric era to which it belongs has been divided up into sequential time periods, based on changing tools and technologies: those of stone, bronze and iron. Stonehenge was built on the cusp of one of these changes, at the end of the Stone Age, just before the first metals began to be used in Britain.

Stonehenge was constructed towards the end of a period we now call the Neolithic (or 'New Stone Age', 4000–2500 BC) when, across Britain, communities were farming and building monuments. This followed the Palaeolithic ('Old Stone Age', *c.*900,000–9700 BC) and Mesolithic ('Middle Stone Age', 9700–4000 BC), both periods when people lived by hunting and gathering their food. Shortly after the large stones at Stonehenge were erected, there were major changes as new people arrived in Britain with the first metals and new types of pottery, heralding the start of the Bronze Age.

Stonehenge was built on Salisbury Plain, a raised plateau of chalk geology in central southern Britain, close to the river Avon, which flows southwards towards the south coast, 32 miles (51km) away. This was a well-connected place, at the heart of a network of routeways linking southern Britain to areas bordering the Irish Sea. The stone circle was built in a landscape that had been frequented by Mesolithic hunters, and by early Neolithic farmers, who had already built several monuments: places of gatherings, funerary rites and ceremonies. At the heart of this cluster, in about 3000 BC, the first phase of Stonehenge was created – a circular ditch with a bank on either side, forming an enclosure about 110m across. This type of prehistoric site is known by archaeologists as a 'henge'. This monument was the resting place of about 150 people, whose cremated remains were buried here. At this time there was a large circle of 56 pits just inside the ditch, which may have held standing posts or stones, and there was probably a timber structure in the centre of the enclosure.

About 500 years later, enormous upright stones linked by horizontal lintels were set in the centre of the henge, forming a stone circle and a horseshoe, with smaller stones set among them. All these stones were carefully arranged to align with the movements of the sun, framing the midwinter and midsummer solstices. It must have taken hundreds of people to move, shape and raise the stones: an astonishing communal feat. The monument and its landscape remained significant into the Bronze Age, when hundreds of round barrows, covering the burials of important people, were built nearby.

Stonehenge, together with the remains of earlier and later sites, forms the heart of a complex of prehistoric monuments, protected today within the Stonehenge and Avebury World Heritage Site, and visited by more than a million people every year. To understand the henge and stone circle of Stonehenge, we need to look at the whole story of this landscape and put the monument into its wider context.

All these stones were carefully arranged to align with the movements of the sun, framing the midwinter and midsummer solstices.

OPPOSITE This bird's-eye view clearly shows the concentric layout of the stone monument. Only part of the outer stone circle survives.

OVERLEAF At Stonehenge the earliest part of the monument – the surrounding ditch and banks known as the 'henge' – are clearly visible as earthworks, as are the remains of the later Avenue, which approaches from the north-east (visible bottom right).

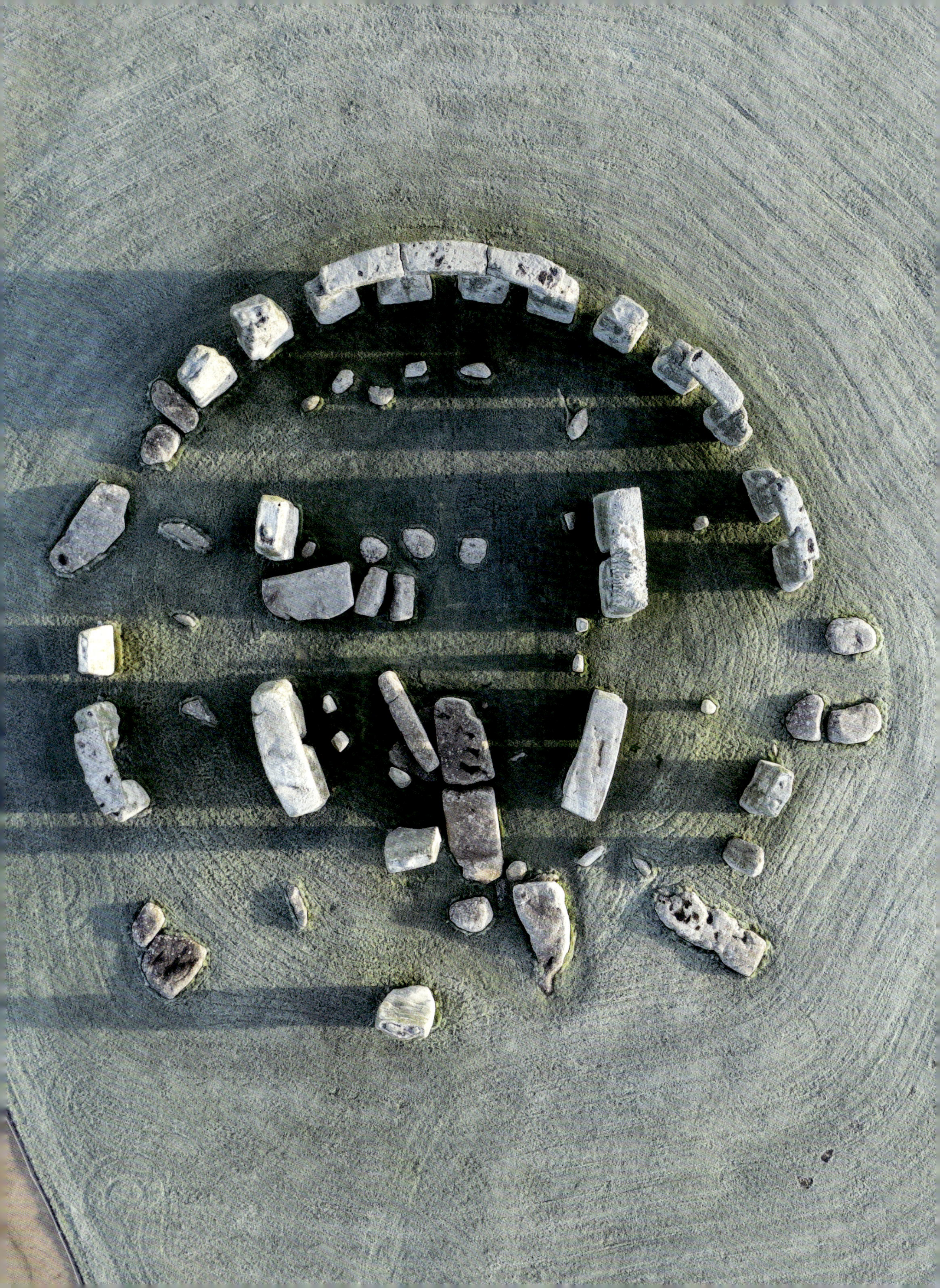

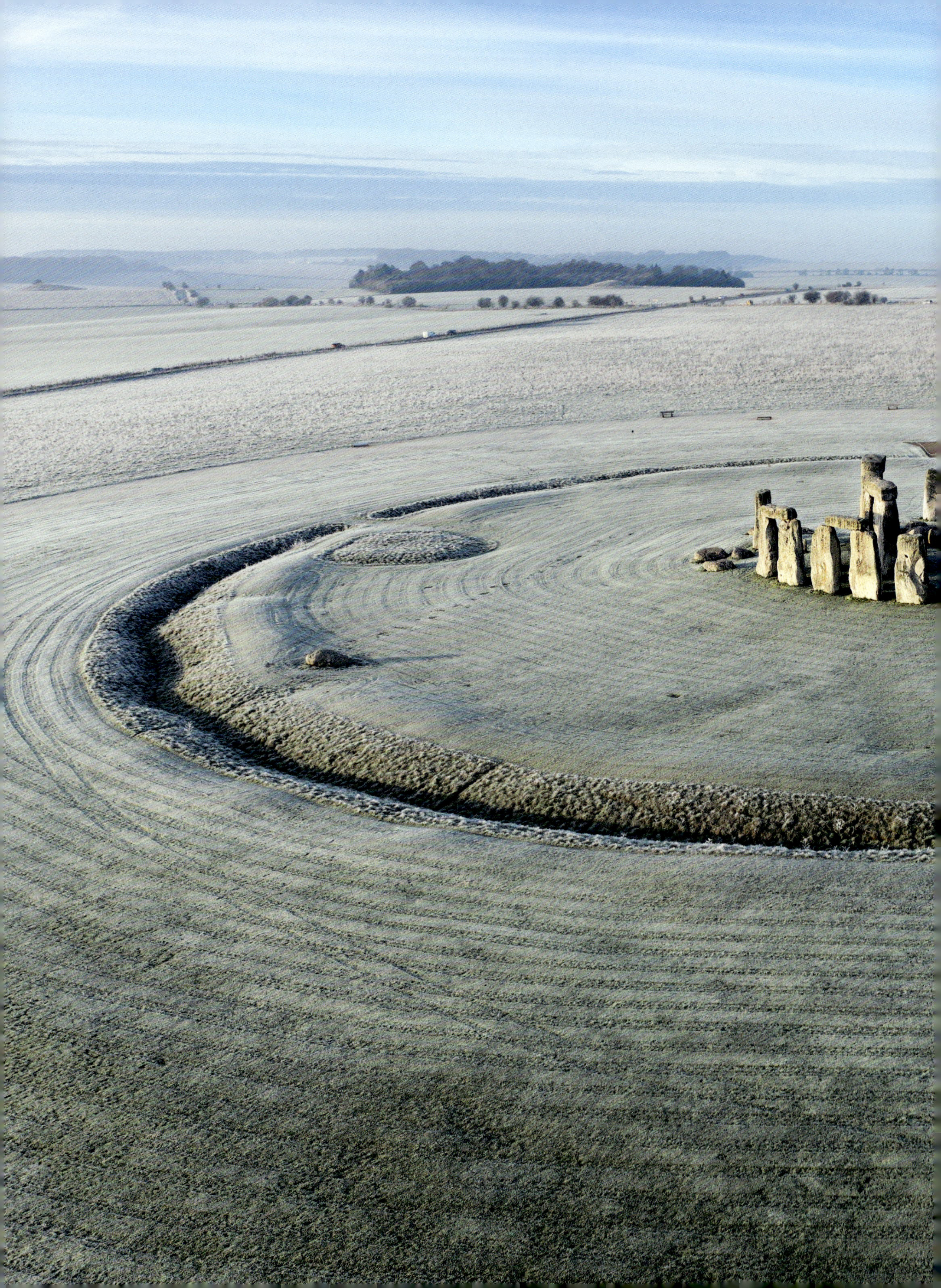

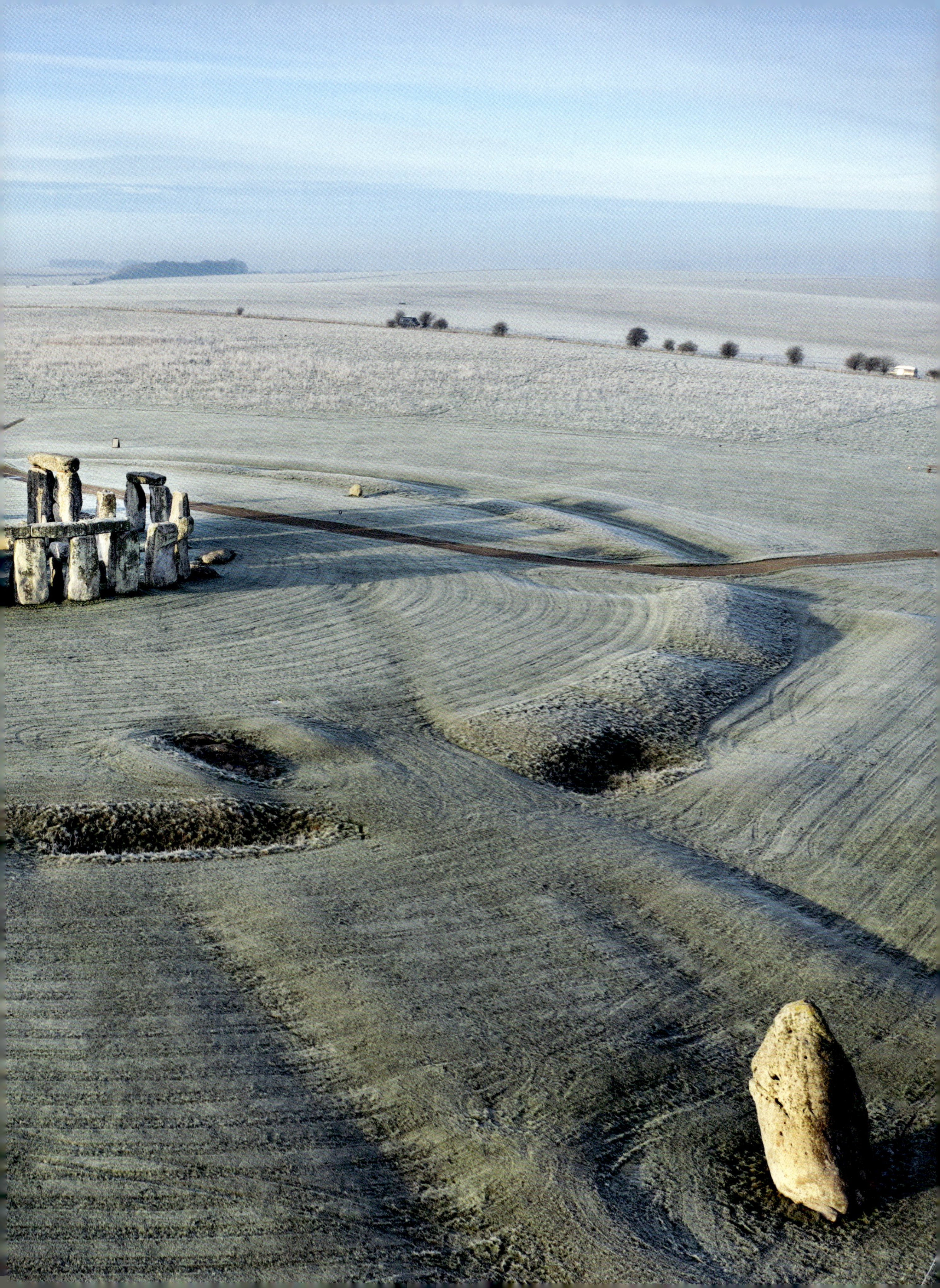

BEFORE STONEHENGE

THE MESOLITHIC LANDSCAPE (9700–4000 BC)

Thousands of years before Stonehenge was built, before the arrival of farming in Britain, people who lived by hunting and gathering wild food were regularly visiting the Stonehenge area. Traces of their activities still survive in the landscape here, and there are clues that this was an important place.

The Mesolithic period in Britain began at the end of the last Ice Age, in about 9700 BC. After the retreat of glaciers and ice sheets, trees, plants and animals were able to recolonise the land, which was still connected to mainland Europe. Groups of people followed reindeer herds northwards, gradually spreading across the whole of Britain, and settling permanently for the first time. Over the next 6,000 years, these people lived in small groups that moved through the landscape, often staying along river valleys or in coastal areas, where they left behind scatters of worked flint – the debris from the manufacture of stone tools.

These communities fished, collected shellfish, hunted or trapped deer, wild boar and aurochs (the extinct ancestor of modern domestic cattle), and gathered fruits, roots and leaves. During this period, in about 6000 BC, geological and coastal changes led to Britain becoming an island, permanently separated from the rest of Europe.

About 1.5 miles (2.4km) east of Stonehenge, on a terrace adjacent to the river Avon, was a major Mesolithic settlement at a site now known as Blick Mead. Here, large quantities of animal bones and chips of flint were found near a natural spring. The presence of this spring must have made this an attractive place to live. Radiocarbon dates from the bones suggest that people returned to this place repeatedly over a period of roughly 3,000 years, from about 7500 BC to 4500 BC. Traces of other camp sites and areas where flint tools were being made have been found at various places along the river valley, suggesting this was a favoured location for mobile groups of hunter-gatherers.

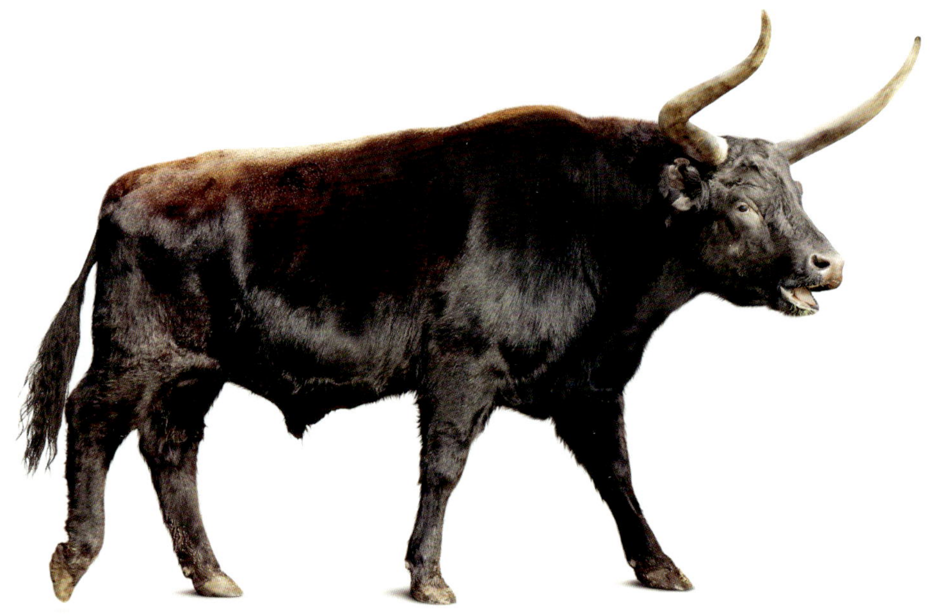

LEFT A reconstruction of an aurochs, a species of now-extinct wild cattle hunted by Mesolithic people. Males had a shoulder height of up to 180cm and horns that reached 80cm in length, making them formidable prey.

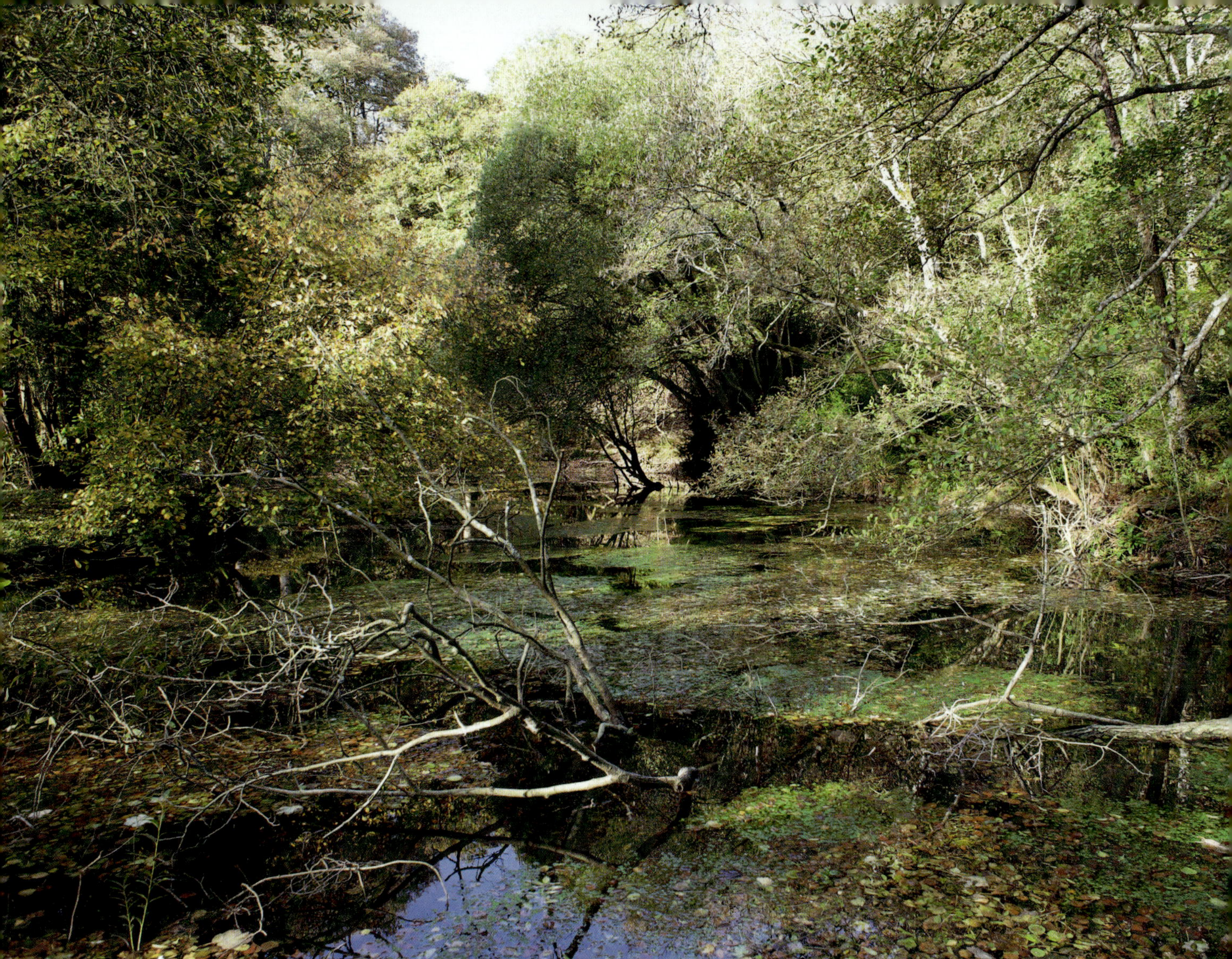

ABOVE At Blick Mead, in shallow water fed by springs, Mesolithic people left large quantities of worked flint and animal bones, presumably from nearby settlements or camps.

Unlike the rest of southern Britain, which was mostly dense woodland at this time, the area around Blick Mead was open grassland – ideal grazing for animals and easy hunting grounds for Mesolithic people. The animal bones found at Blick Mead were mostly those of aurochs. These large, wild cattle with huge horns were extremely dangerous prey and one way of hunting them would have been to drive them into holes dug as traps; one such hole, measuring nearly two metres deep, has been excavated not far from Stonehenge.

Five other smaller Mesolithic pits that do not appear to be hunting traps have been found about 250m north-west of where Stonehenge now stands. Four of these pits were arranged in a line running from east to west. They aligned with a fifth, irregularly shaped pit left where an ancient tree had fallen. They may have contained large standing posts, perhaps markers for a routeway – a rare early monument. Or they may have been dug to mark an important place or for some other purpose. The hollows of these backfilled pits may still have been visible 4,000 years later, when the first phase of Stonehenge was built, although it may simply be coincidence that they were in the same location. Today, the positions of these Mesolithic pits are shown by markers near the shuttle bus stop.

These pits or postholes, the settlement at Blick Mead, the hunting trap and other scattered finds and features, provide a glimpse into the lives of Mesolithic hunter-gatherer communities in this area in the time before Stonehenge.

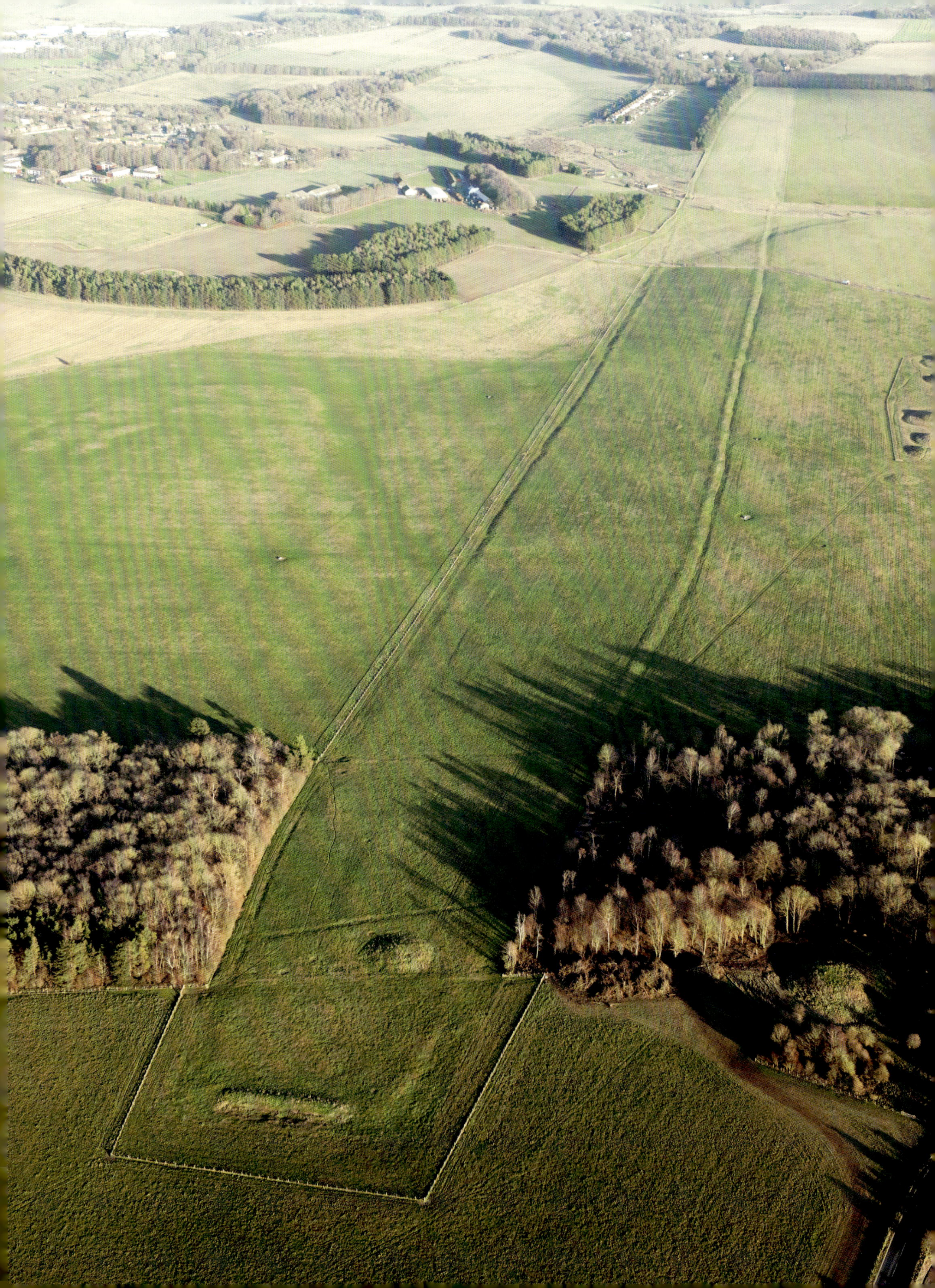

THE EARLY NEOLITHIC LANDSCAPE (4000–3200 BC)

OPPOSITE This long, rectangular enclosure, the Stonehenge or Greater Cursus, was one of several monuments built in this area in the early Neolithic period, long before Stonehenge itself.

Long before Stonehenge was built, this landscape was a place where encounters, negotiations and major communal building projects took place. In the early Neolithic period people built a variety of monuments, including circular ditched features, mysterious, long, rectangular enclosures called cursus monuments, and long mounds, known as barrows, for the burial of their dead and perhaps for other ritual purposes. These monuments tell us that this was a busy and important landscape.

In about 4000 BC, early farmers began to move from different parts of Continental Europe across the Channel to Britain, bringing their domestic animals and crops, as well as pottery vessels and polished stone axes. The arrival of this entirely new way of life and novel technologies marked the start in Britain of what we now call the Neolithic period. The Mesolithic hunter-gatherers living here had dwindled in numbers, and those that remained probably soon adopted farming practices from the incomers.

Early farming communities may have been attracted to Salisbury Plain by the wide expanses of grassland, unusual in the largely wooded Britain of that time. It would have been an ideal place for gathering in large groups or for bringing together their cattle. As these communities spread, they would have interacted with the few hunter-gatherer groups already in the area. An astonishing site not far to the south-east of Stonehenge, known as the Coneybury Anomaly, may provide evidence for one such encounter. Here, in about 3700 BC, people dug a large pit and buried within it the remains of a feast: mostly the bones of domestic cattle and wild roe deer, as well as pig, brown trout, red deer and beaver, and at least 40 ceramic bowls. Chemical analysis of the cattle and deer teeth has shown that they had been brought from at least three different areas within 13 miles (20km) or so of the site. Perhaps this feast marked a meeting between several communities of farmers and hunter-gatherers to negotiate their relationship or agree sharing of land and resources.

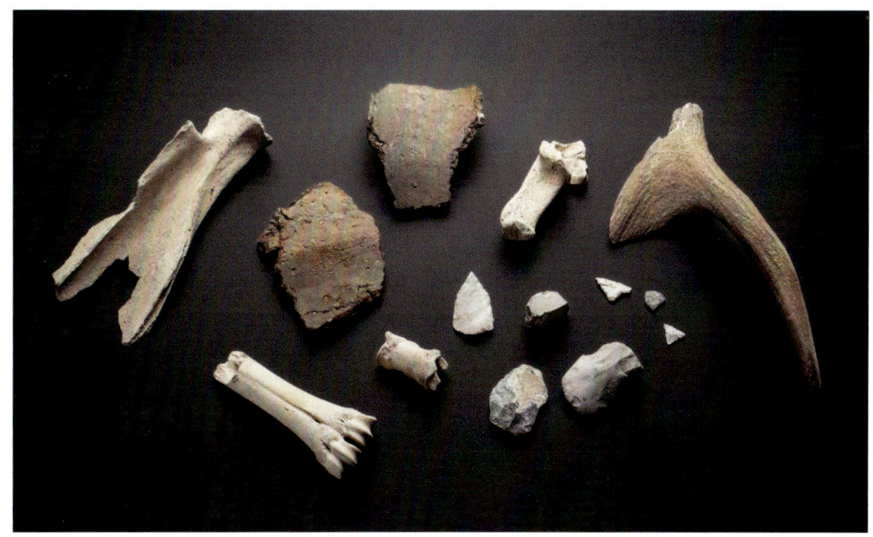

RIGHT Some of the artefacts found in the Coneybury Anomaly: fragments of pottery bowls, red deer and cattle bones, a deer antler and flint tools and cores (lumps of flint from which flakes have been struck to make flint tools).

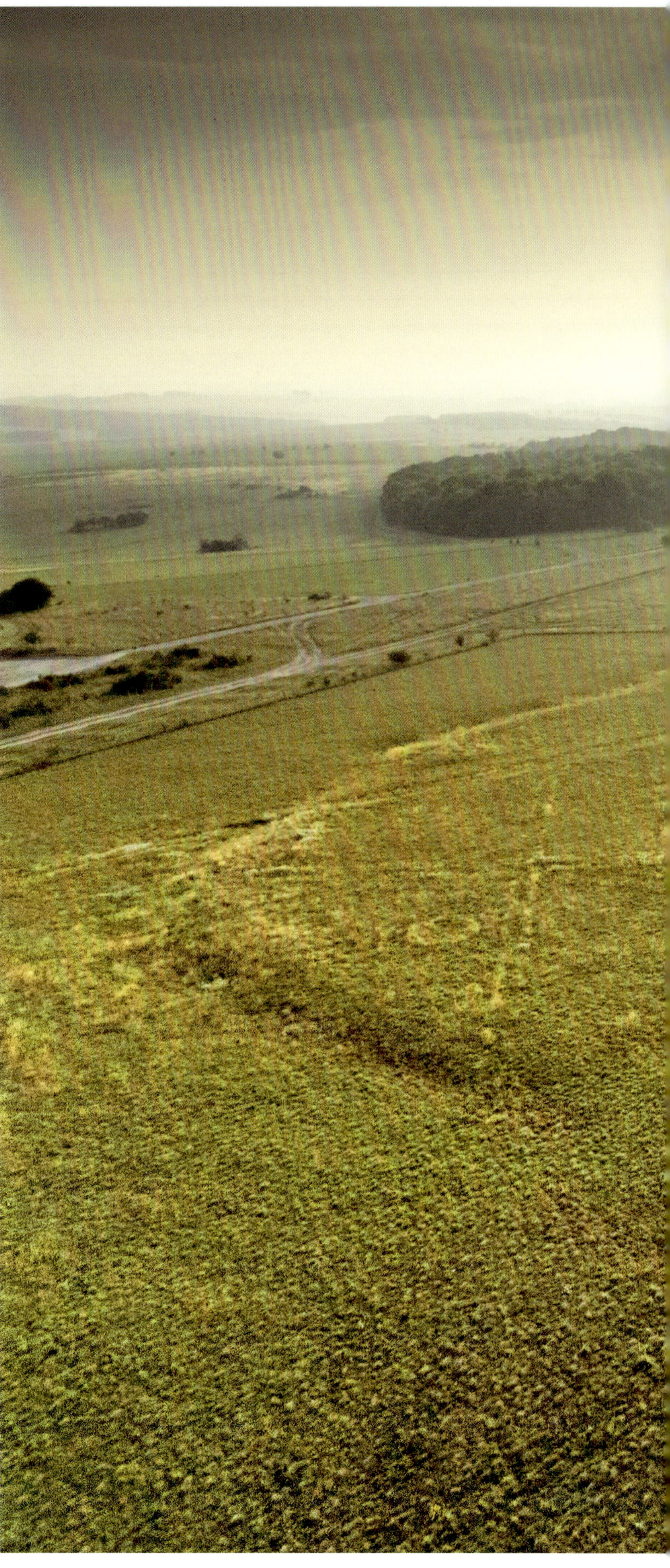

RIGHT Two concentric ditches formed the causewayed enclosure at Robin Hood's Ball. These ditches contained early Neolithic pottery, flint tools and animal bones.

At a similar date, a pair of what are known as causewayed enclosures were built about 1.8 miles (2.9km) to the north of Stonehenge. These were probably the earliest monuments to be constructed in the Stonehenge landscape. These enclosures, at Robin Hood's Ball and Larkhill, were formed of one or two circuits of ditches dug in short segments, enclosing roughly circular areas of about 8.6 acres (3.5 hectares). Excavations here found animal bones, pottery fragments, quern stones for grinding cereals and hundreds of flint tools as well as a few human bones, indicating that both sites were intensively occupied. Some of the pottery was made using a type of clay found only on the Lizard Peninsula in Cornwall, suggesting that people were either travelling to these enclosures from far away or had access to long-distance exchange networks. These were places where dispersed groups of early farmers met to conduct ceremonies, take part in feasts, share news and exchange goods.

No houses from this period have been found in the Stonehenge landscape, although early Neolithic houses are known from other places in Britain. It is likely that any traces of such structures have been lost through generations of ploughing and other activities, so that today settlement sites can only be identified through scatters of flint – the remains of flint tool making – or pits filled with domestic rubbish. We do not therefore know whether people lived in permanent settlements or moved seasonally between different areas.

We do have evidence, however, for the 'houses' Neolithic people built for their dead. These took the form of long barrows, consisting of long mounds flanked on either side by ditches. At least 17 of these are known within a 3.7-mile (5.9-km) radius of Stonehenge. None

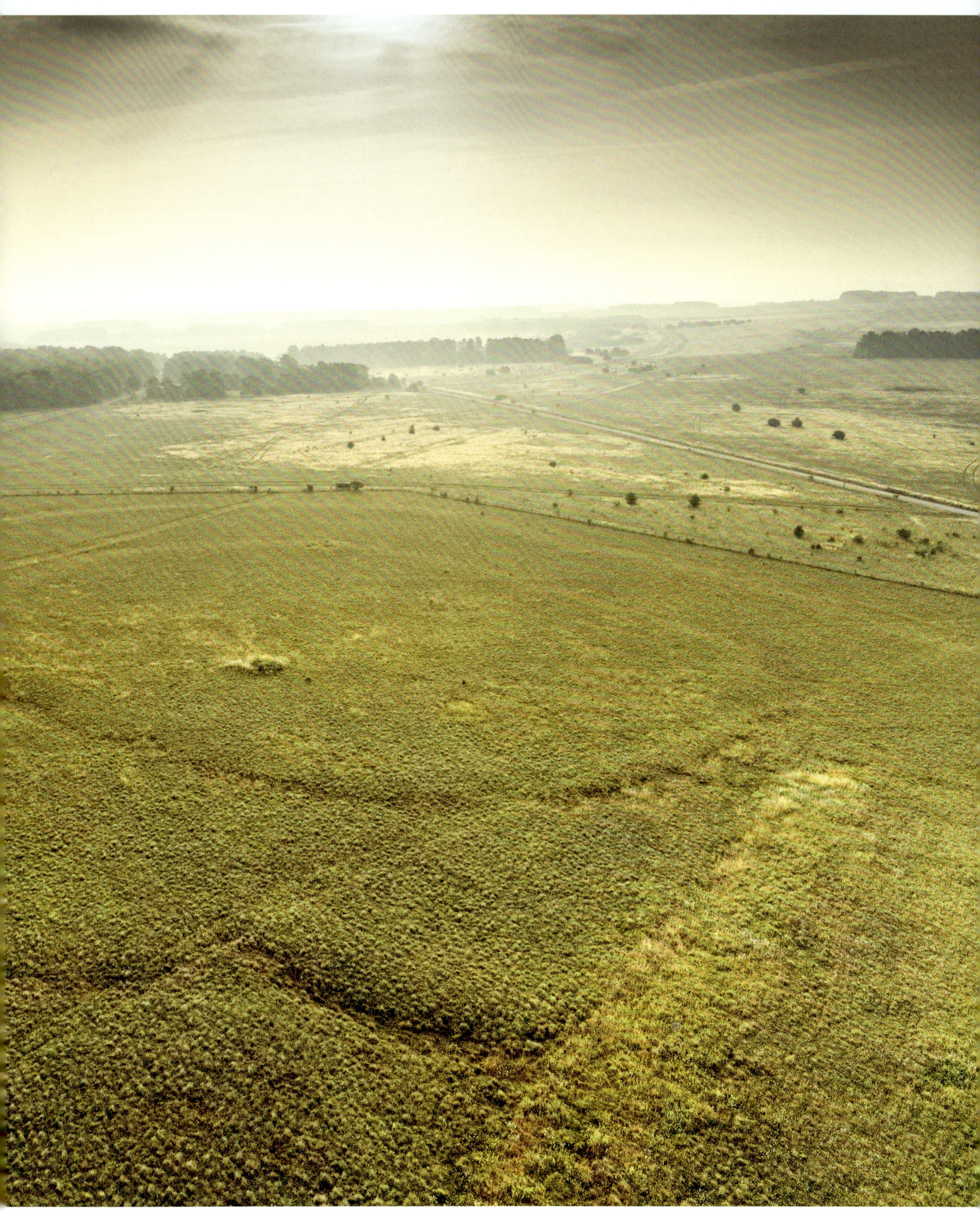

In the years before Stonehenge, this was already a busy landscape, with signs of human activity, filled with stories and memories of past gatherings and feats of construction.

appears to have contained a stone burial chamber, as found within some long barrows elsewhere in Britain (such as West Kennet, 16 miles, or 26km, north of Stonehenge), but some had timber chambers and elaborate façades of wooden posts. Long barrows were usually built on ridges or high ground, with the larger or more elaborate end of the mound orientated towards the eastern part of the horizon, perhaps facing the sunrise. Most long barrows contained human remains, but one, known as Amesbury 42, a mile north-east of Stonehenge, contained only cattle skulls and feet. These animals must have had significant economic, social and perhaps ritual importance for people in this period, being treated in death like humans. Other long barrows may have been built to link communities to the land or as a focus for rituals.

One of the largest and best-preserved long barrows lies at Winterbourne Stoke Crossroads, just under a mile south of the Stonehenge Visitor Centre. Excavations here in 1863 by John Thurnam, an antiquary interested in human bones, uncovered the burial of a man at the eastern end, accompanied by a long flint nodule of a type found only in eastern England. Analysis of chemicals in the man's teeth suggests that he grew up some distance away, perhaps in western Britain. This adds to the picture that early Neolithic people travelled long distances and that the Stonehenge area was a central place in these journeys.

BELOW The spectacular West Kennet Long Barrow near Avebury, which contains stone burial chambers. Although none of the long barrows in the Stonehenge landscape has evidence for stone chambers like this, their timber façades and large earthen mounds would have been equally impressive in the landscape.

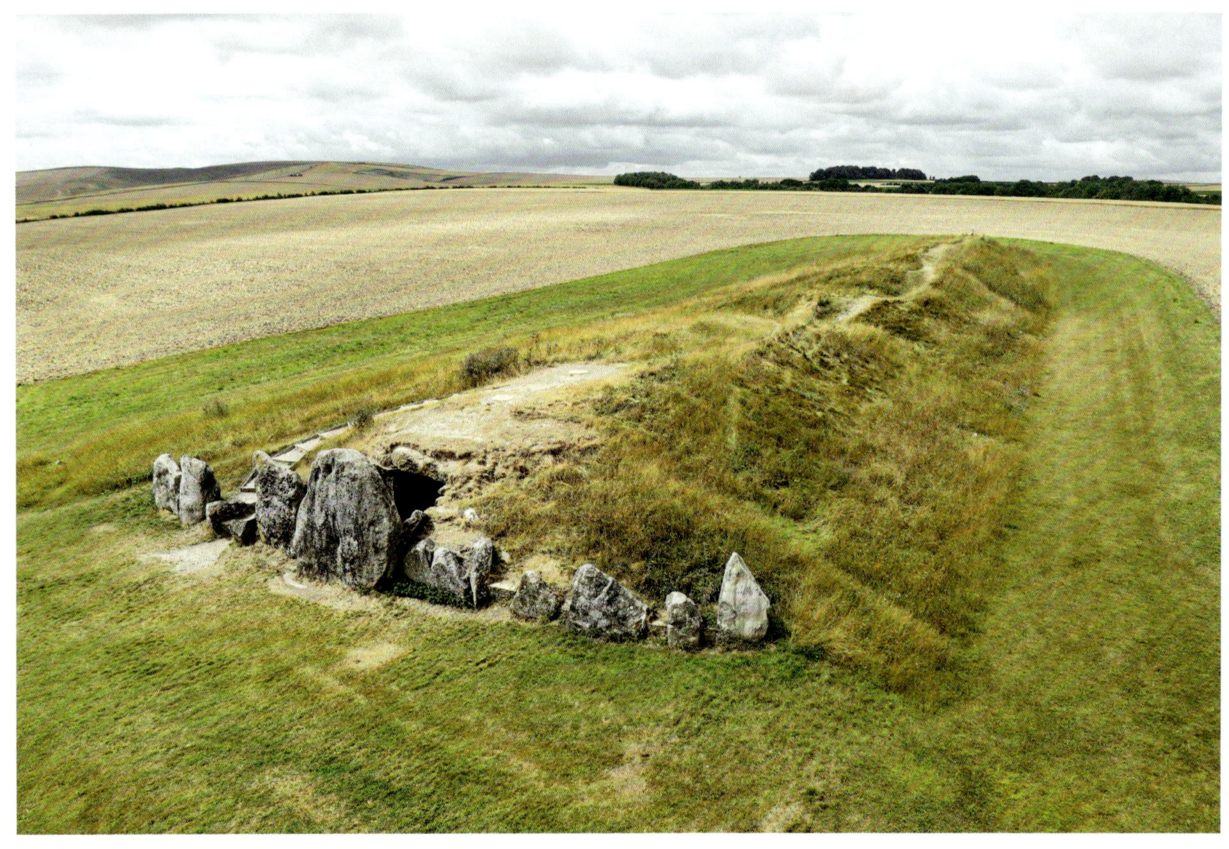

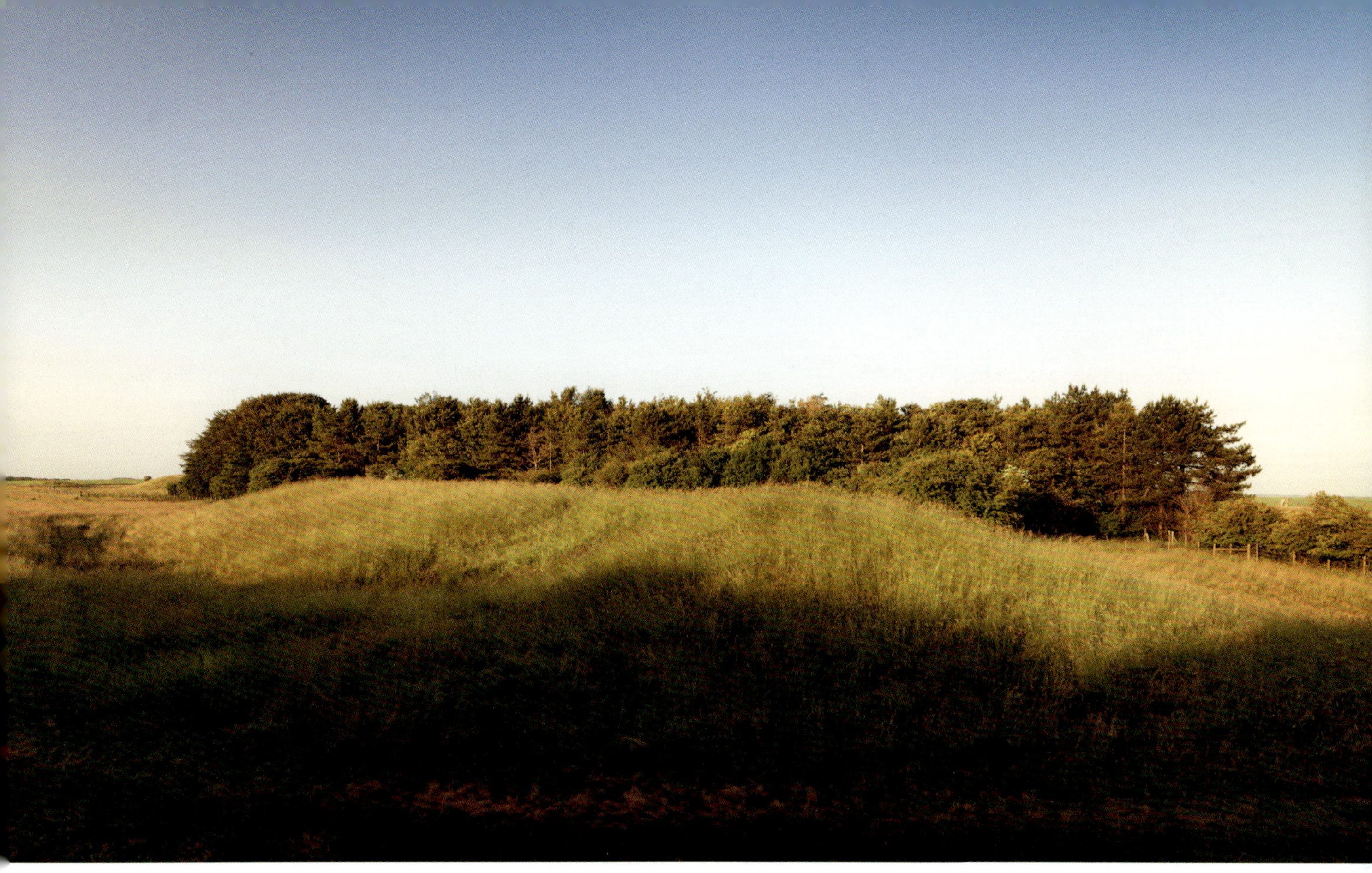

ABOVE The long barrow at Winterbourne Stoke Crossroads was excavated by the antiquary John Thurnam in 1863. He found the burial of a man within.

Two enormous rectangular areas, enclosed by low banks and ditches, known as cursus monuments, were also created in this landscape by early Neolithic communities in the years around 3500 BC. Less than a mile (about 800m) north of Stonehenge is the larger of the two – the Stonehenge or Greater Cursus – which is about 100m wide and just under two miles (3km) long, extending from Winterbourne Stoke Down to King Barrow Ridge. A smaller monument, the Lesser Cursus, lies along a flat ridge about 1.5 miles to the north-west of Stonehenge, measuring 400m long and 60m wide.

These rectangular spaces were defined by ditches about 1m deep and low chalk banks, which, when originally built, would have stood out a stark white against the green grass. Unlike the causewayed enclosures, these sites do not appear to have been places for feasting, gathering or settlement: they have no internal features and very little evidence of any human activity at all. Their purpose remains entirely enigmatic. Some have argued that cursus monuments were processional routeways, but they had narrow openings in the ditches in their long sides, suggesting that people crossed them rather than moved along them from end to end. They may have been used for elaborate races and contests, or perhaps acted as some sort of boundary to control the movement of people or their cattle.

These two cursus monuments, together with the two causewayed enclosures and the scatter of long barrows, formed the core of a distinct cluster of early Neolithic monuments. In the years before Stonehenge, this was already a busy landscape, with signs of human activity, filled with stories and memories of past gatherings and feats of construction.

We know that these monuments remained important for a long time. About 1,000 years after the Greater Cursus was constructed, at the time that Stonehenge was built, pits were dug into the silted-up ditches to gather chalk, which was spread onto the banks, making them white again. People were making sure that the long history of this landscape was known and visible.

Stonehenge in its Global Context

When Stonehenge was being built from about 3000 BC there was huge variation in human societies around the world. While some communities practised farming, many others, for example in Japan and North America, sourced their food by hunting, fishing and gathering. In some regions, such as the Indus Valley and Mesopotamia, the first cities had been built and the earliest writing had developed, but these innovations would take some time to be adopted more widely.

BELOW This life-sized limestone statue, nicknamed Urfa Man, was carved about 11,000 years ago during the Pre-Pottery Neolithic period. He was found near Urfa, in modern-day Turkey.

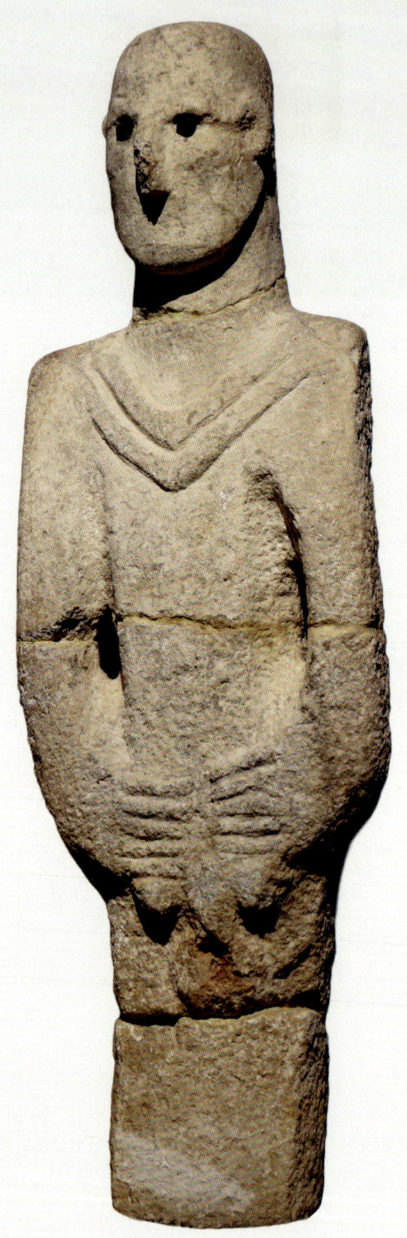

Between 12,000 and 10,000 years ago, foraging societies in south-west Asia, in an area often known as the 'Fertile Crescent' (spanning modern-day Israel, Palestine, Jordan, Lebanon, Syria and Iraq), began to experiment with planting wild species of wheat and barley, and selectively breeding wild sheep, goats, pigs and cattle. Eventually a standard set of agricultural practices developed and spread across Europe. This marked the start of what we now call the Neolithic period. By the time Stonehenge was built, the inhabitants of most parts of central and southern Europe had adopted a farming lifestyle. Other centres of agriculture developed independently at different times across the world, including in Mesoamerica, western Africa, southern India and New Guinea. Practices often spread rapidly to neighbouring regions, but it was not a linear progress: we know of some areas, such as the American south-west, where farmers abandoned the growing of maize and beans to return to a foraging way of life.

For a long time, it has been assumed that the construction of megalithic and other major monuments such as Stonehenge took place when communities had adopted farming and settled down in villages, with surplus time and food allowing them to devote attention to such projects. Although this is often the case, there are some exceptions. In prehistoric (late Jomon) Japan, for example, at about the same time that Stonehenge was built, hunter-gatherer communities were building flat stone circles with standing stones aligned on the solstice. About 11,000 years ago at Göbekli Tepe in modern Turkey, spectacular circular structures with massive carved stone pillars were built by nomadic populations who hunted wild gazelle and gathered wild cereals. Here, it has been suggested that the demands of monument construction fuelled the transition to agriculture, rather than the other way around.

As complex monuments demanded immense amounts of labour and co-operation to build, it has also been assumed that the societies who built them must have been deeply unequal, with permanent leaders and organisers, such as chiefs, able to command and direct a large workforce. However, we do not have proof of this at Stonehenge, such as rich graves or larger houses.

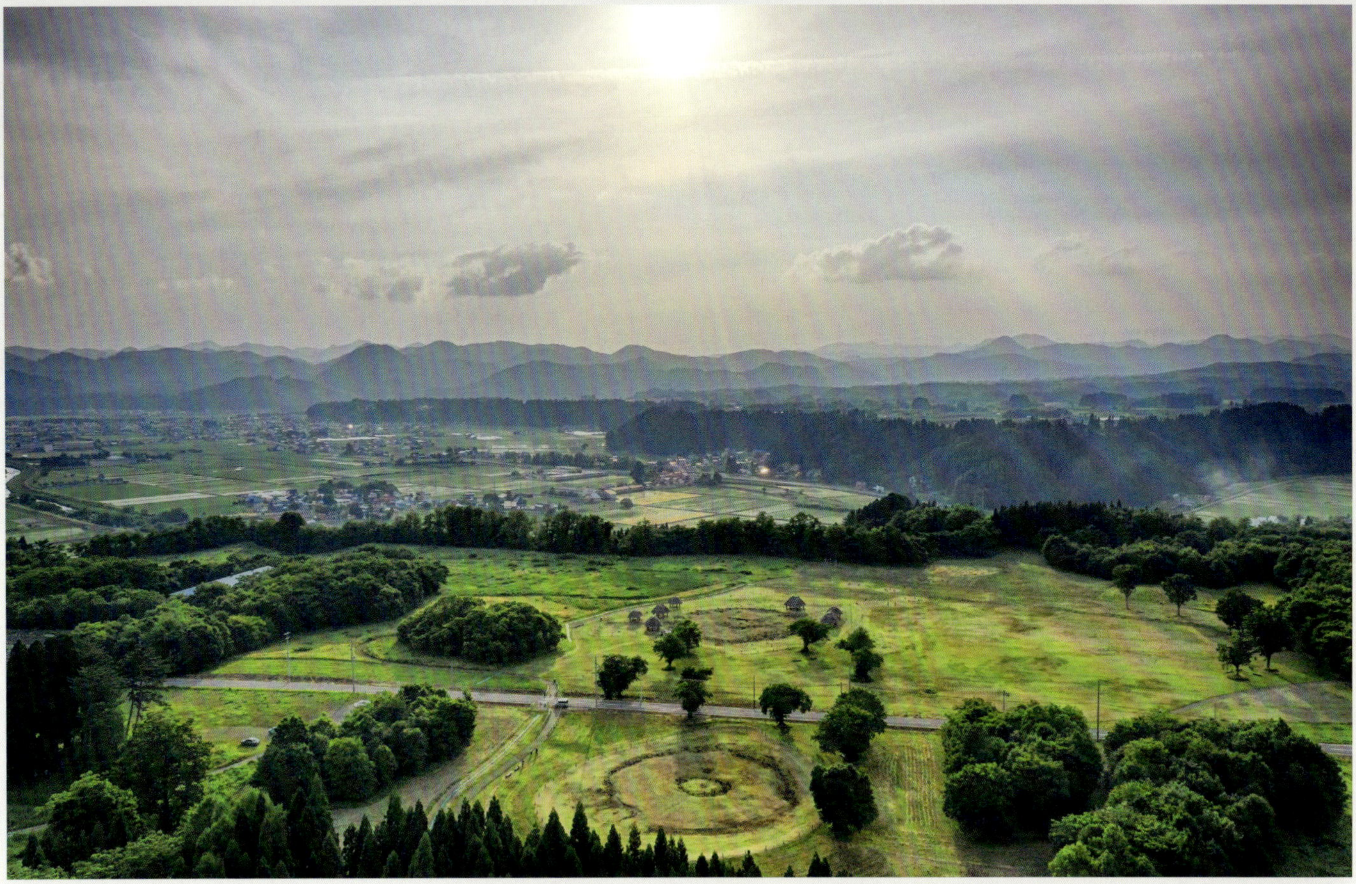

ABOVE The Oyu stone circles in northern Honshu, Japan, were built using flat boulders, groups of which covered graves, forming a ring. They date from a similar time to Stonehenge.

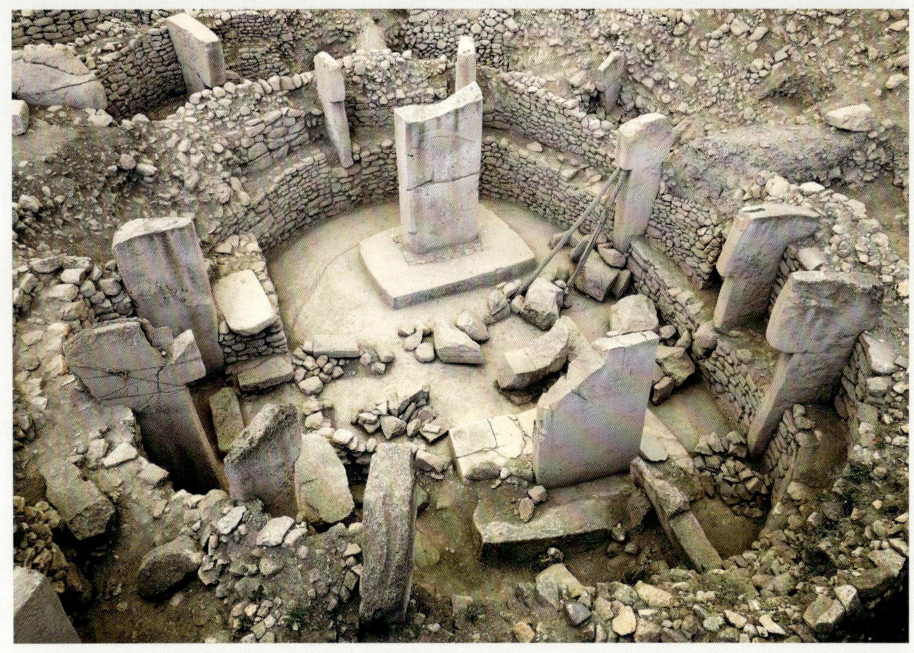

RIGHT Göbekli Tepe in modern Turkey is a cluster of monumental stone buildings featuring pillars carved with animals and abstract motifs, dating from the very earliest stage of the Neolithic period, more than 6,000 years before Stonehenge.

By the time Stonehenge was built, the inhabitants of most parts of central and southern Europe had adopted a farming lifestyle.

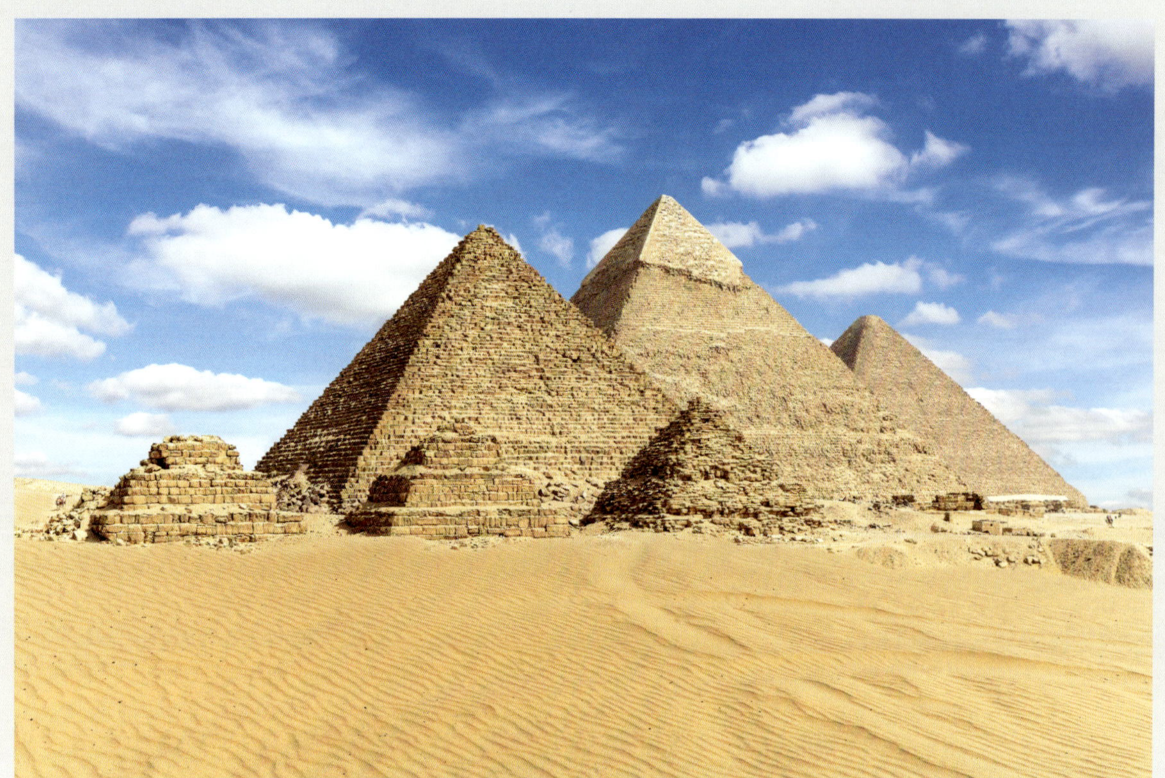

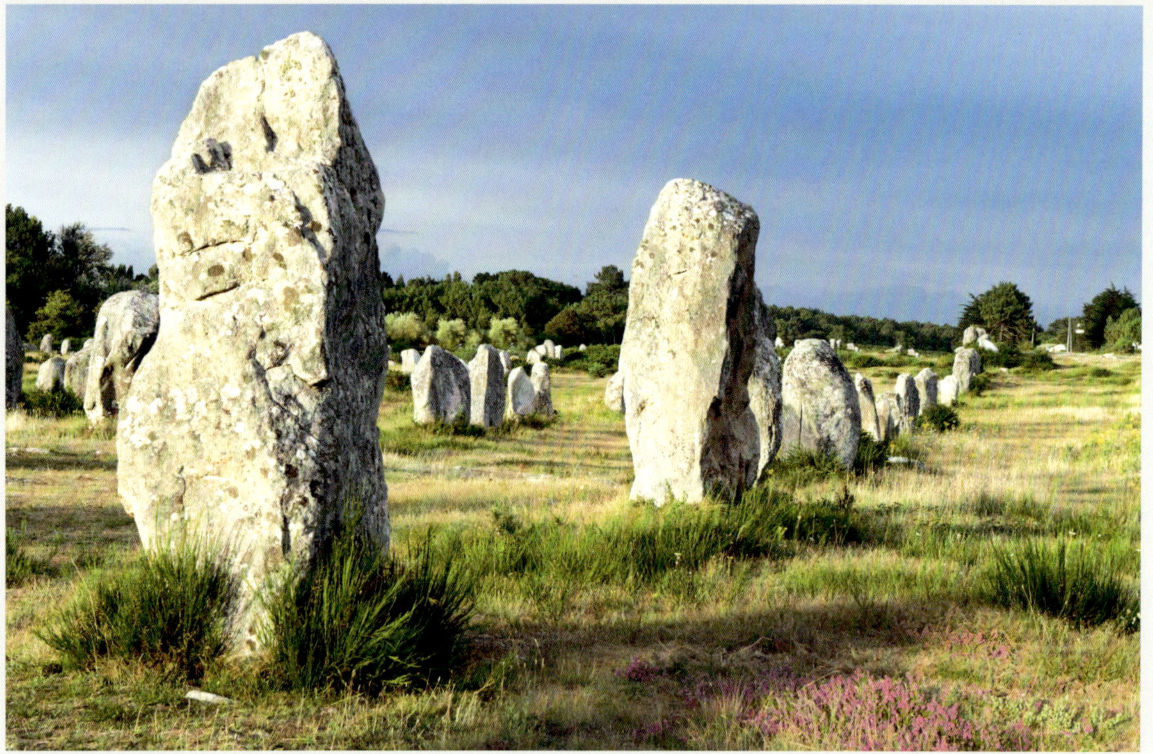

TOP The three large pyramids at Giza in Egypt were built between 2560 and 2500 BC, roughly the same date the sarsen stones were put up at Stonehenge.

ABOVE The multiple rows of standing stones in the Carnac region of Brittany, France, such as this one at Kermario, were built between 4700 and 4200 BC, at least 2,000 years before Stonehenge.

BELOW A reconstruction of Ötzi the Iceman, who died after being wounded by an arrow. His amazingly well-preserved body, naturally mummified in ice, was found with clothing including goatskin leggings and equipment such as a longbow made of yew.

Bronze-working can be traced back to about 3200 BC in the area around the Aegean Sea where, by 2500 BC, the famous Minoan civilisation had developed on Crete.

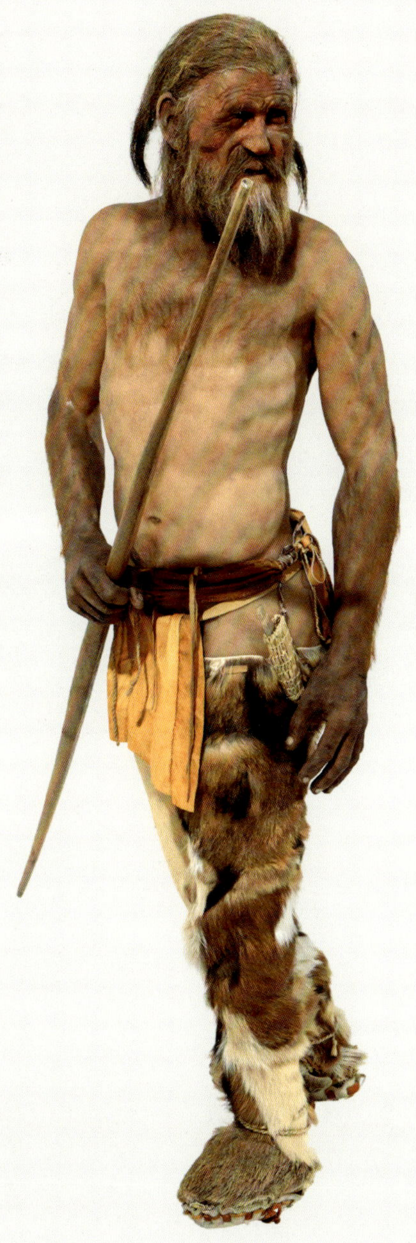

It may be an unfounded assumption, as we know that many societies around the world, such as the Angami Naga people of north-east India, have erected megaliths without any permanent hierarchies in place.

The earliest urban centres emerged a long time before Stonehenge. In Europe, there were 'mega-sites' in modern-day Ukraine, clusters of hundreds of houses laid out in vast circles, which were occupied from about 4000 BC, and cities such as Troy, in what is now Turkey, were established by 3000 BC. Major urban settlements such as Uruk in Mesopotamia had emerged by at least 3500 BC, where the world's earliest writing is recorded. By the time that Stonehenge was built, there were also fortified palace-cities such as Wangchenggang in the Yellow River valley in modern-day China, as well as in Peru and Pakistan. In Africa, the Old Kingdom Egyptian civilisation was flourishing, with the construction of the Great Pyramids at Giza taking place in about 2500 BC.

The earliest European megalithic structures, small stone tombs, were built from about 4700 BC in modern-day France and Iberia. In north-west France, especially the Carnac region, larger and more complex monuments were built including tombs and standing stones. The idea of building megalithic monuments spread to other regions of western Europe, but did not take hold in Britain until after 4000 BC, with the arrival of the first farmers.

At the time that the large stones were being raised at Stonehenge, in about 2500 BC, much of northern Europe and Scandinavia was occupied by interlinked communities known today as the Corded Ware culture, named after their distinctive pottery, decorated with cord impressions. Some of the ancestors of these people had been pastoral communities who had migrated from the Pontic-Caspian steppe, north of the Black and Caspian Seas. Both groups buried their dead in single graves, sometimes in stone cists or under barrows, and often accompanied by grave goods. Communities in central and southern Europe, meanwhile, were already working and trading metals, including gold and copper. The frozen remains of a man who lived between 3350 and 3120 BC, now known as Ötzi the Iceman, were found in the Alps in 1991. He had a copper axe dating from at least 800 years before the earliest metal objects known from Britain. Bronze-working can be traced back to about 3200 BC in the area around the Aegean Sea where, by 2500 BC, the famous Minoan civilisation had developed on Crete.

In the mid 20th century some archaeologists argued that because of Stonehenge's unique structure it must have been designed by, or at least influenced by, the more advanced Minoan and Mycenaean civilisations of the Mediterranean. The advent of radiocarbon dating in the 1960s, however, proved that Stonehenge predated any contact between the two areas, and we now know that it was built by the late Neolithic inhabitants of Britain.

AT THE TIME OF STONEHENGE

THE EARLY MONUMENT (3000–2600 BC)

During its earliest phase, Stonehenge was a place for the dead, where the cremated remains of at least 150 people were buried. They were interred within the feature known by archaeologists as a 'henge', the first part of Stonehenge to be built in about 3000 BC. This was a circular ditch 110m in diameter between two concentric banks. Just inside the inner bank was a circuit of pits, which may have held standing stones, and within and around which the cremated remains of many individuals were placed.

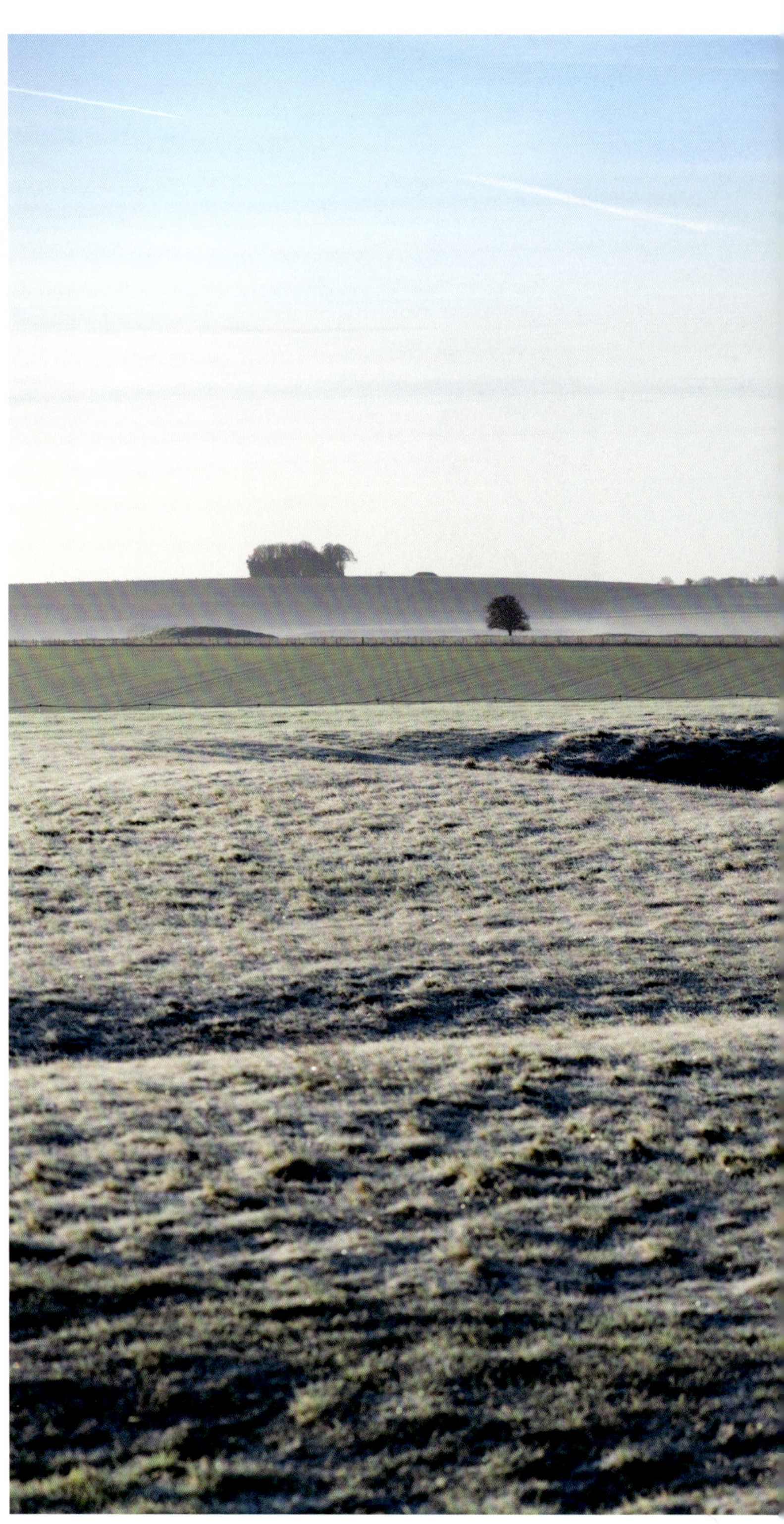

In the middle Neolithic (between about 3400 and 3000 BC) there was a gap of several hundred years when no new large monuments were begun in the Stonehenge area. We know that people continued to visit the area regularly, however, as their settlements can be identified by clusters of pits containing the style of pottery used in this period (known as Peterborough Ware), as well as animal bones, flint and antler tools, carved chalk and beads.

Pit digging was a common practice in the Neolithic period. Many had a practical purpose: for food storage, or to clear away rubbish. Some pits, however, had more unusual objects, such as decorated chalk plaques, and others contained ordinary objects, such as pieces of pottery, that had been carefully arranged. These may have been offerings or were part of ceremonies to mark the end of a stay in a certain place. These pits have been found across the landscape, but particularly to the east of Stonehenge.

Several such middle Neolithic pits were excavated in 2015–16 near West Amesbury, a mile to the south-east of Stonehenge. One contained the burial of a man who had moved to the area from the west, perhaps Ireland, showing that people continued to travel over

BELOW The circular ditch surrounding Stonehenge is still clearly visible. Although the inner bank survives, the outer bank has been largely destroyed by ploughing.

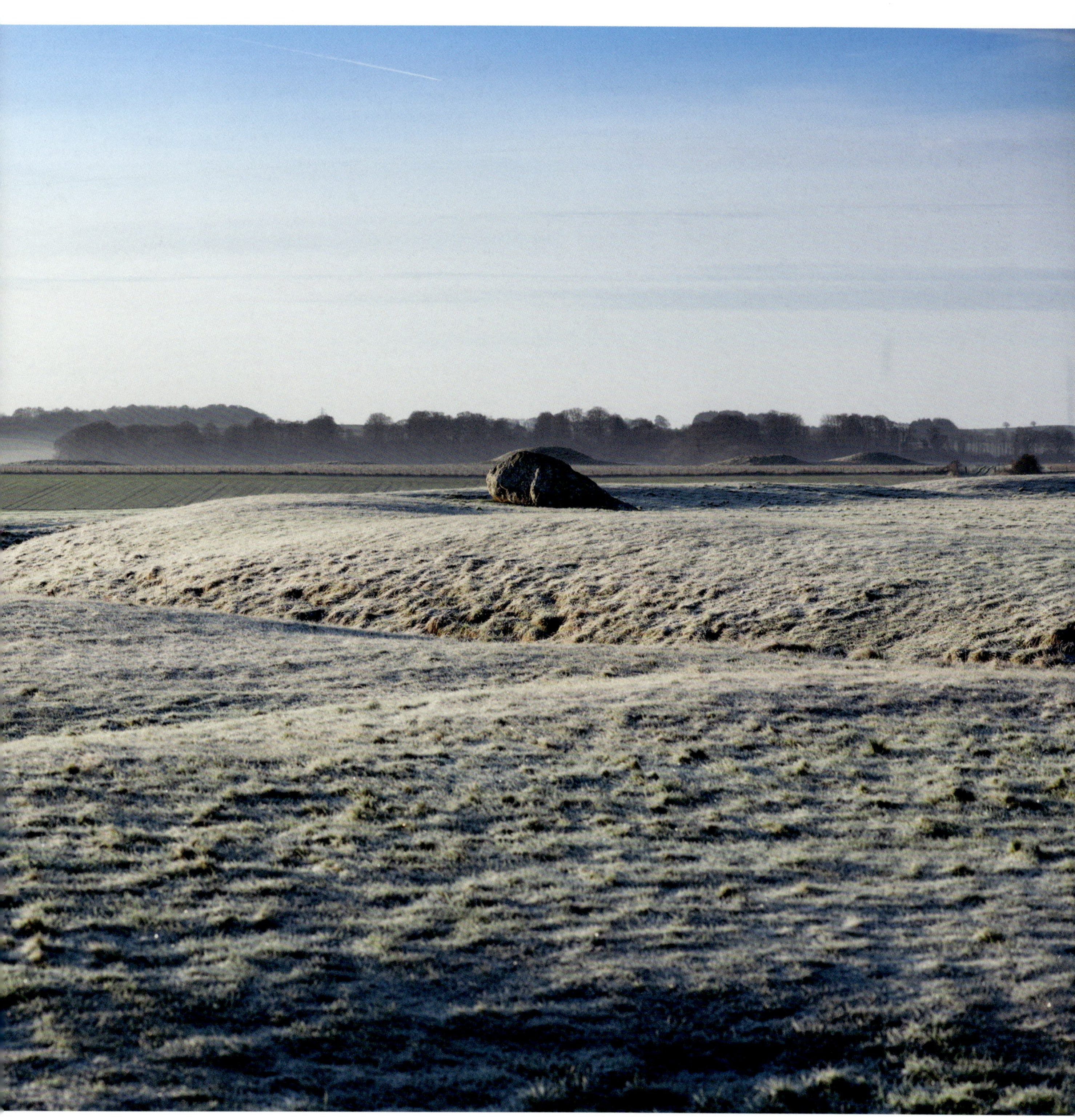

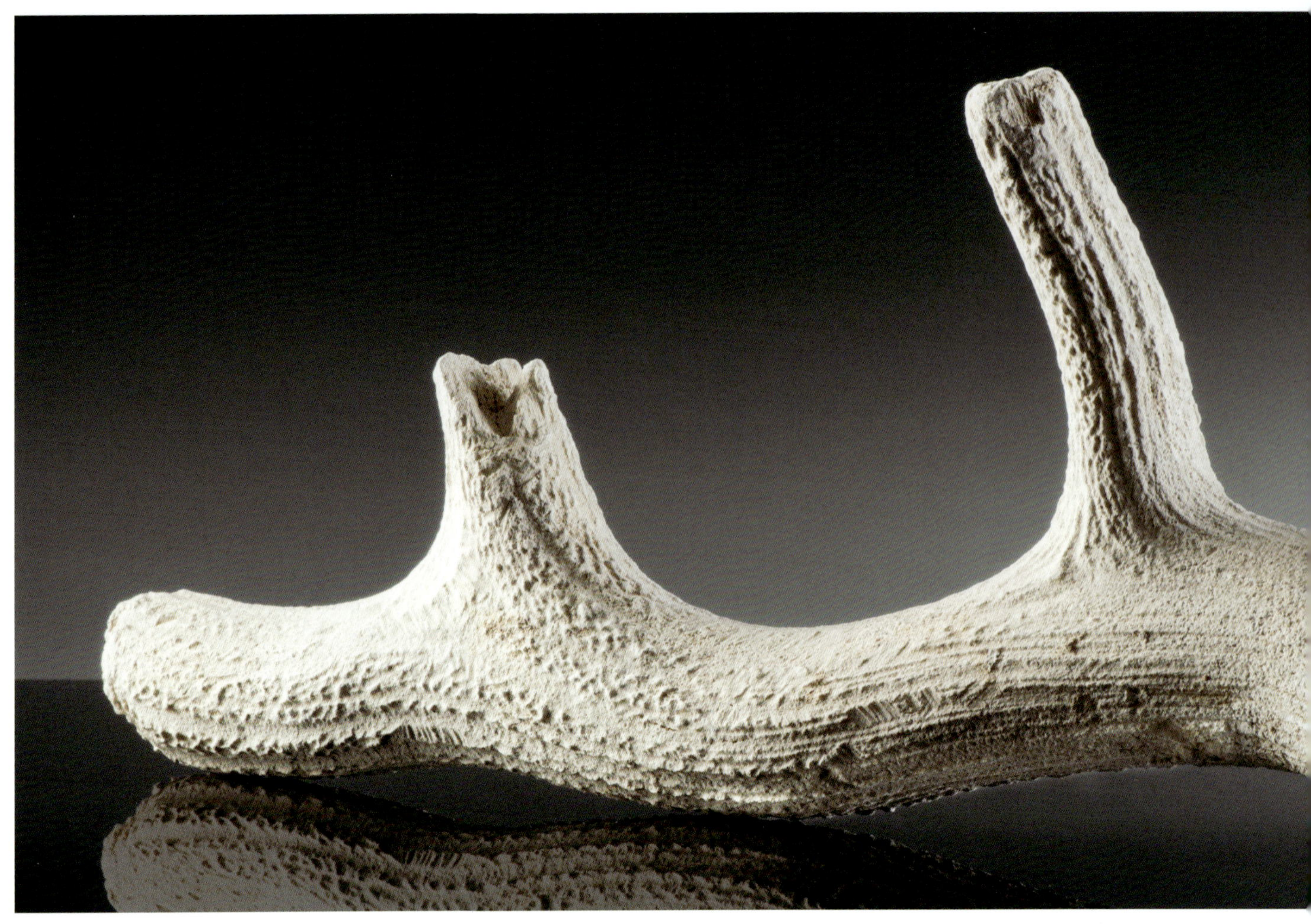

ABOVE Antlers shed by red deer in early spring were collected and modified by removing the tines to make effective digging tools. This Neolithic example was found in the ditch at Stonehenge.

long distances in this period. If people built any houses in the landscape at this time, however, they have not survived.

In the decades around 3000 BC, following the time when relatively few monuments were constructed, an important new place of burial was established: the first phase of Stonehenge. The circular earthwork enclosure, or henge, at Stonehenge was built at the east end of a broad spur above the dry valley of Stonehenge Bottom. This was not the highest point in the landscape, but one that provided extensive views in all directions. This first earthwork phase of Stonehenge is technically known by archaeologists as a 'proto-henge' or 'formative henge', a rare type of monument that is earlier than many other henges, which mostly date from the late Neolithic period. These early henges are markedly circular in shape, measure 80–110m across, and are formed of a ditch with one or two banks crossed by narrow entrances. All of those so far excavated have revealed evidence that they were used for funerary activity, in the form of cremated remains or burials.

The ditch at Stonehenge, dug into the chalk using antler picks, was originally about 1.2m deep. The chalk and soil dug out of the ditch were heaped up to form two flanking banks which were originally about 1m high. The enclosure had a wide entrance or causeway to the north-east and two narrower ones to the south and south-west. Discarded antler picks, animal bones and flint tools were found at the base of the ditch. Radiocarbon dating of the antler picks has shown that the ditch was dug shortly after 3000 BC. In the ends of the ditch on either side of the southern entrances,

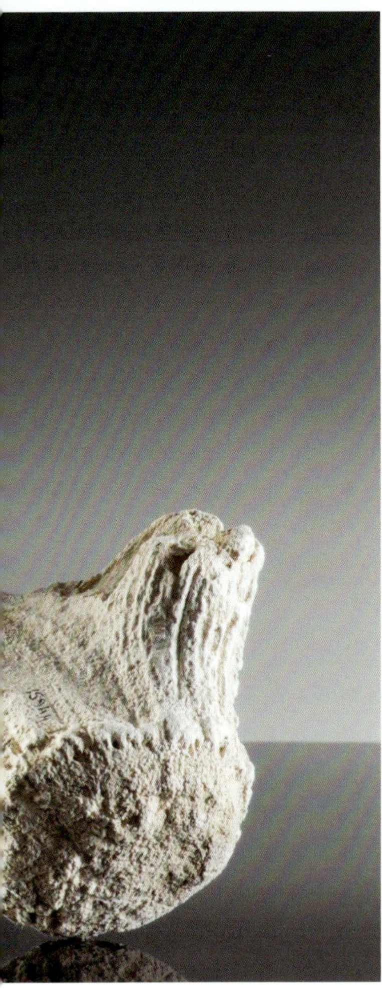

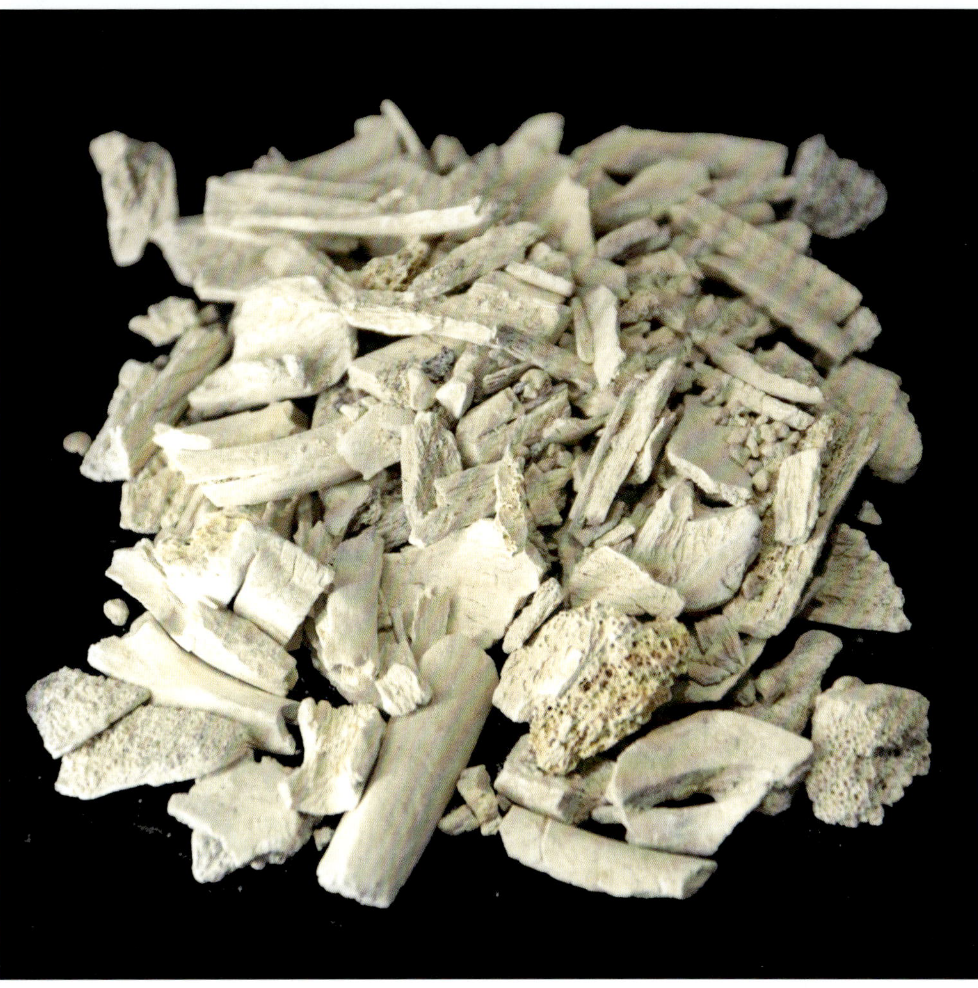

ABOVE RIGHT The cremated remains of a person who died in about 3000 BC. These burnt bone fragments were collected from the pyre and placed into one of the Aubrey Holes at Stonehenge.

some older animal bones were found, including a cattle skull, two cattle jaws and a red deer leg bone. These items, dating from several hundred years before the ditch was dug, may have been relics, kept for a long time before they were placed in the ground, or perhaps were deposited in an earlier circuit of pits that may have existed on the same line as the later ditch.

Lying just within the henge was a precisely circular ring of 56 pits with an average diameter of just over 1m. These are known as the Aubrey Holes, named after John Aubrey, the antiquary who was the first to notice them as shallow depressions when he carried out a survey of the site in 1666 (see page 102). Just over half of these roughly circular pits have been excavated, and most were found to contain at least one deposit of cremated human bones. The Aubrey Holes have been the subject of much debate – did they hold standing stones, or upright timber posts? Or were they simply pits into which cremations were placed? It is difficult to draw firm conclusions, as most of these pits were excavated in the 1920s and few records of what was found survive, but their size and depth suggest that they are unlikely to have been dug

In the decades around 3000 BC, following the time when relatively few monuments were constructed, an important new place of burial was established: the first phase of Stonehenge.

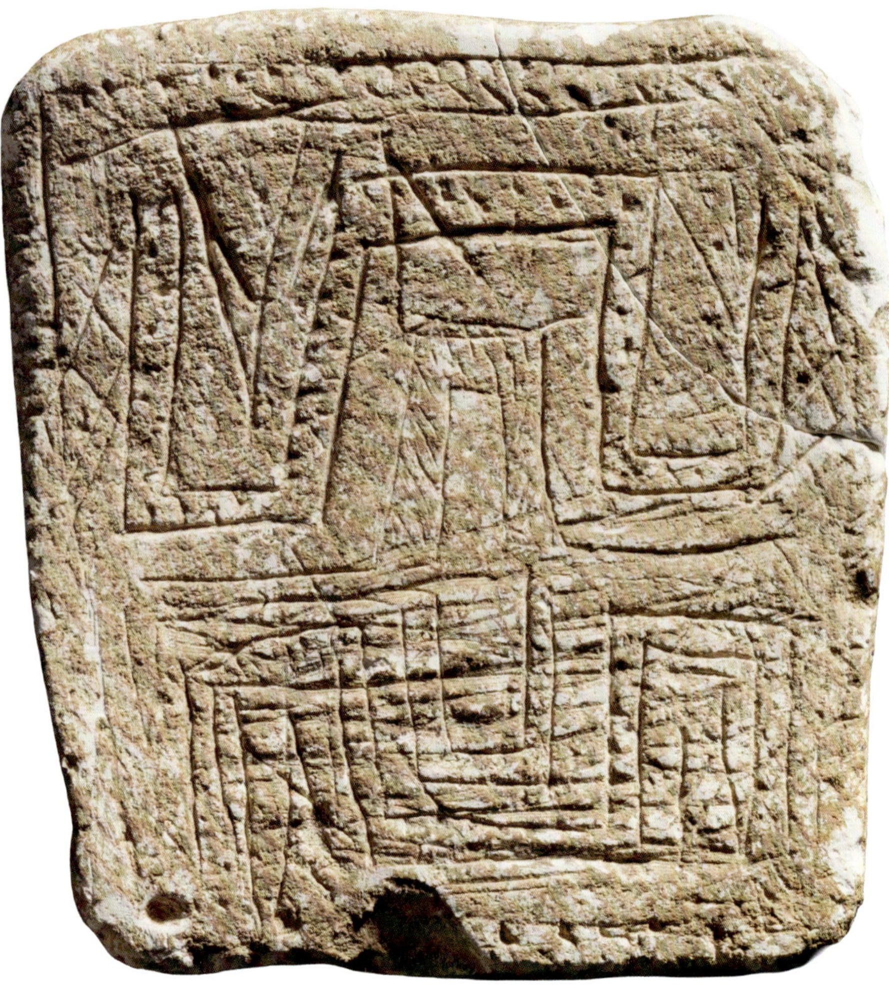

ABOVE This chalk plaque carved with geometric designs, dating from about 2700 BC, was found in a pit just over half a mile (1km) from Stonehenge. With it was another plaque, animal bones and sherds of Grooved Ware pottery, probably the remains of a feast.

to hold timber posts. Some were found to have had sloping sides and chalk rubble packing, suggesting that they held standing stones. These stones would have been similar in size to the smaller standing stones that can be seen today in the centre of the henge at Stonehenge, known as bluestones. These bluestones were transported from the Preseli Hills in south-west Wales, over 140 miles (230km) away (see page 34). It is possible that these bluestones were brought here early in Stonehenge's history to form part of this first phase of the monument, and were later taken down and moved into the central arrangement of stones.

It is not known exactly what stood in the centre of the monument during this earliest stage. Excavations have, however, uncovered many postholes and stakeholes that would have held upright timbers of various sizes, many of which date from before the positioning of Stonehenge's large central standing stones. The arrangement of these holes suggests that a wooden structure once stood in the middle of the henge. This appears to have been formed of an array of concentric posts with a porch-like feature within the south-east part of the henge, as well as a passageway lined by posts and blocked by a timber screen, which extended towards the henge's southern entrance. It is impossible for us to now know exactly what this structure looked like, its purpose or how it was used. Whatever stood in the centre of the earthwork, however, must have been dismantled before the bluestones and sarsens were erected there.

At the time the henge was built, the surrounding landscape was becoming busy, with people making camps and settlements.

These finds suggest gatherings, feasting and rituals ... these people were well connected, or had perhaps travelled to the Stonehenge area from far away.

Evidence for these settlements comes from numerous pits excavated on either side of the river Avon, near to Stonehenge. These pits were packed full of flint flakes and tools including chisel arrowheads, as well as animal bones and a type of pottery known as Grooved Ware, which was beginning to be used in southern Britain at this time. These finds suggest gatherings, feasting and rituals. Unusual items, such as a scallop shell from the coast and a fragment of polished stone axe from North Wales have also been found, suggesting that these people were well connected, or had perhaps travelled to the Stonehenge area from far away.

On the far side of the river Avon, east of Stonehenge, at Bulford, was perhaps the largest settlement in the area. Here, a cluster of 48 pits containing similar artefacts and an early type of Grooved Ware pottery may have been the place where people stayed when they brought their dead for burial at the monument. Nearby, at Ratfyn, a brown bear scapula (shoulder blade) found in a pit shows that people were hunting bears (before they became extinct in Britain), most likely for their fur and skins, which could be tanned to form leather.

In the centuries before 3000 BC this part of the Salisbury Plain landscape was clearly a busy area, where people regularly stayed in temporary settlements. It is likely that they were attracted by the open landscape, ideal for grazing, but perhaps they were also returning to earlier monuments – places of memory and stories. They chose this important location as a suitable place for a new circular form of monument, where they buried members of their community.

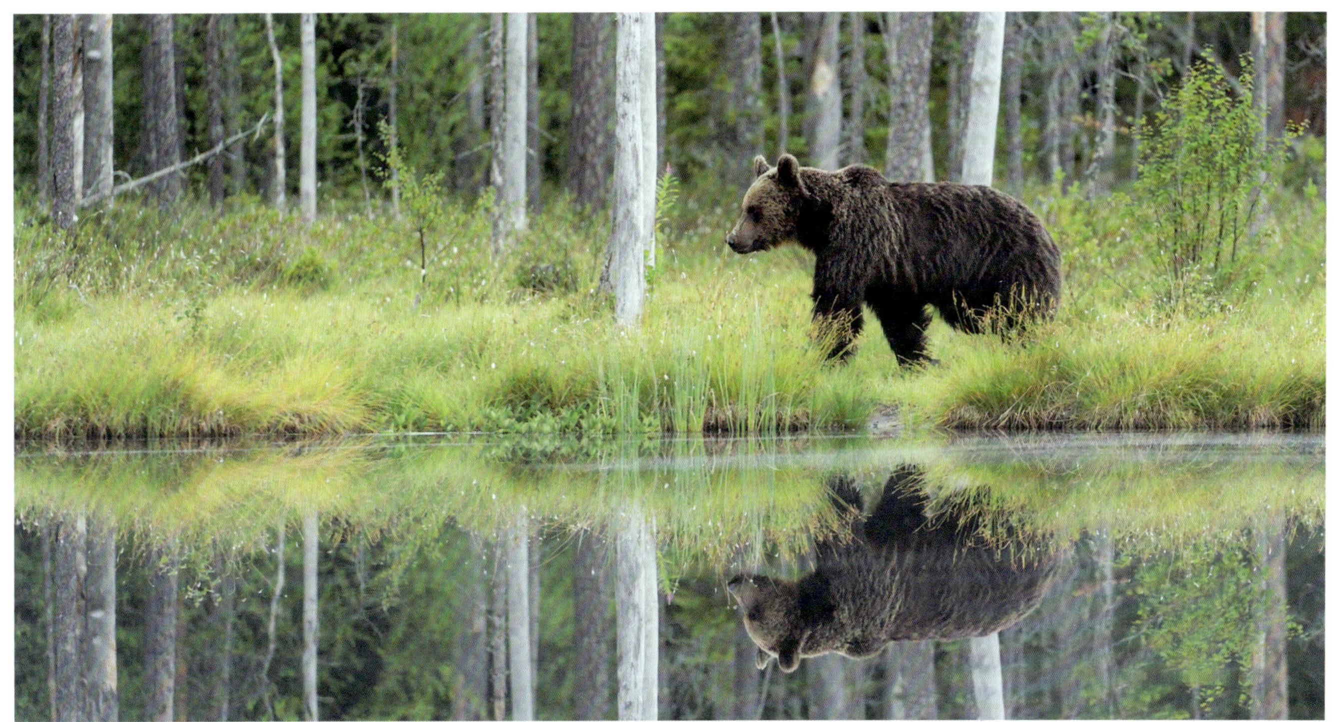

BELOW Neolithic people in Britain inhabited the landscape alongside large predators now no longer found here, including wolves, bears and lynx. Remains of a brown bear were found in a pit at a site not far from Stonehenge.

A Place of Burial

Excavations at Stonehenge have discovered many clusters of cremated human bones, which were buried here in Neolithic times. But who were these people and why were they buried at Stonehenge?

The burials ranged from a single piece of burnt bone to the remains of an estimated four individuals placed together in one deposit. These cremated remains were placed into or close to the Aubrey Holes (see page 29), as well as in the henge ditch and adjacent banks. A distinct concentration of burials was found towards the south-east part of the monument. Radiocarbon dating suggests that the majority of these people died between 3090 and 2745 BC and were buried during the first phase of Stonehenge, before the large sarsen stones were erected in the centre of the monument.

Many of these cremations were excavated during archaeological work at Stonehenge in the 1920s. At that time, the excavators did not have the scientific methods to analyse the fragments of burned bone, and so they were reburied on site within one of the emptied Aubrey Holes. These reburied fragments were retrieved in 2008. Careful analysis using techniques developed since their initial excavation has revealed that they represent the remains of at least 26 separate people, although this is a minimum number; the remains are so fragmentary that it is hard to calculate the total number of people buried here, and there are likely to be far more. Of the 26 individuals, 14 could be identified as female, nine as male and three were impossible to classify. There were at least five children ranging in age from newborn babies to juveniles, and some

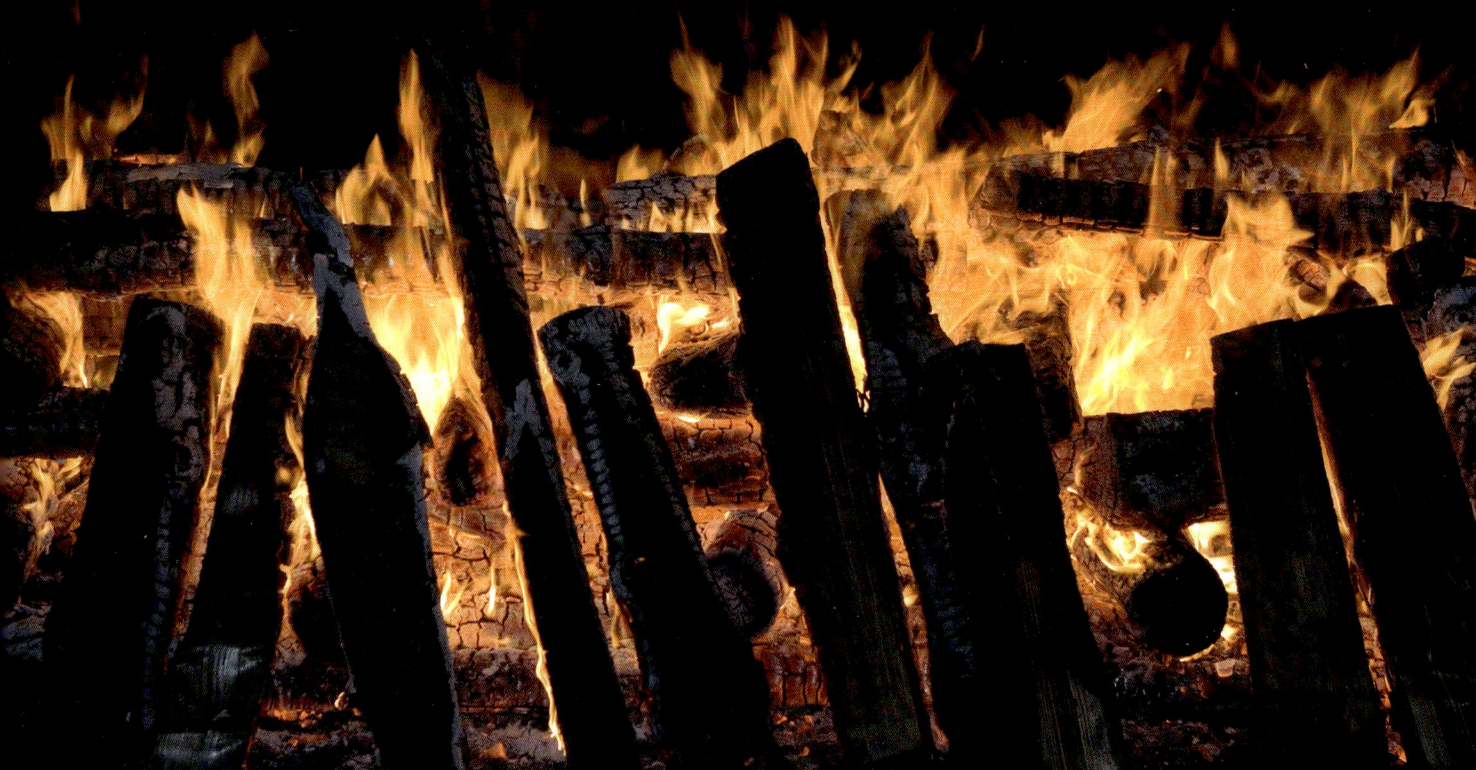

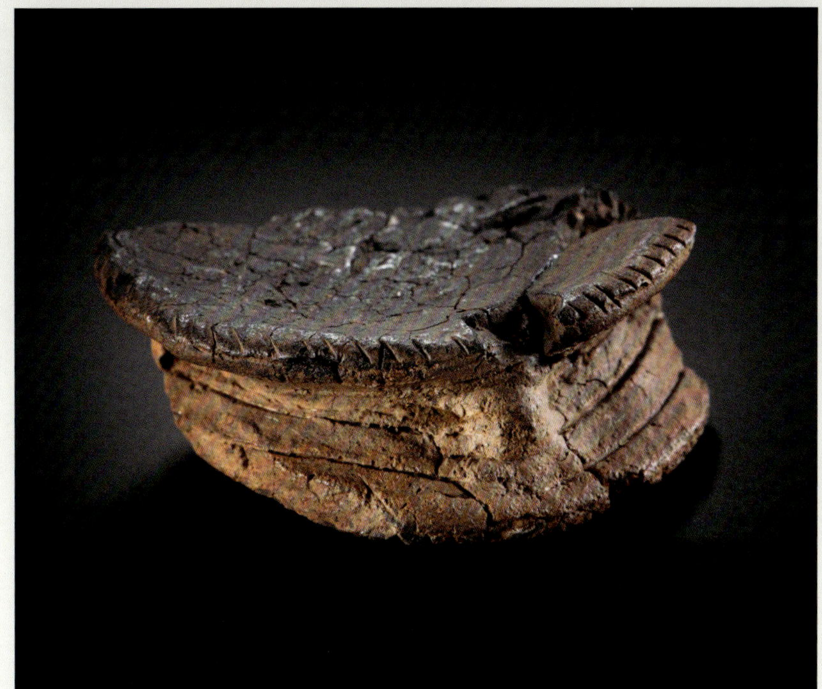

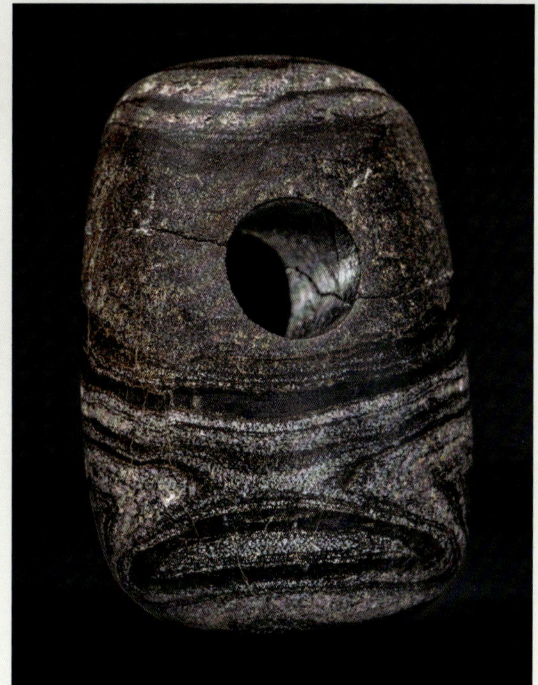

OPPOSITE During the middle and late Neolithic periods, people cremated their dead, burning their bodies on wooden funeral pyres – a dramatic and memorable event that would have lasted several hours.

OPPOSITE TOP These bone skewer pins, which perhaps fastened a shroud, were found with cremation burials at Stonehenge. Similar pins have been found with burials and cremations at sites contemporary with Stonehenge as far apart as Oxfordshire, North Yorkshire and West Lothian, suggesting they formed part of a widely practised rite.

ABOVE LEFT This small ceramic dish with a burnt upper surface was found in the upper layers of earth filling one of the Aubrey Holes at Stonehenge, in which cremated bones had been buried.

ABOVE RIGHT This small stone 'mace-head' was found with another of the cremation burials. It is made from a highly polished gneiss stone and was probably mounted on a wooden handle.

individuals have signs of osteoarthritis, meaning that they were middle aged or older. The burials therefore represented a cross-section of the community, rather than a single group (such as adult males, for example).

Chemical analysis of the bone fragments from 25 of these people revealed that 15 of them spent their last ten years or so living in places with chalk geology, perhaps in the local area. The other ten had lived in a variety of places across south-west England, Wales, and further afield. Some may have travelled to the area late in life or their cremated remains may have been brought to Stonehenge after their deaths. This suggests that Stonehenge was well known to communities living across southern Britain at this time.

Only a few of the burials at Stonehenge were associated with objects. Several were accompanied by bone pins of a long, slender type known as skewer pins. These were burnt and may have been used to hold together a shroud on the funeral pyre. One burial was found with a unique, small, polished stone 'mace-head' – a rounded object pierced with a large hole, made of gneiss rock from western Scotland or the Outer Hebrides. This was perhaps a symbol of high status and connects Stonehenge to communities living much further north. An unusual, small, ceramic dish found with another cremation may have been used to burn incense or perfume as part of the funerary rites.

Many more burials may still lie under the ground, but it has been estimated that perhaps 150 people were buried here in total, over a few centuries. This would make Stonehenge the largest known Neolithic cremation cemetery, as burials from this period are extremely rare. We may never know why these particular people were selected for burial at Stonehenge. Perhaps they belonged to one extended family or were people somehow connected to this place. It has been suggested that the later stone monument was a memorial to these individuals.

A TEMPLE OF STONE (2600–2400 BC)

In about 2500 BC a remarkable stone circle was built within the earlier henge enclosure. It was an architectural and technological masterpiece, apparently unlike anything that had been built in stone before, or that has been constructed since.

The stone circle is made of two different types of stones. The larger stones are sarsen (a form of silcrete), which were transported on sledges from the edge of the Marlborough Downs, about 15 miles (24km) to the north. The much smaller stones are known as bluestones. These are a mix of geological types, including dolerite, spotted dolerite, rhyolites and volcanic tuffs, all quarried from outcrops on or near the Preseli Hills in south-west Wales, 143 miles (230km) away. They were probably transported overland on sledges and then by boat along the South Wales coast and up the river Avon. Although both types of stones now look similar due to millennia of weathering, when the stone circle was first built, the freshly worked dark blue-grey bluestones would have contrasted strongly against the light grey-white sarsens.

Excavations within the ditch and banks at Stonehenge have uncovered very few artefacts such as pottery or animal bones, with little sign of feasting or fires here. It seems to have been kept deliberately clean and free of everyday debris, perhaps showing that it was a sacred space. As such, there is little evidence beyond the stones themselves to help us understand the purpose and function of the monument.

Today, Stonehenge has four concentric rings of stone. The outermost ring originally had 30 upright sarsens, capped by 30 horizontal stones, or lintels. Each upright was positioned to reach the same height, enabling the lintels to be level, despite the slight slope of the ground. The most regularly shaped stones are found on the north-east side of the circle opposite the entrance causeway, suggesting that this was seen as the 'front', perhaps important for creating a dramatic impression as people approached or entered the monument.

BELOW Carn Gyfrwy, one of the outcrops of the Preseli Hills in Pembrokeshire, Wales, from where some of the spotted dolerite bluestones were sourced.

OPPOSITE The sarsen stones chosen for the 'front' face of the outer circle were the largest and most regular in shape, giving an impression of uniformity and solidity. Their trapezoidal shapes give an illusion of height.

OVERLEAF While great care was taken to ensure the lintels of the outer sarsen circle were level, the trilithons of the inner horseshoe were graded in height. Only one of the stones of the tallest trilithon still stands at the head of the horseshoe.

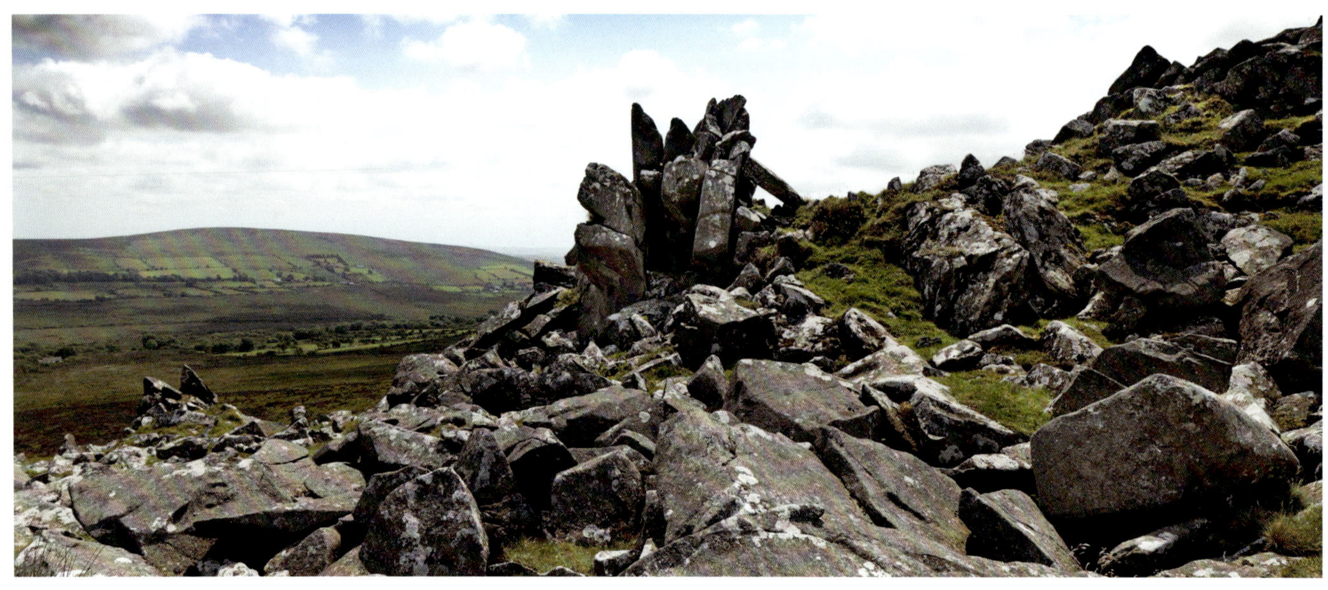

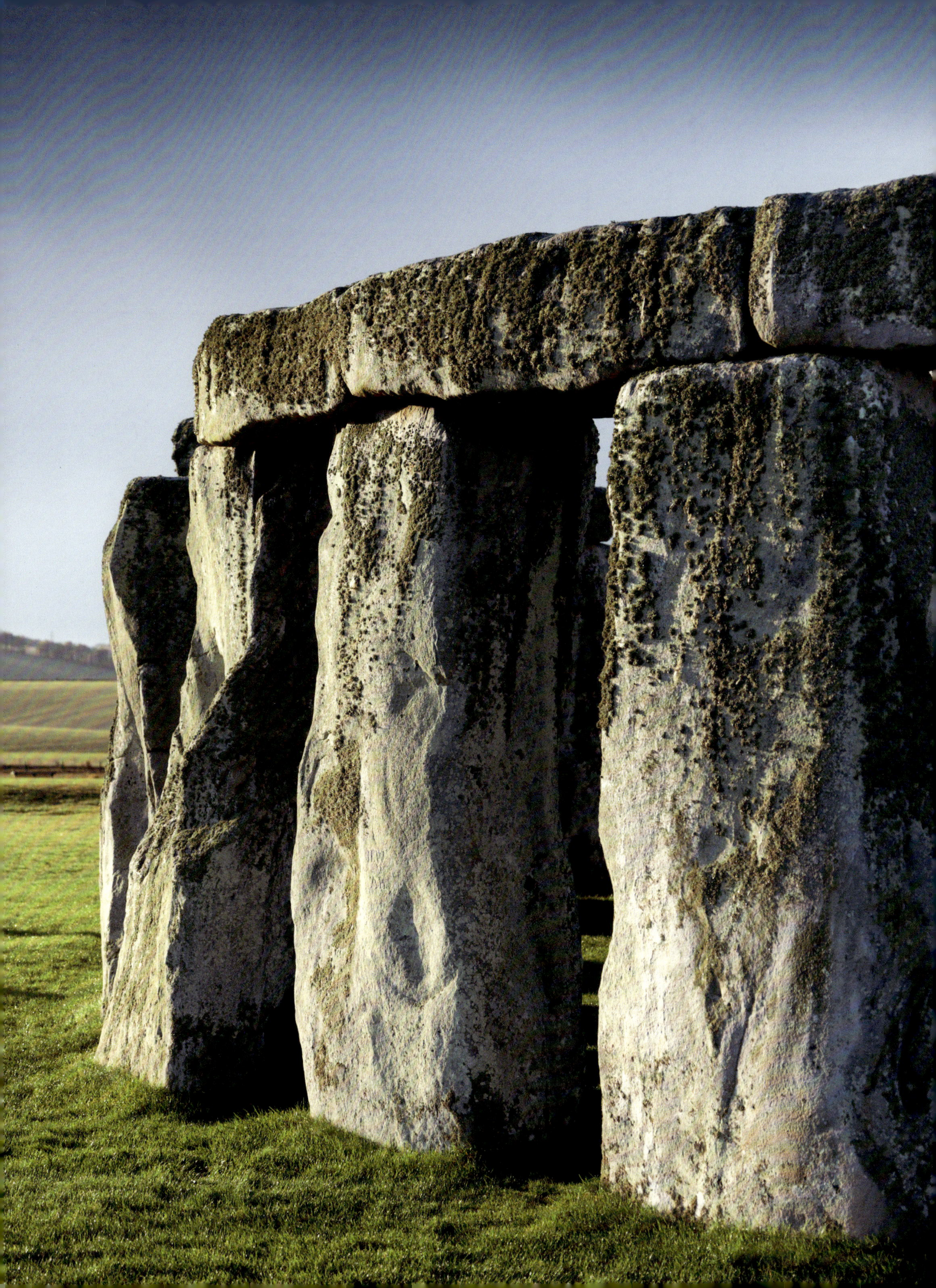

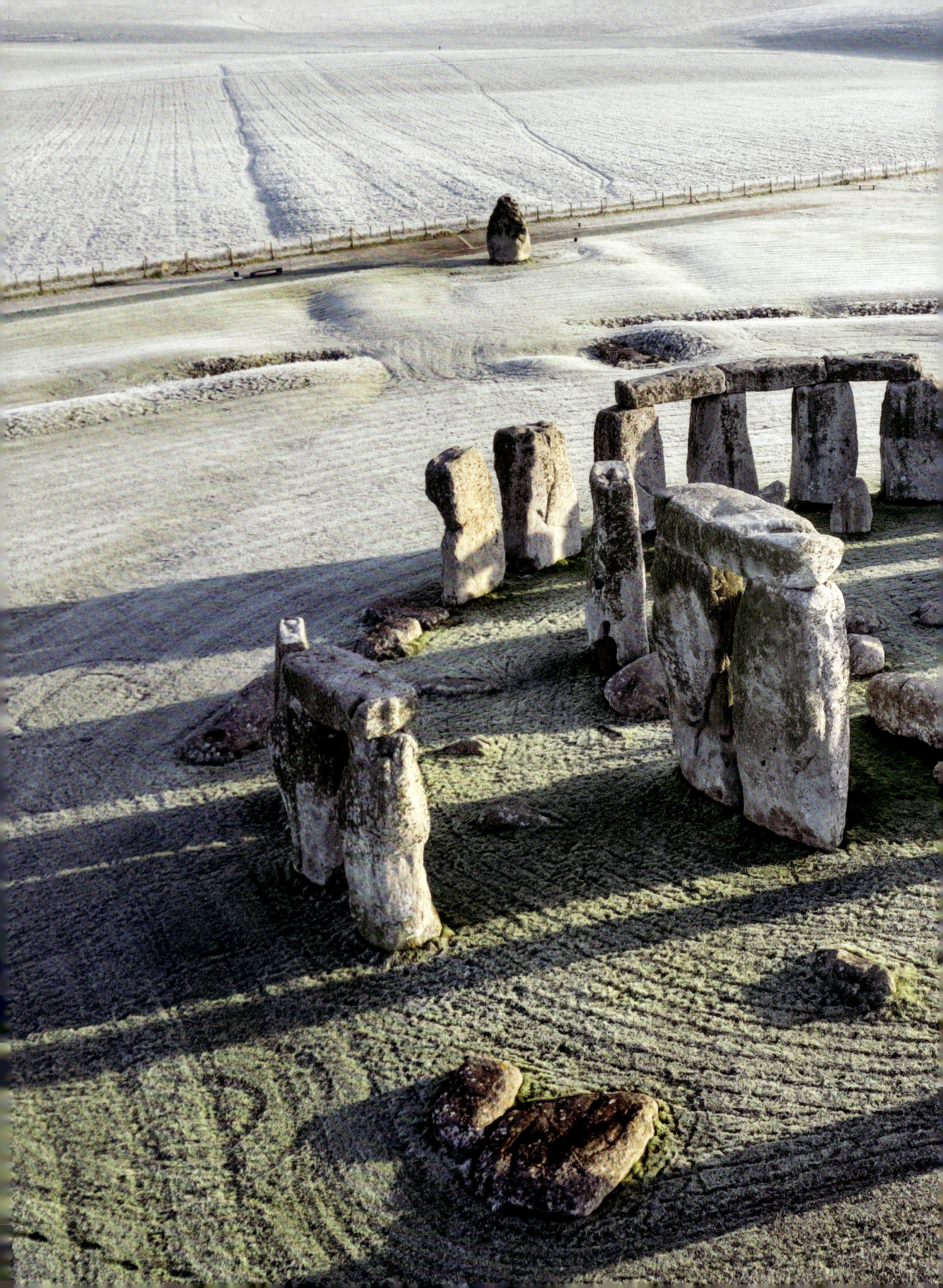

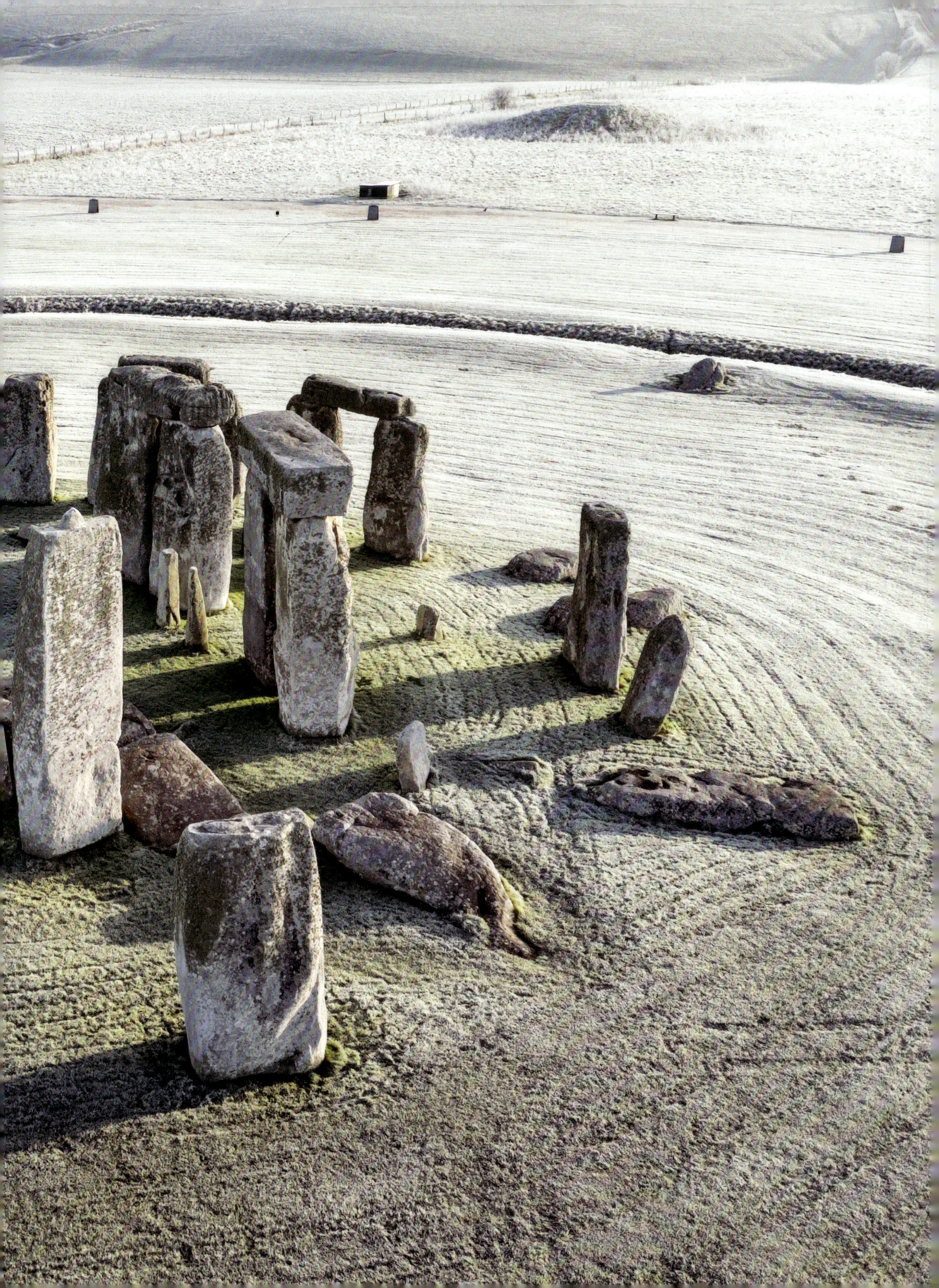

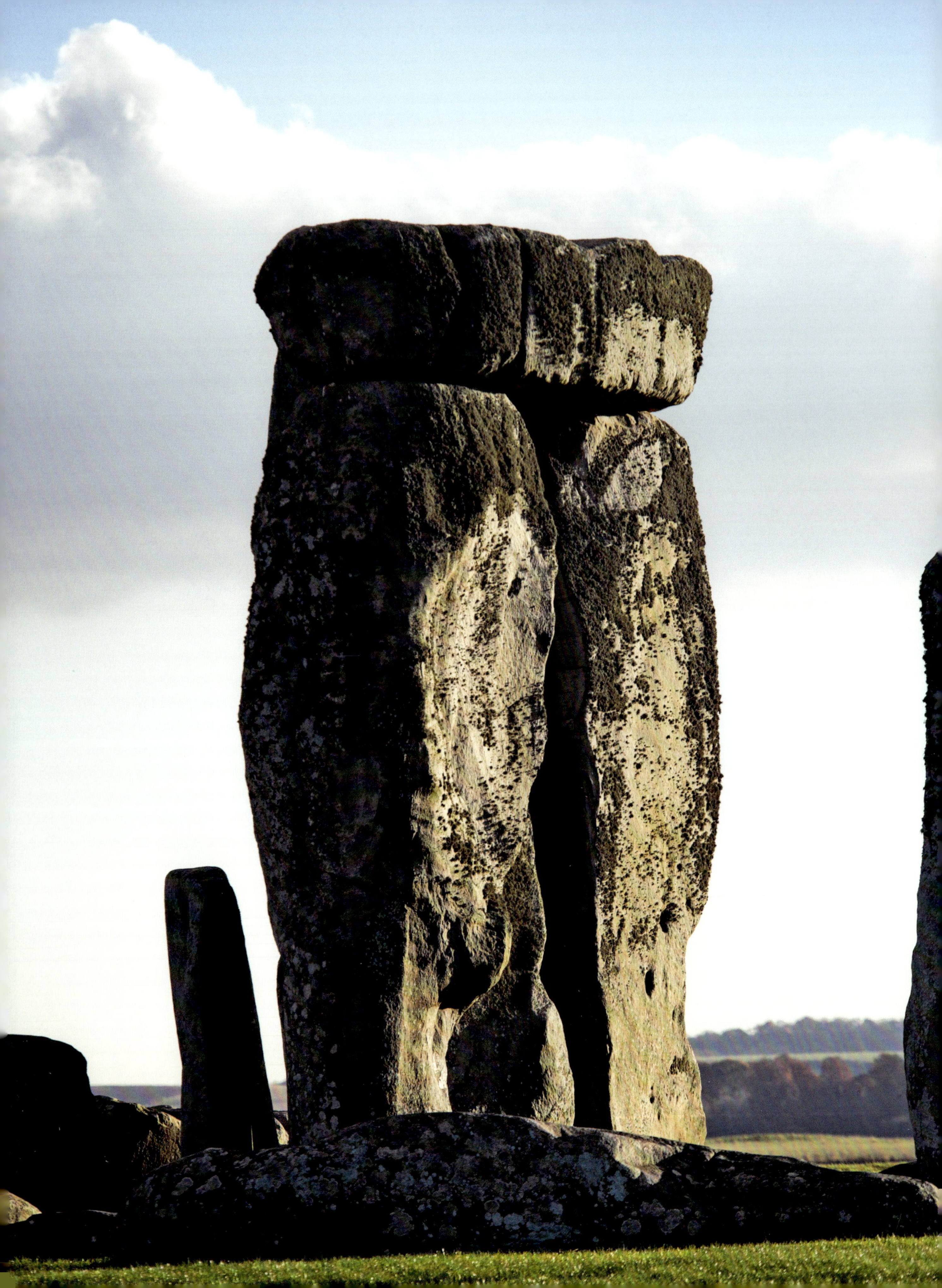

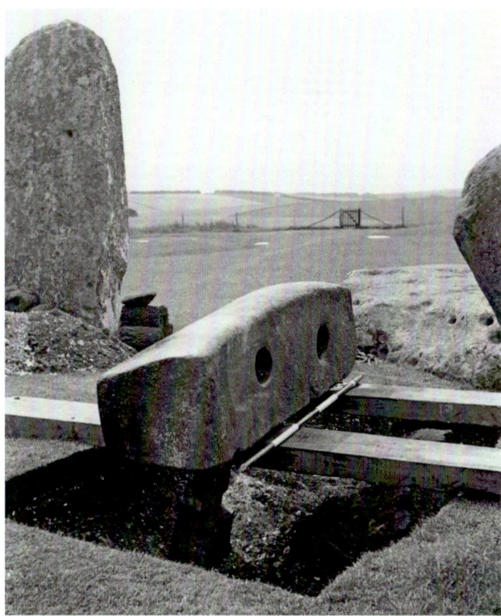

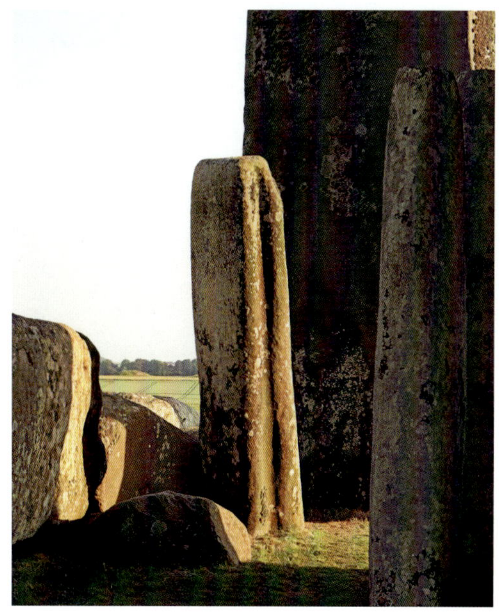

OPPOSITE The monumental sarsen trilithon on the west side of the inner horseshoe. These three stones fell in 1797, and were put back into position in 1958.

ABOVE LEFT One of the fallen bluestones raised on planks during excavations in 1954. It has been carefully shaped and has two mortise holes, showing that it was at some point used as a lintel. It is one of two bluestone lintels known from Stonehenge.

ABOVE RIGHT This bluestone pillar has a distinct groove running lengthways down one side, which shows that it once slotted together with another one.

OVERLEAF The rising sun creates a dramatic silhouette of the Heel Stone and the misty landscape around Stonehenge.

Each stone was shaped using hammerstones (see page 45) to form interlocking joints. The uprights were connected to the lintels with mortise-and-tenon joints, where a single projection, or tenon, on the upright stone fits into a socket, or mortise, on the underside of the lintel. The lintels in the outer circle were connected together by tongue-and-groove joints, where a narrow projection along the end of one lintel stone slots into a groove chipped into the adjacent lintel.

Inside the outer sarsen ring are the fragmentary remains of a circle of bluestone boulders and pillars of different shapes and sizes, all originally from the Preseli Hills in Wales. They include rhyolites, volcanic tuffs and dolerites. Within this circle of bluestones are five sarsen trilithons arranged in a horseshoe formation. Trilithon is a word created from the Greek words for 'three' and 'stone' – two uprights and a horizontal lintel. These trilithons include some of the largest sarsens at Stonehenge, with several weighing over 30 tonnes and the tallest standing at over 7m high. The trilithons were carefully graded in height, with the highest at the head of the horseshoe, towards the south-west.

Within the trilithon horseshoe is a horseshoe of tall, slender bluestone pillars. Most are of spotted dolerite, a dark blue stone flecked with white quartz, resembling the night sky.

Finally, within the arc of the inner bluestone horseshoe lies the Altar Stone. This is a grey-green sandstone of a different type to all the other stones. Geological research has shown that it was brought to Stonehenge all the way from the far north of Britain, probably from north-east mainland Scotland. Today it lies buried and broken under one of the fallen sarsens of the tallest trilithon. The architect Inigo Jones (1573–1652) was the first to describe this stone as an altar (see page 100); whether it stood upright or has always been horizontal is not known.

The large sarsen stones of the outer circle and inner horseshoe appear never to have been moved. The bluestones, on the other hand, have not always stood in the circle and oval arrangement we see today, but instead have a long history of being moved to stand in different places. The bluestones may initially have stood in the Aubrey Holes (see page 29), but their first definite placement was in a curving double arc within the sarsen stone circle. This arrangement included interlocking pairs of stones, as shown by the presence of bluestones with long grooves or tongues down their sides. There were also at least two small trilithons: two of the bluestones have been

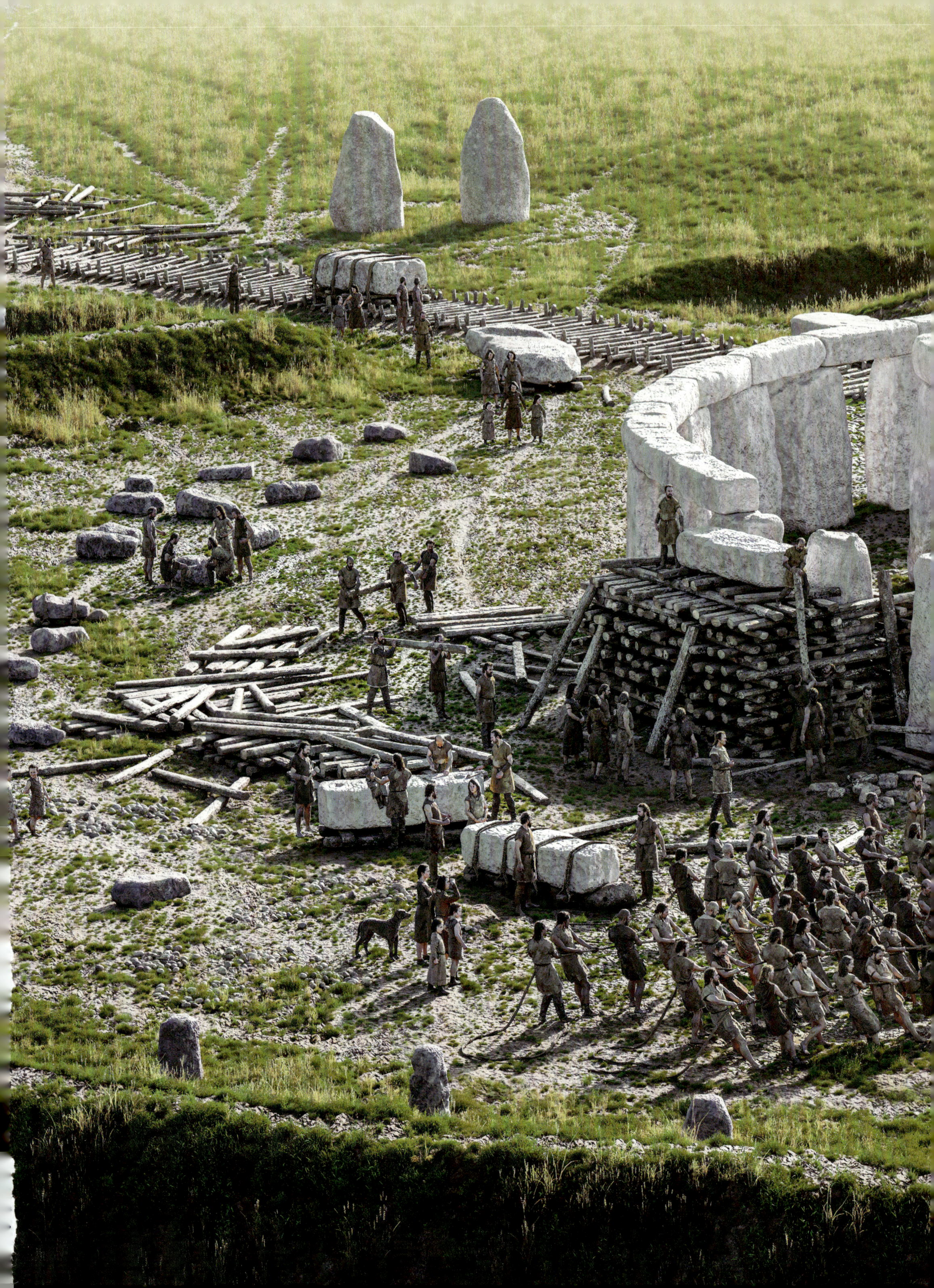

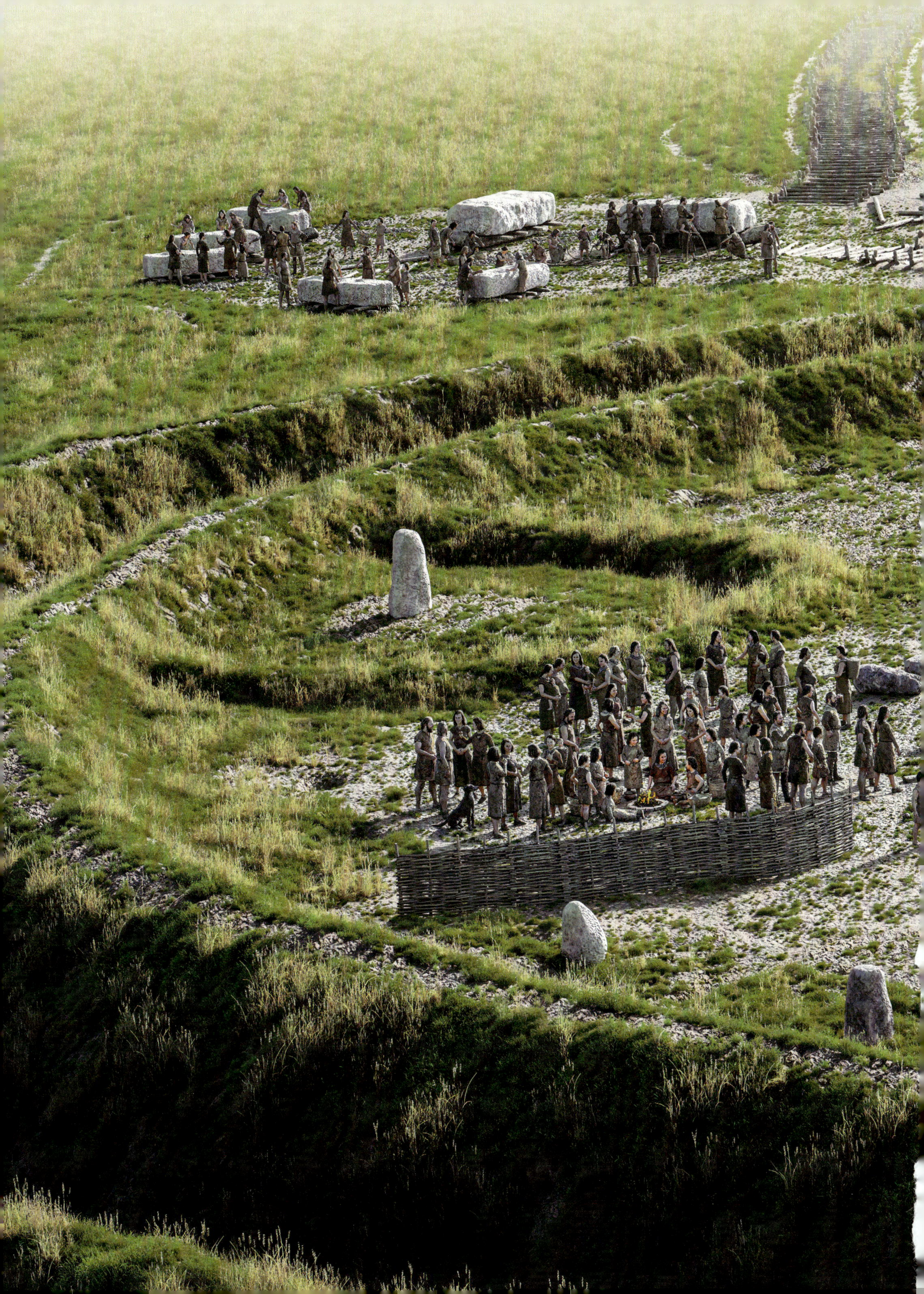

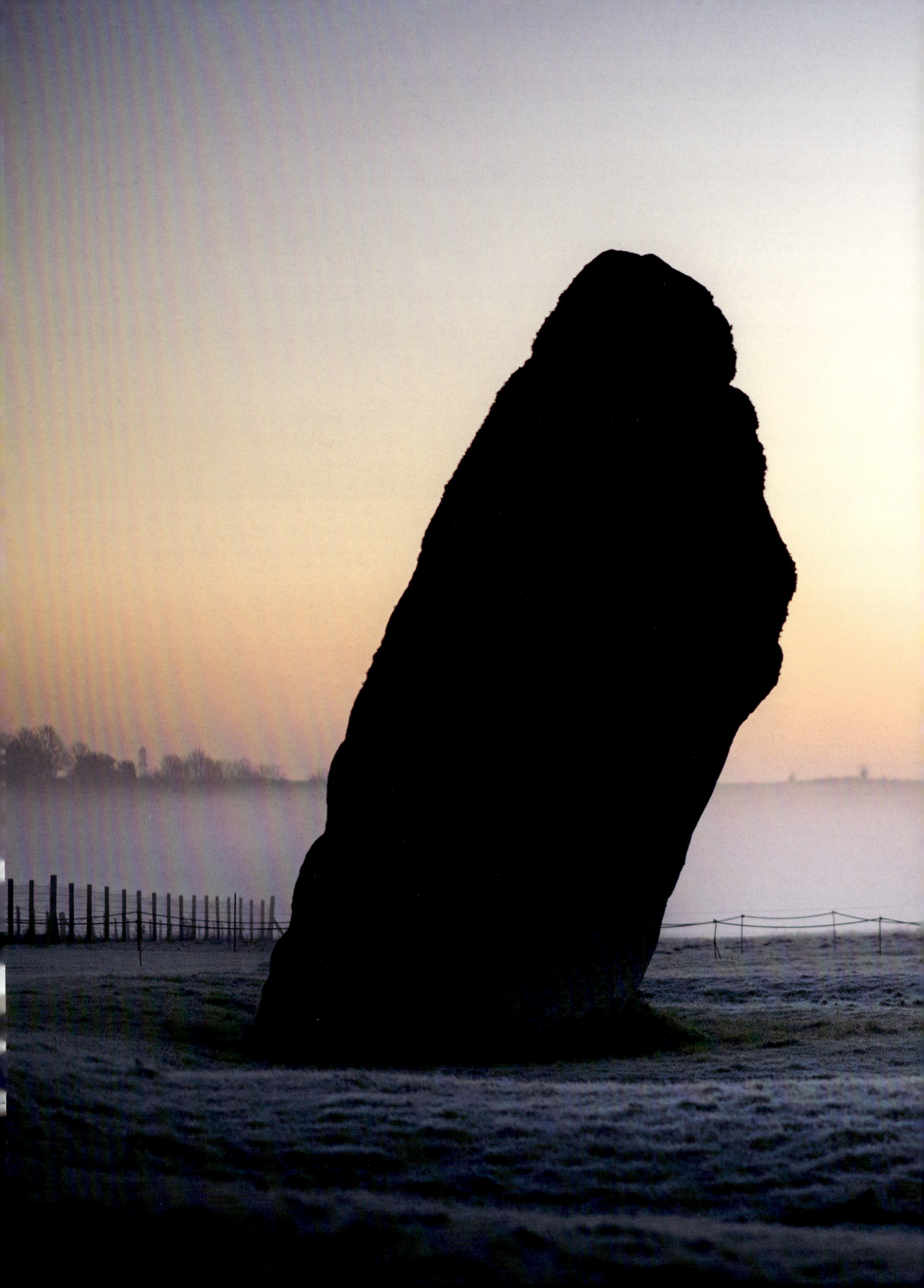

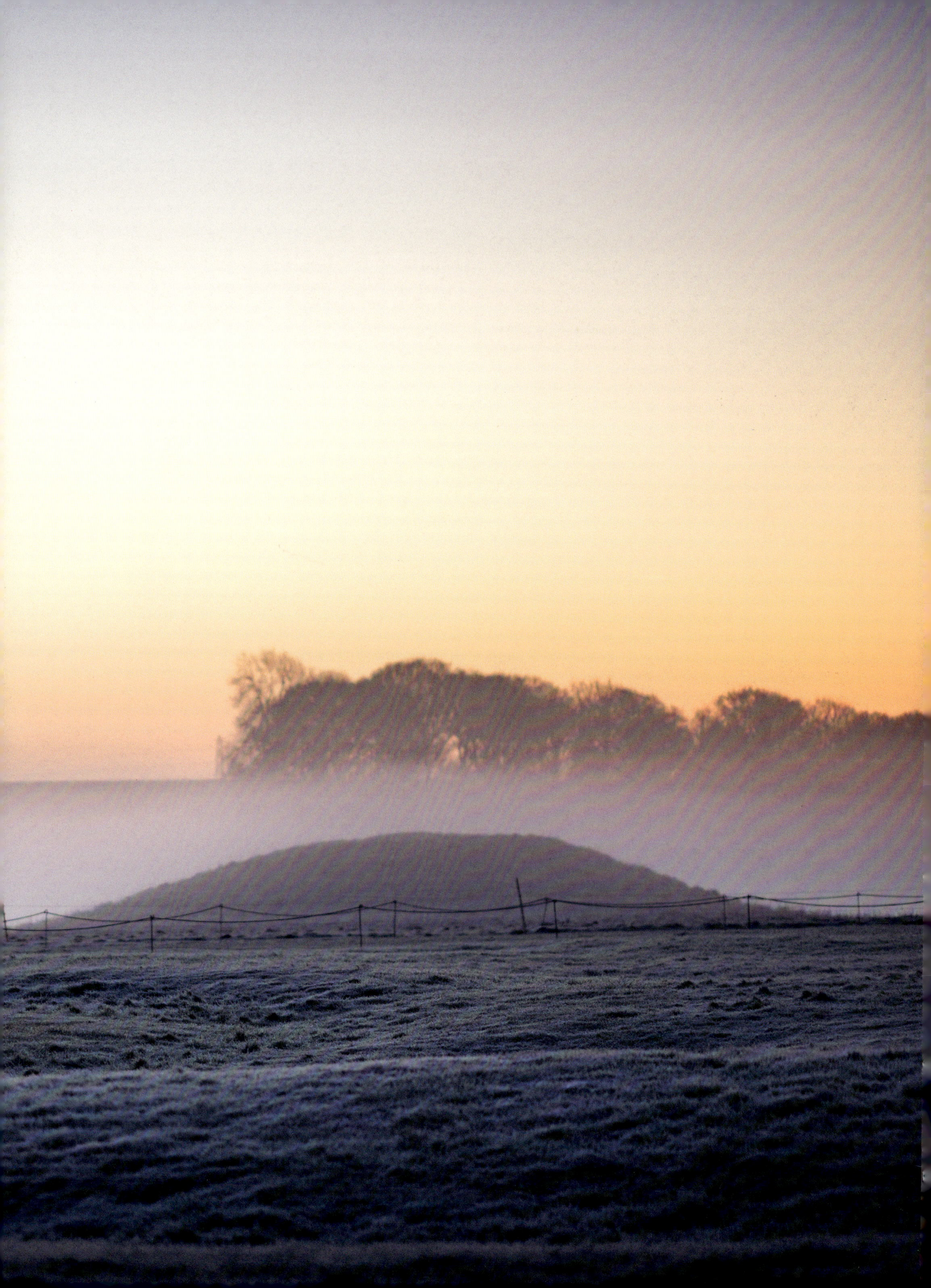

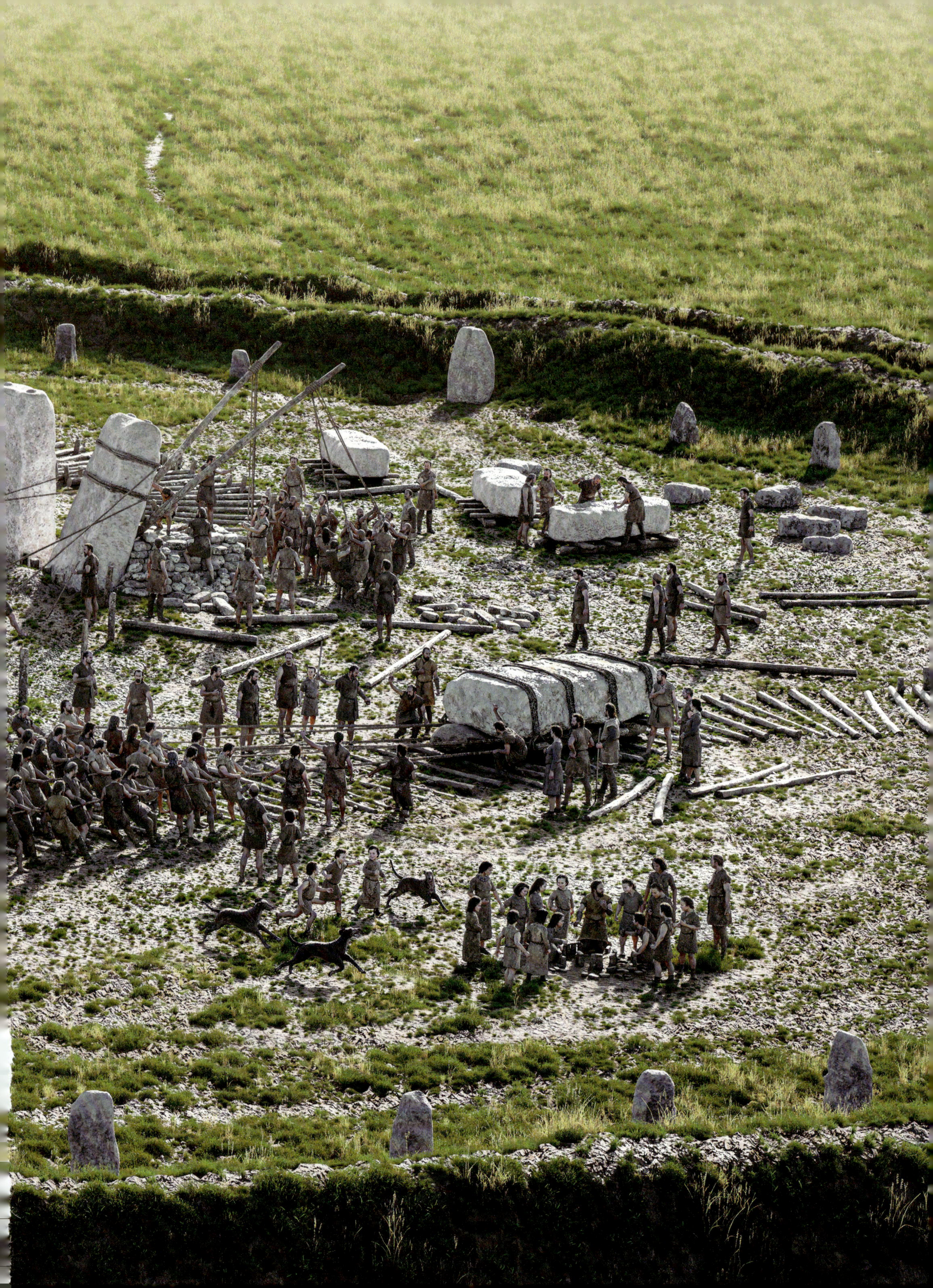

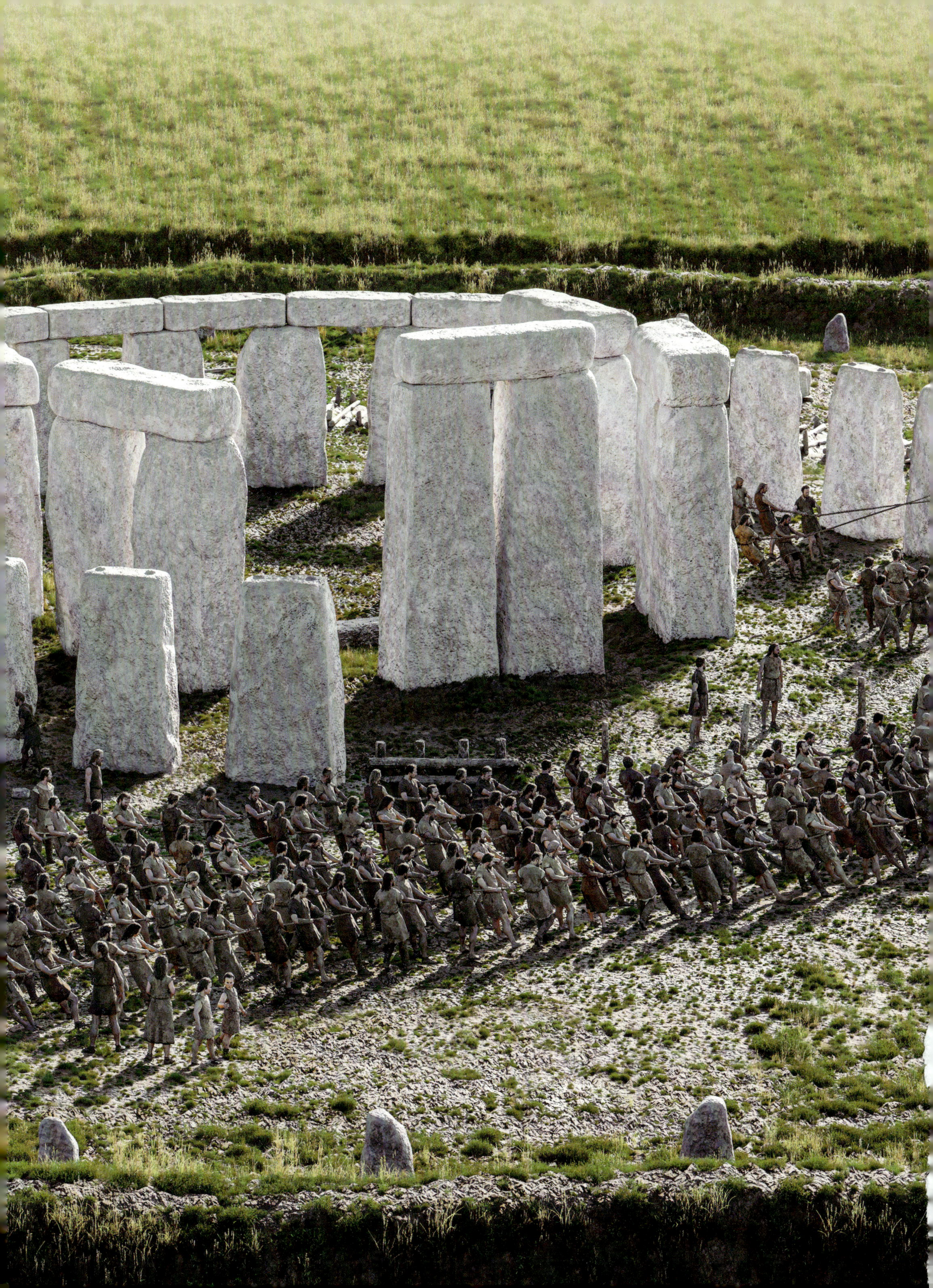

We do not know why people moved the bluestones, but these alterations suggest that they were key to the significance and meaning of Stonehenge and that perhaps that meaning changed over time.

GATEFOLD An artist's reconstruction of Stonehenge from the south-west in about 2500 BC. The sarsen trilithons are already in place in the centre of the monument. Around them, the sarsen circle is being constructed. One of the stones is being pulled to vertical using wooden levers and a pile of chocking stones. Meanwhile, another sarsen is being dragged on sledges along a wooden trackway. To the north, other stones are being worked into shape using hammerstones. Scattered about are the smaller bluestones, some still standing in their previous settings in a circle inside the outer bank, and others already removed and ready to be moved into their new locations.

shaped to form lintels with mortises, and others have vestiges of tenons on top. It is not known exactly where these bluestone trilithons stood, but they were perhaps placed to frame the rising and setting sun at different times of the year (see page 48).

This early arrangement of bluestones was dismantled and, together with more bluestones relocated from a stone circle that stood near the river Avon (see page 64), were arranged among the sarsens into the inner oval and outer circle that we see today. We do not know why people moved the bluestones, but these alterations suggest that they were key to the significance and meaning of Stonehenge, and that perhaps that meaning changed over time.

Several other sarsen stones stood outside the stone circle, probably set up at the same time. These include four 'Station Stones', positioned just inside the outer enclosure ditch to form a rectangle. They were named by the antiquary Edward Duke (1779–1852), who thought that they were 'astronomical stations' for observing the solstice sunrises and sunsets. Only two of the original four stones survive today. Two or three further sarsen stones stood across the entrance causeway. Only one of these now remains, lying fallen in the entrance and known as the 'Slaughter Stone', a name first recorded in 1799, inspired by the idea that it was a table used by the ancient Druids to slay or prepare their victims (see page 104). Outside the enclosure ditch, marking the entrance, is the enormous 'Heel Stone', surrounded by a small circular ditch. It was possibly one of a pair. The origin of this name is a little more obscure, but it probably derives from an ancient legend that when the wizard Merlin was conveying the stones here (see page 98), the Devil hit him in the heel with one of the stones and left a print there. There is a distinctive foot-shaped hollow on Stone 14, one of the stones of the outer circle, which appears to have been known as the Heel Stone. Later accounts transferred the name to the outlying marker stone, by which it has been known ever since.

It is clear that the presence of all these stones at Stonehenge represents a vast outlay of effort. So why did people drag enormous sarsens from the Marlborough Downs 15 miles away, bring bluestones all the way from Wales and transport the central Altar Stone over 460 miles (750km) from north-east Scotland to build Stonehenge? No one knows for certain. The sarsens probably come from an area now known as West Woods, near the town of Marlborough, where large sarsens that match the geology of the stones at the monument still survive despite extensive 19th-century quarrying. Sarsens had been used to build monuments, such as West Kennet Long Barrow, in this area since the early Neolithic period. This was the nearest source of large, regular stones which are almost entirely absent from Salisbury Plain. The Preseli Hills in south-west Wales, from where the bluestones originate, may have held a deeper meaning.

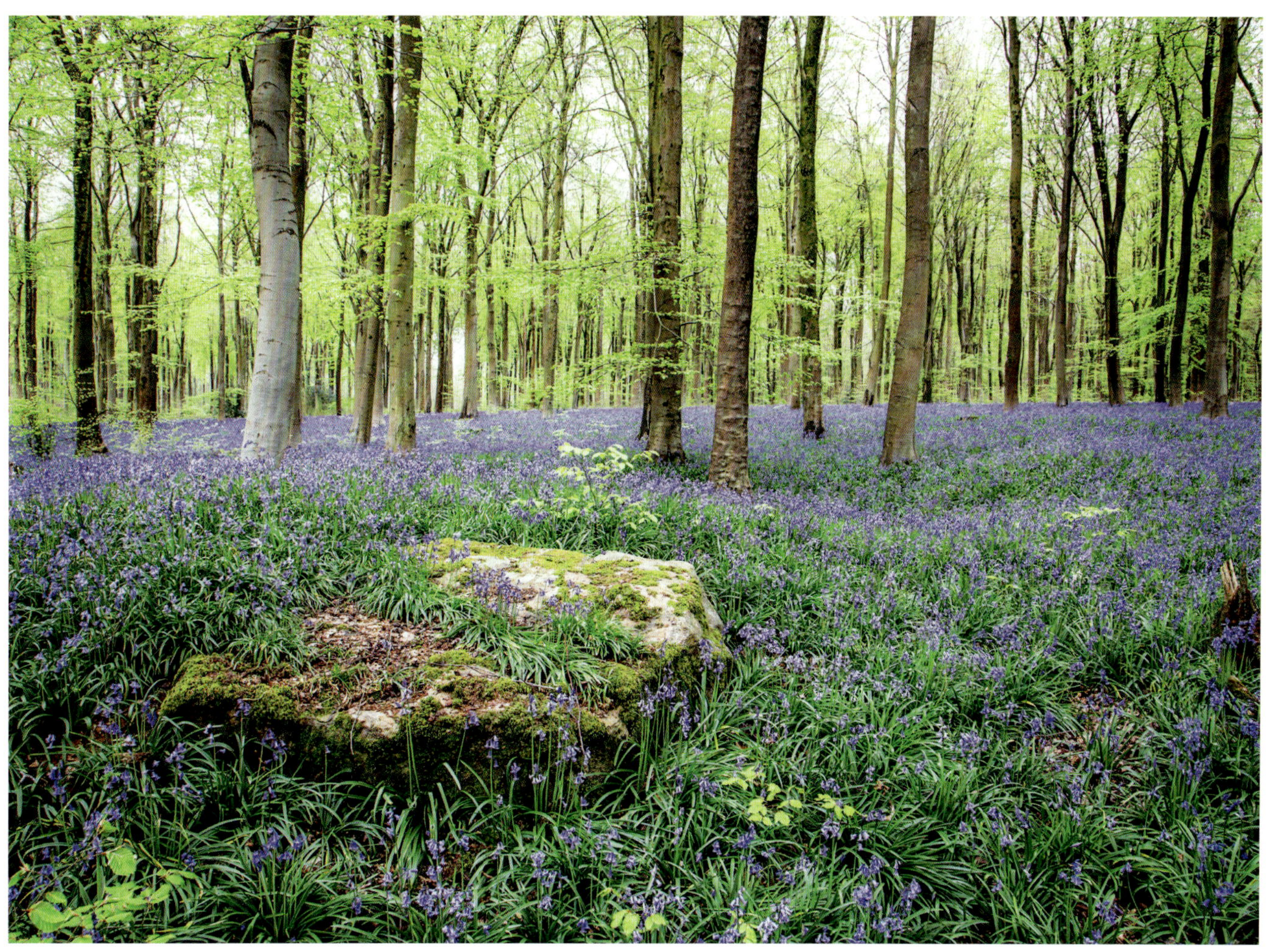

ABOVE Most of the sarsens used to build Stonehenge were transported from West Woods on the Marlborough Downs, where large sarsens still lie among the trees.

It is possible that the hills were regarded as sacred mountains or were viewed as the ancestral home of the people who built Stonehenge. Perhaps prehistoric people believed the bluestones had special healing powers. Detailed geological research has indicated the specific outcrops where the stones were obtained, and excavations in 2015–16 uncovered evidence for quarrying having taken place there in the Neolithic period. The journey of the Altar Stone is perhaps the most astonishing and suggests that there were links between Neolithic communities living in north-east Scotland and the people who built Stonehenge. We do not know if the stone was brought as a gift or tribute, but its position in the centre of the monument on the solstice axis suggests that this stone, and the long-distance connection it represented, was of supreme importance.

The architecture of Stonehenge reveals the sophisticated thought, organisational skills and engineering ability of people in late Neolithic Britain. It would have required hundreds of people working together to move, shape and raise the stones, others to collect and make equipment such as antler picks and ropes, and still more to provide the builders with food and shelter. The builders may have lived in a settlement at nearby Durrington Walls (see page 60), which was occupied for up to 55 years, suggesting the sort of timescale over which the main stone circle could have been constructed. The project was a massive investment of time and resources, involving communities from across Britain, suggesting that Stonehenge was not only a hugely important place for Neolithic people, but also that their beliefs were strongly held and widely shared.

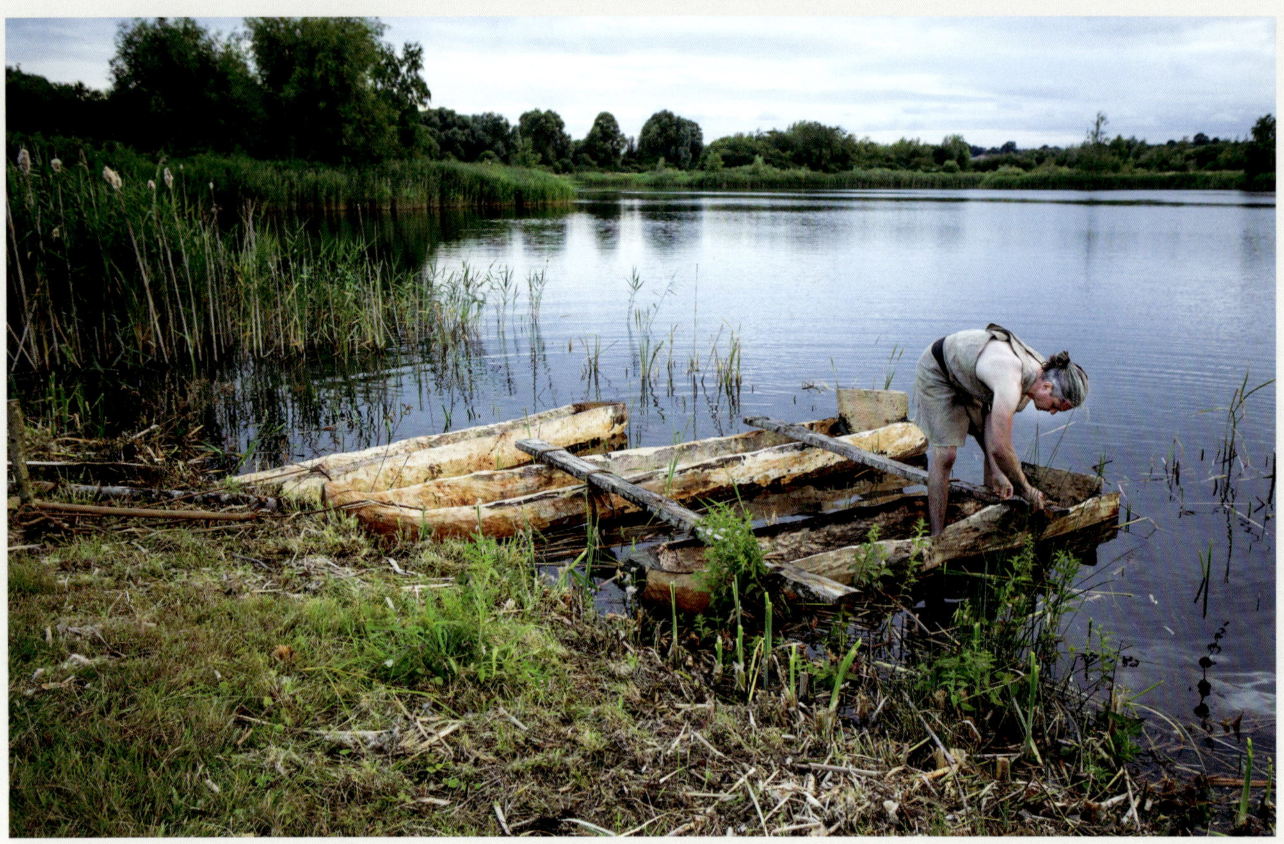

Moving and Raising the Stones

ABOVE An experimental archaeologist with recreated log boats made with authentic stone tools. It is possible that several boats like these, bound together, may have been able to carry a bluestone on part of the journey from Wales to Stonehenge, or perhaps a more elaborate type of boat was used.

Building Stonehenge was an enormous undertaking that demanded the labour of hundreds of people, many resources and a considerable amount of planning and organisation. Much of the equipment for moving and raising the stones was made of perishable materials that have not survived and many activities did not leave behind archaeological traces. Nevertheless, we can make informed conjectures about their methods and techniques, thanks to experimental archaeology and observations of other communities around the world that have built megalithic monuments.

The sarsen stones, some weighing over 30 tonnes, were probably moved from the Marlborough Downs to Stonehenge using wooden cradles or sledges pulled using ropes. Hundreds of people would have been needed, as well as lots of rope, probably made from the inner bark of lime trees. Images from ancient Egypt and Mesopotamia, and records from Madagascar and parts of Indonesia, show how large statues or stones were moved using similar methods. Experiments have shown that it is possible to pull stones on such sledges quite successfully over grass. It is likely that laid wooden trackways aided passage through wet or

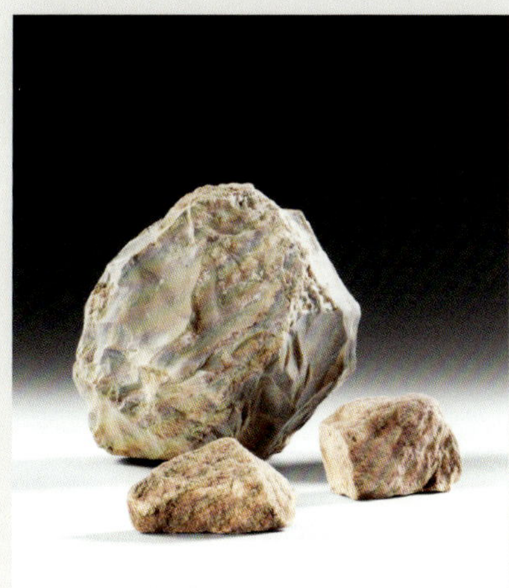

ABOVE Each stone at Stonehenge was laboriously shaped and dressed using flint and sarsen hammerstones such as these examples, found near Stonehenge.

BELOW RIGHT In 1954 archaeologist Richard Atkinson demonstrated that a stone could easily be punted along the river Avon using shallow boats.

muddy areas, such as the Vale of Pewsey, although no evidence for these has survived. Cattle may have been used to help pull the stones, although the more precise movements at Stonehenge itself would have been carried out by people.

The bluestones, although a lot smaller (up to 3 tonnes), were brought over a much longer distance, from south-west Wales. It is quite likely that boats were used to take them around the coast, up the Severn estuary and along the Bristol Avon. Similarly, a much longer maritime route following the western coast of Britain seems most plausible for the Altar Stone, although some archaeologists have argued for an overland route for both this and the bluestones.

On arrival at Stonehenge, the stones were shaped by bashing off larger chunks and then 'pecking' surfaces using hammerstones. Excavations in the fields to the north of Stonehenge have uncovered hundreds of stone chips and broken hammerstones, showing where this long, arduous work took place.

To position the upright sarsen stones, holes were dug using antler picks to about a metre deep, with one sloping side, and sometimes wooden stakes placed against the opposite, vertical side. The stone was manoeuvred into place, and the base slid over the hole. The stones may have been raised using ropes, weights and a timber A-frame, although some have suggested that they were slowly levered up into position using ramps of stone rubble. The lintels must have been raised using timber platforms, and then slid sideways into position. We know that the tenons on top of the stones were initially oval in shape, but each was then worked to fit precisely into its corresponding lintel mortise.

Each part of the project, such as gathering materials, as well as feeding and sheltering the workers, would have needed careful organisation, and transporting the stones, working them into shape and raising them into place would have taken many years. For some of the time, the builders probably lived at Durrington Walls (see page 60). That settlement lasted for about 55 years, giving an indication of how long this extraordinary project may have taken.

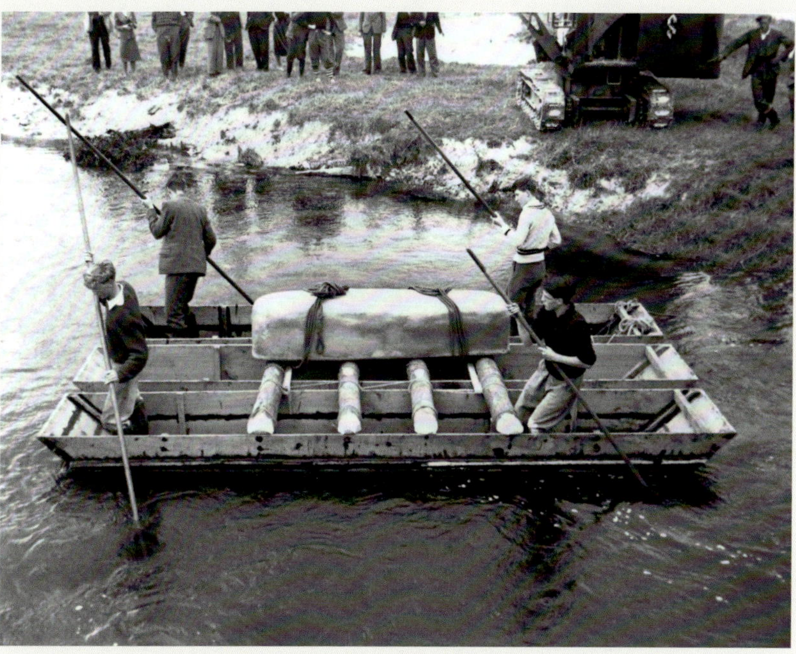

The Missing Stones

Many of the stones that make up Stonehenge are now fallen or missing entirely. Some may have fallen in prehistoric times, perhaps even during the construction of the monument. The bluestones were broken and chipped from prehistoric times onwards, with some surviving only as stumps below ground. Fragments may have been broken off these stones because of their perceived magical powers, and some were made into axeheads, discs and amulets, found dispersed across the region.

Some archaeologists have argued that the south-west side of the sarsen circle was never completed, as the stones here are more irregular in shape and one is only half the height of the others. Enough remains, however, to show that a large amount of stone must have been removed from Stonehenge at some point in the past: in dry weather, parch marks in the grass show the position of long-lost holes where the missing stones would have stood.

There are no written records of this taking place, however, unlike at the stone circle at Avebury, where there are accounts of stones being broken up and then buried or removed in the 17th and 18th centuries. This was partly due to their 'pagan' associations, but also because they were a useful source of building stone, and their removal cleared the way for agriculture. These reasons do not apply to Stonehenge, as very few buildings in the area are built of sarsen and the land cleared was not extensive. Instead, it is likely that the stones were broken up for roadstone, perhaps in the 17th century. All the evidence suggests that the circle was originally complete.

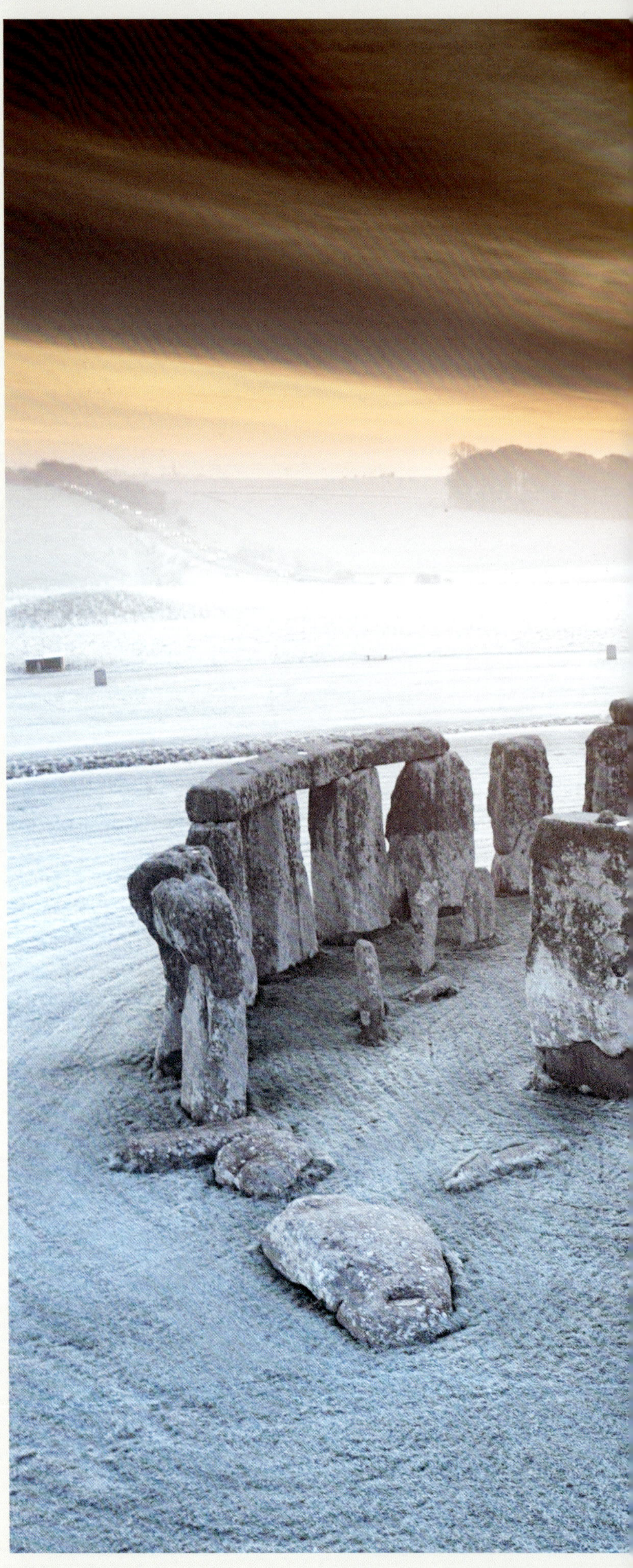

RIGHT Many of the stones that formed part of the outer sarsen circle on the south-west side of the monument have fallen, and most are either partly or entirely missing.

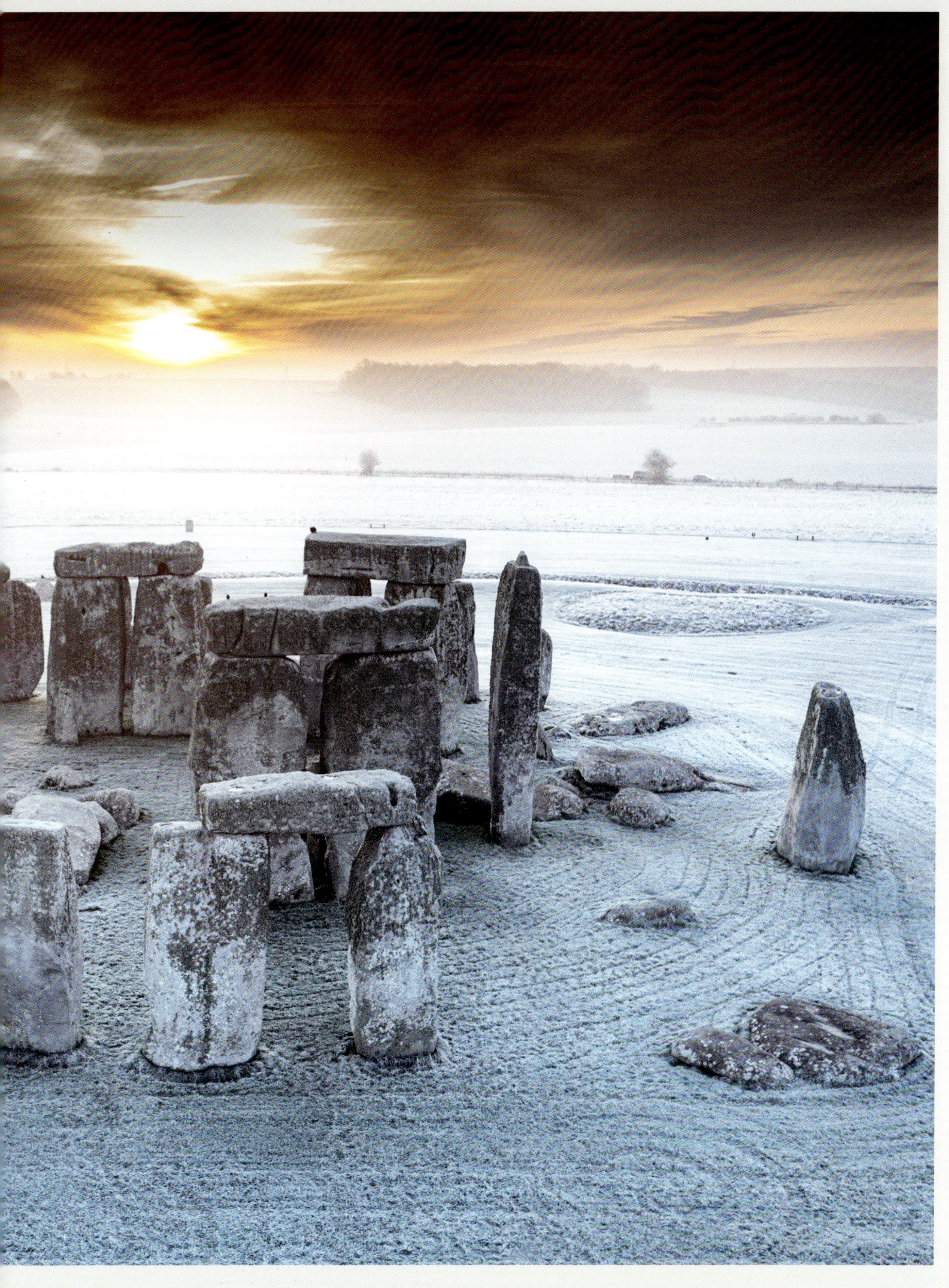

The Power of the Sun

In the modern world, the skies and the movements of the celestial bodies go largely unnoticed by people in their day-to-day lives. But for prehistoric people the sky and, in particular, the movements of the sun, would have been a vital source of practical information for predicting weather and for navigation, as well as for tracking time and the seasons. Their observations of the sun, moon, stars and planets were fundamental to their beliefs about the cosmos and the world they lived in.

Stonehenge was carefully designed to align with the movements of the sun. When the sun is observed from the centre of the monument on Midsummer's Day, the longest day of the year, it rises on the north-east horizon just to the left of the outlying Heel Stone. Excavations have shown that the Heel Stone may originally have been one of a pair and that the rising sun would have been framed between the two stones. The first section of the Stonehenge Avenue, a route between Stonehenge and the river Avon marked by parallel banks and ditches (see page 64), is also aligned on this same axis.

Six months later, on the shortest day in midwinter, the sun sets exactly opposite on the south-west horizon. Originally, the setting sun would have been framed within the gap between the two uprights of the tallest trilithon at the head of the sarsen horseshoe. The effect is lost today because one half

THIS PAGE On a winter's evening close to the winter solstice – the shortest day of the year – the last glimmer of the setting sun shines through the stones at Stonehenge.

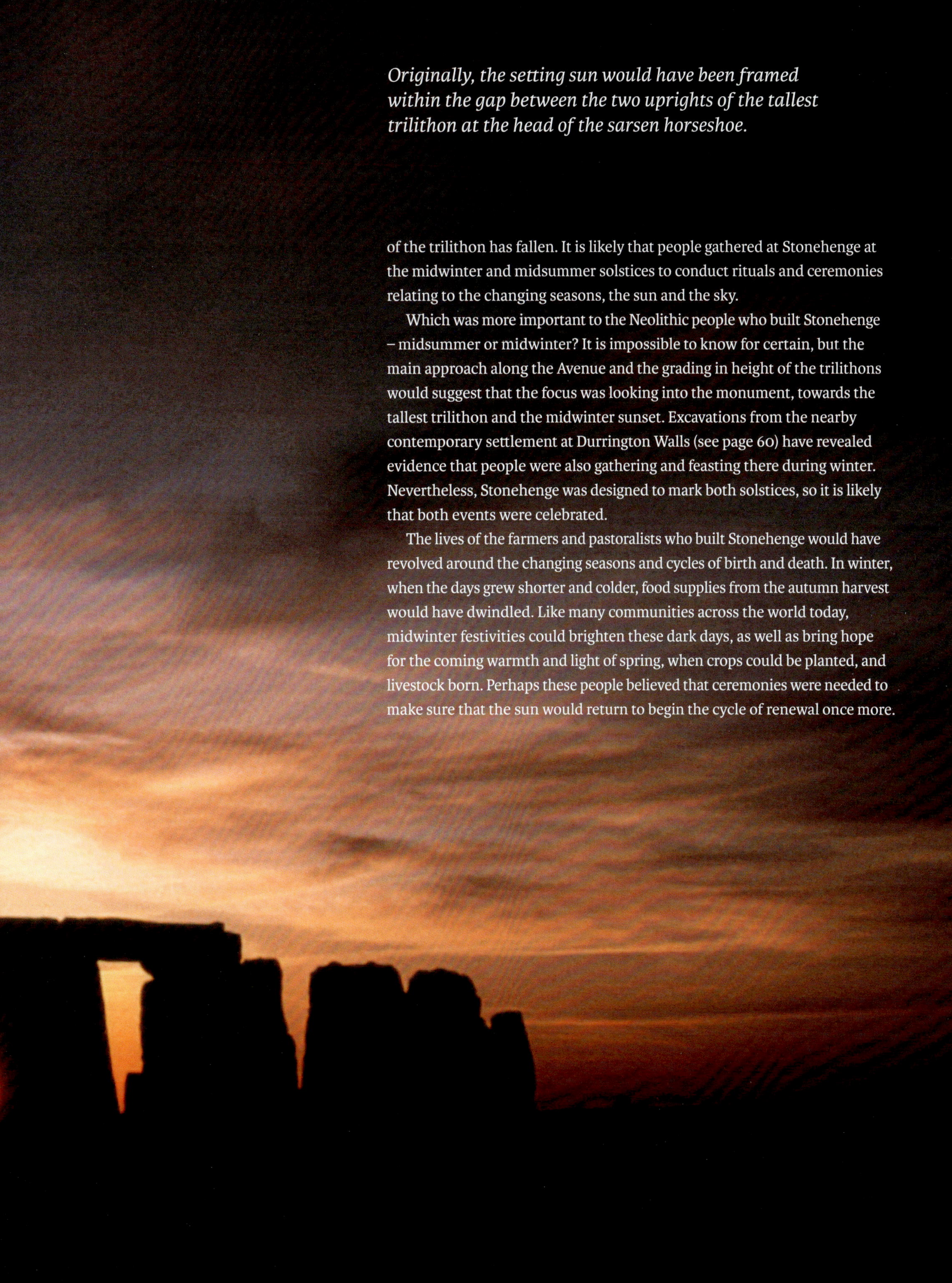

Originally, the setting sun would have been framed within the gap between the two uprights of the tallest trilithon at the head of the sarsen horseshoe.

of the trilithon has fallen. It is likely that people gathered at Stonehenge at the midwinter and midsummer solstices to conduct rituals and ceremonies relating to the changing seasons, the sun and the sky.

Which was more important to the Neolithic people who built Stonehenge – midsummer or midwinter? It is impossible to know for certain, but the main approach along the Avenue and the grading in height of the trilithons would suggest that the focus was looking into the monument, towards the tallest trilithon and the midwinter sunset. Excavations from the nearby contemporary settlement at Durrington Walls (see page 60) have revealed evidence that people were also gathering and feasting there during winter. Nevertheless, Stonehenge was designed to mark both solstices, so it is likely that both events were celebrated.

The lives of the farmers and pastoralists who built Stonehenge would have revolved around the changing seasons and cycles of birth and death. In winter, when the days grew shorter and colder, food supplies from the autumn harvest would have dwindled. Like many communities across the world today, midwinter festivities could brighten these dark days, as well as bring hope for the coming warmth and light of spring, when crops could be planted, and livestock born. Perhaps these people believed that ceremonies were needed to make sure that the sun would return to begin the cycle of renewal once more.

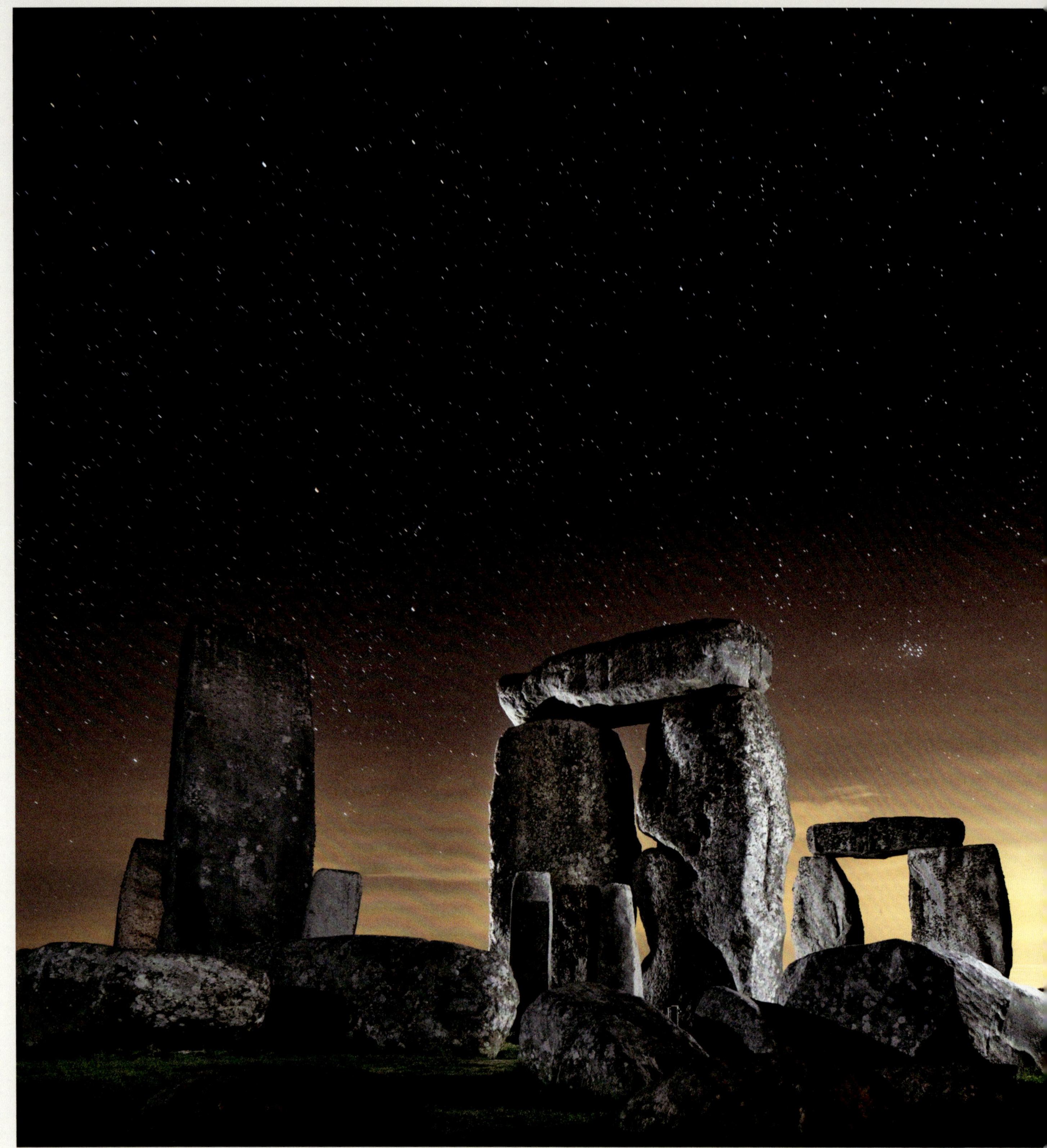

ABOVE The night skies over Stonehenge today can be spectacular, despite modern light pollution. In prehistoric times, without any artificial light other than small fires, the stars and visible planets would have been familiar companions.

People may have undertaken processions between these monuments to observe these different celestial events. Clearly the sun, and key directions in the solar year, were integral to their religious beliefs.

Although Stonehenge was clearly built to focus on the midsummer sunrise and midwinter sunset, other alignments may also have been marked. The Altar Stone and tallest trilithon are at a slight skew to the rest of the horseshoe, and align with two other important solar events – the midwinter sunrise and the midsummer sunset. A south-easterly focus towards the southernmost moonrise at the major lunar standstill (equivalent to a solstice of the sun) also seems to have been important. The four Station Stones form a rectangle, the long axis of which points in this direction, and a seemingly distinct cluster of cremation burials is located on the south-eastern edge of the henge.

Stonehenge is not the only Neolithic monument in this landscape with solar alignments. Two miles (3km) north-east, a series of concentric timber ovals, forming a monument known as Woodhenge (see page 67), were orientated on the same midsummer sunrise and midwinter solstice axis as Stonehenge. At the nearby Neolithic site of Durrington Walls another concentric timber structure, known as the Southern Circle, was aligned on the midwinter sunrise and a short roadway or 'avenue' connecting it to the river Avon was aligned on the midsummer sunset. People may have undertaken processions between these monuments to observe these different celestial events. Clearly the sun, and key directions in the solar year, were integral to their religious beliefs.

It is possible that the idea of precise alignments at Stonehenge was adopted from older monuments. In about 3000 BC, Neolithic people in different parts of north and west Britain and Ireland built passage tombs aligned on solstices and the mid-points of the solar cycle – the equinoxes – for example at Newgrange in Ireland, Maeshowe in Orkney and Bryn Celli Ddu on Anglesey in North Wales. These monuments were different to Stonehenge, however, being enclosed tombs accessed by narrow passages, where a select few, or perhaps only the dead, could observe the solar alignment.

Neolithic monuments built with such specific alignments as these are rare, however. More often, Neolithic people built monuments that were only generally orientated towards solar events or along principles relating to a quartering of the horizon or key directions in the sky. Early Neolithic long barrows in southern Britain, for example, were often orientated towards the sunrise. Later, stone houses in places such as Orkney were laid out with reference to the key solstice directions. Timber structures made of four large posts and encircling fences, were also built with their entrances facing towards the south-east. Known as 'square-in-circle' monuments, these temple-like structures were built across Britain and Ireland (see page 64). All these examples suggest that, throughout the Neolithic period in Britain, it was important that certain structures reflected and were aligned with wider solar principles.

THE WORLD OF STONEHENGE (3200–2400 BC)

Stonehenge was built at the end of the late Neolithic period (3000–2400 BC), at a time when extraordinary communal building projects were taking place in several different parts of Britain and Ireland, where people gathered to bury their dead and to conduct ceremonies. People were moving huge stones, setting up thousands of timber posts, and moving tonnes of earth and chalk to create large earthworks. They were radically altering their environment, creating powerful places, changing both the landscape, and themselves, in the process.

At this time, people were building many different types of monument including henges, palisaded (fenced) enclosures, stone circles, timber structures and mounds. Although these features are scattered widely across Britain, many were built in areas where earlier monuments existed, and went on to attract more in turn, becoming distinct clusters or 'complexes' of monuments. Some of these are well known, such as the cluster of monuments at Avebury, 17 miles (28km) to the north of Stonehenge and part of the same World Heritage Site. Here, the spectacular henge, stone circles and avenues form part of a complex that includes an enormous artificial mound (Silbury Hill), a causewayed enclosure, a scatter of long barrows, some large, palisaded enclosures at West Kennett and several smaller types of Neolithic enclosures and monuments.

Another such area is on the western Mainland of Orkney. Here, there are two major stone circles, the Ring of Brodgar and Stones of Stenness, set within henges, as well as groups of monumental houses at the Ness of Brodgar, chambered tombs and standing stones.

Other complexes are less famous, such as the cluster of monuments set within and around a large, palisaded enclosure at Forteviot, Perth and Kinross, including a cremation cemetery, a timber structure and several small henges, or at Milfield in Northumberland, where five henges are associated with alignments of pits, cremated remains and enclosures, or the three large henges and nearby cursus at Thornborough, North Yorkshire. These monument complexes appear to have been important places in late Neolithic networks of communication.

Towards 2500 BC, particularly innovative and radical monuments were built at some of these complexes. In the north of Wiltshire people built Britain's largest known stone circle at Avebury and its greatest artificial mound at Silbury Hill; to the south, in Dorset, an enormous timber and earth enclosure, another palisaded enclosure and a henge with extraordinarily deep shafts were all built in the Dorchester area. It is difficult to know what caused such an explosion of innovation and intensive activity. Some archaeologists have suggested that communities were in competition with one another, building ever bigger and more complex monuments to prove

Although these features are scattered widely across Britain, many were built in areas where earlier monuments existed, and went on to attract more in turn, becoming distinct clusters or 'complexes'.

OPPOSITE TOP The henge at Avebury, north Wiltshire, is over 400m in diameter and contains the largest stone circle in Europe, as well as two smaller inner circles. The enormous ditch was dug ten metres deep.

OPPOSITE BOTTOM The Ring of Brodgar on Orkney is a stone circle surrounded by a large rock-cut ditch. Originally there were about 60 standing stones placed in a circle 104m in diameter, very similar to the first phase of Stonehenge.

OVERLEAF Silbury Hill, near Avebury, is Europe's largest artificial mound, over 30m high. It was built in several stages between 2400 and 2300 BC on low-lying ground near the headwaters of the river Kennet.

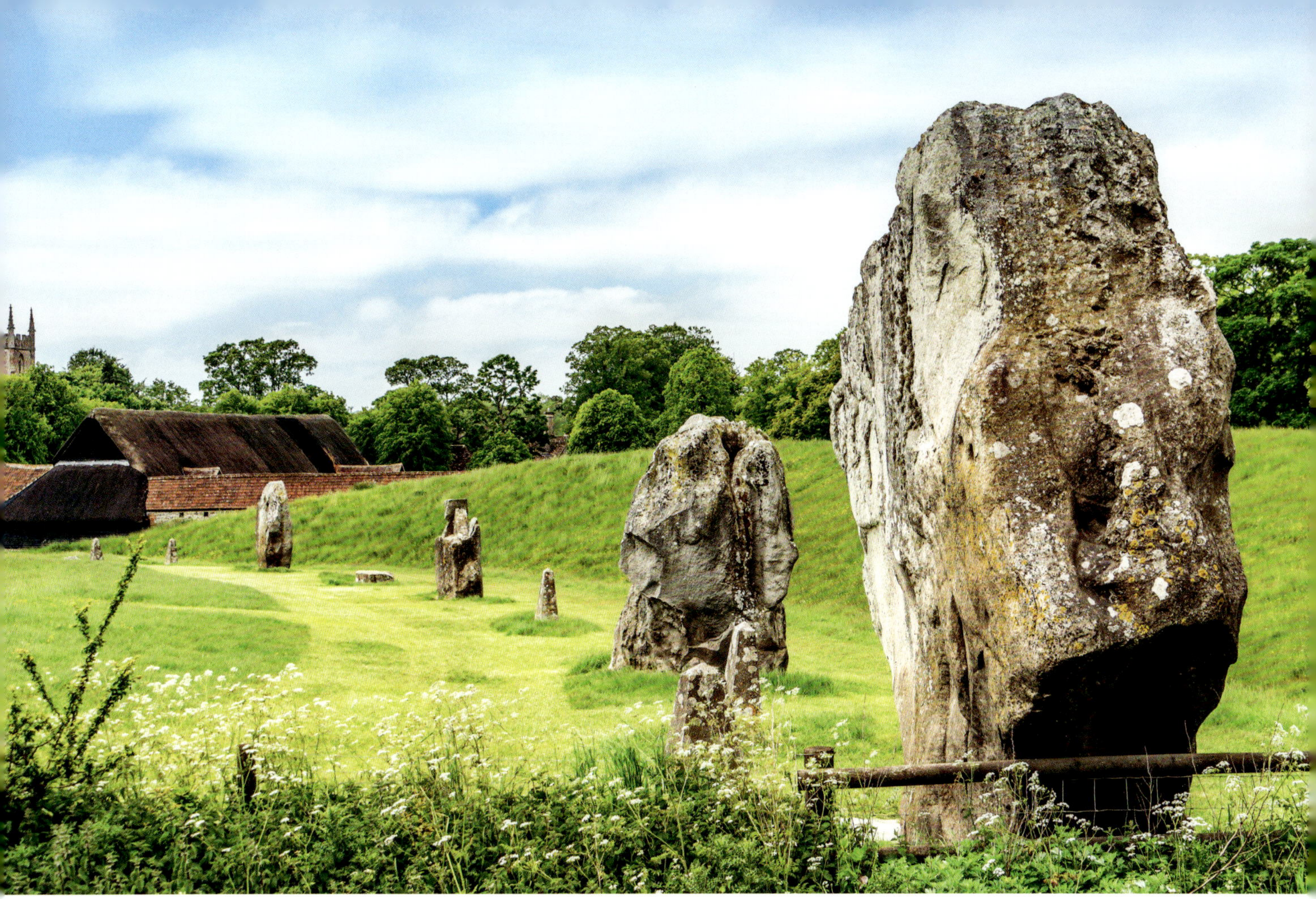

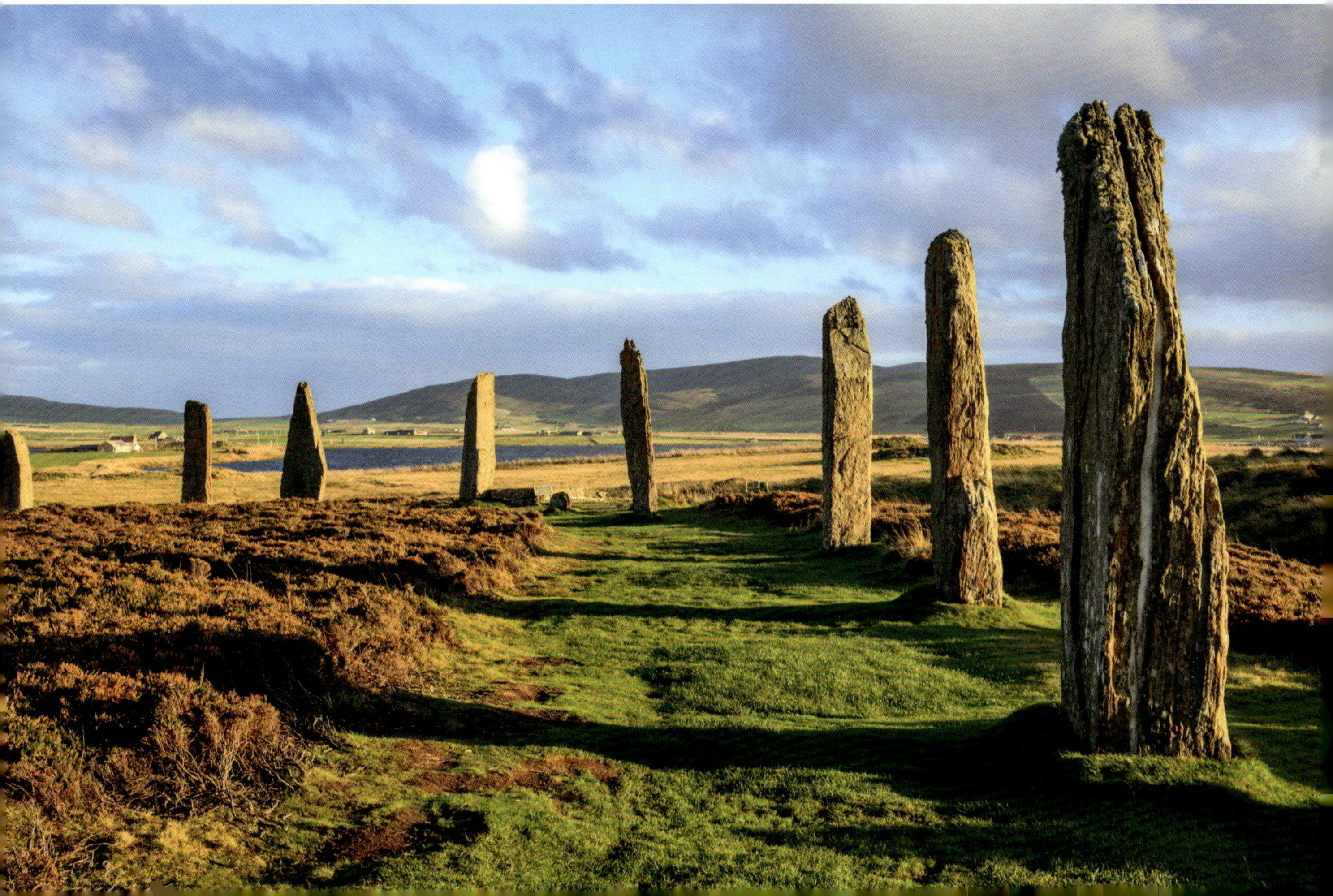

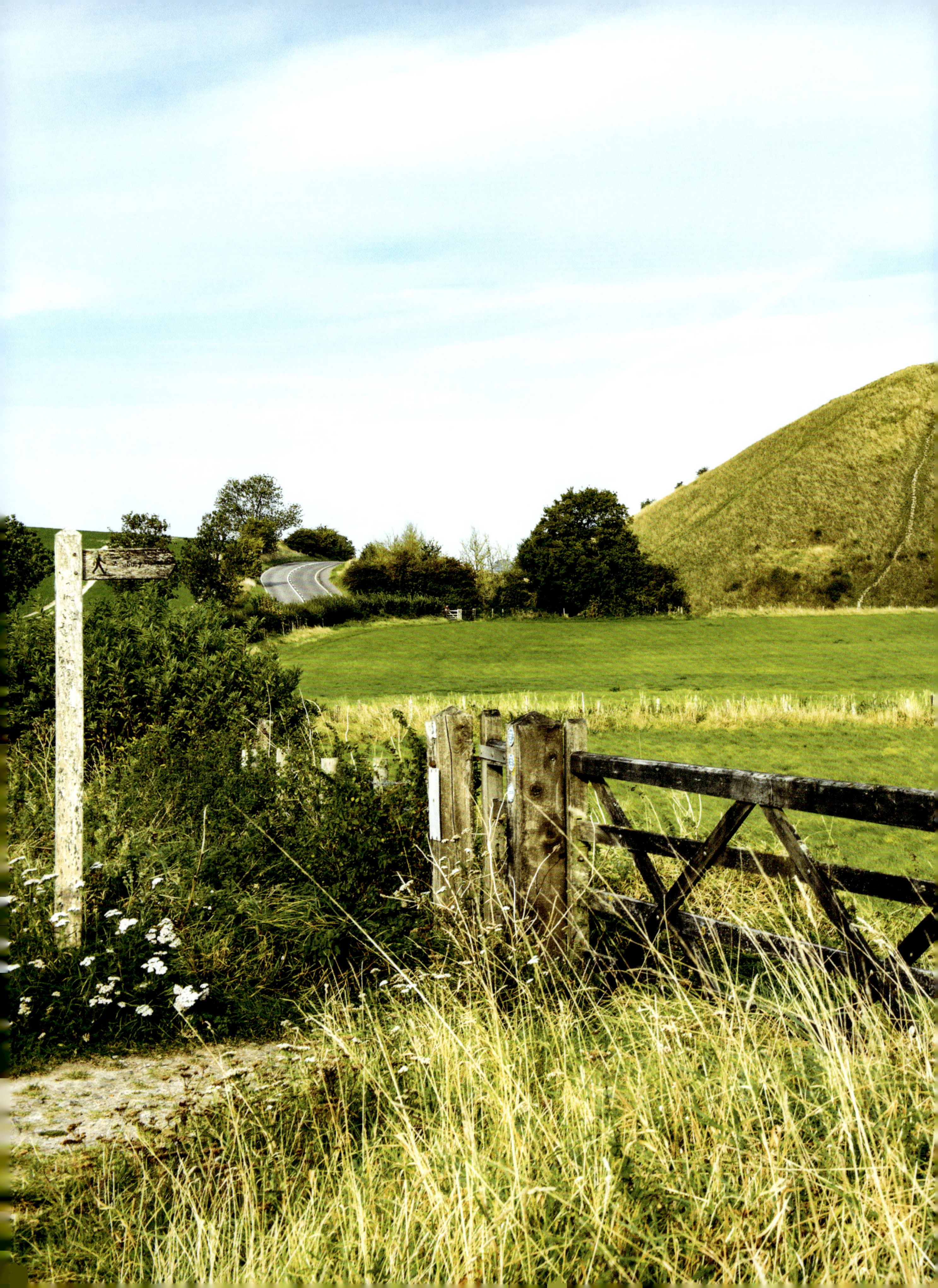

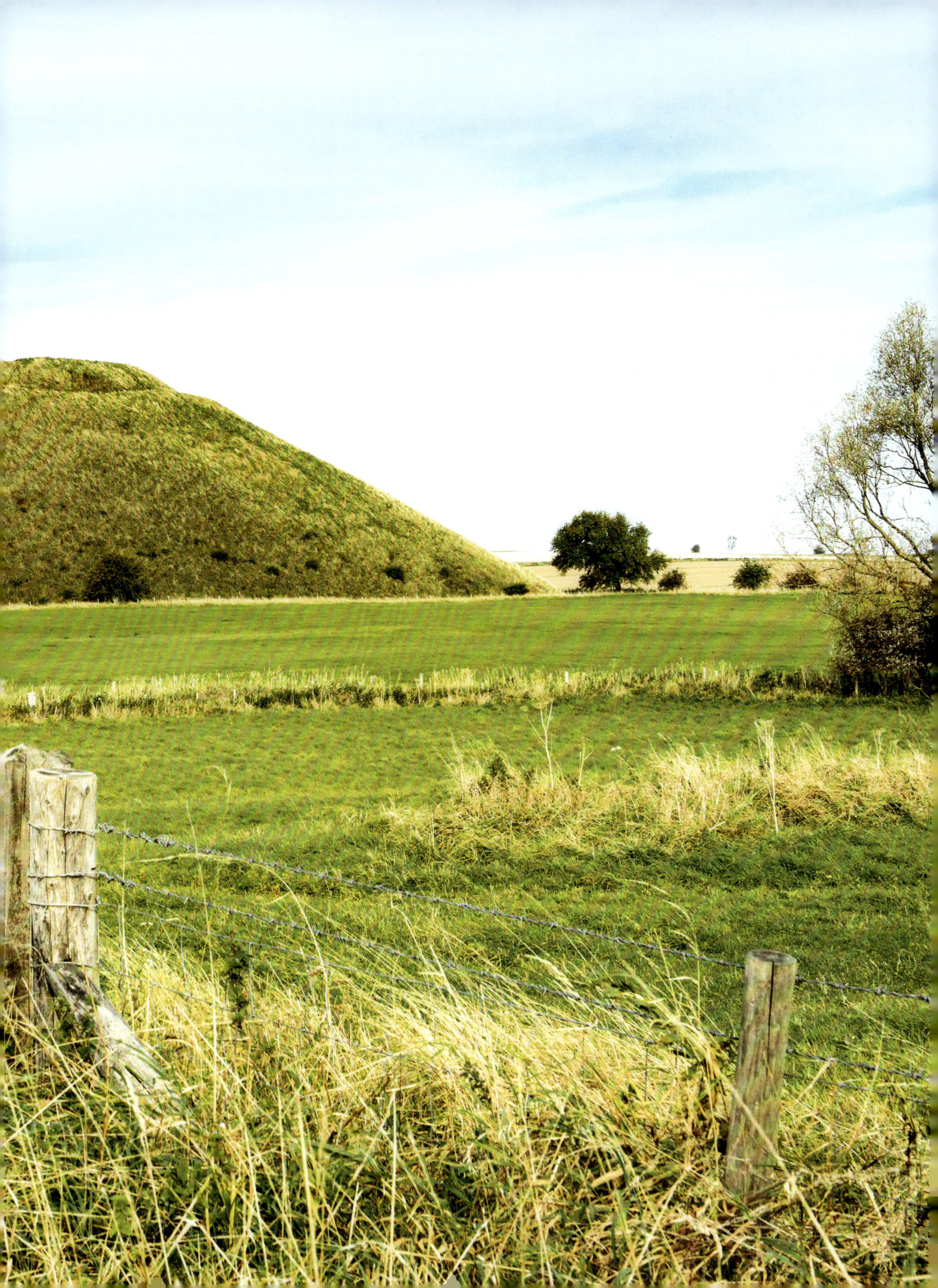

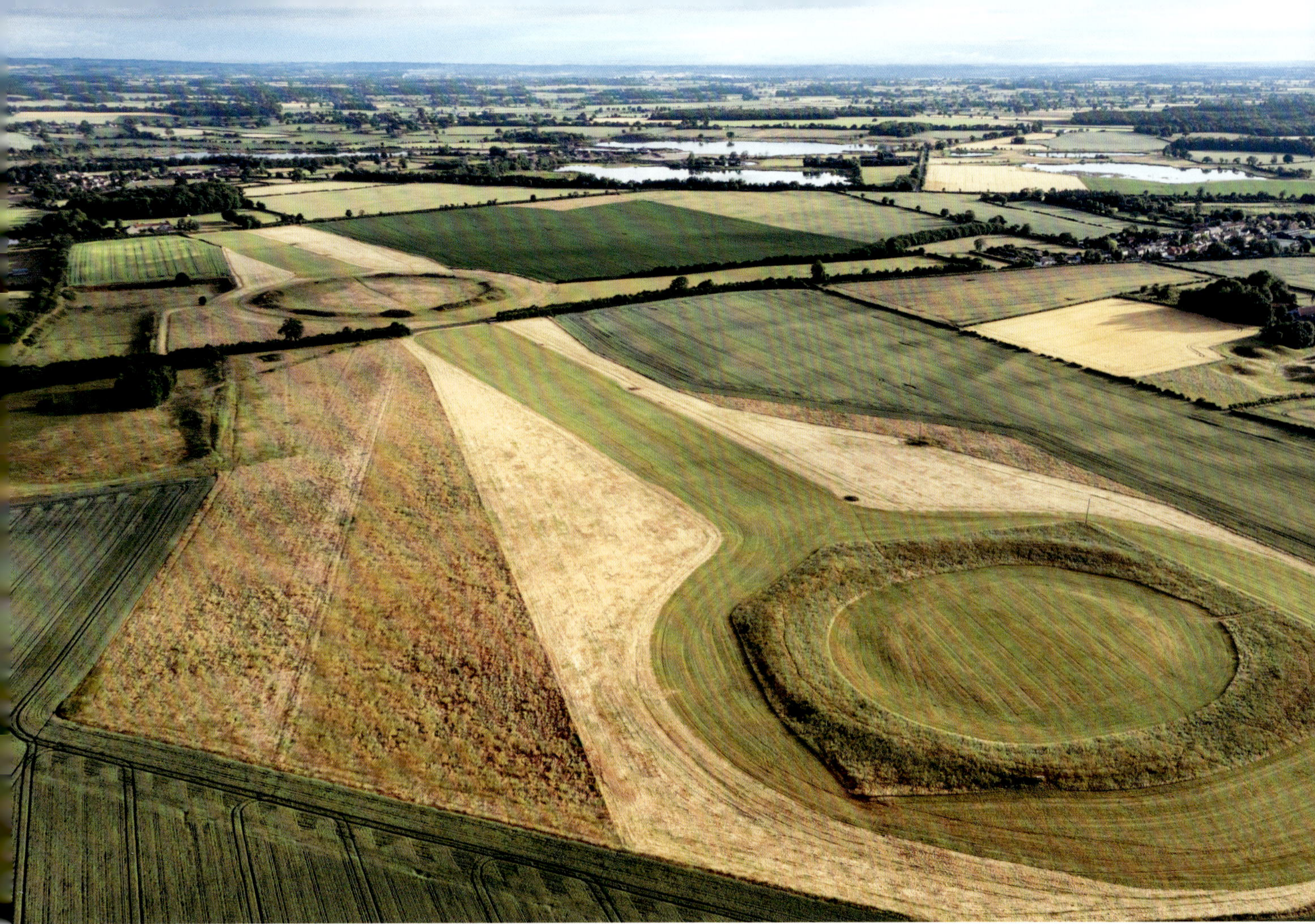

ABOVE At Thornborough in North Yorkshire three spectacular and near identical henge monuments were laid out over an earlier cursus monument in the middle or late Neolithic period.

themselves more powerful than their rivals. Or perhaps these projects were driven by religious fervour or led by charismatic individuals.

The immense labour and co-operative demands of such building projects must have required careful organisation and planning. We do not know, however, how late Neolithic societies were structured. No burials accompanied by valuable objects have been found, and burials of any kind from this period are extremely rare. Cremation cemeteries such as that at Stonehenge date from slightly earlier and are unusual: most late Neolithic people must have been cremated and their ashes perhaps scattered on the ground or placed into rivers. Similarly there are very few clearly defined settlements from this period, so evidence that might indicate something about social hierarchy, such as the discovery of houses of different sizes, is also lacking. The houses at Durrington Walls (see page 60) are an exceptional survival, and although some of the buildings there were larger and surrounded by ditches, these may have been shrines or cult buildings rather than the homes of chiefs.

Did people live in the same place all year round? Did they reside together as part of extended families or other groups? We simply do not know the answers to these questions. The sharing of ideas and practices across different parts of Britain and Ireland does indicate, however, that long-distance travel was common. Across these islands monuments with similar architectural features were built, Grooved Ware pottery of the same type and decoration was made, and objects were carved and painted using distinctive geometric art styles.

Scientific evidence, particularly isotopic studies of the bones and teeth of people and animals, and the geological origins of different

BELOW LEFT A polished stone axehead made of volcanic tuff from the Langdale Pikes in Cumbria, found in Wiltshire. Langdale axeheads were exchanged or traded across much of Britain and Ireland and must have been highly valued.

BELOW RIGHT One of the artificially created galleries dug by hand, deep below the ground at the flint mines known as Grime's Graves, Norfolk. Here, Neolithic flint miners sought out seams of high quality black flint, which they extracted and used to make axeheads, knives, arrowheads and scrapers, which were transported across Britain.

raw materials, provides more evidence for long-distance contacts between groups. We know that the bluestones and the Altar Stone were moved hundreds of miles to Stonehenge, but much smaller objects were also transported far from their places of origin. For example, objects made of pitchstone from the Isle of Arran in Scotland, flint from the Yorkshire coast and mines in East Anglia (Grime's Graves), and gneiss (banded rock) from western Scotland have been found at sites across Britain. Some archaeologists have suggested that it was only the elite who travelled between places, but perhaps a variety of people travelled as tradespeople, pilgrims or explorers. Annual or cyclical journeys by larger numbers of people may have revolved around synchronised times of feasts and gatherings, and events of monument construction. Ideas, objects, art styles and traditions flowed through these inter-regional networks, brought in the minds and belongings of travellers who came by sea and by land, and shared with those who were eager to learn new ideas and adopt innovative styles.

In the late Neolithic, there was very little figurative art, depicting life-like people or animals. Instead, art was almost always abstract – geometric shapes, lines and zig-zags carved onto chalk, incised into the wet clay of pots, or etched into stone. The Grooved Ware bowls and tubs made and used at the time of Stonehenge were decorated with similar geometric incised patterns and applied lines of clay. Large and particularly ornate versions of these pots appear to have been used during feasts. Wooden objects or clothing may also have been decorated with geometric designs, but, unlike pottery, these do not survive. In northern and western parts of Britain and Ireland, concentric circles and dots were often pecked into rocks in upland areas, typically marking routeways or overlooking harbours, although their meanings are now entirely lost.

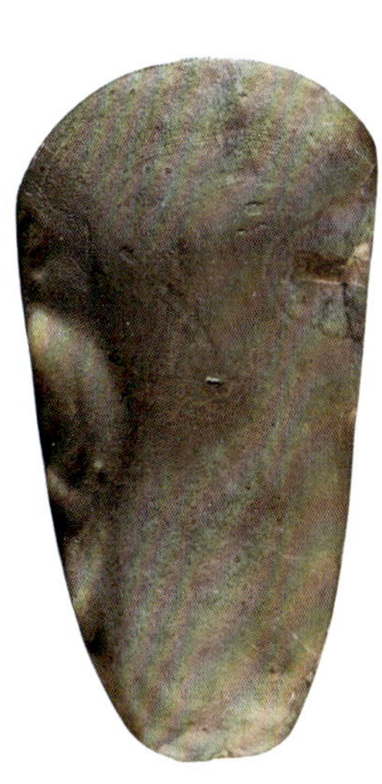

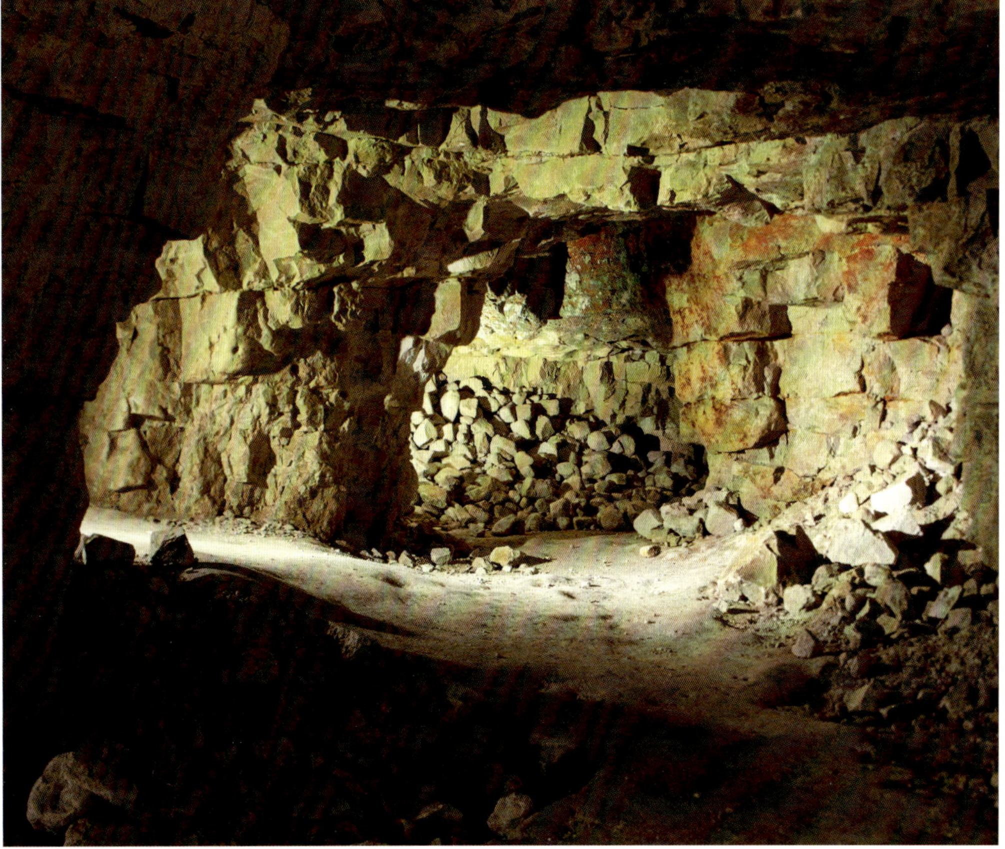

RIGHT A highly decorated Grooved Ware vessel, the type of pottery used at the time of Stonehenge. This example was placed in the ditch of a henge in Dorset.

FAR RIGHT Cattle were important to the people who built Stonehenge, for meat, milk and pulling simple ploughs. People probably moved seasonally, herding their cattle to fresh pastures, as depicted in this artist's reconstruction.

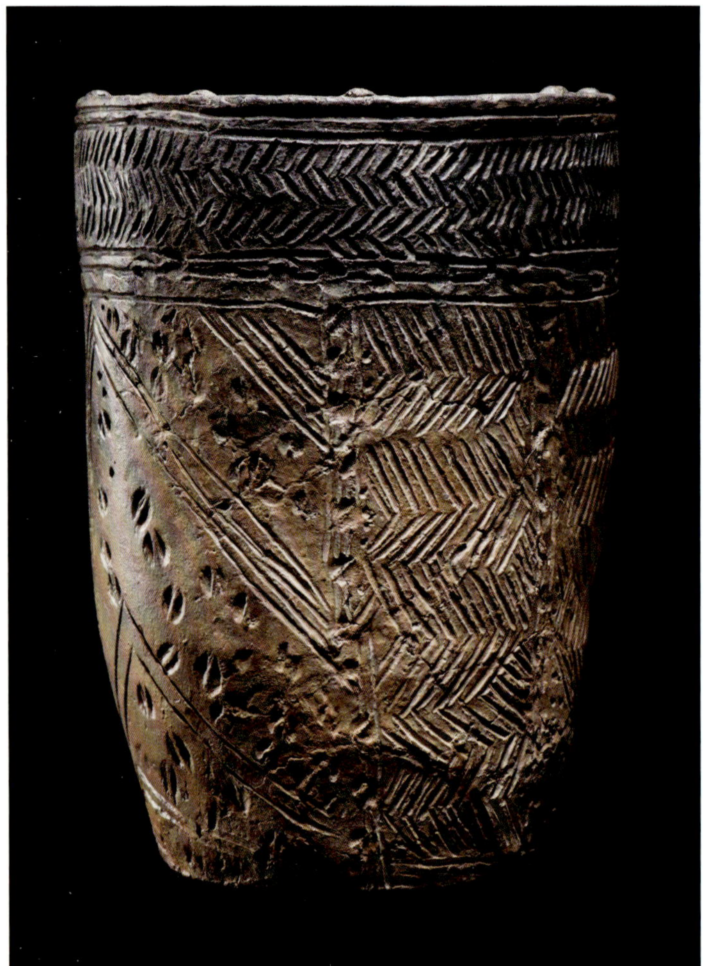

At the time that Stonehenge was built, people had been farming in Britain for 1,500 years, and had become expert pastoralists, keeping pigs and herds of cattle for meat and dairy products, as well as growing crops such as wheat, barley and rye, which they ground to make flour or fermented into beer. People occasionally hunted red deer, wild boar and waterfowl, and continued to gather and eat wild plants, particularly hazelnuts, but also crab apples, autumn berries, tubers, and probably leafy vegetables and herbs as well as mushrooms. By the late Neolithic, however, crops were grown less often and people were more reliant on their herds of animals, particularly cattle, and may have moved them seasonally to different areas of pasture.

The people who built Stonehenge would have known their homelands and the locations of useful resources intimately: groves of lime trees, the bark of which could be stripped to make ropes, riverbeds where flint nodules could be found for making tools, good places for finding mushrooms, the easiest locations to water cattle, the best sources of clay for the crafting of pots, the glades where freshly shed deer antlers could be gathered. These people would have moved through a landscape full of stories, told and re-told with each encounter: that old mound where the ancestors are buried, that hollow where grandmother came across the wild bear, that dwelling place where the family used to live. Around the fire in the evening people would have listened to these stories as they stripped and twisted nettle fibres to make clothing, or polished their stone axeheads to a fine sheen.

What did these people look like? We know from ancient DNA evidence that people in Britain

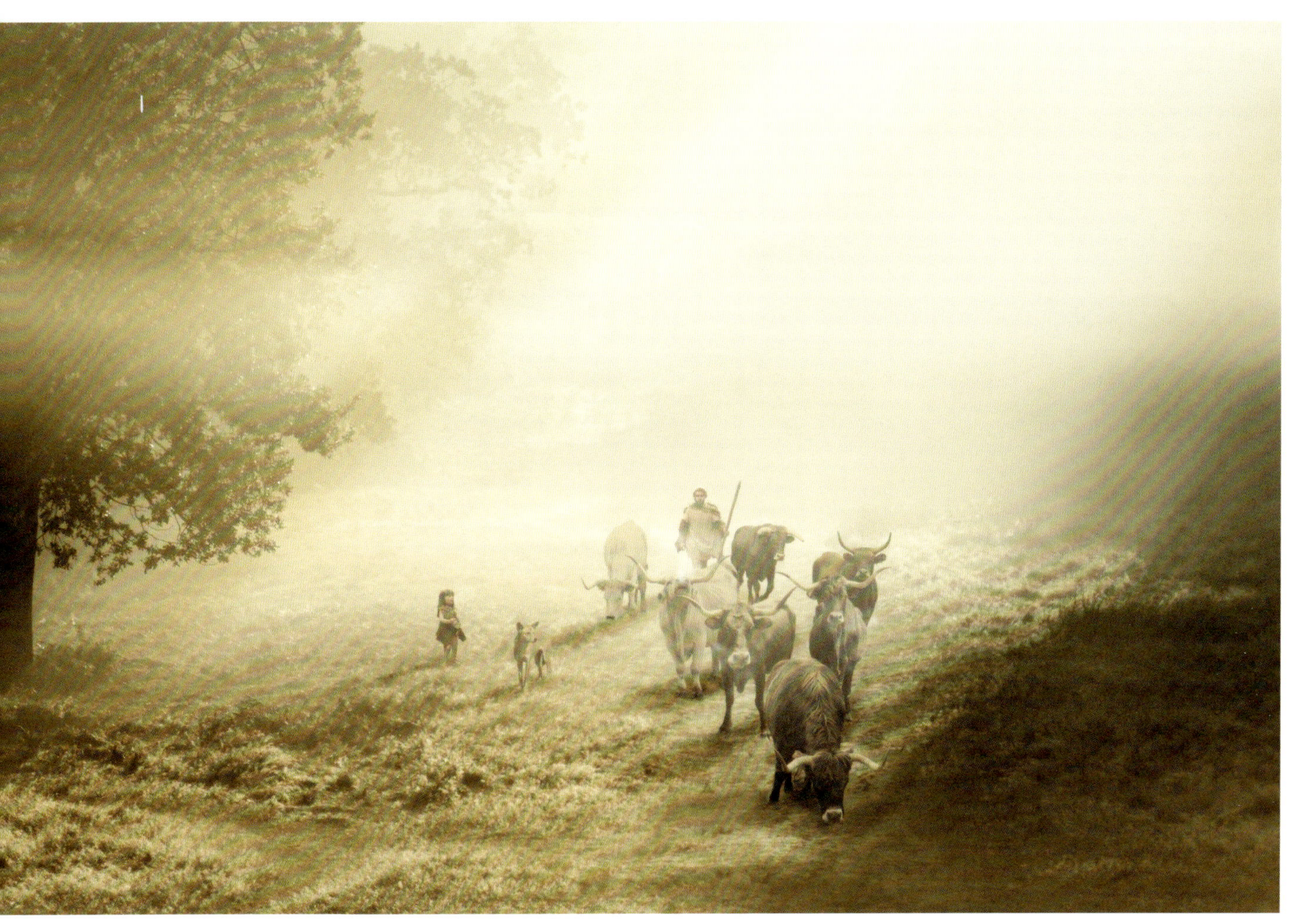

in the Neolithic generally had dark hair and eyes, and dark to intermediate skin, perhaps not unlike communities from Mediterranean regions today. Men and women were only slightly shorter than modern European populations. Their relatively hard physical lifestyles would have given them strong muscles and bones. Small items such as beads, pendants and pins show that people wore accessories, and needles tell us that they wore finely sewn clothes made of furs, leather and plant fibres.

Estimating how many people were living in late Neolithic Britain remains very difficult, but as more sequences of ancient DNA from individuals become available, it will be possible to look at patterns of relatedness in order to estimate the total population. Projects such as the construction of Stonehenge or the building of Silbury Hill, which would have required many hundreds of people, certainly suggest relatively large numbers were able to dedicate their time to such projects, and perhaps for a short while, the presence of charismatic leaders who could organise and motivate others.

Late Neolithic people were resourceful, organised, well travelled and thoroughly connected with their landscape. Life may not have been easy, however, and at times the demands of monument building, and their associated ceremonies, may have been onerous. This was a physically tough, not necessarily peaceful, and probably unequal society. Nevertheless, by working together people achieved extraordinary feats of transport, engineering and construction, some of which have lasted as monuments to their achievements to this day.

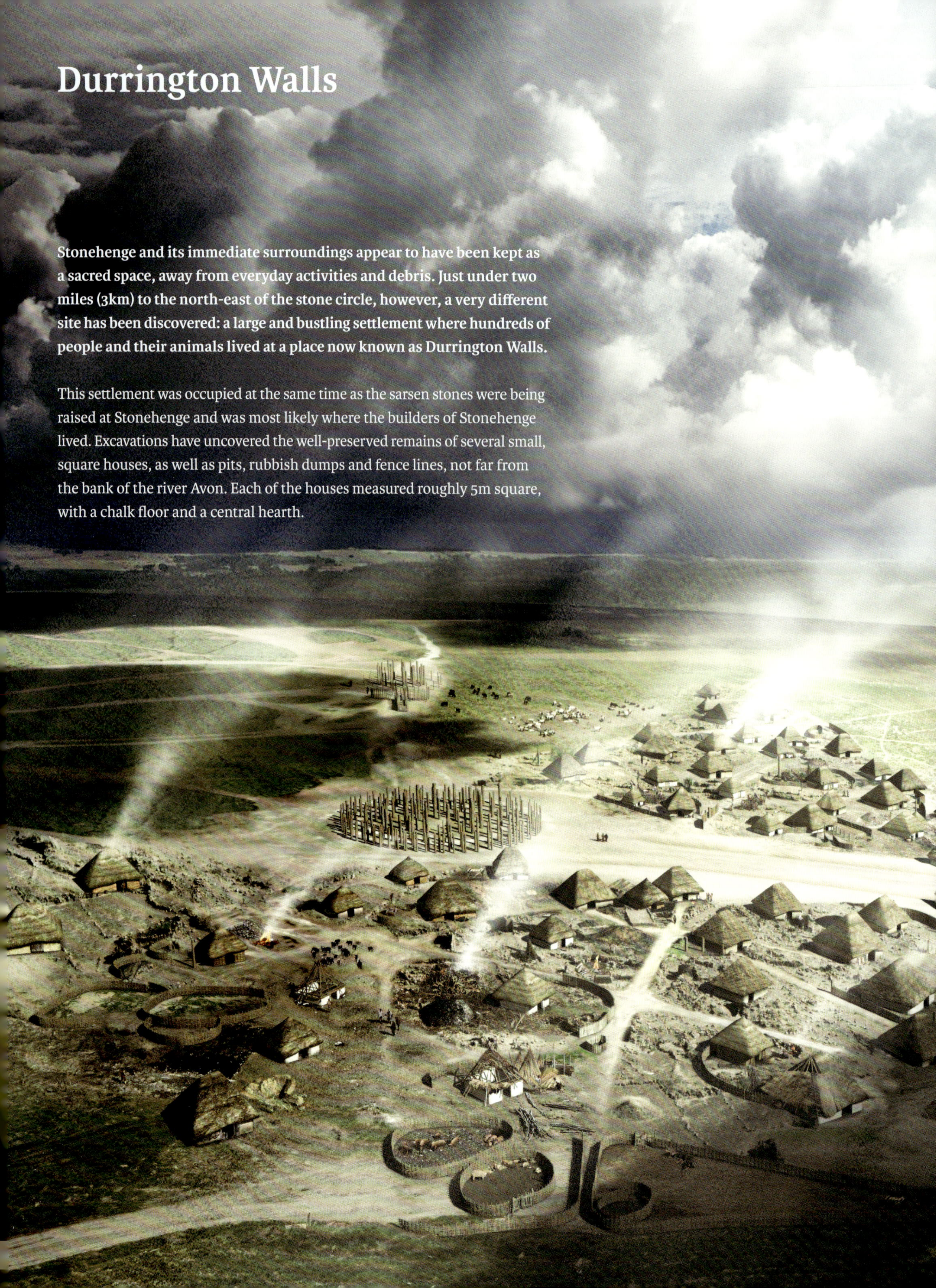

Durrington Walls

Stonehenge and its immediate surroundings appear to have been kept as a sacred space, away from everyday activities and debris. Just under two miles (3km) to the north-east of the stone circle, however, a very different site has been discovered: a large and bustling settlement where hundreds of people and their animals lived at a place now known as Durrington Walls.

This settlement was occupied at the same time as the sarsen stones were being raised at Stonehenge and was most likely where the builders of Stonehenge lived. Excavations have uncovered the well-preserved remains of several small, square houses, as well as pits, rubbish dumps and fence lines, not far from the bank of the river Avon. Each of the houses measured roughly 5m square, with a chalk floor and a central hearth.

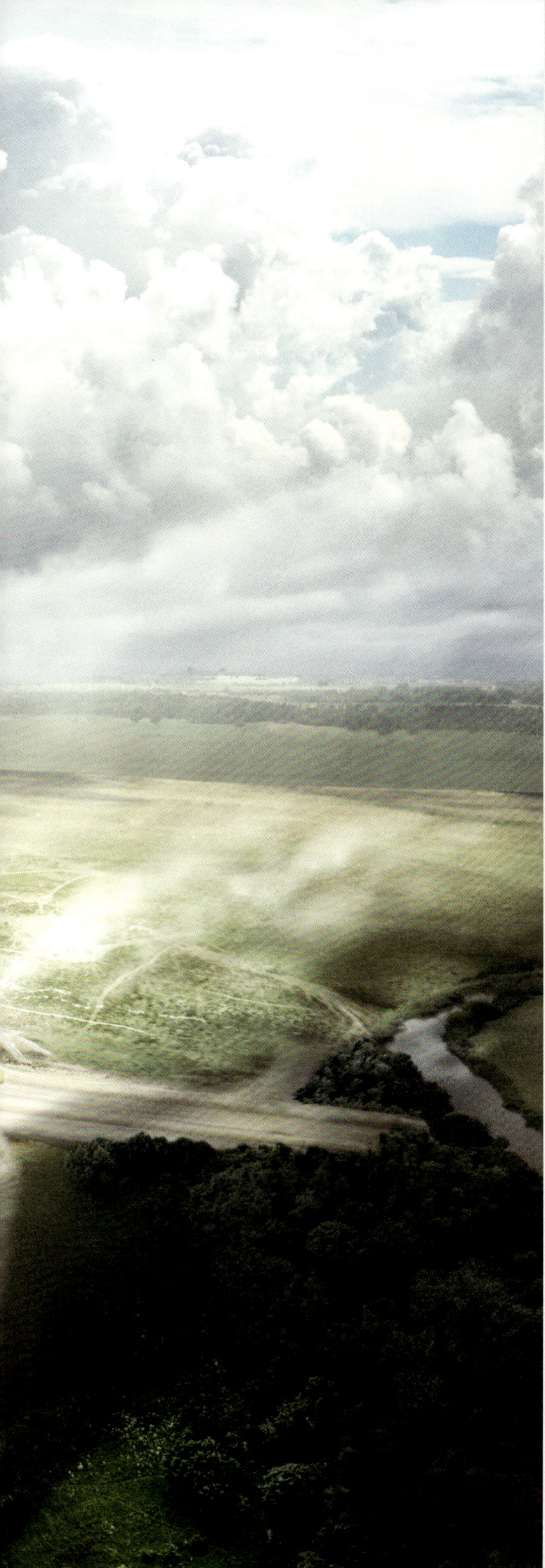

LEFT An artist's reconstruction of the settlement at Durrington in about 2500 BC. The small houses were clustered either side of a roadway or 'avenue' leading down to the river Avon and among them were monuments formed of concentric rings of timber posts.

The walls and roofs were formed of interwoven vertical and horizontal hazel stakes, rather like an upside-down basket, with the lower portion probably covered with chalk daub and the upper part probably thatched. In two of the houses, slots found in the floor showed where wooden furniture, perhaps beds or seating, had once stood. Further upslope were similar structures, surrounded by circular ditches and some by a circuit of standing posts. These may have been the houses of more important people, or perhaps shrines or cult buildings. Surveys have revealed that there were potentially several hundred houses here, although it seems that the settlement was short-lived, perhaps occupied for only 55 years.

When this settlement was discovered in 2006, it was a revelation for archaeologists, who had begun to believe that houses from the late Neolithic would never be found in southern Britain. The site has produced a rich array of finds, including over 80,000 pig and cattle bones and more than 12,500 sherds of Grooved Ware pottery. The sheer quantities suggest feasting on a large scale. Durrington's inhabitants do not seem to have been processing or eating cereals, and only very limited remains of fruits, nuts and tubers have been discovered; Grooved Ware pots found here were used to cook and serve meat and dairy products. All parts of pig and cattle skeletons have been found, but no new-born piglets or calves, suggesting that the animals were brought to the site on the hoof. Analysis of chemicals in the teeth of these animals has shown that these herds were raised in a variety of locations across southern Britain and perhaps further afield, their owners herding them over long distances to reach Durrington Walls. This was a place that attracted people from far and wide, to take part in the great building project of Stonehenge.

Durrington's residents appear to have been slaughtering their pigs mostly at about nine months old, during the winter months. Given the solstice orientations at Stonehenge and other nearby monuments, we might imagine midwinter pork feasts taking place here. Intriguingly, some of the pig and cattle bones found had

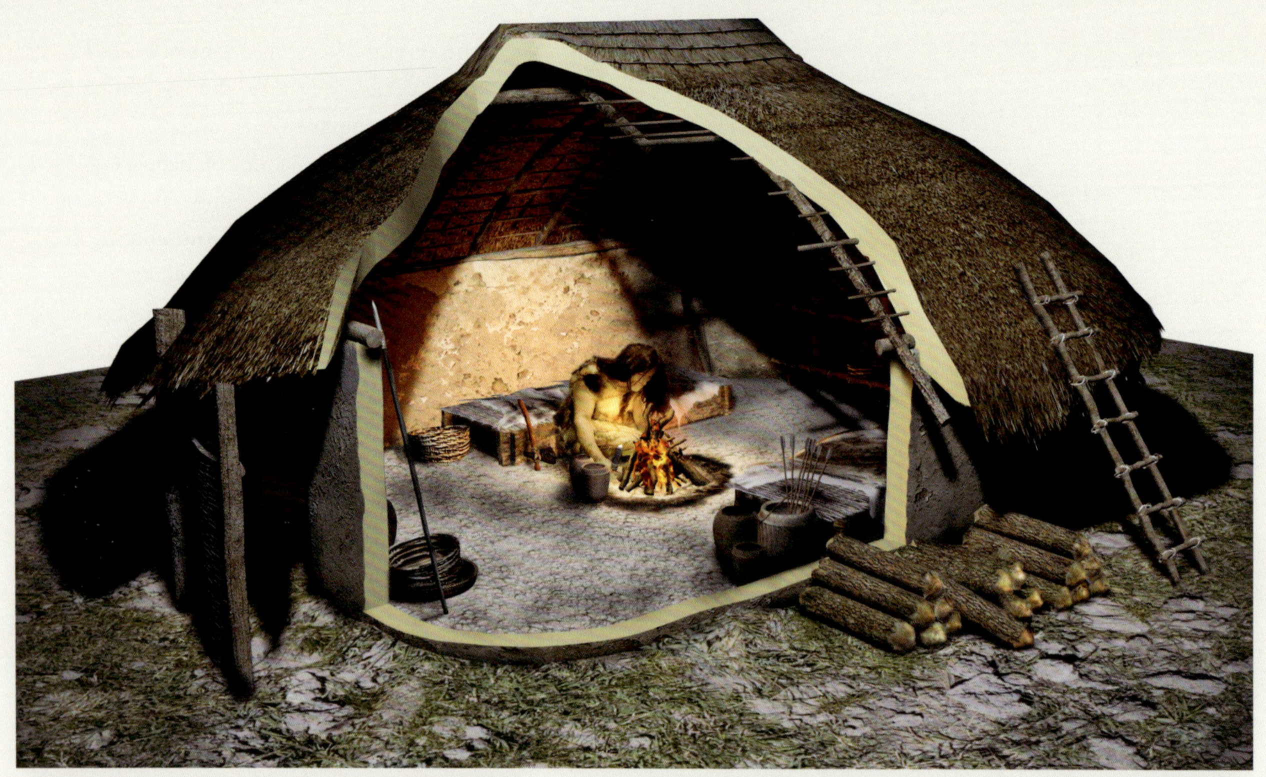

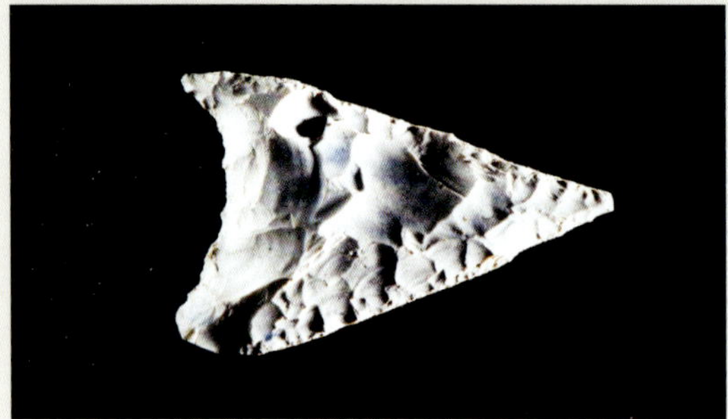

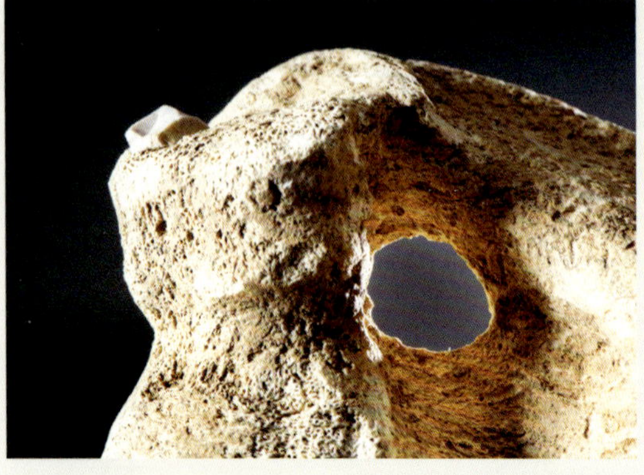

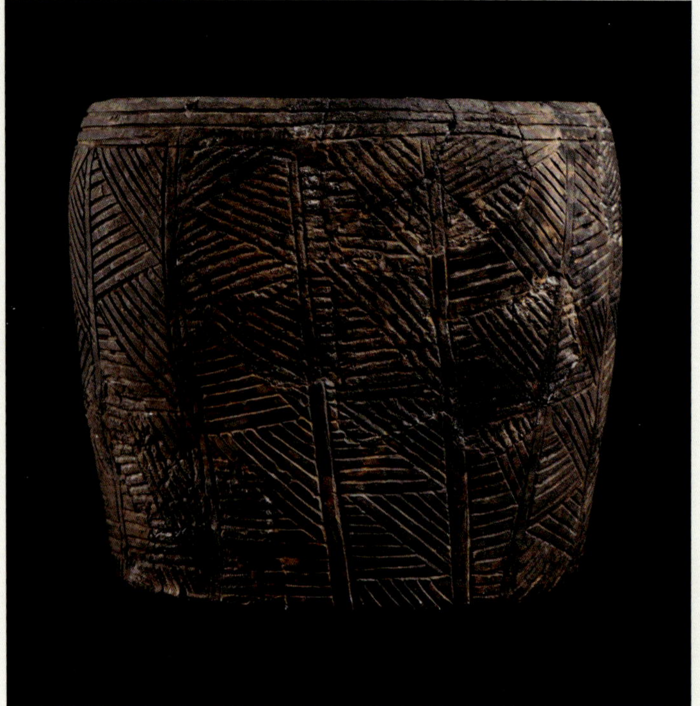

TOP An artist's reconstruction of one of the Durrington houses. The archaeologists found small, square areas of laid chalk – the floors of the houses – with a hearth in the centre and surrounded by the stakeholes of wattle walls.

ABOVE Artefacts found during excavations at Durrington Walls, anticlockwise from top left: a flint arrowhead, a pig bone with the tip of a similar arrowhead embedded in it, and a small Grooved Ware pot.

the tips of finely made flint arrowheads embedded within them. These suggest that, rather than being slaughtered conventionally, these domestic animals were being shot, perhaps during sporting events or ritual hunts.

After the houses at Durrington Walls had been abandoned, people enclosed the old settlement within a 430m-diameter ring of large timber posts, a type of monument known as a palisaded enclosure. These posts, numbering in their hundreds, were a way of setting apart this area of land and marking the important events that had taken place there. The circuit of posts was soon replaced by a bank standing 3m high, with an outer ditch over 5.5m deep – an enormous 'henge' that survives as an earthwork today. This was not the only major landscape feature created to contain the site of Durrington Walls. Surveys have uncovered a ring of 20 large pits outside the henge, enclosing both the location of the settlement and several nearby timber monuments. These pits were up to 5m deep and 10m across and were linked by curving fences of wooden stakes, forming an enormous circuit some 1.5 miles (2.4km) across. Although these are not yet fully understood, the pits appear to have been contemporary with the creation of the henge and represent an extraordinary feat of digging and construction. This enclosure and the henge suggest that the settlement at Durrington Walls was a place of exceptional importance, one that would be remembered for generations.

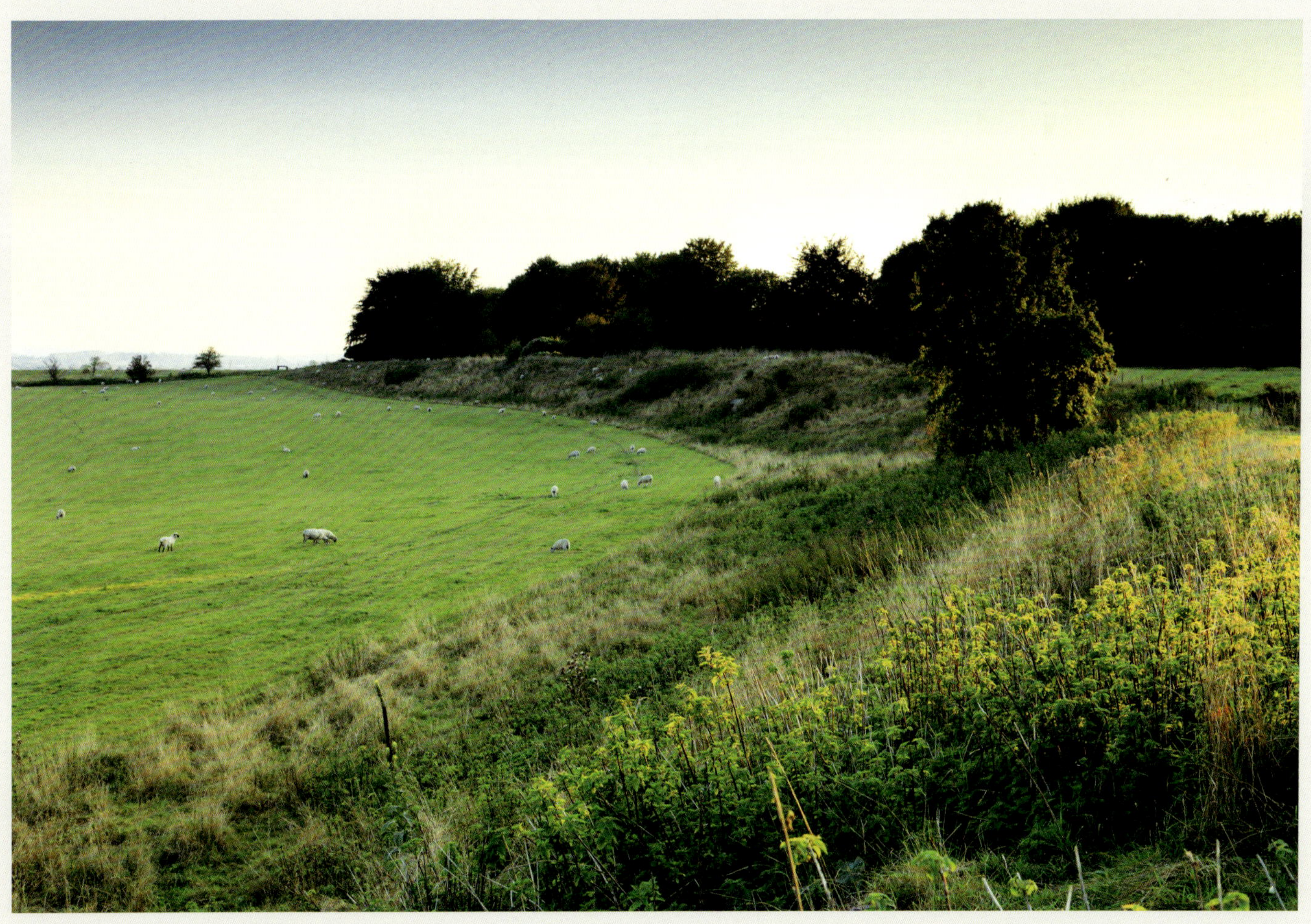

BELOW Durrington Walls today, where the earthwork bank and ditch of the enormous henge are still clearly visible.

A Monument Complex

Stonehenge did not stand alone. The surrounding landscape contains many other places of ritual and burial, as well as the dwelling places of prehistoric people. Some monuments date from the early Neolithic, before Stonehenge was built, and many more were created long after major construction activity at Stonehenge had ended. But others are contemporary with the main phases of Stonehenge and were built and used by the same people. Many components of this complex of prehistoric monuments are today protected within the Stonehenge World Heritage Site.

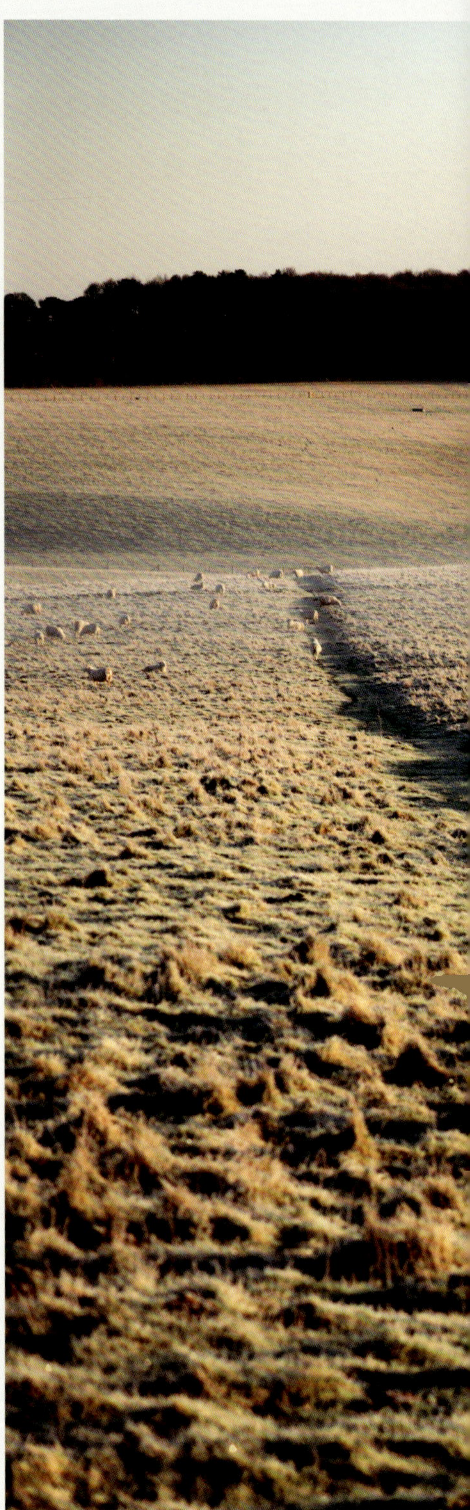

This relatively open, easily accessible, raised grassland plateau forming part of Salisbury Plain had attracted people and animals for millennia, and many different features (including cursus monuments, causewayed enclosures and long burial mounds) show that this landscape was an important place for early Neolithic people before Stonehenge was built (see page 17). The creation of the first phase of Stonehenge, however, seems to have acted as a catalyst for people to build other monuments and for intense episodes of activity, reaching a peak at the end of the late Neolithic period in about 2500 BC. Earlier monuments were not forgotten. There is evidence that the banks of the Greater Cursus, and the long barrow at its eastern end, were re-capped in white chalk at this time, making them visible against the green pastureland and renewing their importance.

Shortly after the sarsens were raised at Stonehenge, a pair of parallel banks and ditches about 20m apart were created. These formed a feature now known as the Avenue, which extended for more than 1.5 miles (2.7km), connecting Stonehenge's north-east entrance to the river Avon near the modern village of West Amesbury. This may have been a processional route for people approaching Stonehenge, although, as there is little evidence that it was heavily used, it may instead have formed a symbolic connection between Stonehenge and the river, with its probable sacred or funerary importance. On the riverbank at the end of the Avenue stood a circle of about 20 bluestones, surrounded by a circular ditch and bank – a small henge. These bluestones were later removed to form part of the settings at the centre of Stonehenge (see page 42).

Another monument built at a similar time was Coneybury Henge, located on a hill just under a mile south-east of Stonehenge. Here, four great timber posts were set up in a square, surrounded by a circle of smaller posts with a porch-like entrance facing towards the north-east. This type of monument, known as a 'square-in-circle' monument, was built across Britain and Ireland in the late Neolithic period, particularly at monument complexes. The four posts may have supported some sort of platform, possibly related to funerary rituals, or was perhaps a roofed structure, forming a temple or shrine.

BELOW The parallel ditches and banks of the Stonehenge Avenue, created more than 4,000 years ago, are still visible in low sunlight, leading away from the monument and down into a valley on the approach to the river Avon.

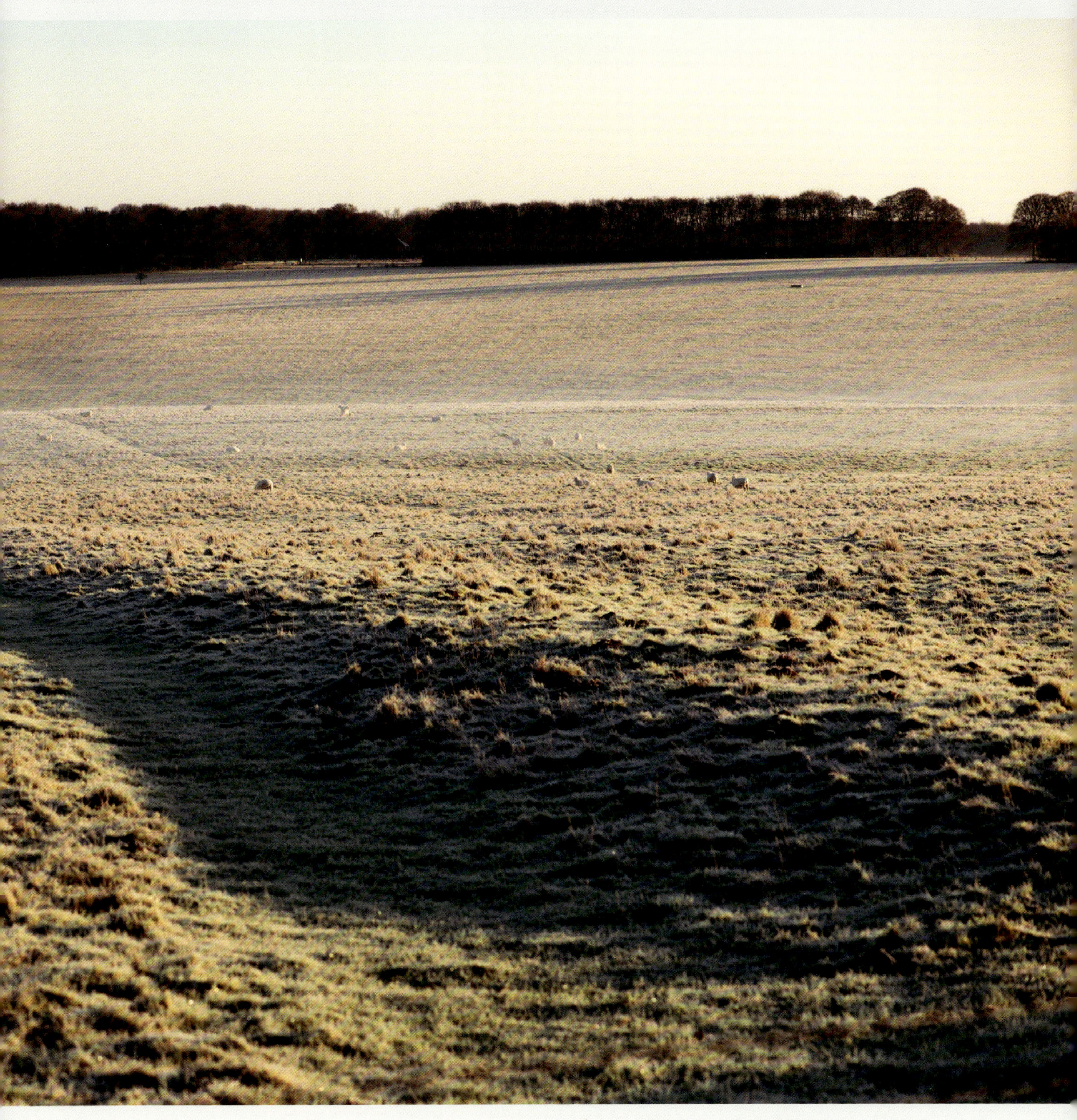

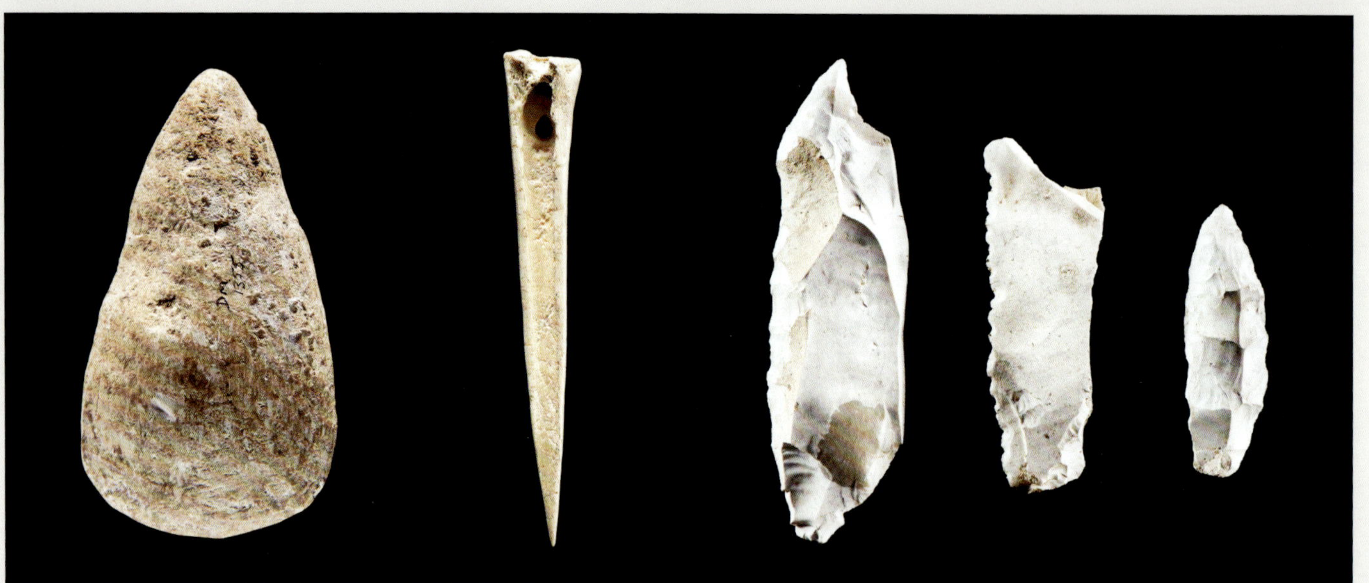

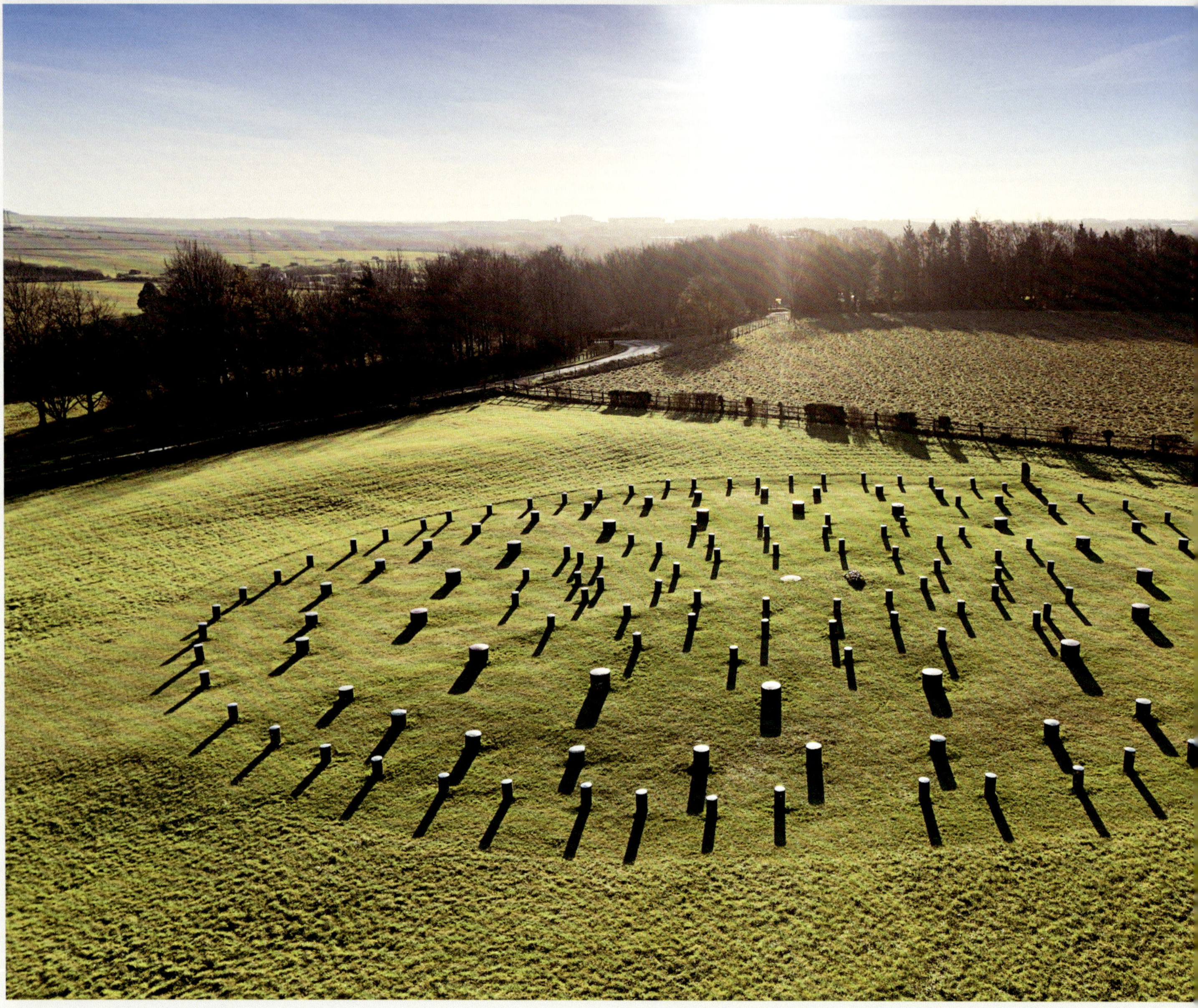

OPPOSITE A small selection of the great many objects deliberately buried at Woodhenge in the Neolithic period (from left to right): a model axehead carved from chalk, a bone pin and three flint tools. These tools were an awl for piercing wood or leather (left), a saw, probably for processing plant materials (middle) and a tool known as a fabricator (right), used for firelighting.

Leading from the Southern Circle was a surfaced roadway flanked by ditches and banks, like the Stonehenge Avenue ... It had been extensively trampled, as if people had regularly walked between the timber monument and the river, perhaps during ceremonies.

At Coneybury, animal and bird bones, flint tools, such as arrowheads, and Grooved Ware pottery were found, and the whole monument was surrounded by a ditch and bank. This was one of several small henges across the Stonehenge landscape; perhaps some of these unexcavated enclosures also contained similar timber structures.

Several more of these square-in-circle timber monuments were built close to the settlement at Durrington Walls. Three examples that are smaller than Coneybury have been excavated along the ridge 500m to the south. Two more (known as the Southern and Northern Circles) stood among the houses and had façades that would have screened the view of their interiors. Soon after it was built, the Southern Circle was transformed into a more elaborate monument, when the original posts were replaced by six concentric rings of oak timbers. People placed all kinds of objects among the posts and in the postholes: Grooved Ware pottery, animal bones, flint and bone objects. This practice continued for a long time after the posts had rotted and fallen. Leading from the Southern Circle was a surfaced roadway flanked by ditches and banks, like the Stonehenge Avenue. It extended 100m to a cliff edge above the nearby river Avon. It had been extensively trampled, as if people had regularly walked between the timber monument and the river, perhaps during ceremonies.

A similar monument of concentric timber posts arranged in ovals, known as Woodhenge, was built to the south of Durrington Walls. Like Stonehenge, it was aligned on the midsummer solstice sunrise, but unlike the stone circle, where few objects have been found, this was a place where people left pottery, antler picks, carved chalk objects, animal bones, flint tools, fragments of human bone and the cremated remains of at least one individual. Again, the deliberate placing of objects here continued after the posts had rotted away.

By the end of the Neolithic period, about 2400 BC, the huge, newly built banks of Durrington Walls must have risen above the debris of an abandoned settlement and the decayed and fallen posts of timber monuments, vestiges of remembered temples. It had been a messy and busy place, very different to Stonehenge, only a short distance away, which seems to have been kept clean and clear of everyday debris. However, the two places were closely linked, like two sides of the same coin. The riverside was where the builders and pilgrims gathered for feasts and rituals, but once the stone monument had been completed, it was the focus for different kinds of ceremonies.

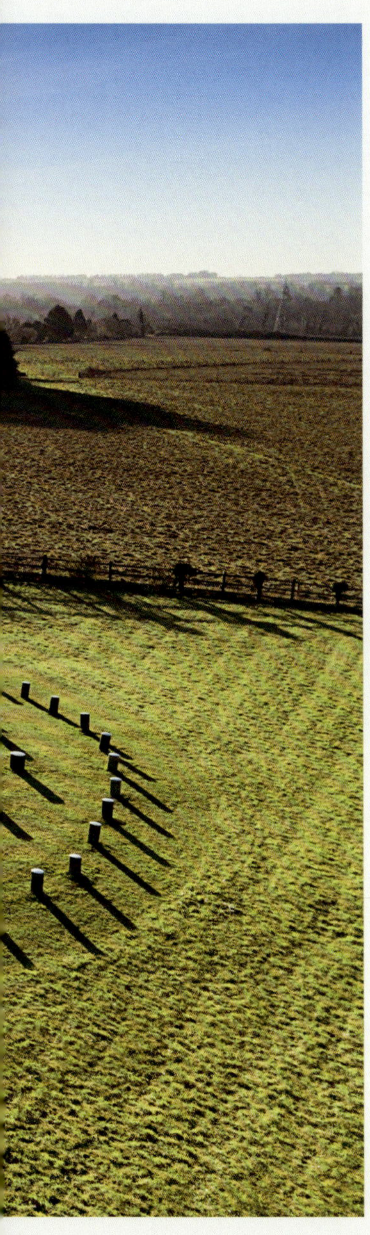

LEFT Woodhenge was excavated in the 1920s by pioneering archaeologist Maud Cunnington. Its six oval rings of postholes, which originally held upright timbers, were marked by short concrete posts.

THE CHALCOLITHIC AND BRONZE AGE

NEW PEOPLE, NEW IDEAS (2400–2200 BC)

Shortly after Stonehenge was built, great changes began to sweep across Britain, during a short period known as the Chalcolithic, or 'Copper Age', an overlap between the late Neolithic and early Bronze Age. People from Continental Europe arrived, bringing new objects, skills and ideas with them, including the first metal items and new types of finely made ceramic pots, now known as Beakers. These exotic incomers held different beliefs to the resident Neolithic population and may well have spoken an unfamiliar language. Their ideas and technologies soon spread, representing a distinct shift in social and cultural practices.

The frenzy of monument building across Britain and Ireland in the centuries around 2500 BC came to a sudden end shortly after the stone circle at Stonehenge was built. Although a variety of smaller cairns, tombs, stone circles and rows were built in northern and western Britain and Ireland in the early Bronze Age (up to about 2000 BC), no major communal monuments were built after about 2300 BC. It is quite possible that the demands of building such structures, including transporting heavy stones and timber over long distances, placed a strain on the daily lives of entire communities. Increasing demands for labour may have led some people to question their beliefs and the

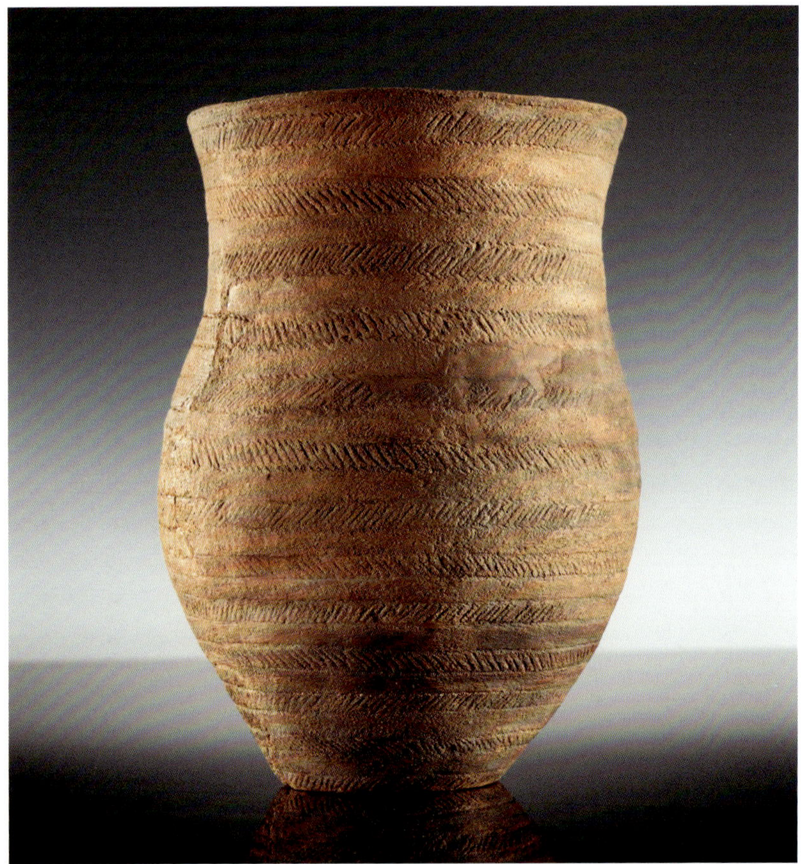

LEFT This pottery vessel has been reconstructed from large fragments found within a burial mound on Wilsford Down, south of Stonehenge. It is an early style of Beaker, typical of those made in southern Britain in about 2300 BC.

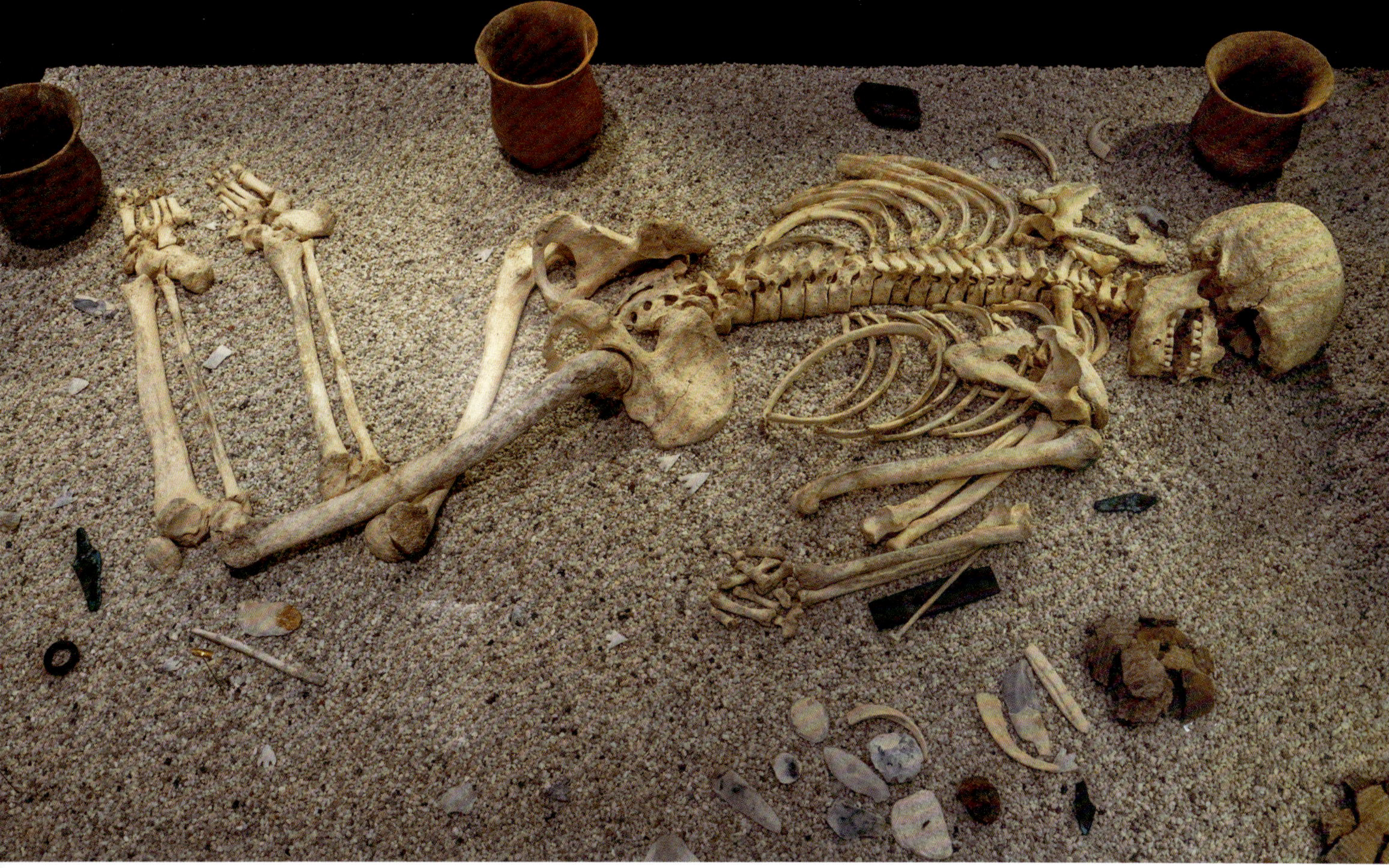

ABOVE The skeleton of the so-called Amesbury Archer, now on display at the Salisbury Museum, laid out exactly as he was placed in his grave, surrounded by pottery, flint tools and other objects.

religious fervour involved, to resist authority, to down tools and to move away. On the other hand, such communal projects may have ceased because of the impact of new people arriving with radical ideas and seemingly magical skills in the production of shiny metals. Suddenly it was possible to see different ways of living and relating to the world, and perhaps it was no longer considered useful or necessary to create the older types of monuments.

Only a few first-generation migrants from Continental Europe have been identified from archaeological excavations. These people were buried with a variety of objects in flat graves or under small round mounds – a very different funerary rite to late Neolithic cremation. In these graves, the body was often accompanied by one or more ceramic drinking vessels, known as Beakers. These were finely made and decorated with lines and geometric patterns by pressing cord, combs or fingernails into the wet clay, and were quite unlike the larger Grooved Ware pots otherwise in use. Archaeologists have traditionally called people buried with this distinctive type of pottery 'Beaker People' or the 'Beaker Folk'. There has long been debate as to whether these people were new arrivals, or whether they were locals adopting new practices. Analysis of chemicals in the teeth of skeletons from Beaker graves has shown that some were men and women who had been brought up in Europe, and their DNA shows that they were descended from Continental European populations. It seems that first-generation Beaker-using immigrants were soon having children and prospering in Britain, although rarely mixing with the resident Neolithic population.

One of the earliest Beaker graves found in Britain has been dubbed the 'Amesbury Archer'.

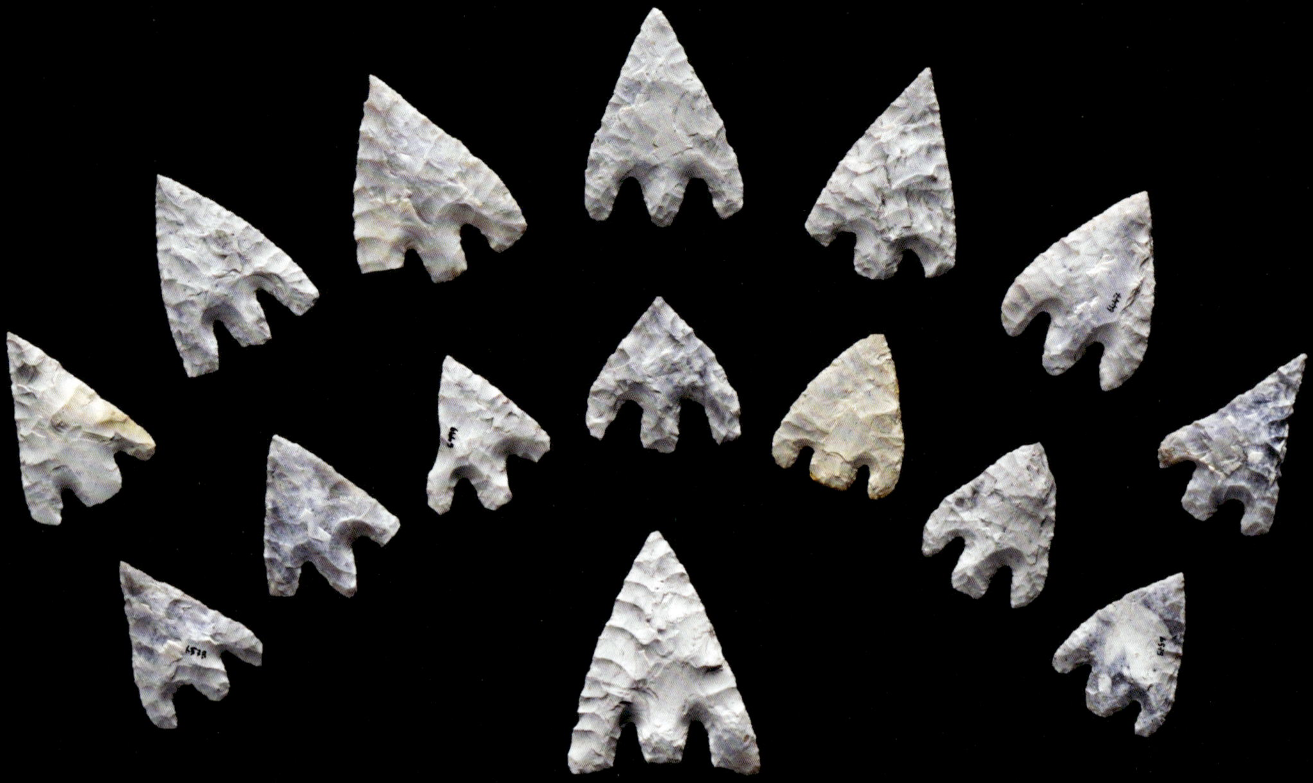

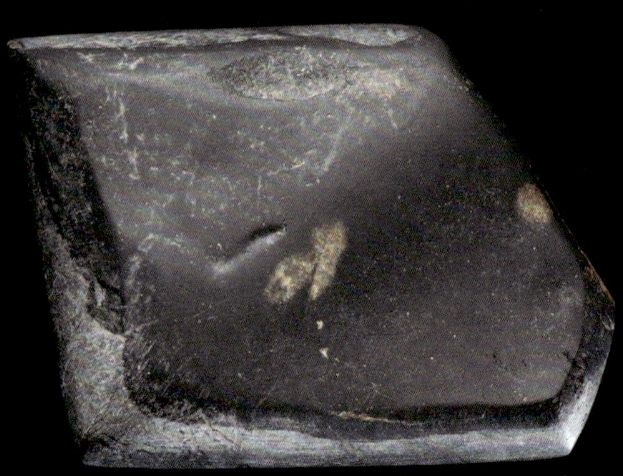

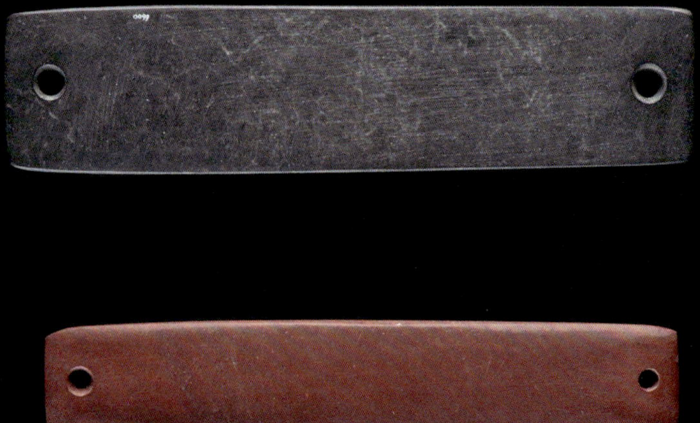

TOP Lying over and around the body of the Amesbury Archer were flint arrowheads of a new, Continental European type, known now as 'barbed and tanged' because of their backwards-pointing barbs and the tang, which fitted into a slot in an arrow shaft.

ABOVE LEFT The Amesbury Archer's burial included this smooth black rock, known as a 'cushion stone', which would have been used as a small anvil on which to work copper or gold.

ABOVE RIGHT The Amesbury Archer was found with these two stone wrist guards. These would have been worn on the forearm to protect from the recoil of the string when firing a bow, but may also have been symbols of status.

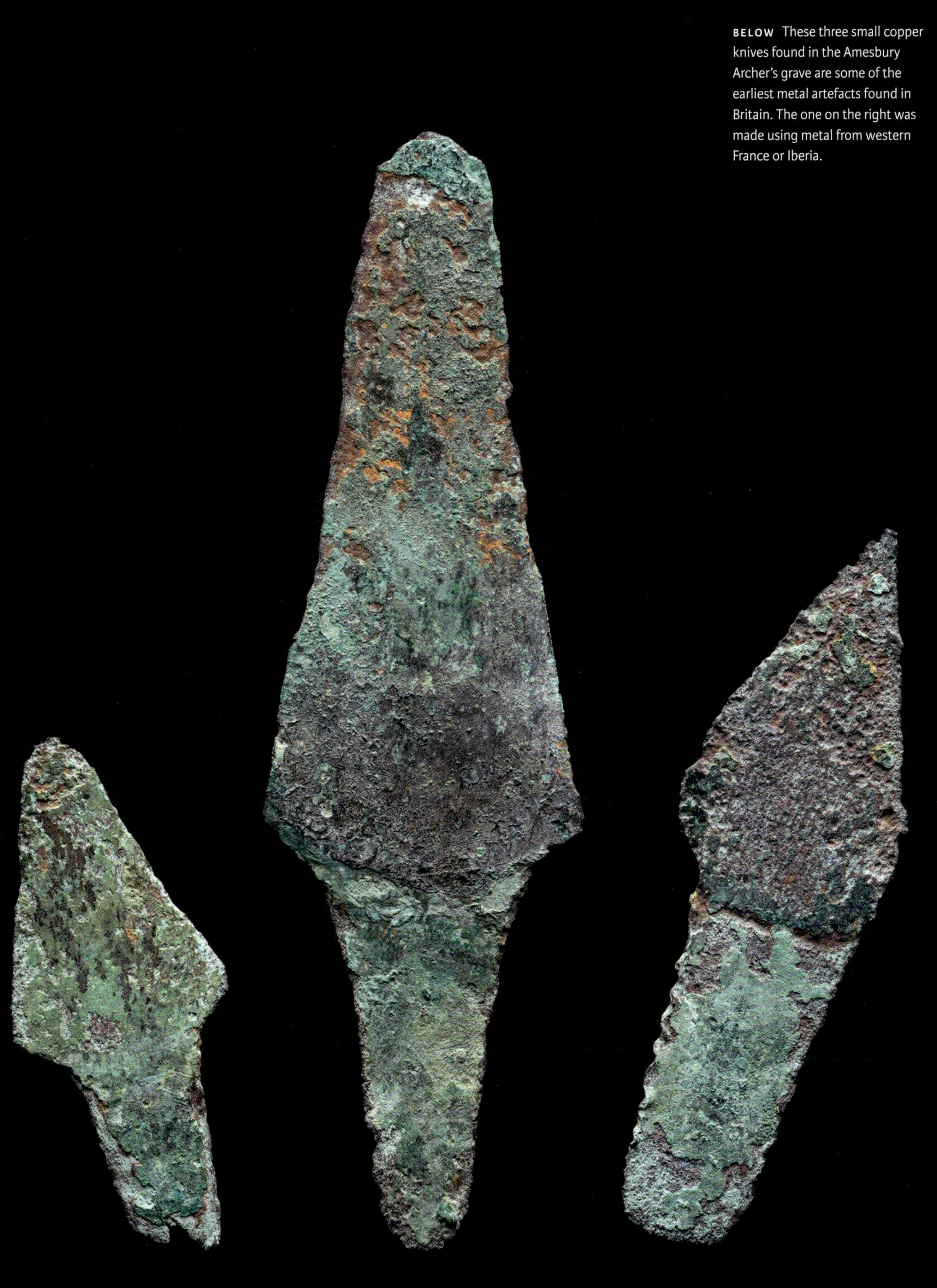

BELOW These three small copper knives found in the Amesbury Archer's grave are some of the earliest metal artefacts found in Britain. The one on the right was made using metal from western France or Iberia.

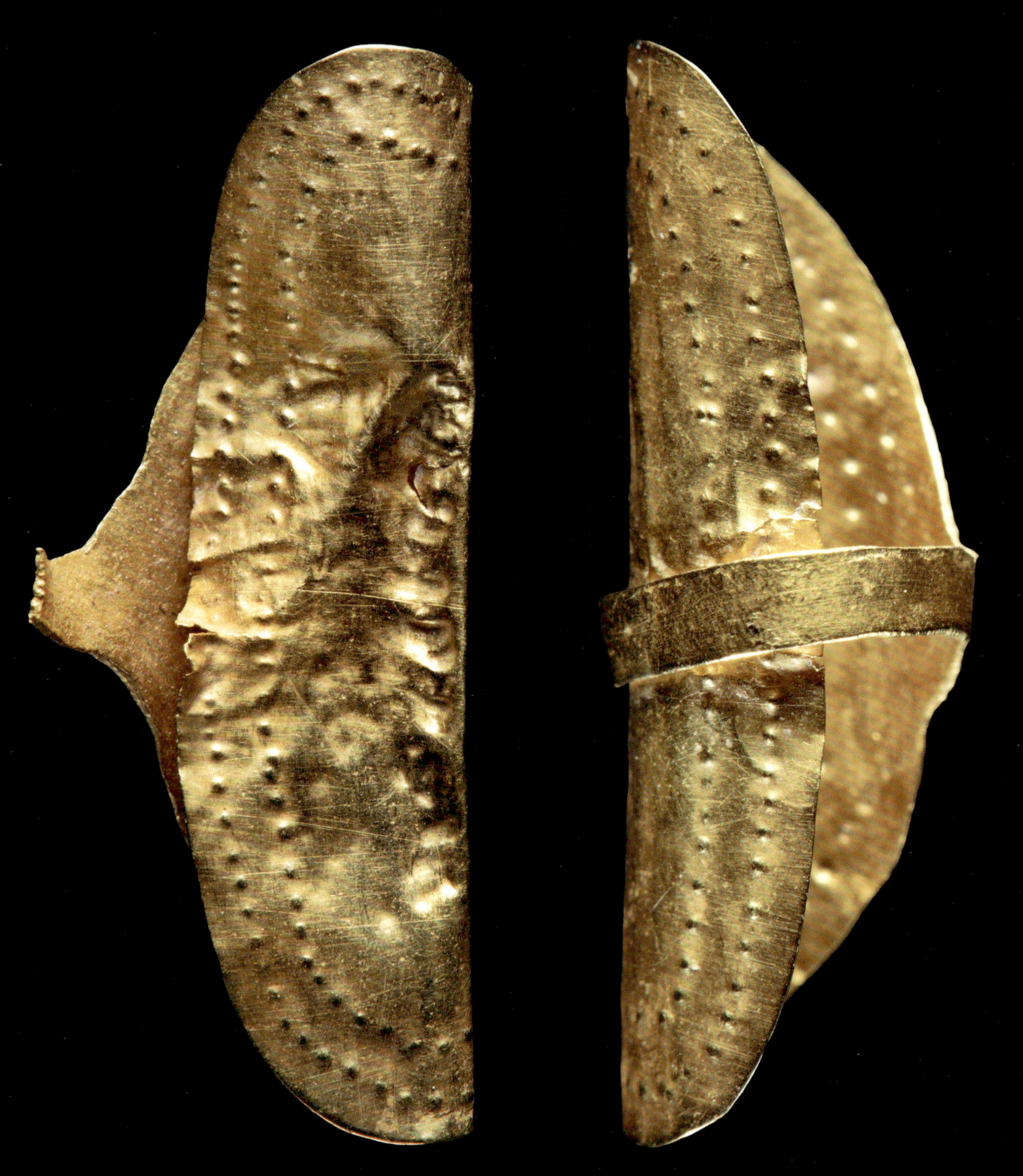

OPPOSITE This pair of delicate basket-shaped gold ornaments, about 3cm in length, were found with the Amesbury Archer. An identical pair was found with another man, buried close by at a slightly later date. Perhaps these gold objects signified that these men shared a similar role in life.

His burial, dating from about 2300 BC, was discovered in 2002 about 3 miles (5km) from Stonehenge, on the far side of the river Avon. His mourners had buried him in a wooden chamber with about 100 objects, among which were 16 flint arrowheads, five Beaker pots, two sandstone wrist guards (used during archery), boars' tusks, various flint tools, a bone pin, an antler spatula, and a shale belt ring. The Amesbury Archer was between 35 and 45 years old when he died, with robust bones, but a damaged knee that would have made it difficult to walk in the last few years before his death. Chemicals laid down in his teeth show that he grew up in central Europe, probably in the western Alps, and his DNA shows he was descended from European communities. He must therefore have been one of the pioneering settlers who had arrived in Britain at the end of the Neolithic period.

From where did these people originate? Beaker pottery was first made in about 2700 BC by people living in present-day Spain, Portugal and south-west France. From there, this type of pottery spread north between communities along the Atlantic coast and was adopted across western Europe. At the same time people moving eastwards, who had been part of northern European cultures that made distinctive Corded Ware pottery, brought with them the practice of burying their dead in single graves and accompanied by different types of objects. From various parts of the Continent, people began to travel to Britain, bringing with them these amalgamated traditions, and started to interact more regularly with the people living here, creating connections that would last for centuries.

These Continental people may have been in search of new sources of precious raw materials: gold, copper and tin. As well as the objects mentioned above, the Amesbury Archer was buried with two tiny rolled-up discs of gold, perhaps earrings, or hair or beard tresses, and three knives, made using copper from central Europe. These are the earliest metal objects known in Britain. Not only was this man buried with these extraordinary items, he appears also to have had the knowledge to craft them: buried with him was a 'cushion stone' used in the shaping of small metal objects. These early prospectors would have struck lucky in Britain and Ireland, which have plentiful resources of precious metals, such as tin in Cornwall, copper at the Great Orme, North Wales, and gold from Ross Island in south-west Ireland.

The ability to take dull stone and transform it into lustrous metal may well have been viewed as otherworldly or magical. The method may have been secret, known only to a few metalworkers who had specialist status in the community. The Amesbury Archer may have been one of these people. He certainly lived during a short but momentous 'Copper Age', a radical time of change in both technology and society.

The Amesbury Archer was buried with two tiny rolled-up discs of gold ... and three knives, made using copper from central Europe. These are the earliest metal objects known in Britain.

Beaker Burials (2400–1800 BC)

The Amesbury Archer was just one of several burials with Beakers found in the Stonehenge area, and part of a cluster of particularly early burials discovered on Boscombe Down. Perhaps having heard tales of this extraordinary monument, travellers were attracted to Stonehenge, settled in the nearby landscape and buried their dead in the area.

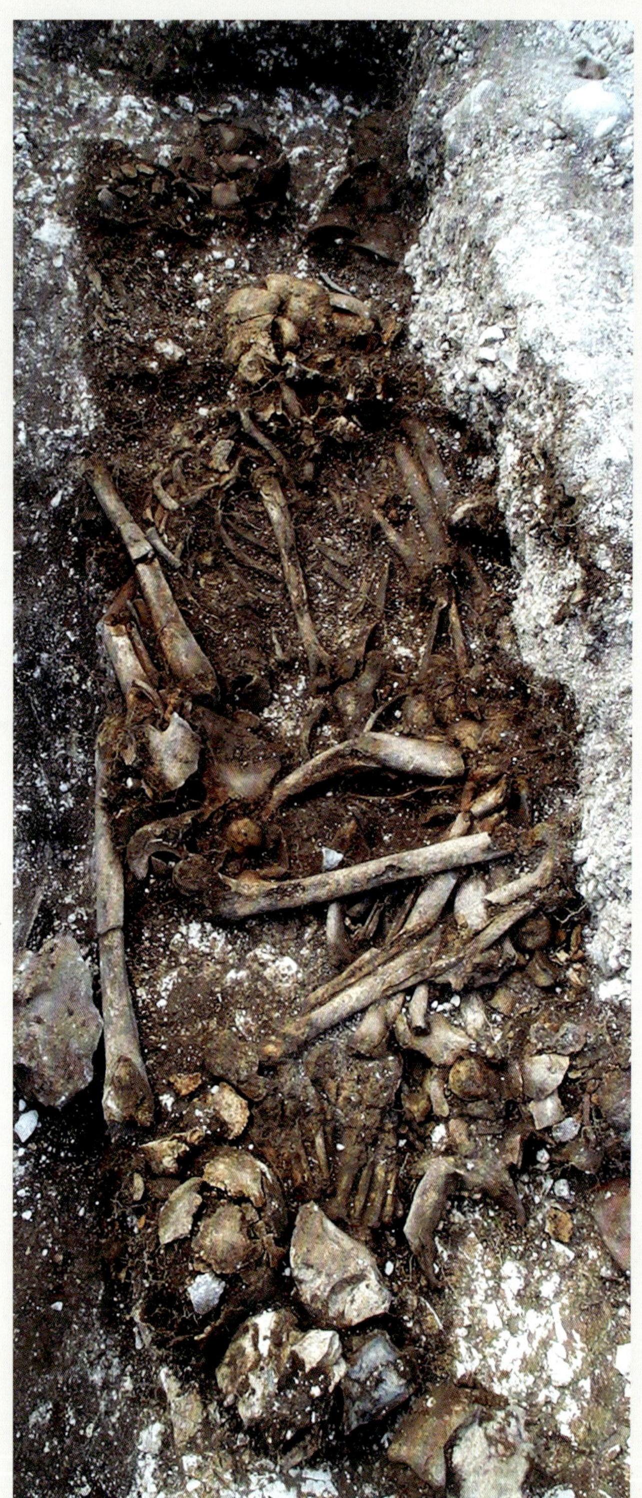

The earliest male Beaker burials in Britain were usually accompanied by a distinctive range of objects deliberately placed into the grave. These included copper knives, Beaker pots, stone wrist guards (which protected an archer's arm from being whipped by the bowstring when firing a bow) and flint arrowheads made in 'barbed and tanged' shape (triangular, with a projection at the base and two smaller points on either side). These may have been personal belongings, but could also have been symbols of an idealised warrior-archer identity, or part of what was considered a suitable costume to enter an afterlife. Female Beaker graves are rarer, and usually less well equipped. Sometimes the graves of both men and women were left unmarked, but often they were covered by a small mound of earth or surrounded by a circular ditch. Some of these early burials were located within sight of Stonehenge, such as that of a woman and several children buried in a cemetery (known as Wilsford G1 – see page 85) just under a mile (1.2km) to the south-west of the monument.

Across the river Avon on Boscombe Down, just 3m from the Amesbury Archer grave, was another early burial, of a young man who was between 20 and 25 years old. This man is known as the Amesbury Archer's 'companion' because he was buried with an identical pair of rolled gold ornaments to his neighbour, as well as a child's tooth, a boar's tusk and several flint flakes and tools. DNA from both individuals has shown that the two men were not closely related family members, but both had a rare skeletal variation in the bones of their feet, suggesting that they were distantly related. Analysis of the chemicals in the companion's teeth tells us that he

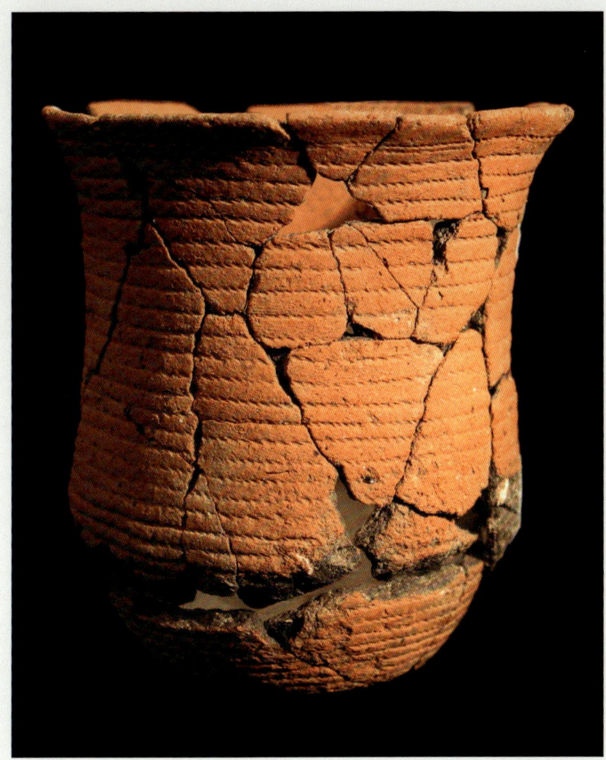

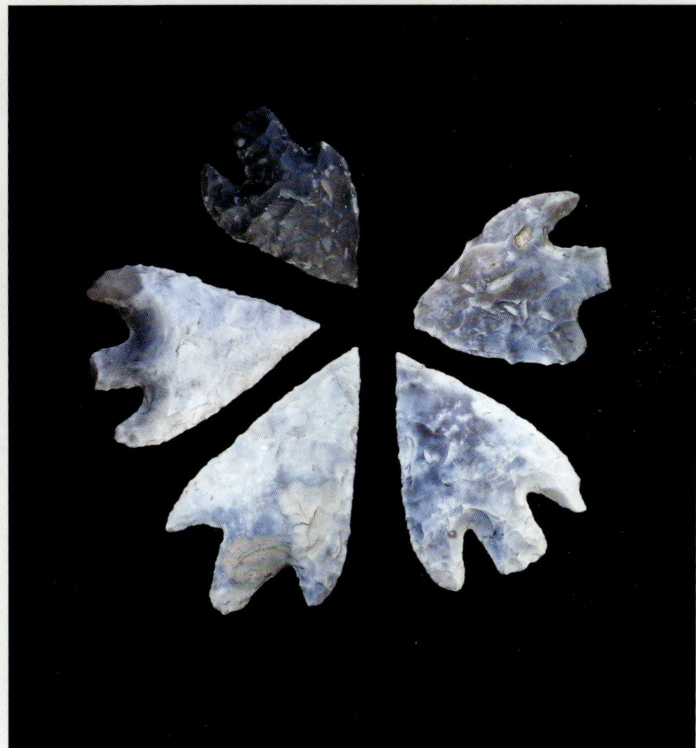

OPPOSITE The grave of the 'Boscombe Bowmen', which included five adult men, a teenage boy, two or three children and an infant. They were buried successively in a timber chamber.

ABOVE LEFT One of the Beaker pots found in the grave of the Boscombe Bowmen. It has been decorated all over by impressing a cord into the wet clay.

ABOVE RIGHT Barbed and tanged arrowheads found with the Boscombe Bowmen. Four of the five were clustered together, perhaps in a bundle or quiver.

grew up in an area of chalk soils, probably in southern England, but between the ages of about nine and thirteen he travelled to central Europe for a time, probably to the area where the Amesbury Archer had grown up. This suggests that communities in these two areas were connected over a considerable distance, across the Channel and many weeks' journey on foot.

Dating from a similar time, not far from the graves of the Amesbury Archer and his companion, at least nine people of various ages were buried within a large rectangular timber chamber, together with at least eight Beaker pots, as well as flint and antler items. These individuals are known as the 'Boscombe Bowmen' because of the discovery of flint arrowheads in the grave. From chemicals in their teeth, we know that the three adult men placed in this chamber (two of whom were cousins or half-brothers) had shared a pattern of long-distance migration during their lives. They spent their early childhood living in an area with granite or older geologies (perhaps Wales or south-west England), before travelling to another location during early adolescence and finally travelling to the Stonehenge area later in life. DNA extracted from their remains tells us that the mother of one of these men is likely to have been a Neolithic inhabitant of Britain, but his father was clearly of European ancestry.

These early Beaker burials show that complicated journeys and relationships were involved in the arrival of new people to Britain from Continental Europe. This was not necessarily a pattern of one-way immigration, but of moving back and forth between different areas. Crucially, these long-distance links with other communities were maintained for generations, well into the Bronze Age.

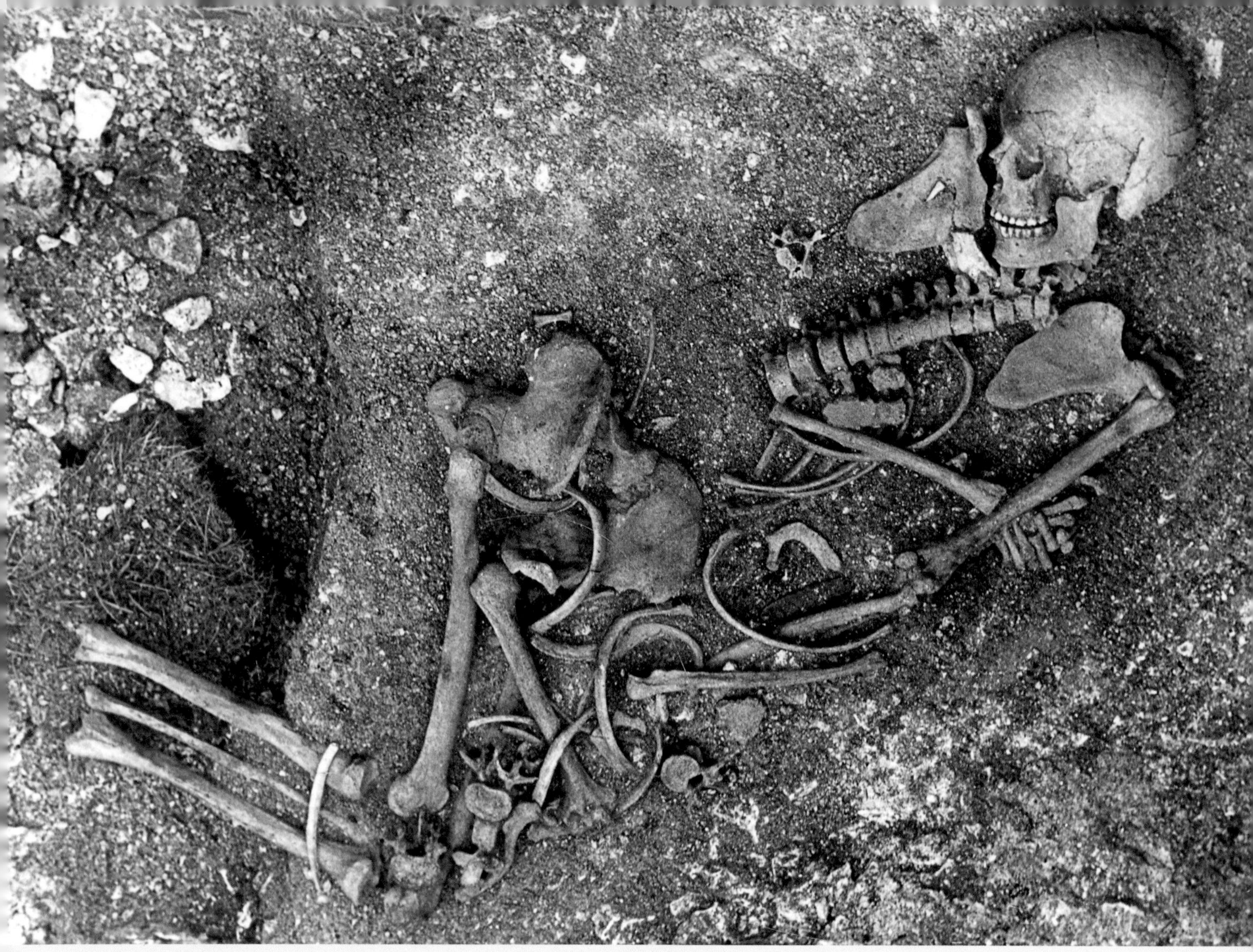

The Stonehenge Archer (*c.*2350–2200 BC)

ABOVE The Stonehenge Archer burial during excavation in 1978.

In 1978, archaeologist John Evans was excavating a small trench across the henge ditch not far from the Heel Stone at Stonehenge. He was looking for evidence to understand the prehistoric environment at Stonehenge, but unexpectedly found the burial of a man, uncovering something of a murder mystery.

The aim of the excavation was to take soil samples from the layers in the ditch to look for tiny snail shells. As different species of snail are very particular about the habitats in which they live, the variety of species in a sample of soil can tell us about the local vegetation and landscape in the past. On the penultimate day of the excavation, however, the section excavated across the ditch collapsed, revealing the leg bones of a human skeleton.

Closer analysis of the skeleton, however, revealed that the arrowheads were not his own hunting tools. One of them was embedded in his sternum and two others had damaged his ribs: he had been fatally shot at close range, and from behind.

A man aged between 25 and 30 had been buried in the ditch, wearing an archer's stone wrist guard and with three barbed and tanged arrowheads, leading him to be dubbed the 'Stonehenge Archer'. These finds are typical of the sorts of objects found in graves from the Chalcolithic period, and radiocarbon dating of his bones confirmed that he died between 2345 and 2195 BC. Closer analysis of the skeleton, however, revealed that the arrowheads were not his own hunting tools. One of them was embedded in his sternum and two others had damaged his ribs: he had been fatally shot at close range, and from behind, and had been buried with the murder weapons.

Was this a human sacrifice or a ritual execution? Had the man been murdered during a dispute or conflict? Perhaps the man had been trespassing at Stonehenge and was shot by the monument's protectors. Of course, it is possible that the man was killed elsewhere, and brought to Stonehenge for burial. Analysis of chemicals in the man's teeth tell us that he grew up on the chalk soils of southern Britain and is likely to have lived locally. His violent death may indicate that relations were not always cordial between different groups at this time. Whatever the reason for his death, the recently completed stone circle was still an auspicious place to be buried. Some archaeologists have suggested that the Stonehenge Archer was the last in the long line of prehistoric people to be buried at Stonehenge, although his burial was some 400 years after the earlier cremation burials.

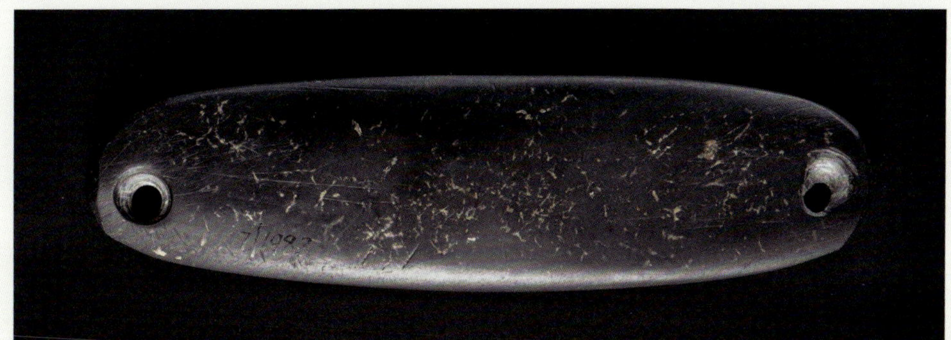

RIGHT This wrist guard, or bracer, made of a dark grey metamorphic rock, was found next to the lower left forearm of the Stonehenge Archer, suggesting that he fired a bow right-handed.

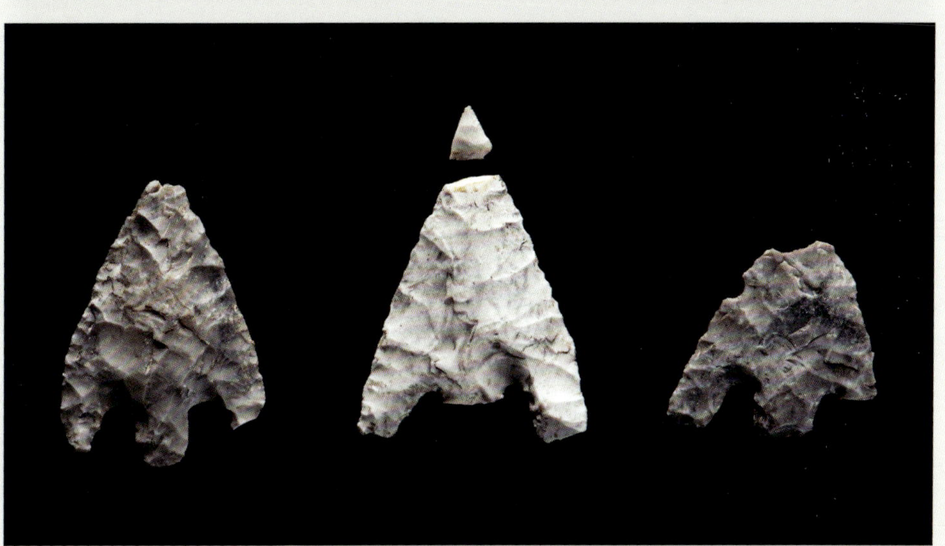

BELOW RIGHT Three barbed and tanged arrowheads discovered in the Stonehenge Archer's grave. The tip of the middle arrowhead was found embedded in his rib and another broken fragment of a fourth arrowhead was found in his sternum.

Parallel Populations?

Recent studies of the remains of people buried under round barrows in the Stonehenge landscape have led to new discoveries about their family relationships, through the analysis of their DNA. On the whole, these individuals did not have children with people descended from the native British Neolithic population, but stayed as a separate community.

Analysis of the DNA from one young man buried under a mound at Wilsford (about 1.2 miles, or 1.9km, south of Stonehenge) with a bronze dagger and stone battle axe, shows that he was probably the uncle of a pair of male cousins, buried in graves three miles to the east on Amesbury Down. One of these cousins was the father of a young woman buried in a cemetery at Porton Down, three miles to the south-east of her father's grave. It appears that, soon after giving birth, both she and her baby died, and she was buried holding the infant.

These relatives were not buried together within one group of barrows, but were dispersed across the local area, showing that previous assumptions that clusters of round barrows might represent individual family plots are wrong. Other relationships or factors in a person's life must have determined where they were buried. None of the members of this family had inherited significant portions of their DNA from the native British Neolithic population. These second-, third- and fourth-generation descendants of Beaker-using immigrants had, for 200 or 300 years, been having children mainly within their own community. In this area, at least, there must have been two populations living largely separately, but alongside one another (although there were exceptions, such as the man buried on Boscombe Down with mixed parentage, see page 75).

It took a long time before the new ideas and religious beliefs of Beaker-using people were fully adopted by the descendants of Neolithic inhabitants of Britain. We can see that this happened from about 2200 BC onwards – the early Bronze Age – when the Beaker pottery that people were making became more regionally distinctive and people buried their dead in more varied ways. Some people continued to be buried with accompanying objects in their graves, as was typical of the early Beaker-using immigrant population, but others were cremated or had only parts of their bodies interred. At this same time, people returned to Stonehenge to make changes to the arrangement of the bluestones.

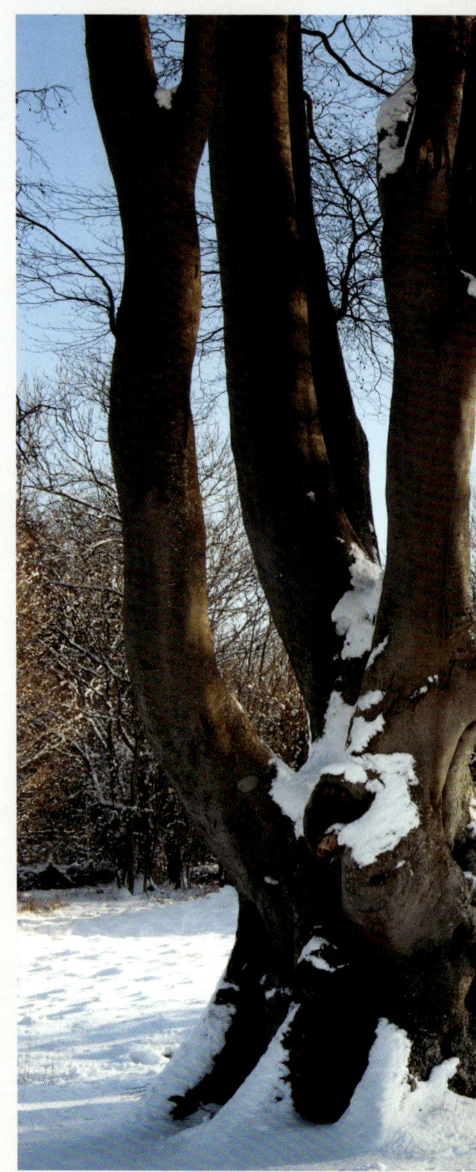

One of these cousins was the father of a young woman buried in a cemetery at Porton Down ... It appears that, soon after giving birth, both she and her baby died, and she was buried holding the infant.

RIGHT Artist's reconstruction of people walking on the Stonehenge Avenue in about 2200 BC. People may have travelled over long distances to see the spectacular monument.

BELOW Barrows forming part of the New King Barrow group, just under a mile east of Stonehenge. Each barrow was probably built in several stages and may cover numerous burials dating from the early Bronze Age.

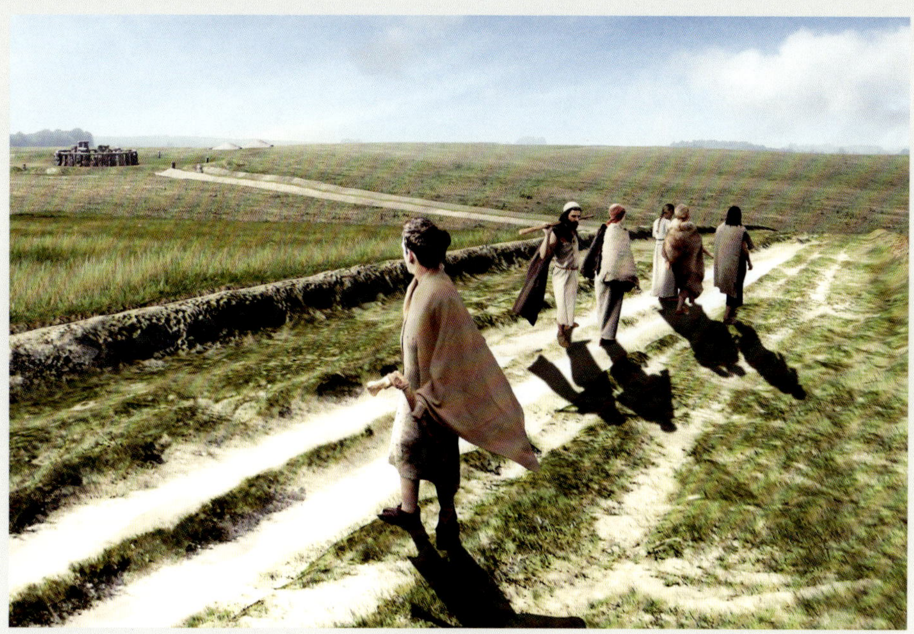

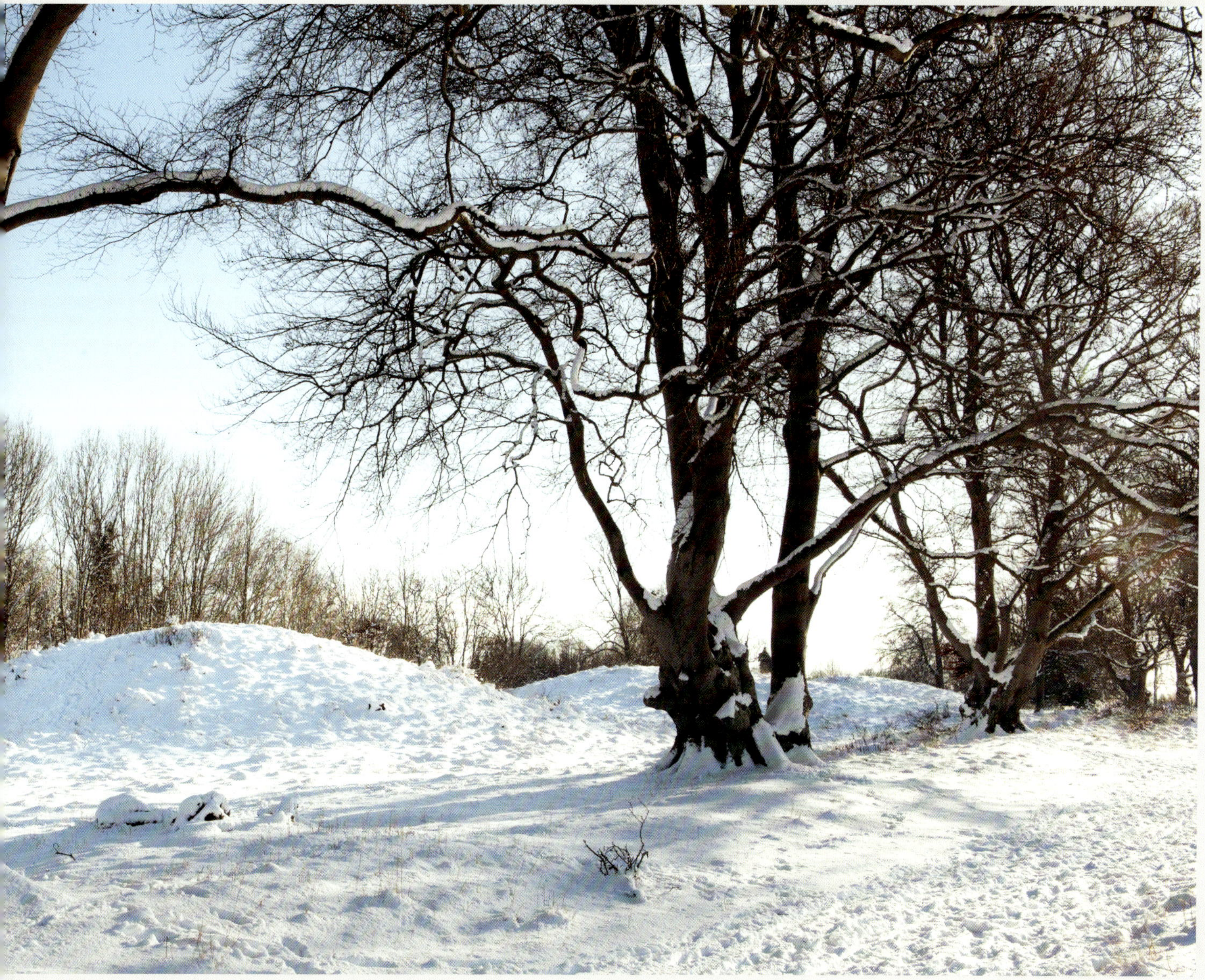

THE EARLY BRONZE AGE (2200–1500 BC)

In the centuries after Stonehenge was built, not only was the monument itself altered, but the landscape around the monument was transformed by the construction of hundreds of burial mounds for the dead. Clustered in groups or strung out in lines along ridge tops, these round barrows contain burials that tell us of journeys, connections, and extraordinary craftsmanship, as well as the continuing importance of Stonehenge.

In about 2100 BC the double bluestone arc that had stood for perhaps 400 years at the centre of Stonehenge was dismantled. The stones were moved to form a central oval and an outer circle, with others brought from the stone circle at the end of the Avenue (see page 64). At a similar time, the Avenue ditches were recut, making the route between Stonehenge and the river visible again as bright white chalk banks against the green pasture. It is possible that these alterations to Stonehenge were carried out by the newly integrated communities living nearby, perhaps returning to older ways but also celebrating new futures together.

At the time these changes were being made to Stonehenge, people had started to build a new type of monument in the surrounding landscape. If you stand at Stonehenge today and look around, low grassy mounds can be seen peppered across the ridge tops in almost every direction, even though many have been lost to the ravages of the plough in recent times. These features, known as barrows, are the burial places of early Bronze Age people. They were built in great numbers across Britain, but there is a distinct cluster of more than 300 within two miles (3km) of Stonehenge; it must have been important to be buried within sight of the famous stone structure.

Many of the round barrows near Stonehenge were excavated by early archaeologists in the 18th and 19th centuries. They found spectacular burial goods, such as gold and amber objects, which they kept for their private museums, but did not usually record any details of how the barrows had been built, or retain the human remains. Nevertheless, it is possible to see from their work, and a few later excavations, that these grass mounds hide complex stories of funerary events and construction phases. Most barrows contain more than one burial with associated objects, and the mounds were often enlarged several times. Most were built of chalk and earth, but some, including those along King Barrow Ridge to the east of Stonehenge, were created by stripping vast areas of downland turf that was cut into blocks and stacked up. Some barrows contained wooden burial chambers, or even standing timbers. Geophysical survey has shown that one burial not far from Stonehenge was surrounded by a ring of posts, which were later covered over with a mound.

One of the most prominent groups of barrows lies along a ridge on Normanton Down, just over half a mile south of Stonehenge. Some of the burials under these barrows were accompanied by truly spectacular artefacts (see page 86).

OPPOSITE A cluster of barrows known as the Cursus Barrows, a linear group of well-preserved early Bronze Age burial mounds, was built along a ridge, parallel to the much earlier Greater Cursus and within view of Stonehenge itself.

OVERLEAF The Normanton Down barrow cemetery, located along a ridge to the south of Stonehenge, includes early Neolithic long barrows and a variety of early Bronze Age round barrows, including the famous 'Bush Barrow'.

If you stand at Stonehenge today and look around, low grassy mounds can be seen peppered across the ridge tops in almost every direction.

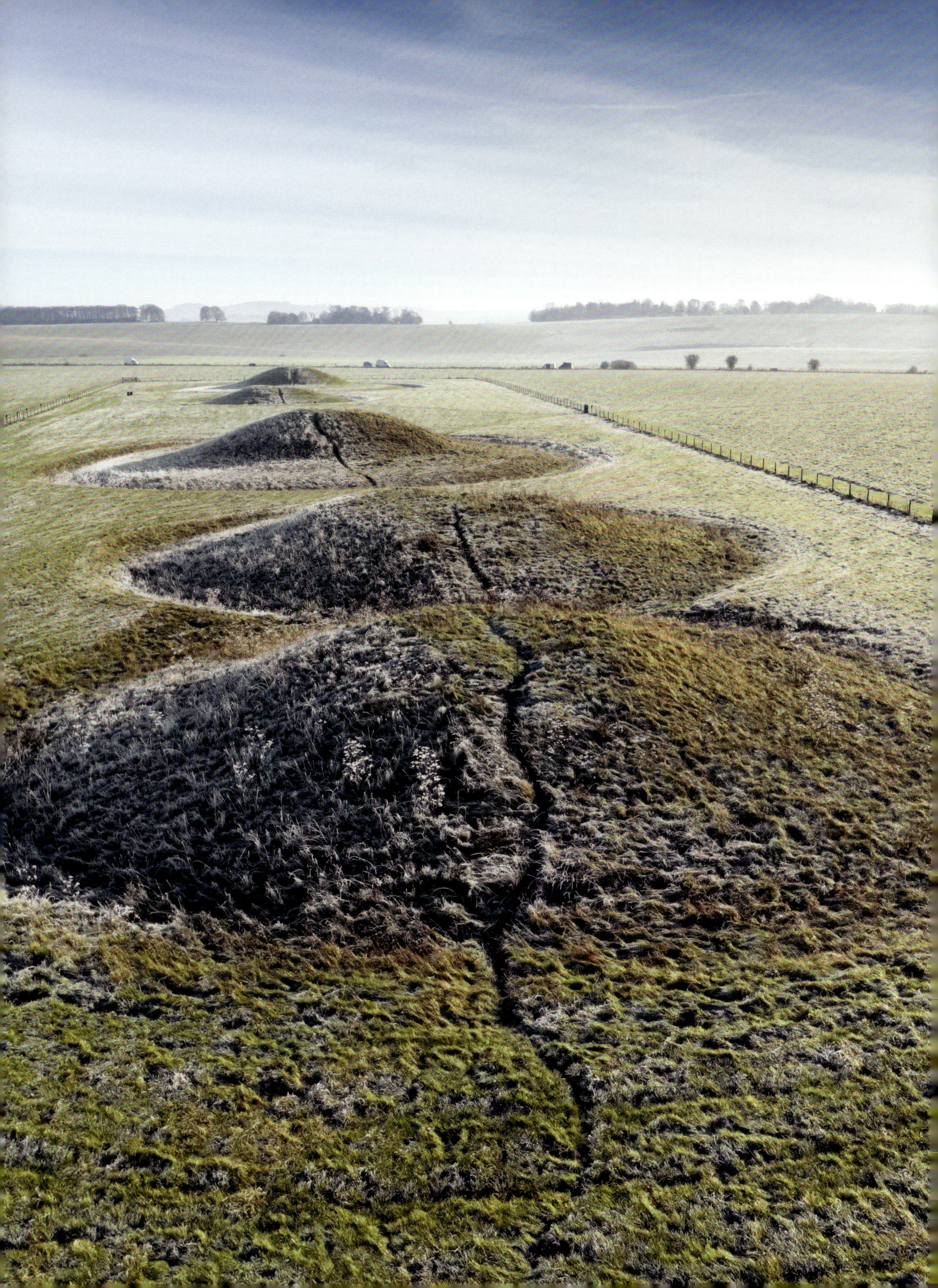

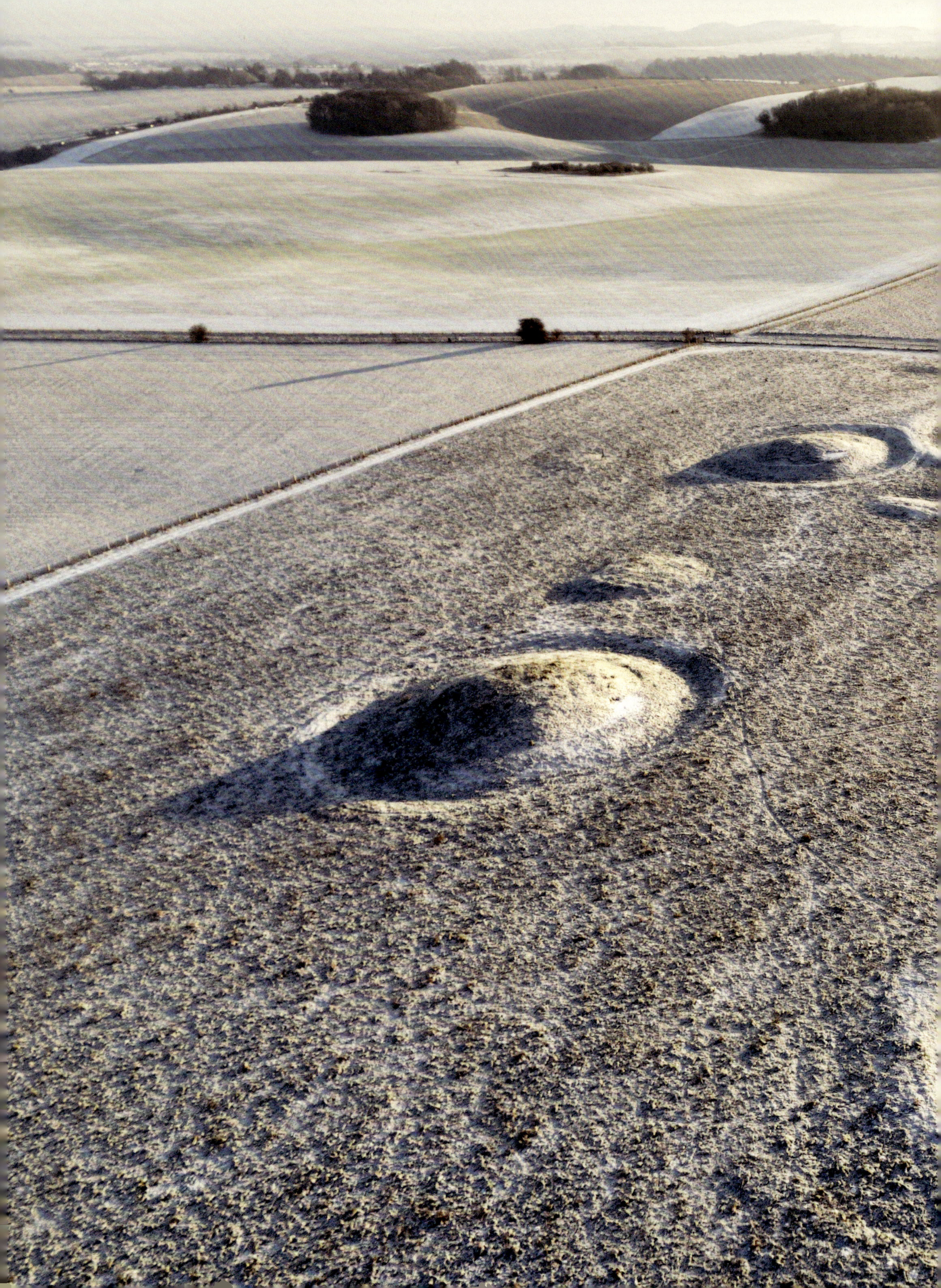

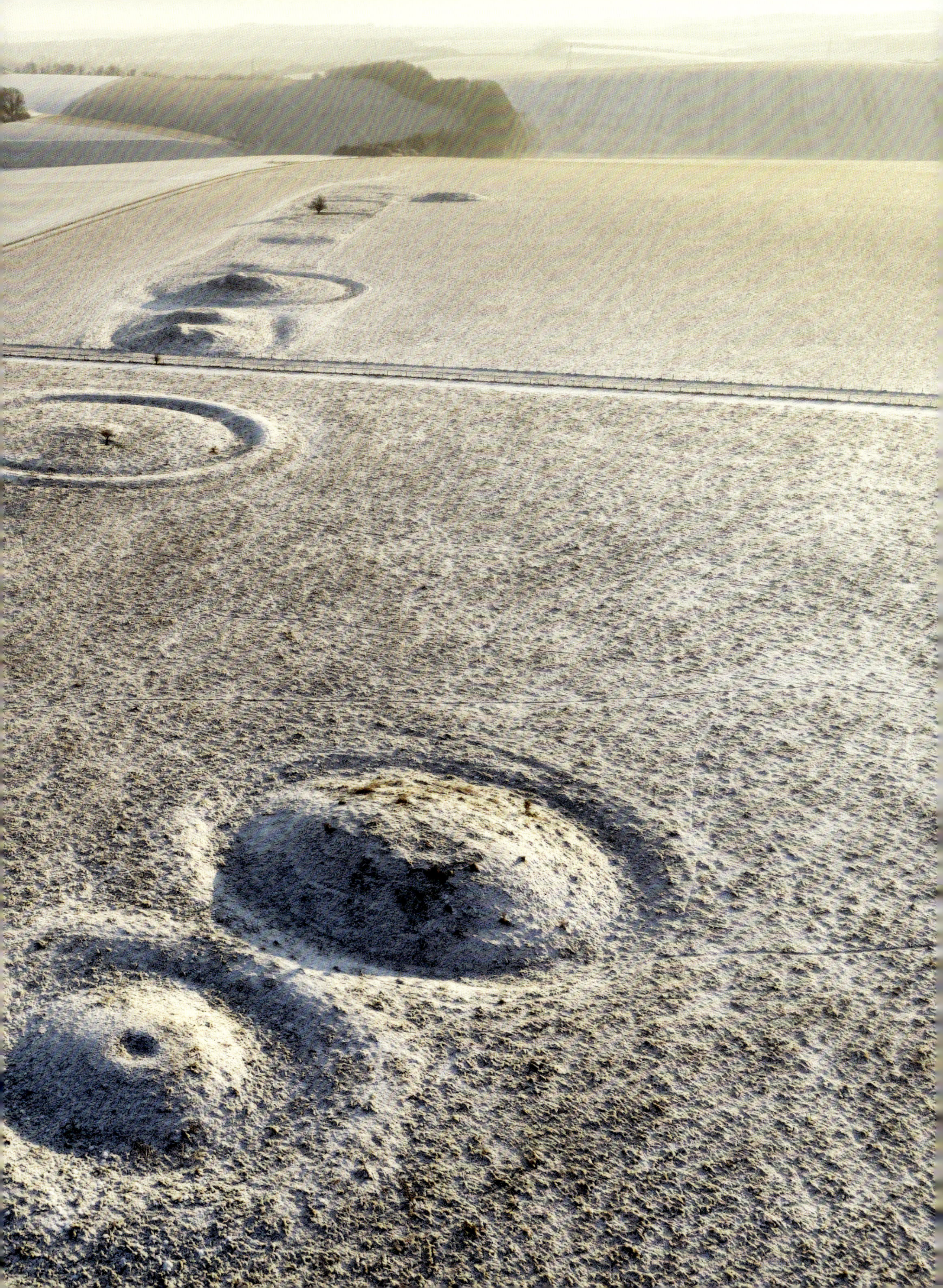

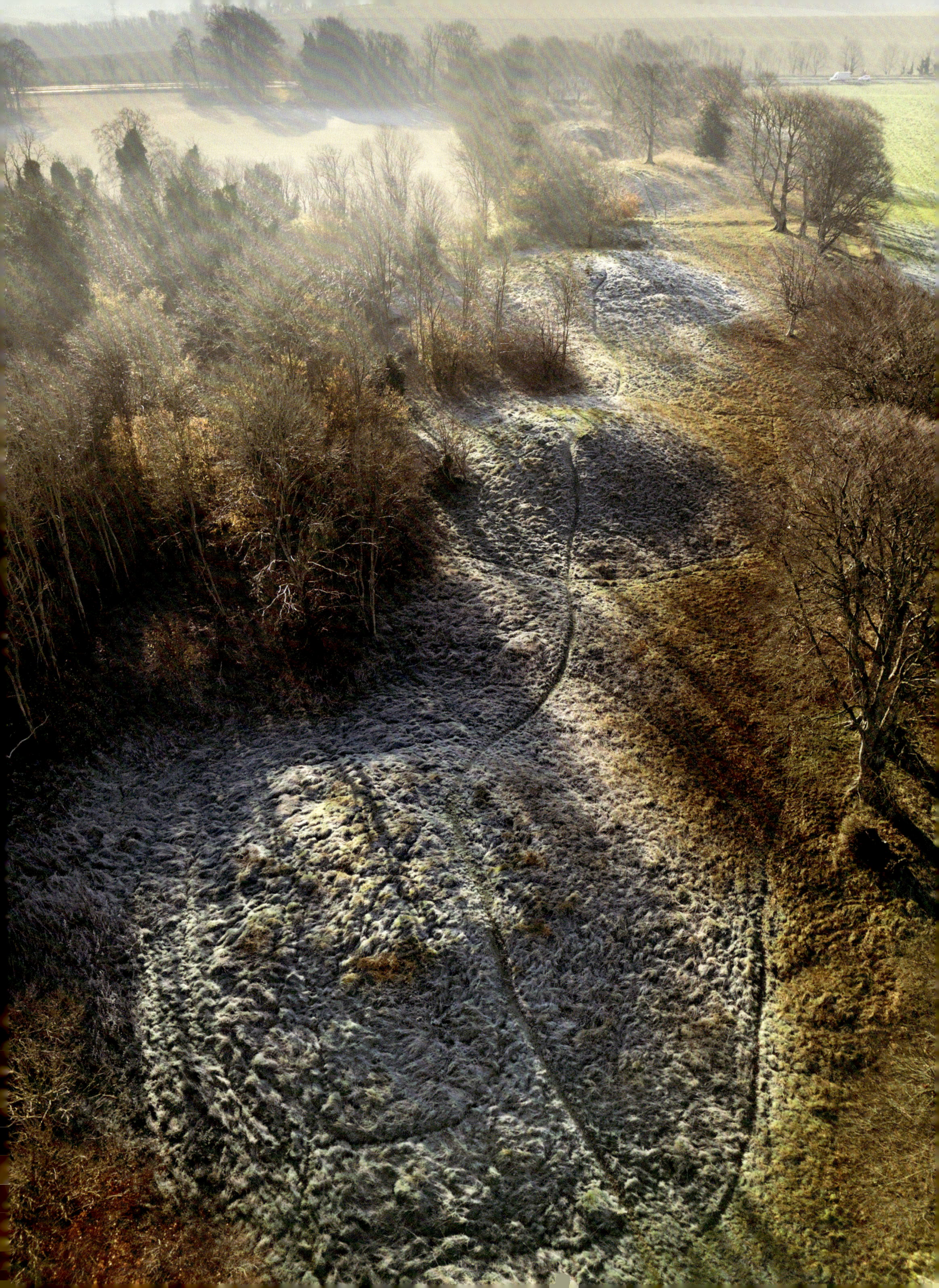

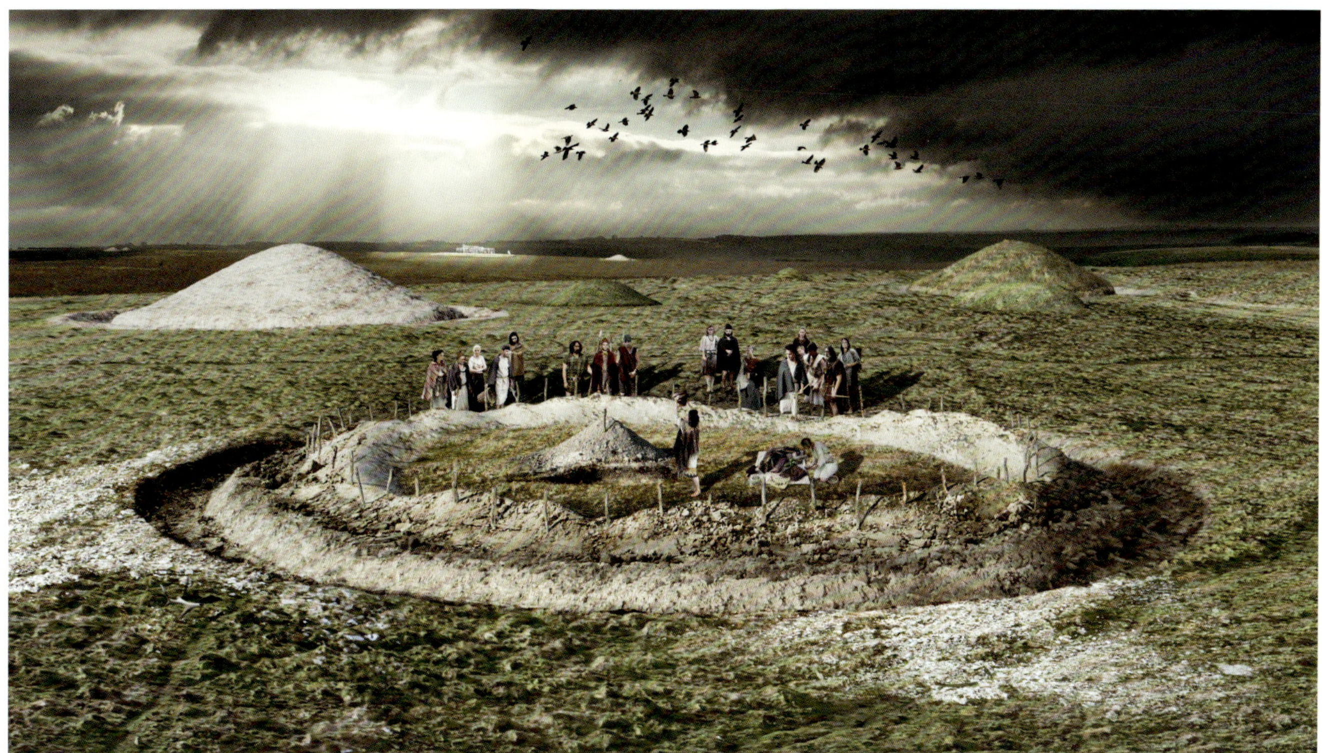

OPPOSITE The 18th-century antiquarian William Stukeley named this group of barrows the 'King Barrows' because of their large size and prominent location flanking the Stonehenge Avenue to the east of Stonehenge. Some appear to have been built using stacks of turf and soil.

ABOVE An artist's reconstruction of the burial of a woman in the barrow cemetery at Normanton Down in about 1800 BC. After interring her body in the ground, the mourners would have raised a mound over her grave.

The round mounds built here were of various types: simple rounded 'bowl' barrows; mounds surrounded by a flat area and outer ditch known as 'bell' barrows; and 'disc' barrows, where a circular bank surrounds a flat area containing a small burial mound. This barrow cemetery was built in a place with a long history, as it includes two small long barrows and a rectangular enclosure, all of which are probably Neolithic. Some of the earliest burials date from the Chalcolithic, clustered near an isolated barrow (known as Wilsford G1) at the far west end of the cemetery. Here, a central grave contained a burial with a Beaker pot and antlers, as well as the fragmentary remains of three other people and two cremated burials. A further nine people, mostly children with Beakers, were placed into a surrounding ditch and in flat graves to the north. Radiocarbon dates show that some of these people were living at a similar time to the Amesbury Archer (about 2300 BC). Like him, they may also have been early immigrants.

Over the next few centuries, probably between 2200 and 1700 BC, about 30 more round barrows were built in a long line running south-east, creating the Normanton Down cemetery. We do not know if the people buried in these barrows lived locally, as settlements from this period of the early Bronze Age have not been discovered. It may be that the dead were brought here from other places, to be buried within view of Stonehenge. Either way, the objects buried with them show that they were certainly well-connected and important people.

At Stonehenge itself, one final episode of alteration took place probably in about 1800 BC. Two concentric rings of pits, today known as the Y and Z holes, were dug around the outside of the sarsen circle, 30 in the outer ring and 29 in the inner. These holes may have been made to relocate the bluestones or were perhaps just intended as simple pits, perhaps some sort of 'closing' event. Whatever their purpose, they were left gradually to fill with windblown sediments. It is quite possible that some of the sarsen stones had already fallen by this date, as there is no hole under the fallen Stone 8 – one of the sarsens of the outer circle. Stonehenge was beginning to become a ruin.

‘Wessex Culture’ Burials (1950–1500 BC)

The burials of some people in Wiltshire and Dorset in the early Bronze Age were accompanied by ornate, rare and precious grave goods. These have been named ‘Wessex Culture’ burials and provide evidence of highly skilled crafts and long-distance connections at this time. Some of the most spectacular, including the famous ‘Bush Barrow’ burial, have been found close to Stonehenge.

From about 2200 BC metalworkers in Britain and Ireland began to combine copper with tin to make bronze, a much harder and more versatile metal. Tin from Cornwall, together with gold and copper, was exchanged between communities up and down the Atlantic coast of Europe. Specialist metalworkers in these areas made ornate and beautiful objects, such as crescent-shaped gold ‘lunulae’, a form of ceremonial necklace. The Stonehenge area, at the gateway to south-west Britain, with overland routes to the Irish Sea, and connected by the river Avon to the south coast, was at the heart of these exchange networks.

In 1808, antiquaries William Cunnington and Sir Richard Colt Hoare were excavating barrows on Normanton Down (see page 106). Under one mound, known as Bush Barrow, they found the skeleton of an adult male in a crouched position, with three large bronze daggers, a bronze axe, a gold belt hook, two gold lozenges decorated with intricate geometric shapes and a mace-head with a decorated handle. It is the richest burial ever found from prehistoric Britain.

BELOW This barrow on Normanton Down, known as Bush Barrow, was excavated in 1808. Inside it was a burial, probably an adult male, accompanied by spectacular gold and bronze objects.

OPPOSITE The Bush Barrow grave goods, now on display at Wiltshire Museum, included a stone mace-head (left), perforated for a wooden handle, which was probably decorated with bone mounts (reconstructed here). The small gold lozenge (right top) was found nearby and may also have been mounted on the handle. This eye-catching weapon may have been an important piece of regalia. The burial also included the decorated gold cover of a large belt hook (right bottom).

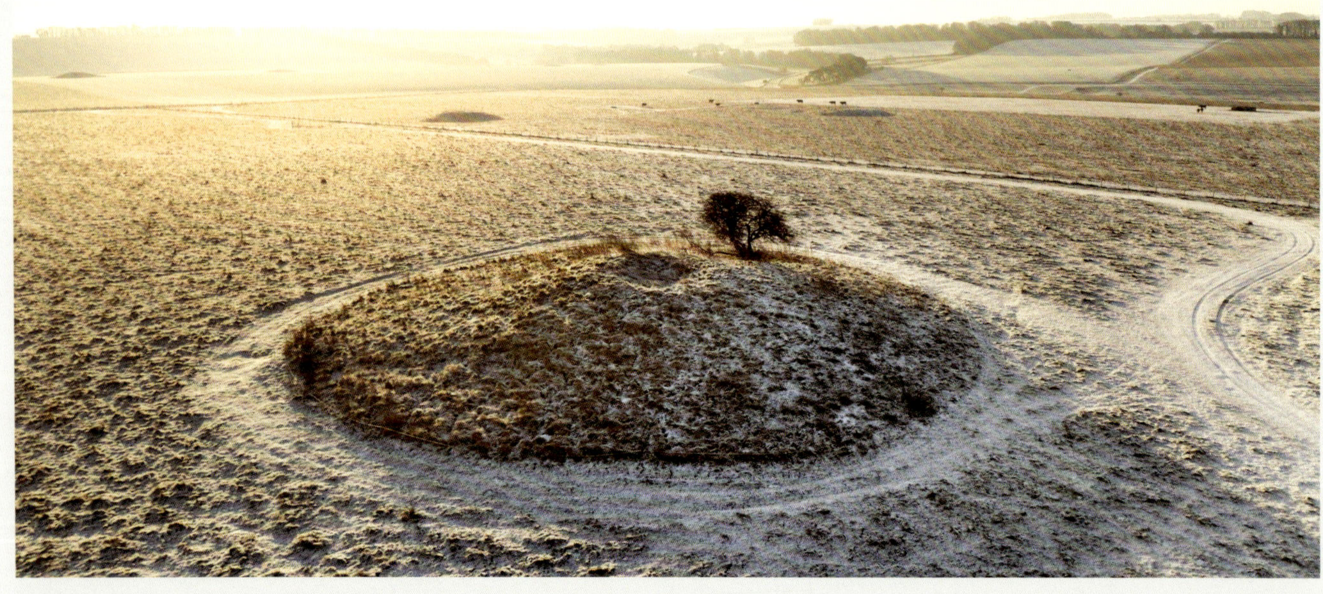

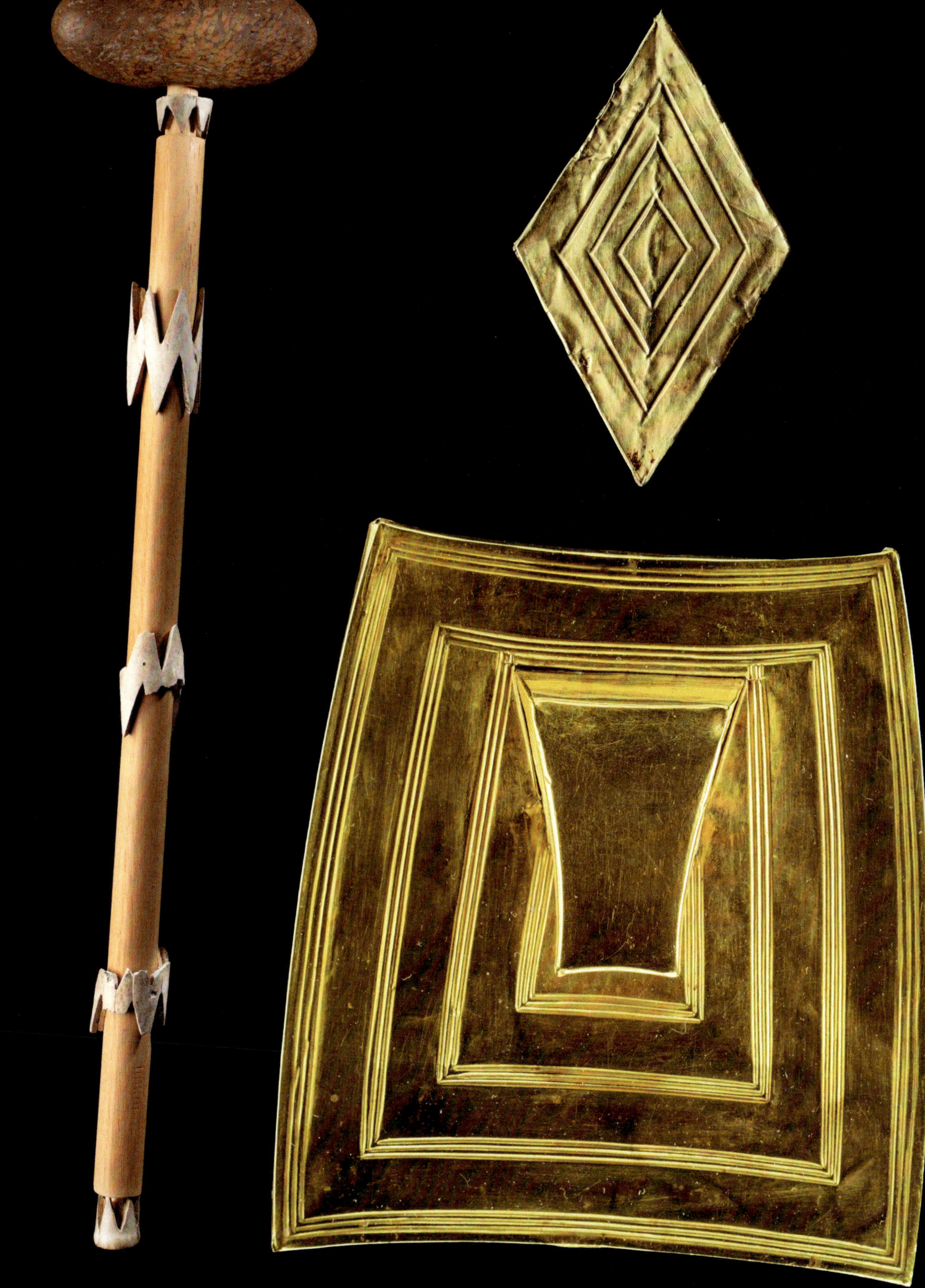

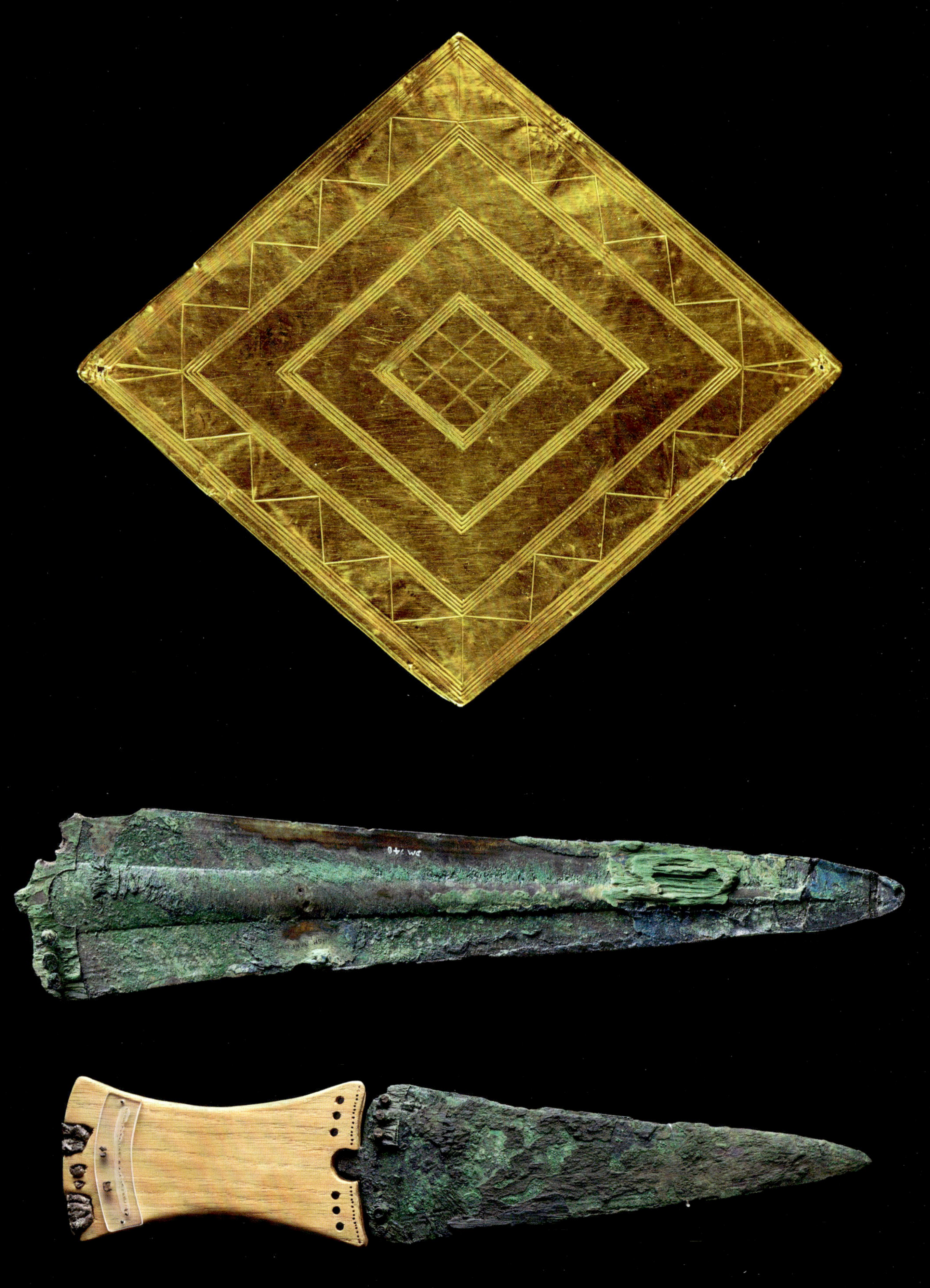

OPPOSITE The Bush Barrow burial also included a large gold lozenge (top). It was found on the skeleton's chest and may have been an elaborate costume fitting. The bronze dagger (middle) was found by the skeleton's right arm and was originally in a sheath of some organic material. A smaller bronze dagger (bottom) had a wooden handle (reconstructed here) decorated with thousands of tiny gold-wire studs, each the width of a human hair and less than 1mm in length.

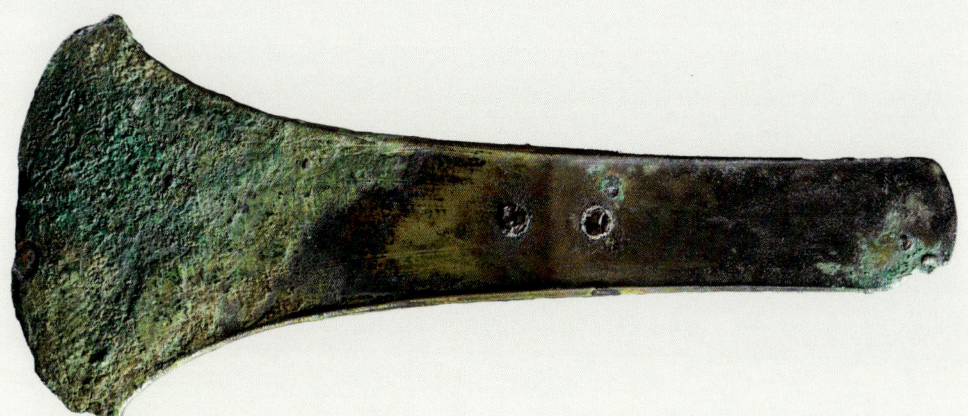

RIGHT This bronze axe was found at the shoulders of the Bush Barrow skeleton. The community who buried him may have become rich through the trade and exchange of copper and tin.

BELOW An artist's reconstruction of the Bush Barrow man adorned with the precious items found in his grave.

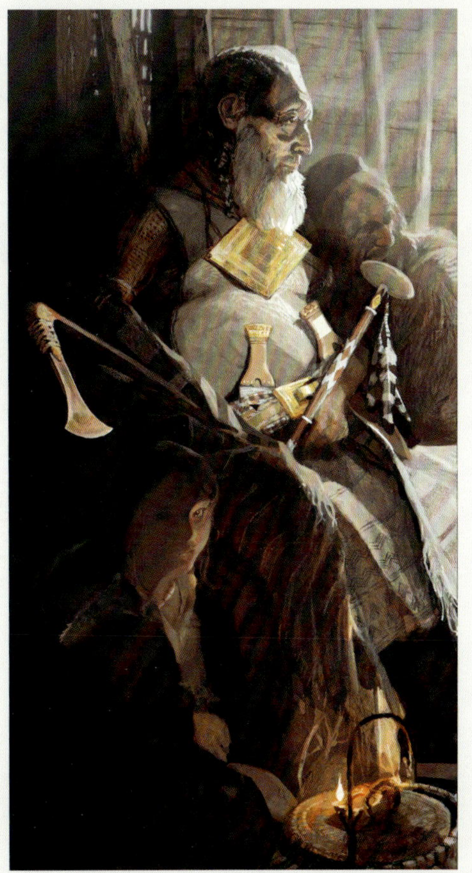

One of the bronze daggers was particularly distinctive. Its handle was decorated with up to 140,000 tiny gold studs in a herringbone pattern. This intricate design could only have been created by someone with extraordinary skill, good eyesight and dextrous fingers, due to the tiny size of the studs. The stone mace-head, likely a symbol of leadership in the community, was made from a fossilised sea sponge, probably from Devon or Cornwall. It was originally fixed to a wooden handle with bone zig-zag decorations and dangling bone rings. The smaller gold lozenge, which was just over 3cm long, may also have been mounted on the handle. The large gold lozenge, measuring 18.5 by 15.6cm, was found on the man's chest. Both lozenges were made of highly polished sheet gold, incised with intricate patterns of lines and triangles.

The man buried under Bush Barrow was no doubt an important figure in the community, although we cannot assume that his costume and equipment were the personal possessions of a wealthy individual. The burial of these valuable objects would have been a striking display of the wealth, skills and power of his wider community, and may have been deliberately buried as part of an offering, as accompaniments for the afterlife, or as appeasement to their gods.

Two nearby barrows (known as Wilsford G7 and G8) that formed part of the same Normanton Down barrow group covered the burials of two people, very likely women, together with other exotic and rare objects. The person buried under Wilsford G7 had a necklace made of amber, shale, jet and fossil beads and pendants. Two of the shale beads had been covered in sheet gold, and the jet pendant was made in the shape of a miniature axe. Also in the grave was a ceramic vessel known as a Collared Urn, and a small cup decorated all over with small balls of clay. The person under Wilsford G8 had been cremated. With the ashes was an ornate amber necklace similar in some ways to a modern-day charm bracelet. As well as eight pendants of amber, two amber discs set in gold and a gold-covered shale cone, this necklace included a tiny gold, bronze and amber pendant in the shape of a halberd (a weapon comprising a blade mounted onto a wooden pole), and a decorated gold pendant encasing a small square of human bone.

The pendants and beads on these necklaces showed varying degrees of wear, suggesting that they had been collected from different people and places over time, mapping a story of relationships and journeys. The amber would have come from the Baltic coasts of the North Sea, the gold from Cornwall or

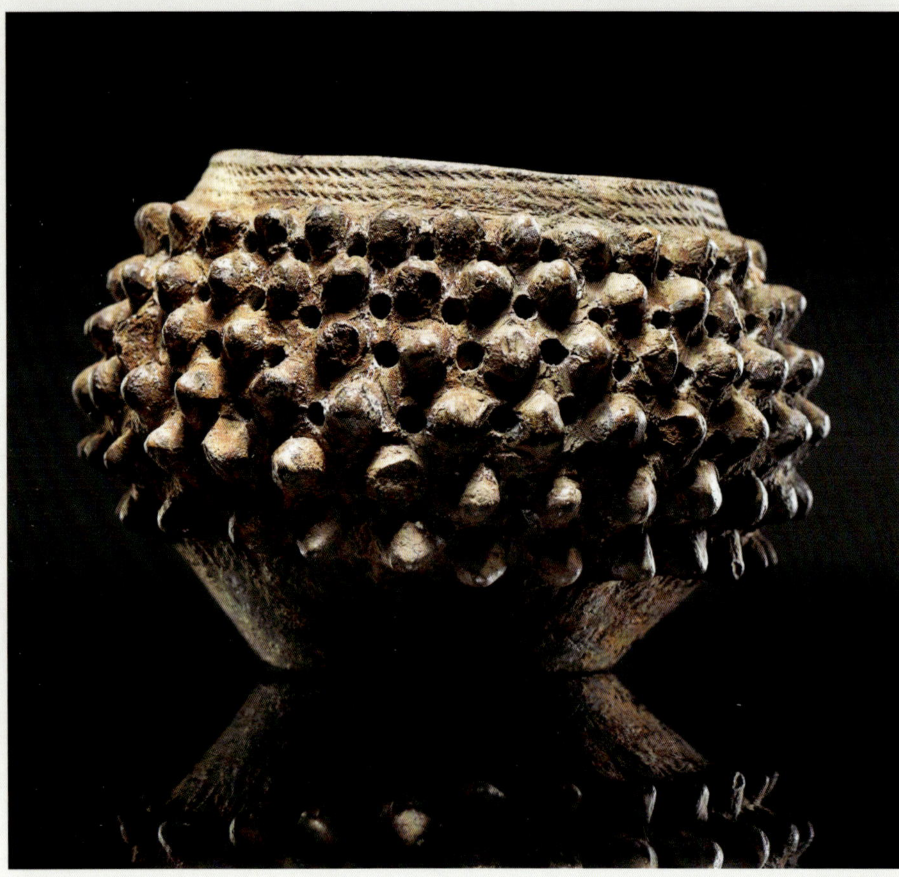

LEFT Accompanying a grave under barrow Wilsford G7 on Normanton Down was this small pottery vessel, known as a 'grape cup'. It was made by applying clay balls onto the perforated walls of the vessel and may have been used to burn fragrant oils.

BELOW A conical button made of shale was capped with this decorative gold cover. It was found with the cremation burial in the barrow known as Wilsford G8.

OPPOSITE The cremation burials under two barrows on Normanton Down – Wilsford G7 and Wilsford G8 – were accompanied by a number of ornate beads and pendants. These were of different types and materials, probably strung together to form a necklace or bracelet, somewhat like modern charm jewellery. Those from Wilsford G7 included two ribbed jet beads, one of which is shown here (1), a spherical gold pendant (2), two amber discs (3 and 5), a miniature axe made of jet (4), a spherical shale bead with a gold cover (6), and two beads made from fossils (7 and 8). Items with the burial in Wilsford G8 included two amber discs with gold mounts, one of which is shown here (9), a miniature halberd (10), a curved gold ornament (11) and a piece of human bone covered in gold (12).

Brittany, the shale perhaps from the Dorset coast, and the jet from Whitby in northern England. The man buried under Bush Barrow and these two women may well have known each other.

Objects covered with thin layers of polished sheet gold seem to have been particularly valued in the early Bronze Age. The transformation of objects by this delicate and skilled process may have been seen as a magical or ritual process, a secret method known only to a few people. A man buried at Upton Lovell, nine miles (14km) west of Stonehenge, was probably one of these specialist gold-workers. He was buried with a variety of different stone tools, such as hammers, anvils and grinding cups, which had been used to work and decorate gold. He was also buried wearing an elaborate costume decorated with many hanging animal bones carved into points, which would have clinked and rattled as he moved, suggesting that he was also seen as a magician or shaman. Perhaps this gold-worker was buried with these tools to enable him to use them in another world.

These elaborate burials did not represent a distinct group of people, as the name 'Wessex Culture' suggests. Instead, they were people with important roles in the wider early Bronze Age community: specialist craftworkers, long-distance traders, or religious experts who could communicate with other worlds. The huge investment of labour and materials that went into these specific burials suggests that these individuals had special status, although we can only guess at how society was organised at this time.

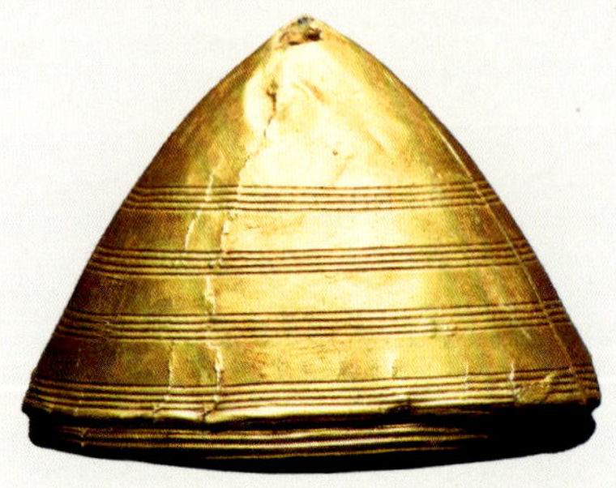

WILSFORD G7 BARROW

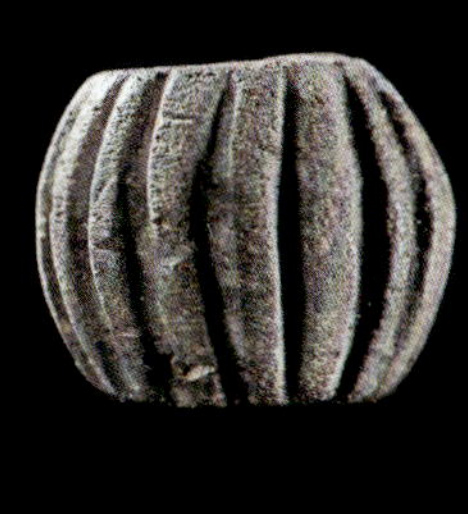

1

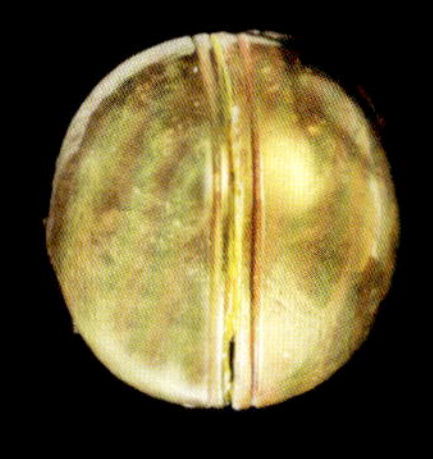

2

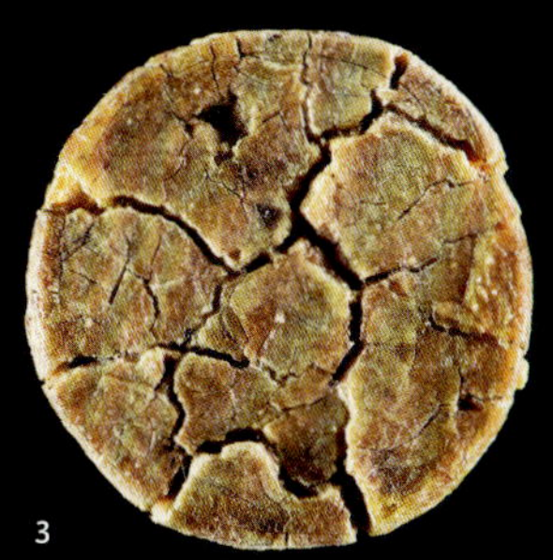

3

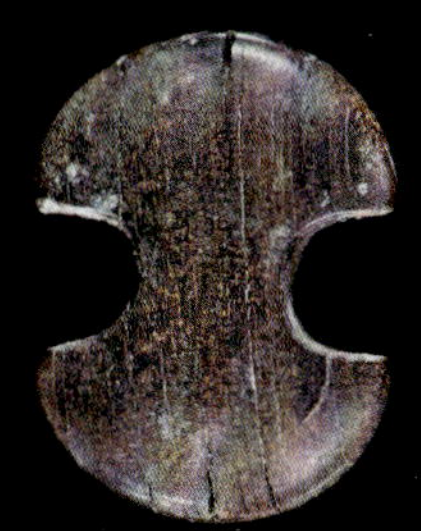

4

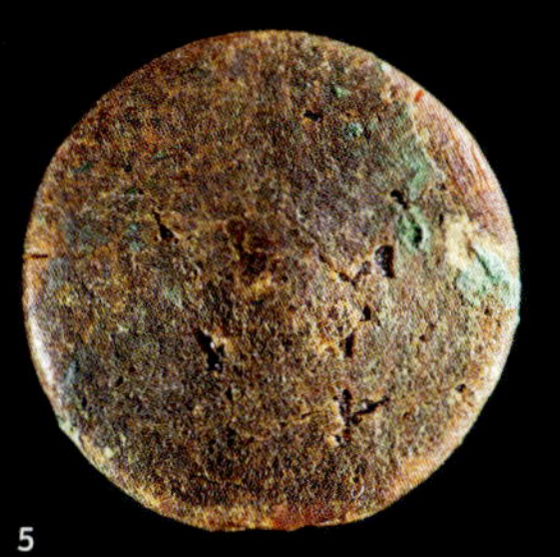

5

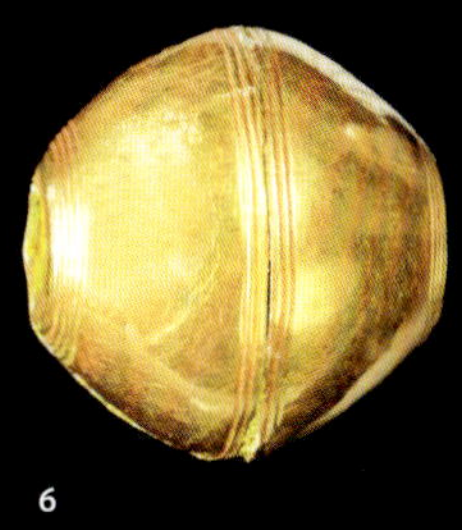

6

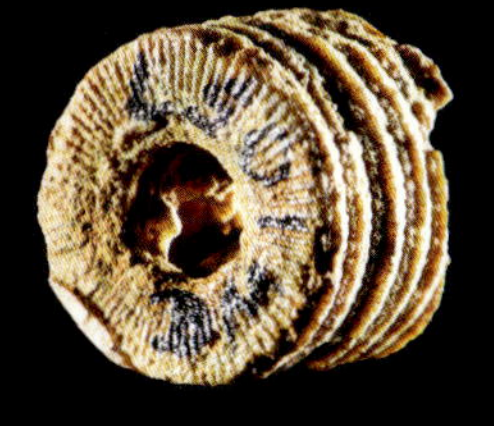

7

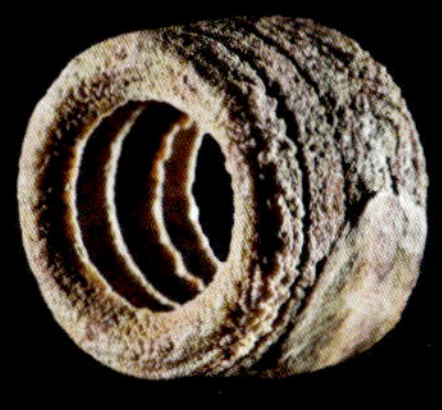

8

WILSFORD G8 BARROW

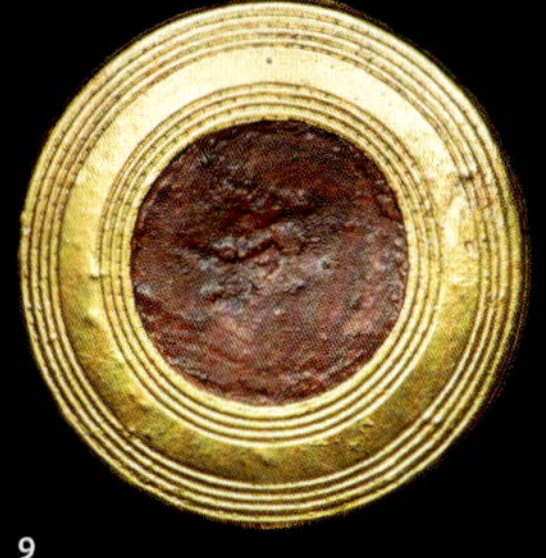

9

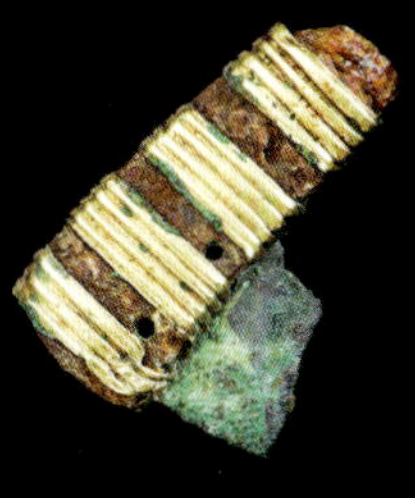

10

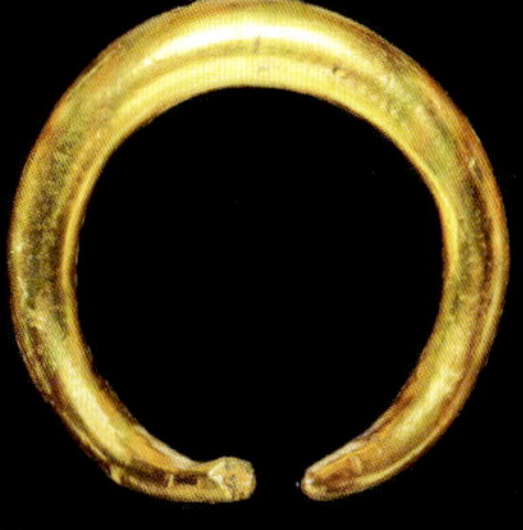

11

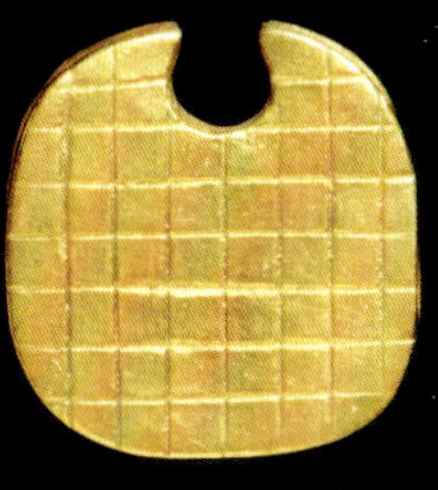

12

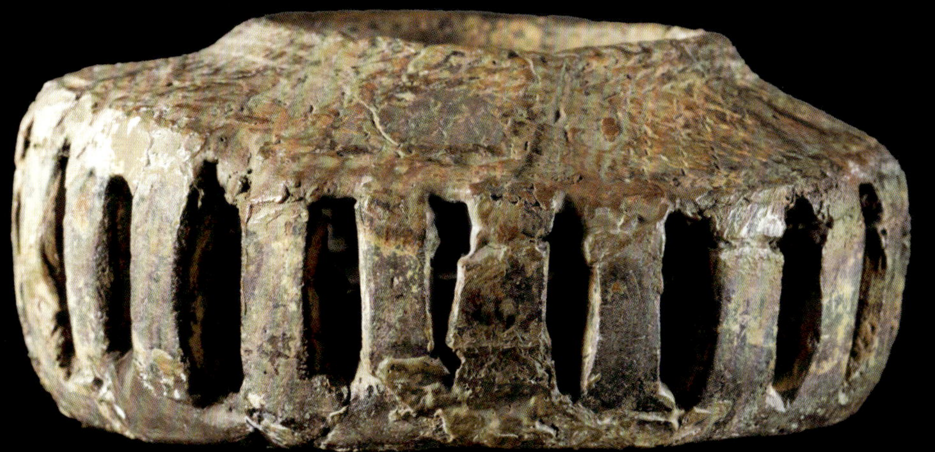

LEFT This miniature pottery vessel found accompanying the cremation burial under barrow Wilsford G8 has vertical slots cut into the sides. Experiments have shown that a lit flame inside casts distinct shadows. Perhaps it was used during the funerary ritual.

Bronze Age Carvings (1750–1580 BC)

In the early Bronze Age, about 800 years after the sarsen stones had been set up at Stonehenge, when the original meaning and purpose of the stone circle was perhaps forgotten, the shapes of over one hundred axes and three daggers were carved onto the stones. We do not know why this was done, but the adding of these symbols of metal tools to the ancient stone monument may reflect the importance of trading and exchanging bronze at this time.

Symbols of axes were carved onto four of the sarsen stones at Stonehenge, each carving carefully placed so as not to overlap with its neighbours. A few of these, in the right light, remain visible to the naked eye, but many more have been found by carefully analysing detailed laser scans of the stones.

The axes, with their splayed, curved blades facing upwards, are a type known as Arreton Down, named after the place where a hoard of them was found on the Isle of Wight. Axes of this type were made between about 1750 and 1580 BC in southern and eastern England. By this time, people were usually cremating their dead, often placing the burnt bones and ashes into large ceramic pots of types known by archaeologists as Food Vessels and Collared Urns. Some barrows were still constructed over these burials, but, more often, these cremation pots were placed into existing barrows, or into flat cemeteries nearby. Instead of being buried with the dead, precious metal objects were buried in hoards or cast into rivers or other watery places.

The four decorated sarsen stones have particularly smooth surfaces but are not in the most prominent places within the monument. It is possible that, by the time the carvings were made, Stonehenge had largely gone out of use, or at least its original purpose had been forgotten. Perhaps these carvings were an adaptation of Stonehenge to a new purpose or to serve changed beliefs. Clearly metal objects held enormous significance at this time, and the carvings may well be related to the burial of the dead close to nearby round barrows.

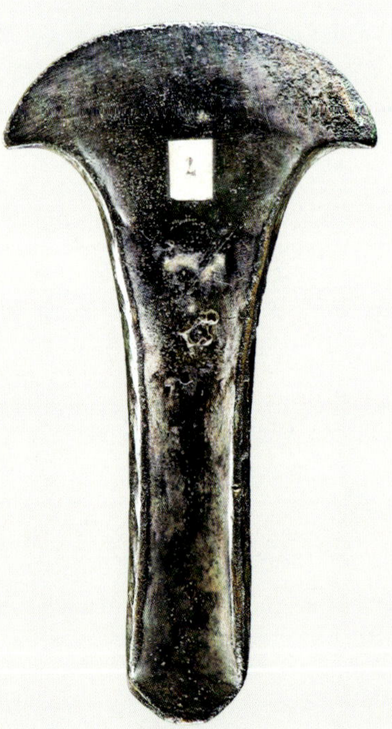

RIGHT TOP Some of the carvings on the stones at Stonehenge resemble Bronze Age daggers like this one found in a barrow of the Wilsford barrow group.

RIGHT The axehead shapes carved onto the stones at Stonehenge are similar to this Bronze Age example.

RIGHT Two of the best-preserved carvings – a dagger with a hilt pointing downwards and an upright axehead, pecked onto one of the sarsen stones of the inner horseshoe at Stonehenge.

BELOW Carvings of Bronze Age daggers and axes are still clearly visible on the inner face of one of the sarsen trilithons at Stonehenge.

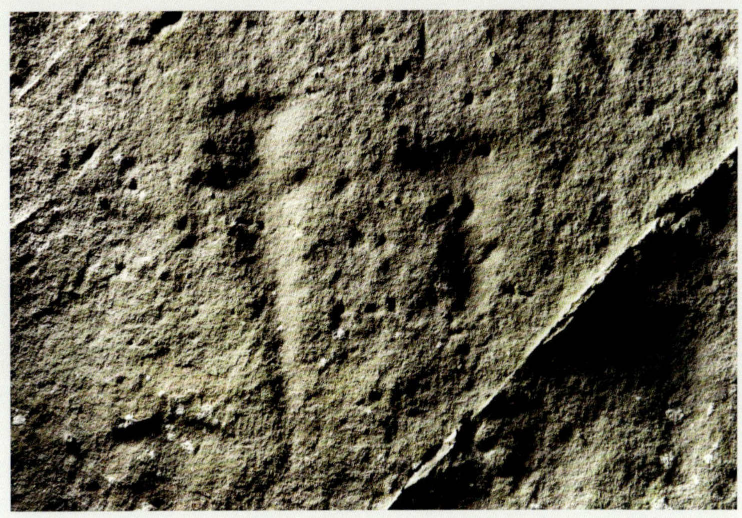

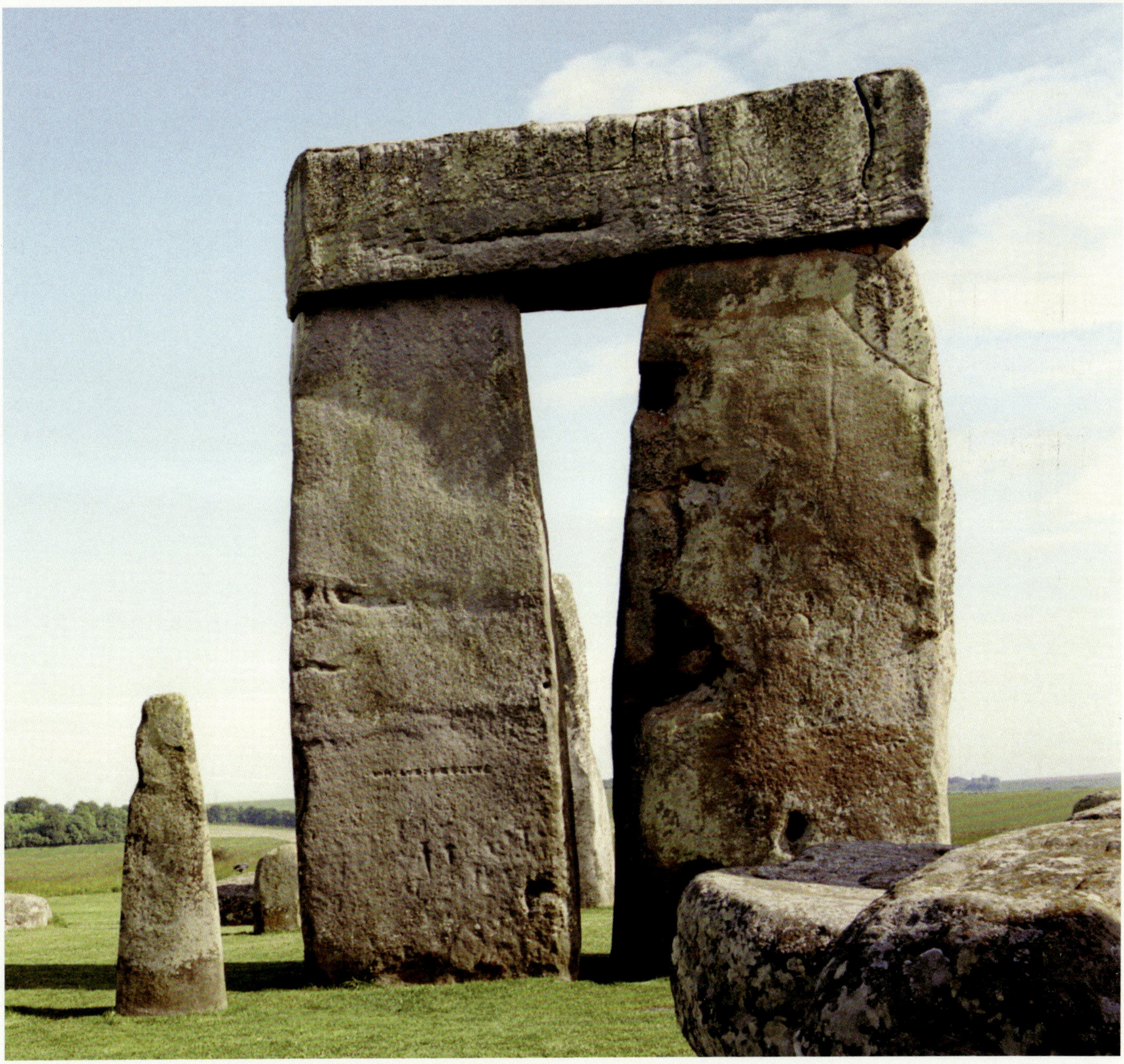

AFTER STONEHENGE

AN ABANDONED RUIN (1500 BC–AD 1200)

For the rest of prehistory, and much of the early historic period, Stonehenge was an abandoned ruin, the lonely stones standing within the wide expanse of Salisbury Plain, visited only by passing shepherds and occasional travellers. In some periods, such as the late Iron Age, the monument may have been deliberately avoided, while at other times it may have been treated as a shrine, or a place for the burial of criminals.

In the middle Bronze Age in southern Britain, after 1500 BC, people began to make large-scale field boundaries, dividing up the land between different communities. There was a shift towards the cultivation of cereals and the keeping of sheep, as well as a continuing reliance on cattle for milk, meat and pulling ploughs. Remnants of these field systems have been found across Salisbury Plain, with fields laid out over much of the Stonehenge landscape, including over older monuments such as the Greater Cursus. The area immediately around Stonehenge and Normanton Down was, however, kept open and undivided. A series of long ditches, some holding rows of standing posts, separated this part of the landscape from the surrounding area where field systems proliferated. This precinct appears to have been kept as a sacred space, distinct from the ordinary farming world beyond.

Throughout the rest of the Bronze Age (until about 800 BC) and the succeeding Iron Age (800 BC–AD 43), Stonehenge was largely abandoned, perhaps only visited by passing travellers or even avoided altogether. Small settlements of round houses were scattered across the area and the landscape was largely used for grazing animals. In about 700 BC, a large Iron Age hillfort was constructed a few miles to the east, given the name Vespasian's Camp by early antiquaries who believed it to be Roman in origin. Little is known about this hillfort, which has seen no modern excavation.

During the late Roman period, in the third and fourth centuries AD, there seems to have been renewed interest in Stonehenge. An astonishing 1,500 objects dating from this time have been found at the site, including coins, pins, brooches and fragments of pottery. For many years it was assumed that these were the losses of careless Roman tourists, but excavations within the stone circle in 2008 revealed a deep hole with abundant Roman pottery, animal bone and a late Roman coin. Perhaps these objects and the other Roman finds had been deliberately left at the site as offerings, and the monument used as some sort of shrine or temple. It is known that the inhabitants of Roman Britain took an interest in earthworks and structures surviving from earlier periods, often choosing them for burials or as the sites of temples.

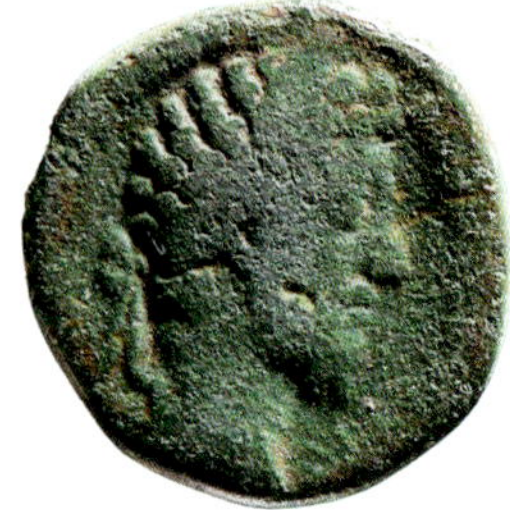

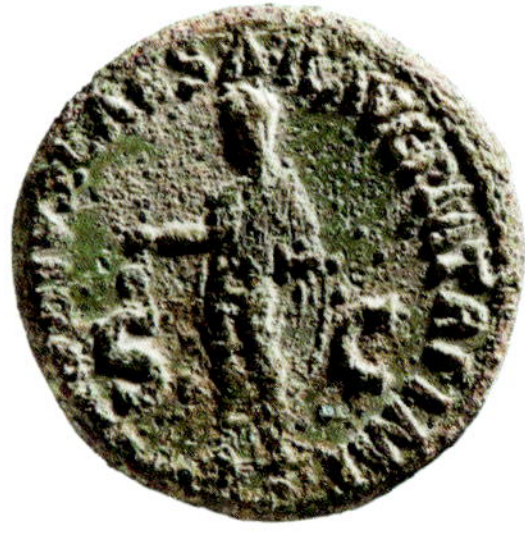

LEFT Two of at least 21 Roman coins that have been found at Stonehenge, perhaps deposited by Roman visitors as offerings.

BELOW Snaking across the landscape about 6 miles (9.5km) north of Stonehenge is a feature known as Old Nursery Ditch. It is one of the longest late prehistoric land boundaries known in the wider Stonehenge landscape. A later field system can be seen to its left.

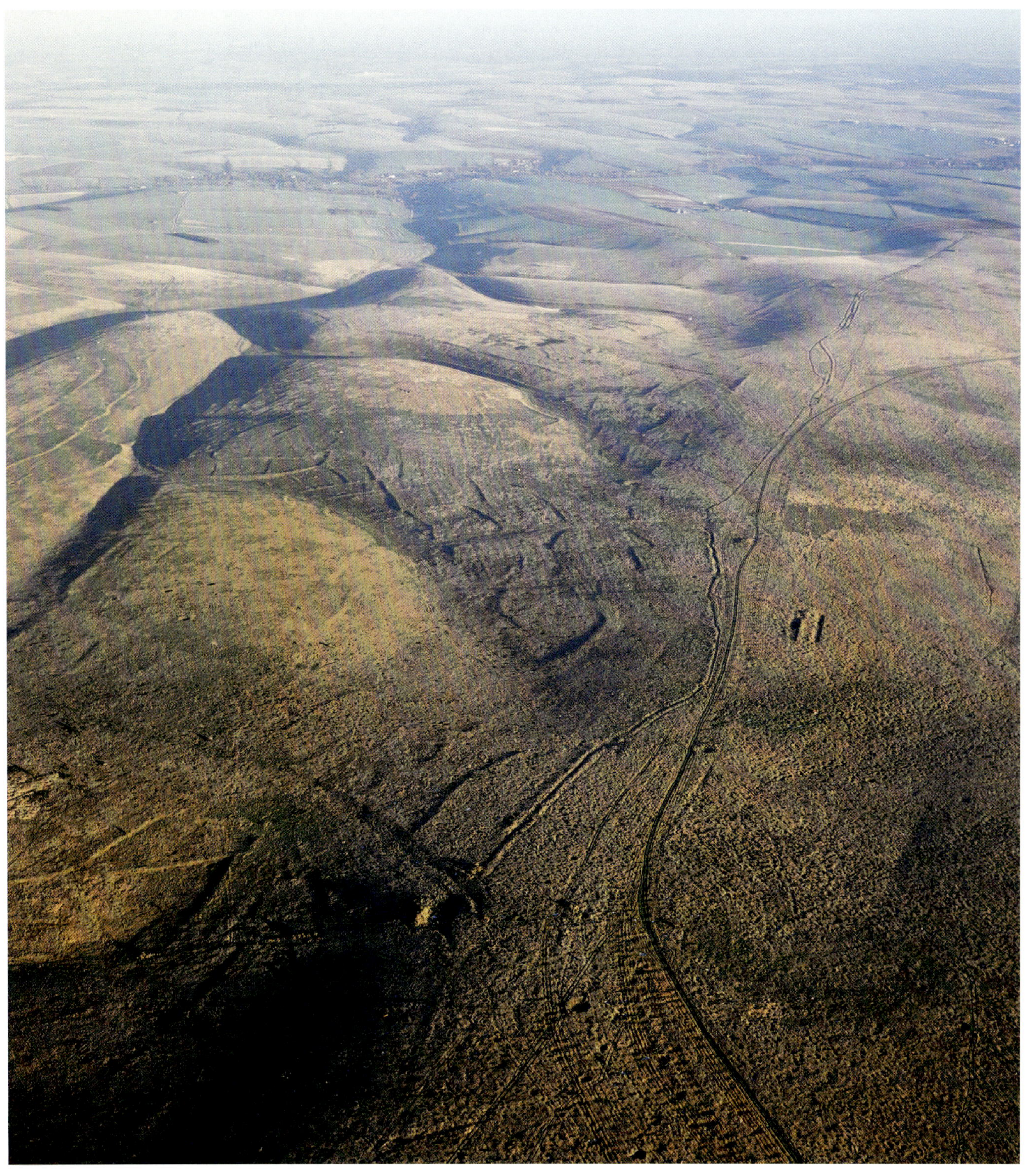

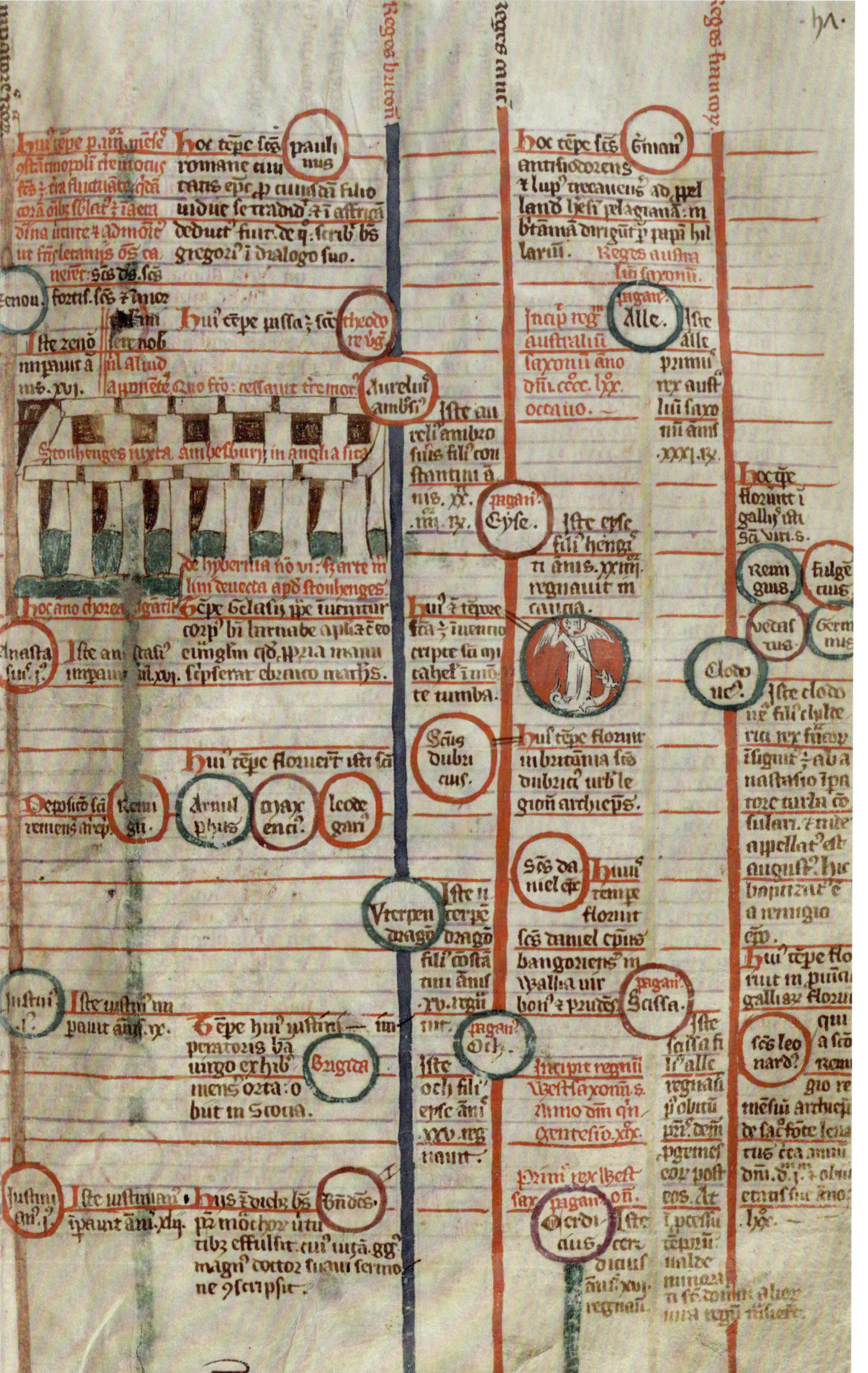
Reges britonum
Reges francorum
Stonhenges iuxta Ambesbury in anglia sita
Alle
Eyse
Brigida
Remigius
Clodoveus

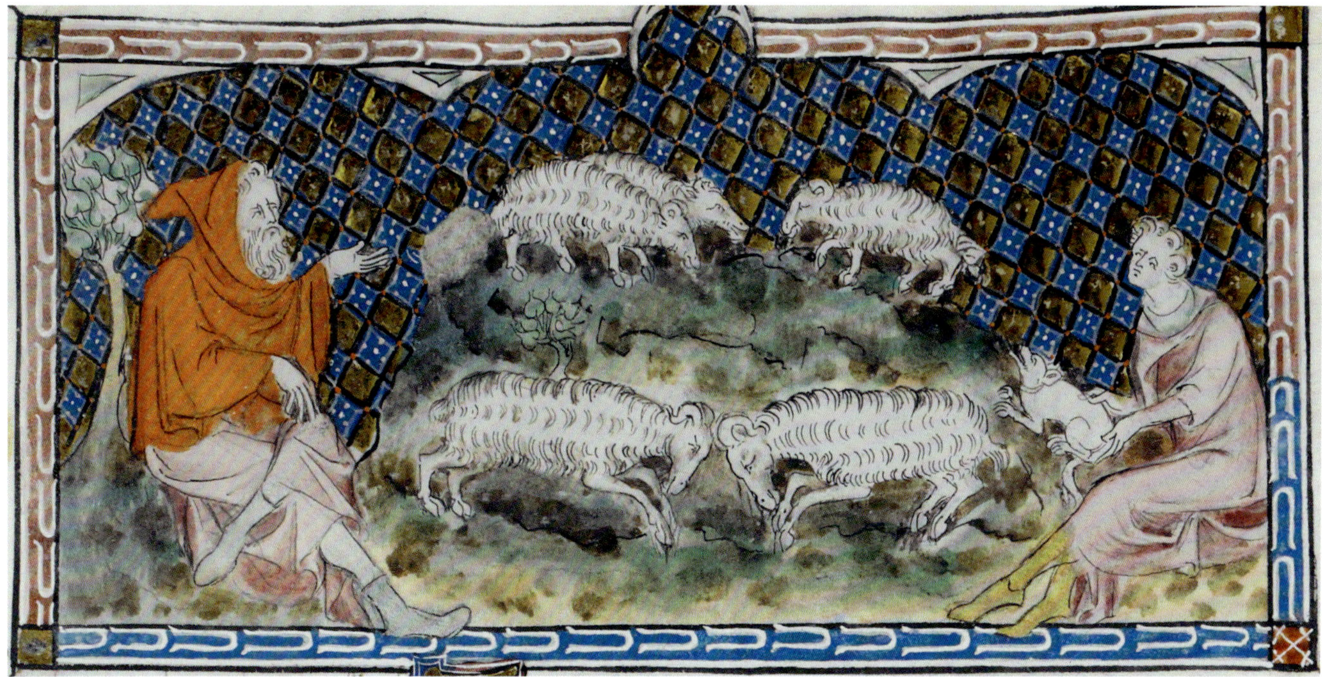

OPPOSITE Stonehenge depicted in the early-14th-century *Scala Mundi* (*Ladder of the World*), a chronicle of world events that incorporated Geoffrey of Monmouth's legend. It places the construction of the monument, by the wizard Merlin, during the post-Roman period.

ABOVE A depiction of shepherds and sheep from an English manuscript of about 1320. Throughout the medieval period the only regular visitors to Stonehenge must have been shepherds moving their flocks across the extensive grazing lands that surrounded the monument.

Whether Stonehenge was simply a local shrine (there were Roman settlements located along the river Avon valley, near Durrington Walls and probably on Boscombe Down) or attracted people from further afield, is not yet known.

In the early medieval period, sometime between AD 660 and 890, a decapitated man was buried just outside the stone circle at Stonehenge. He may have been a criminal or other social outcast, buried at a remote and strange location, well away from contemporary villages along the river valley. There are a handful of other finds from this period at Stonehenge, including a skull fragment, two human teeth, a handful of sherds of pottery and a penny of King Aethelred II (r.AD 978–1013 and 1014–16) which suggest that people visited, albeit infrequently. By this date, the nearby town of Amesbury had developed, possibly as the centre of a royal estate and with an early minster church founded in AD 979.

Despite being abandoned, however, Stonehenge was never forgotten: it was a constant landmark on the rolling downland of Salisbury Plain, a place where several trackways and paths converged. Throughout the medieval period the most frequent visitors were probably flocks of sheep and their attendant shepherds, although travellers must have stopped to marvel at these lofty stones.

Our earliest written reference to Stonehenge dates from about AD 1130, when the medieval historian Henry of Huntingdon wrote in his *Historia Anglorum* (*History of the English People*), 'Stanenges ... where stones of wonderful size have been erected after the manner of doorways ... no-one can conceive how such great stones have been so raised aloft, or why they were built there.' Geoffrey of Monmouth, Bishop of St Asaph, writing a few years later, was less restrained, telling the story of how Stonehenge had been transported by the wizard Merlin as a memorial to a great battle between the Saxons and the Britons. Geoffrey's *Historia regum Britanniae* (*History of the Kings of Britain*) legitimised and captured in writing a legend that was to remain the accepted explanation for Stonehenge until the 17th century. By the time of these medieval writers, the stone circle was ruinous and partly fallen, and people had started to break up the sarsen stones, probably using the material to fill muddy parts of nearby trackways and as roadstone.

Myths and Legends

For over 400 years during the medieval period, one story came to dominate popular narratives about Stonehenge. It formed part of an origin story of Britain involving a great battle, as well as giants, wizards, stones brought from afar, and elements of magic.

In his *Historia regum Britanniae* (*History of the Kings of Britain*), written in about 1136, the medieval writer Geoffrey of Monmouth tells the story that Stonehenge was built during the turbulent period after the end of Roman rule. In his tale, 460 British lords and soldiers under the command of Vortigern, an imposter king, were treacherously slain by an invading Saxon army, led by the warlord Hengist. After returning from exile in Brittany, killing Vortigern and defeating the Saxons, the rightful British king, Aurelius Ambrosius, wanted to set up a fitting memorial to the fallen at the site of the battle. He sent for the wizard Merlin, who commanded that the *Chorea Gigantum*, or 'Giant's Round', be brought from Ireland. This stone monument had been built there by giants, but 15,000 men struggled to dismantle it. So Merlin, using magic, took down the stones himself and transported them to England, erecting them on Salisbury Plain. Geoffrey tells us that Ambrosius was buried within the monument, as was Uther Pendragon, whose son Arthur became the legendary king of Britain.

Geoffrey of Monmouth claimed to have translated the *Historia* from 'a very ancient book in the British language'. Even his contemporaries, however, were sceptical that such a volume existed and it is likely that Geoffrey weaved together his own imaginative narrative, drawing inspiration from various medieval Welsh legends, lists of kings, as well as historical accounts by the early medieval writers Bede and Gildas. The book was hugely popular, with hundreds of copies made, and his account of Stonehenge was widely accepted until the 17th century. All three known medieval depictions of Stonehenge are in manuscripts accompanying versions of Geoffrey's *History*.

The story incorporates the widely held medieval belief that megalithic monuments had been constructed by a race of giants in ancient times. Although this is clearly fantastical, there is an aspect of the tale that rings true: while the monument was not brought from Ireland, the bluestones were brought over the sea from the far west, from south-west Wales, and the Altar Stone from even farther afield in north-east Scotland. Could memories of the construction of Stonehenge have been maintained as part of oral histories over thousands of years? It remains an intriguing possibility.

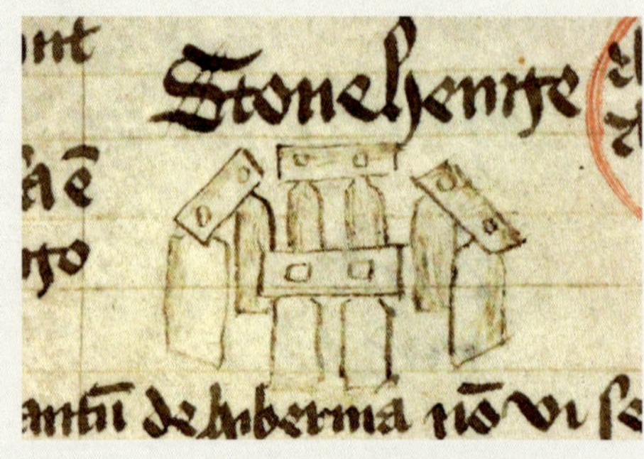

ABOVE A simplified sketch of Stonehenge from about 1440, clearly showing jointed trilithons. It appears in another copy of the *Scala Mundi*.

OPPOSITE Merlin the giant is depicted placing a lintel on top of upright stones in this drawing made between 1338 and 1340. It accompanies a version of the 12th-century poet Wace's *Roman de Brut*, a legendary history of Britain that embellished Geoffrey of Monmouth's account of the building of Stonehenge.

'If you are desirous, said Merlin, to honour the Burying Place of these men with an everlasting monument, send for the Giant's Round, which is in ... a mountain in Ireland. For there is a structure of stones there, which none of this Age could raise ... '.

GEOFFREY OF MONMOUTH, *c.*1136

Cils sunt as pieres alees
Erent devant et de travers
Bien ont empeinte et bien bote
Et bien retraite et bien crole
Une par force a la menour
Ne purrent faire prendre un tour

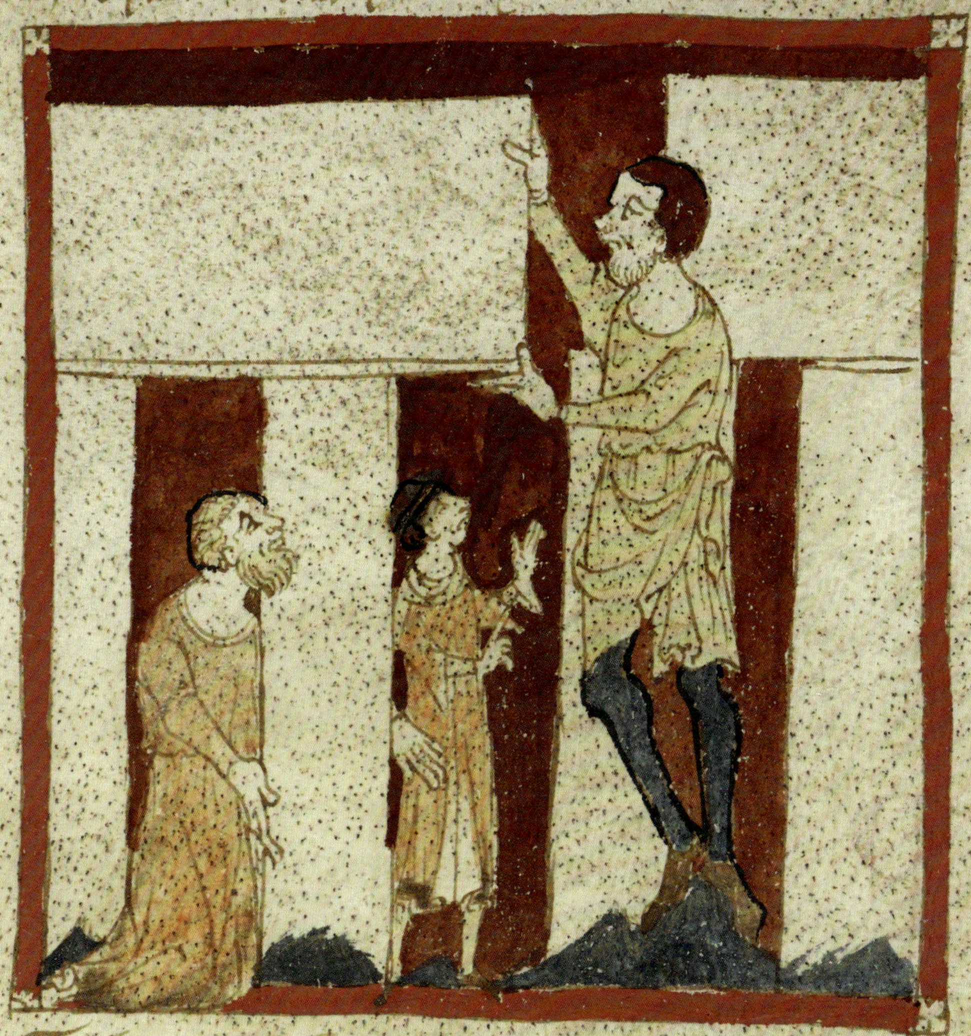

Trahez vous dit Merlin en sus
Ja par force ne ferez plus
Ieo ferrez engine et raison
Mens que vertu de corps valer
Tunc alast avant si festuet
Entour garda le leve mut
Cum hom qe fist oreisun
Ne sai sil fist quiuisoun
Dunc ad les Bretuns rapeles

ANTIQUARIAN INTEREST (1650–1740)

Opinions about the age and purpose of Stonehenge among early antiquaries were divided. Some argued that it was Roman, others that it had been built by the Danes or the Phoenicians. Following the work of scholars John Aubrey and William Stukeley in the 17th and 18th centuries, however, antiquaries reached a consensus – that Stonehenge had been built by the Druids. This erroneous interpretation persisted for at least 200 years.

From the 17th century antiquaries began to cast doubt on Geoffrey of Monmouth's fantastical explanation for Stonehenge involving giants and a wizard (see page 98), and a variety of more scholarly explanations were put forward. The architect Inigo Jones (1573–1652), after conducting a survey of the stone circle commissioned by King James I (r.1603–25), argued that Stonehenge had been built by the Romans. In a book published posthumously in 1655 he set out a reconstruction of the elegant proportions and architectural order of the monument, suggesting that precise geometrical patterns and the crudest form of the classical order had been employed. Jones argued that it was a roofless temple dedicated to the god Coelus, the Roman god of the sky.

Jones's theories were soon countered by the physician Walter Charleton, who claimed instead that Stonehenge was built by the Danes, as a coronation place of kings. In his book *Chorea Gigantum*, published in 1663, he drew parallels between the monument and similar megalithic structures in Denmark, concluding that the Danes, or Vikings, were responsible. Aylett Sammes, in his 1676 book *Britannia Antiqua Illustrata*, instead argued that Stonehenge had been constructed by maritime traders from the Mediterranean – the Phoenicians – who had come to Britain in search of tin. None of these authors could conceive that Stonehenge had been built by

OPPOSITE This sketch plan of Stonehenge by John Aubrey includes the small depressions that he observed just inside the bank and ditch (labelled 'b'). Today we call these the Aubrey Holes.

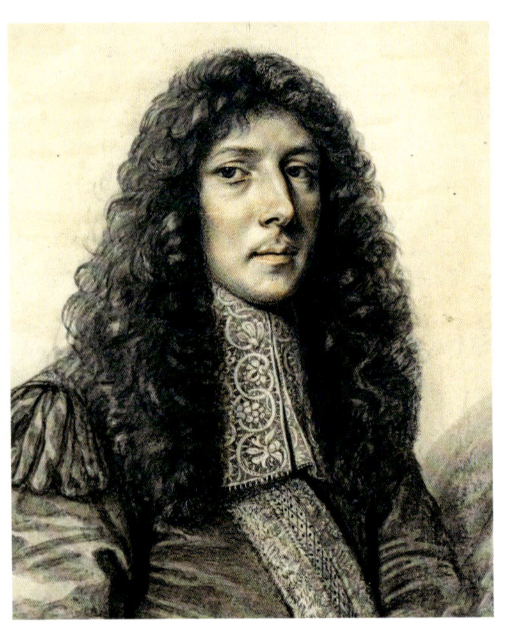

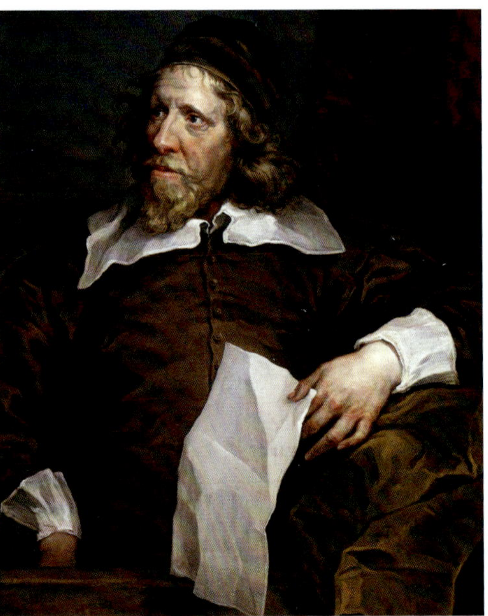

FAR LEFT John Aubrey by William Faithorne the elder, 1666. Aubrey was a polymath who was fascinated by antiquities, folklore and natural history.

LEFT Portrait of Inigo Jones by William Hogarth. Jones was commissioned to survey Stonehenge by King James I.

The Ichnographie of Stoneheng as it remaines this
present yeare 1666.

These ✦ ✦ ✦, that I have
cancelled and struck out with
my pen, should be placed near
the stones of ye outer circ[le]

a

b

b

b

a

c

c

b

b

a a a path[s]
with carts

o
q

~~b b b &c cavities in the
ground, from whence ~~the~~ one may
(conjecture the
stones c c were taken,
wch stood round the trench
as those at Avebury.~~

a. the bank.
q. the ditch.

a

ω

[...] survey all the stones wanting,
[...] Inig: Jon: with the Monument
[i]selfe.

x v In [...]
M[e]m.

Mdm, a [...]
and is not [...]
easily made[...]
Why might [...]
the foregoein[g]
seaven Pla[nets]
not determ[...]

Plate VII

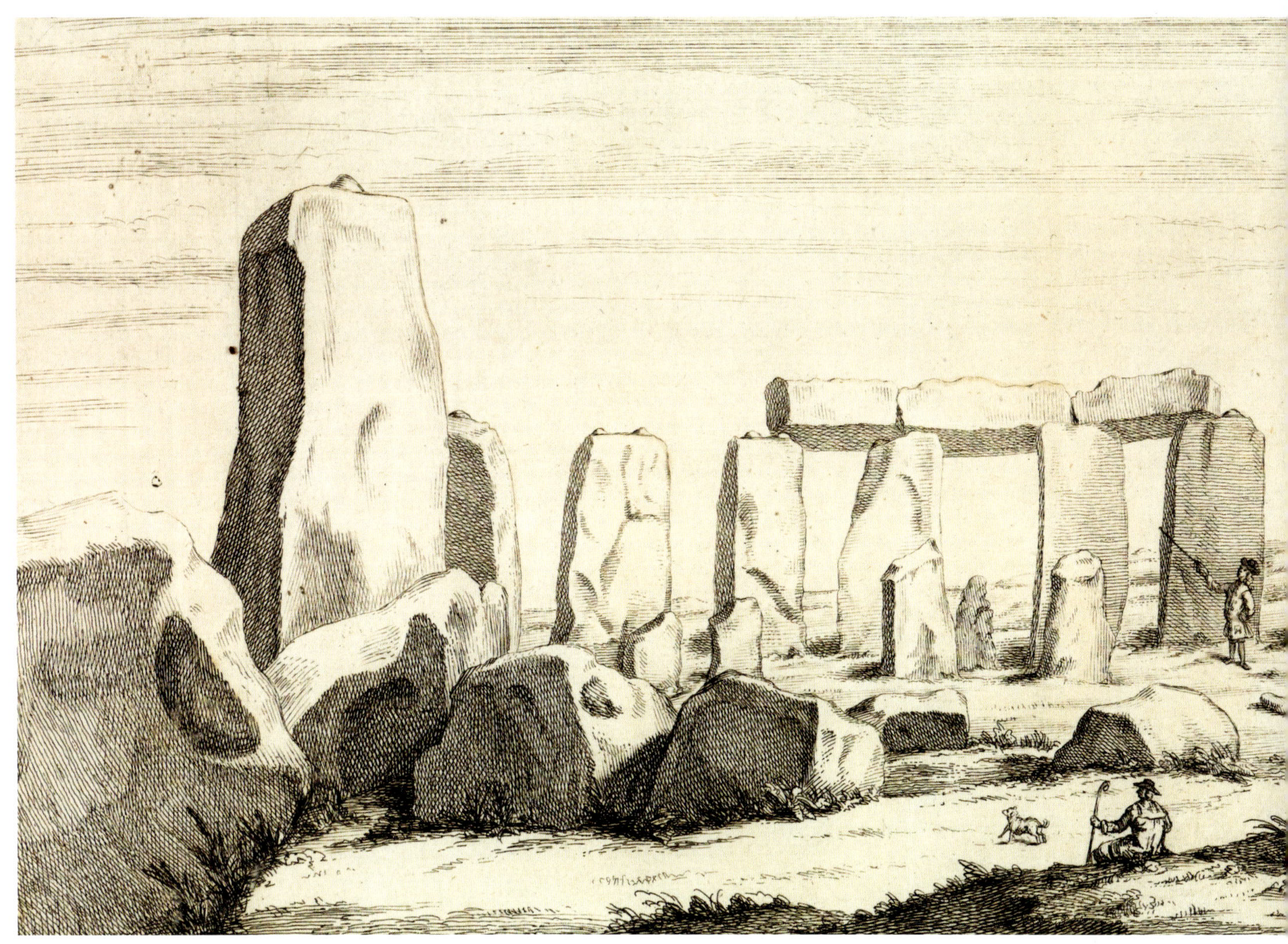

inhabitants of Britain, who were deemed to have been primitive savages, incapable of such an architectural feat.

While hunting with friends in 1649, the antiquary and writer John Aubrey (1626–97) was taken to the village of Avebury, in north Wiltshire, where he was astonished by the enormous stone circle. Fascinated, he went on to spend part of each year there, even taking King Charles II (r.1660–85) on a personal tour of the site. He also conducted a more thorough survey of Stonehenge, comparing it to Inigo Jones's inaccurate reconstruction. Aubrey believed that these sites, and many other megalithic monuments across Britain, were religious temples dating to a time before written records. Noting that they could be found in Ireland and Scotland, areas that had never been conquered by the Romans or the Danes, he correctly concluded that they were not built by visitors from overseas, but by the indigenous pre-Roman population of Britain.

At this time there was no concept of prehistory – the world was widely accepted as having been created in 4004 BC, based on calculations of Biblical time, with Britain estimated to have been first populated in about 2000 BC. The only pre-Roman religious leaders described by the Classical authors at the time of the Roman invasion of Britain were the ancient Druids, who were Iron Age priests, judges and teachers. It was therefore logical for Aubrey to conclude that the Druids were the architects and users of Avebury and Stonehenge. Although he amassed many hundreds of pages of notes, drawings and

ABOVE One of the many detailed illustrations of Stonehenge from William Stukeley's 1740 book *Stonehenge, A Temple Restor'd to the British Druids*. This view is entitled 'Inward view of Stonehenge from the high altar'.

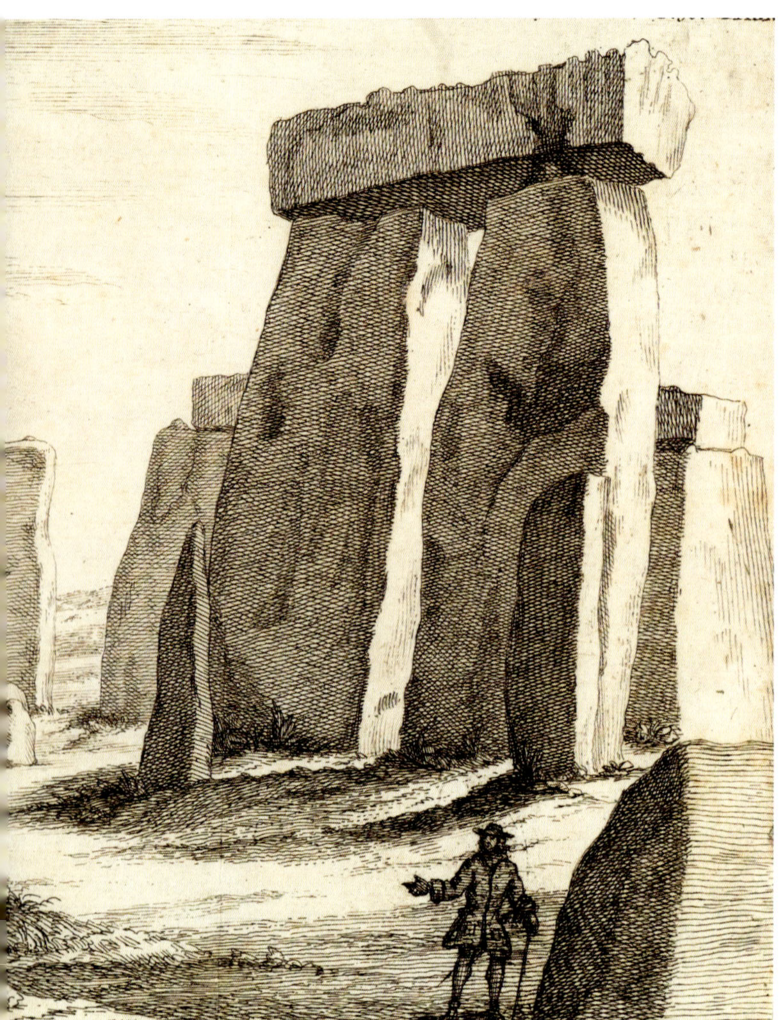

BELOW Portrait of William Stukeley by an unknown artist, about 1740. Stukeley proposed that Stonehenge had been built by ancient Druids, an idea that would endure for the next 200 years.

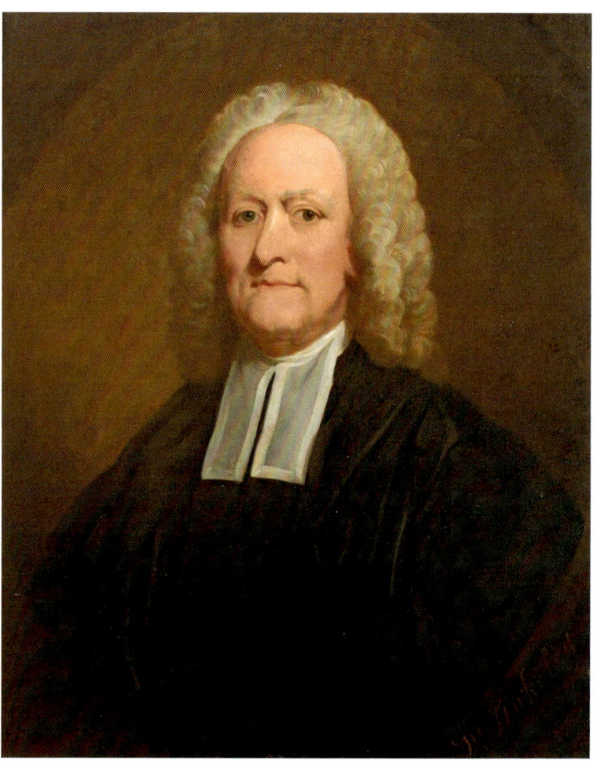

diagrams, Aubrey unfortunately never published his work. Nevertheless, he did discuss his ideas with friends, and his manuscript notes were widely consulted after his death.

Aubrey's ideas influenced William Stukeley (1687–1765), a doctor, antiquary, scientist and later a clergyman, who took a particular interest in megalithic monuments. Between 1719 and 1725 he spent his summers touring Britain, surveying, drawing, and making observations about historical and ancient antiquities. He conducted surveys using a theodolite, made the first accurate plans of many sites and often drew landscape-scale maps or views that are invaluable records today. At Stonehenge, his careful observations led him to recognise the solstice alignment of the stones, to identify the earthworks of the Avenue and discover the nearby Greater Cursus, giving it a name that reflected his opinion that it was a Roman arena for 'games, feats, exercises and sports'. He was also responsible for coining the term 'trilithon' to describe two upright stones capped by a horizontal lintel.

Stukeley's 1740 volume *Stonehenge, A Temple Restor'd to the British Druids* argued that the monument had been built by the Druids, who he thought had practised an early form of Christianity. This, he believed, was not far removed from the original pure world religion originating with, and descending from, Adam and Noah. Stukeley's theories were taken up enthusiastically and were widely accepted by scholars and the general public alike. For the next 200 years, Druids would be firmly associated with Stonehenge.

The Druids

Even today, Stonehenge is strongly associated with Druids. The 18th-century antiquary William Stukeley's theory that Stonehenge had been built by the ancient Druids, who were active before the Roman invasion of Britain, became established fact for over 100 years. His idea had a direct influence on the rise of modern Druidry and, in turn, modern solstice ceremonies, as well as inspiring popular poems and paintings.

The ancient Druids were priests, teachers and judges in late Iron Age Britain and Gaul (an area roughly equivalent to modern France and portions of adjoining countries to the north and east). They were briefly described by Roman writers including Julius Caesar, Tacitus and Pliny, in the first centuries BC and AD. These authors record the various rites and practices of the Druids, which included both cattle and human sacrifice, ceremonies in sacred groves or clearings, gathering mistletoe from oak trees using golden sickles, overseeing disputes, exacting punishments, and educating young men in religious matters.

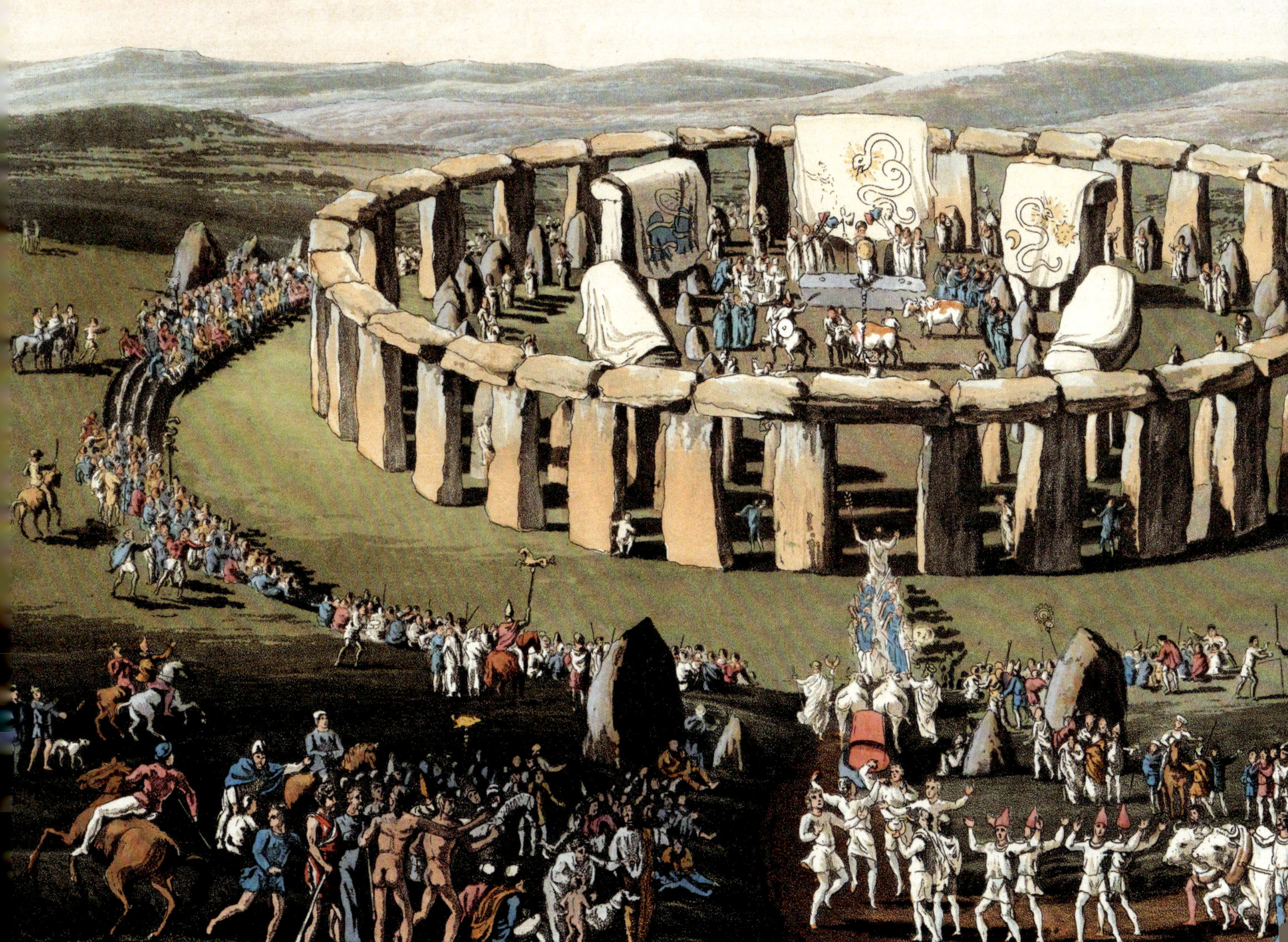

THIS PAGE This image, adapted from a plate in Samuel Rush Meyrick and Charles Hamilton Smith's book *The Costume of the Original Inhabitants of Great Britain and Ireland*, published in 1815, imagines a fantastical Stonehenge festooned with banners for a Druid festival.

BELOW RIGHT The Oxford Druids pose during an initiation ceremony at Stonehenge in 1905. The group were part of the Ancient Order of Druids, a gentlemen's society founded in 1781 based on ideas of justice, benevolence and friendship.

Writers, such as the poet William Blake, who wrote about the Druids of 'Albion' (a poetic name for ancient Britain) in the deep mythological past, similarly created a mythology around the site.

Once William Stukeley's books had popularised the idea that the Druids had built Stonehenge, writers and artists were inspired to combine these scanty, but lurid, Classical sources with their knowledge of the monument. One of the outlying stones became named 'The Slaughter Stone', as the idea took hold that this was where the Druids had conducted their barbaric rites. Artists, such as Samuel Rush Meyrick, depicted fantastical scenes showing elaborate ceremonies with costumes and banners taking place at Stonehenge. Writers, such as the poet William Blake, who wrote about the Druids of 'Albion' (a poetic name for ancient Britain) in the deep mythological past, similarly created a mythology around the site. These images and words made a lasting impression on the public perception of Stonehenge and other prehistoric monuments, enduring long after archaeologists had proven that the monument had been built more than 2,000 years before the time of the Iron Age Druids.

From the late 18th century the Druids were recast in a more favourable light, as ancient and venerable. Various friendly societies and groups were inspired to adopt their name and imagined ethos. The first of these was the Ancient Order of Druids, formed in 1781, although there were many different breakaway groups and factions, and over time they developed increasingly elaborate ceremonies and initiation rites. The association with prehistoric sites only began with the first meeting at Stonehenge in August 1905, when the Ancient Order of Druids, wearing white robes and false beards, held a mass initiation ceremony there. Increasingly these groups practised rites of a more religious nature, and in 1912, the Church of the Universal Bond began holding rituals inspired by Druid rites at the summer solstice. It is from these groups that the modern spiritual movement of Druidry developed.

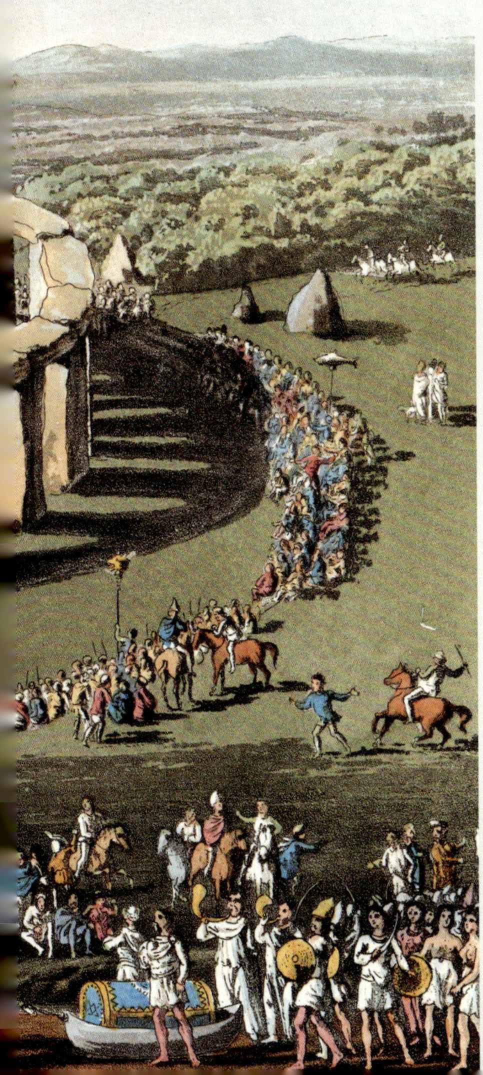

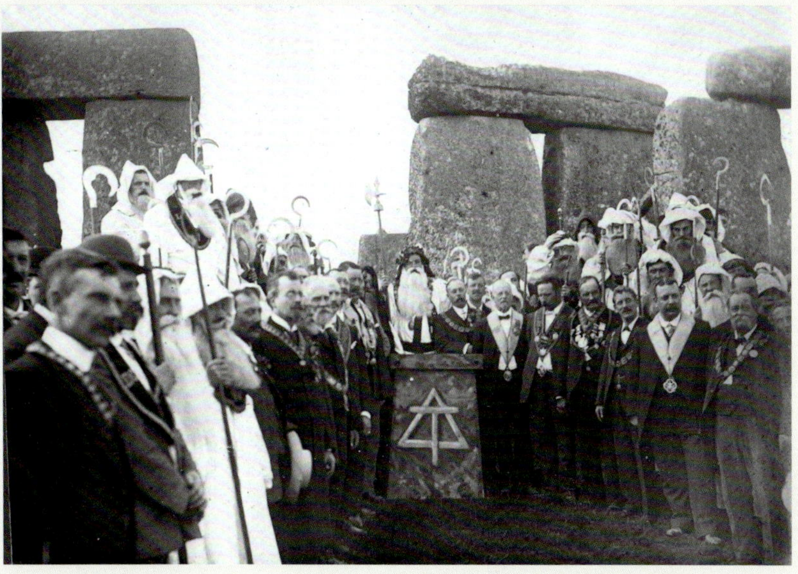

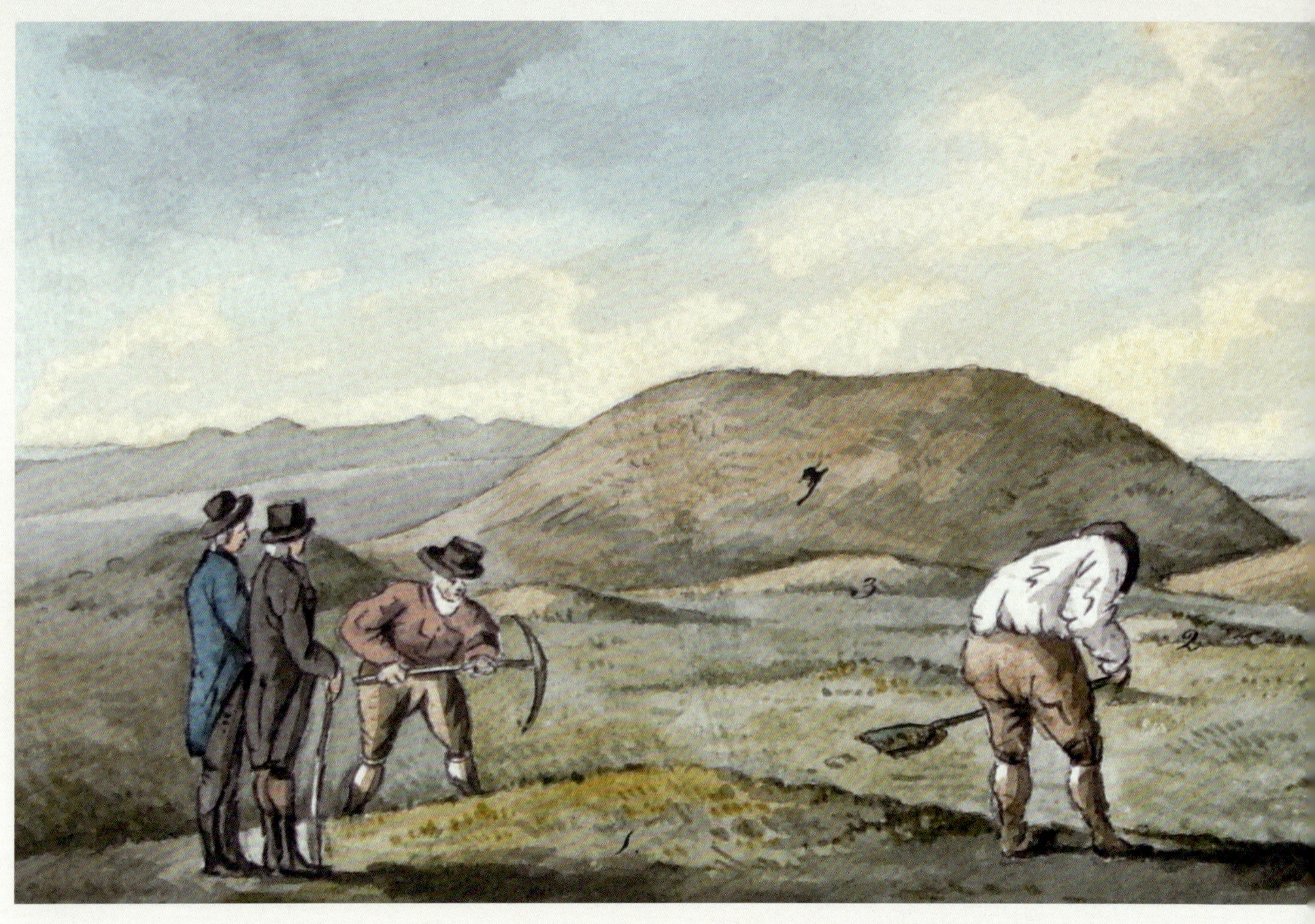

The Barrow Explorers (1720–1880)

The numerous round barrows in the area surrounding Stonehenge excited the curiosity of 18th- and early-19th-century gentlemen who had leisure time and funds to organise excavations into the mounds. They hoped to find intriguing curios to display in their personal collections, but also to understand more about the ancient past.

ABOVE A watercolour of 1805 by Philip Crocker, showing William Cunnington and Sir Richard Colt Hoare looking on as two skilled labourers – Stephen and John Parker – excavate a barrow in the Normanton Down barrow cemetery.

Many early openings of barrows went unrecorded, only evident by distinct hollows now visible in the tops of mounds or by signs of earlier disturbances revealed during later excavations. William Stukeley had opened a few barrows near the Greater Cursus in 1723, but the most prolific barrow diggers were local antiquary William Cunnington (1754–1810) and his friend and patron Sir Richard Colt Hoare (1758–1838), the wealthy owner of Stourhead House, Wiltshire. Cunnington was a retired wool merchant who became interested in burial mounds when told by his doctor, who was concerned about his health, to 'ride out or die', inspiring him to take regular horse rides across Salisbury Plain.

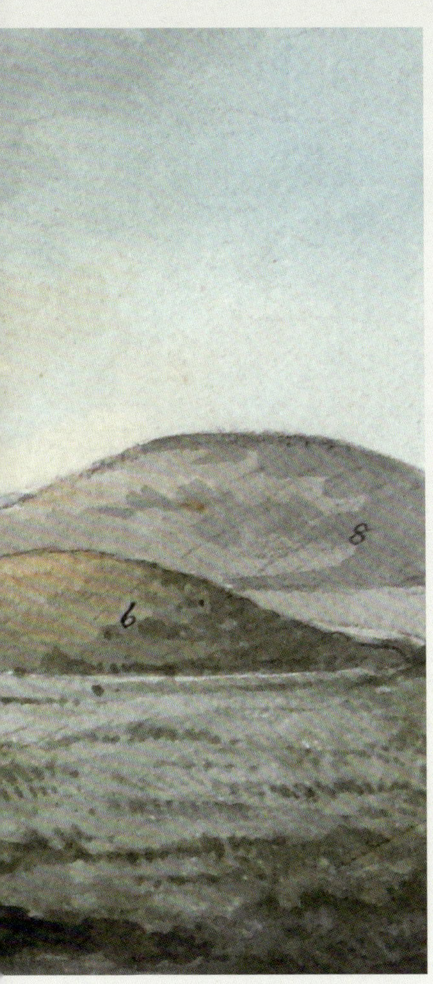

William Stukeley had opened a few barrows near the Greater Cursus in 1723, but the most prolific barrow diggers were local antiquary William Cunnington (1754–1810) and his friend and patron Sir Richard Colt Hoare (1758–1838).

Over a period of seven years from 1798, Cunnington, together with Colt Hoare, with whom he shared a great interest in prehistory, opened over 200 barrows near Stonehenge. Aided by excavators Stephen and John Parker, and surveyor and draftsman Philip Crocker, the pair devised a unique numbering and classification system for the barrows, creating detailed maps of their positions and other archaeological features in the landscape. Their most spectacular discovery was the burial within Bush Barrow, excavated in 1808 (see page 86). They also excavated at Stonehenge itself, digging under two of the fallen stones to prove that they had once stood upright. After Cunnington died in 1810, Hoare bought Cunnington's collection of artefacts from his heirs and published their joint work in a beautifully illustrated volume, *The Ancient History of Wiltshire*. The artefacts that Cunnington and Hoare collected were initially displayed at Stourhead, but in 1883 were sold to become part of the collections of the Wiltshire Museum.

In contrast to these barrow explorers, who left any human remains that they found in the ground, John Thurnam (1810–73), a medical doctor, opened barrows to obtain skeletal material. He had become interested in skeletal remains after excavating a large Saxon burial mound near his hospital in York, and became an authority in craniology, the now-discredited study of human skulls to determine race. Between 1863 and 1868, while medical superintendent of the Roundway Hospital in Devizes, he excavated several long and round barrows near Stonehenge in pursuit of skulls, publishing papers on his discoveries.

None of these early barrow diggers excavated to modern standards, and the information they left behind is often patchy or difficult to interpret. Nevertheless, their work in many cases provides the only information we have about the people and the objects buried within the barrows near Stonehenge.

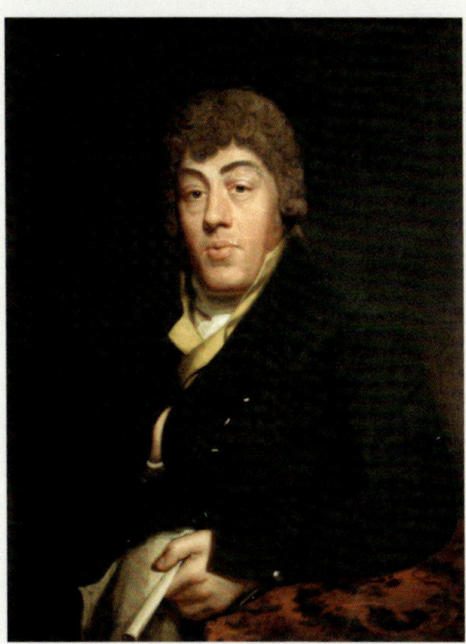

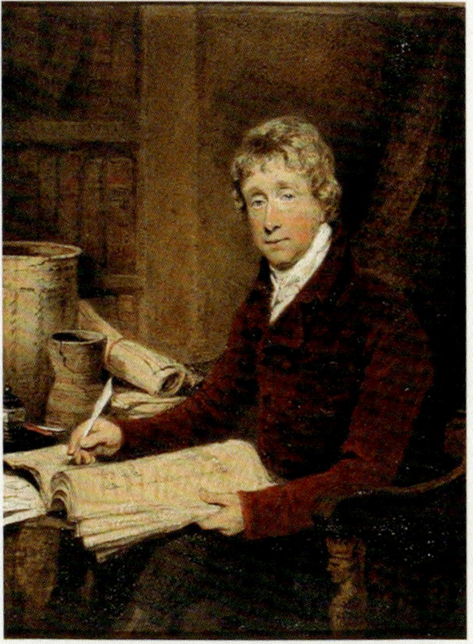

RIGHT William Cunnington, painted by Samuel Woodforde in 1808, the same year he oversaw excavations at Bush Barrow.

FAR RIGHT Sir Richard Colt Hoare, painted by Henry Edridge in about 1820. He is depicted writing, with prehistoric vessels on his desk.

Early Visitors (16th to 18th Centuries)

It is likely that Stonehenge attracted visitors sporadically throughout its history, and that these people had various motives for coming, such as Romans who left offerings and those, probably from the medieval period, who broke up the stones and carted them away. It is only from the 16th century onwards that we have clear evidence for the first tourists visiting Stonehenge, some of whom left their mark on the stones.

During the 16th century wealthy individuals, who could afford the time and money to undertake extensive journeys for pleasure, began to visit the stones. The earliest record of a visit to Stonehenge was written by Herman Folkerzheimer from Switzerland who, in 1562, was staying with John Jewel, Bishop of Salisbury. The bishop took him to see several notable ancient sites, including Old Sarum and Stonehenge. Folkerzheimer, writing to a friend back home, found the monument 'incredible' and wondered at how and why the stones had been raised.

'Upon the whole, we must take them [the stones] as our ancestors have done; Namely, for an erection, or building so antient, that no history has handed down to us the original, as we find it then uncertain, we must leave it so: 'Tis indeed a reverend piece of antiquity, and 'tis a great loss that the true history of it is not known ... '.

DANIEL DEFOE, c.1727

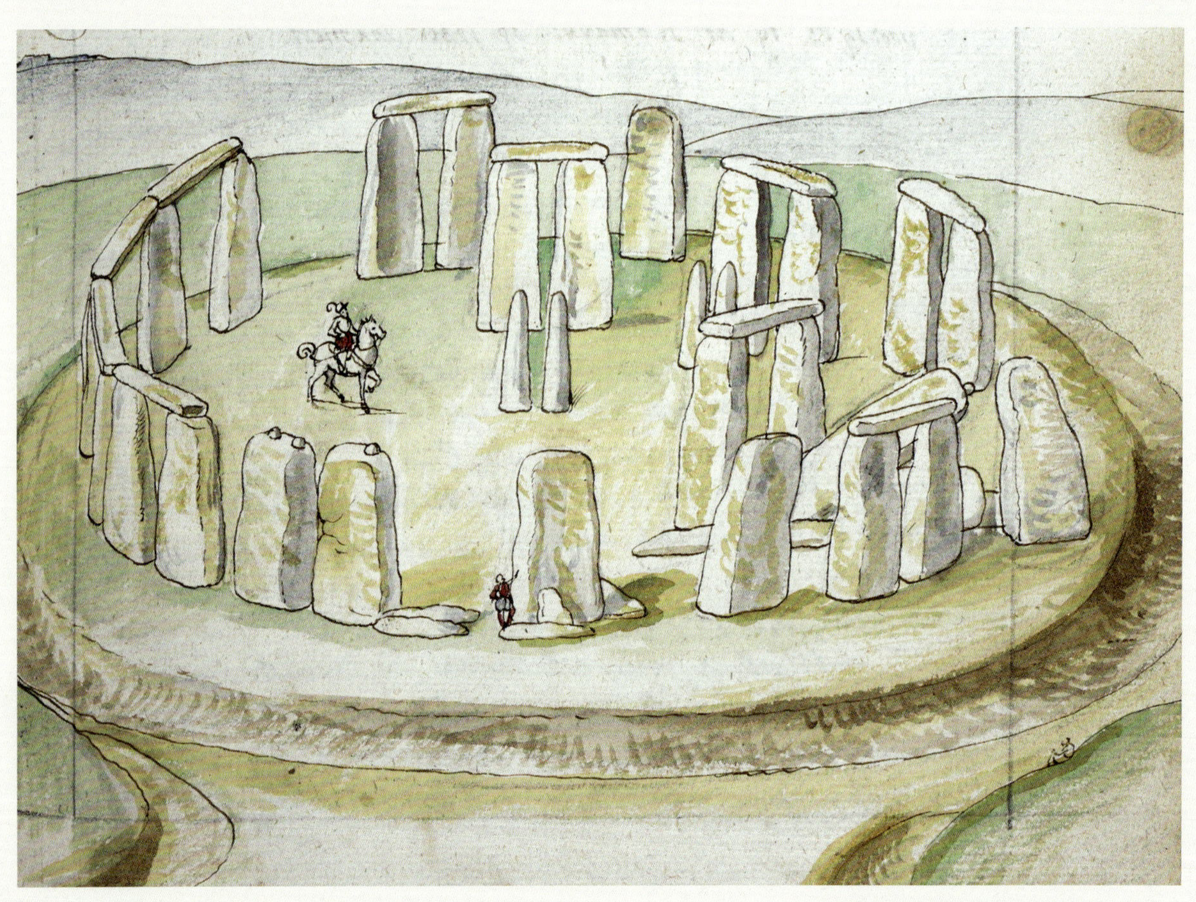

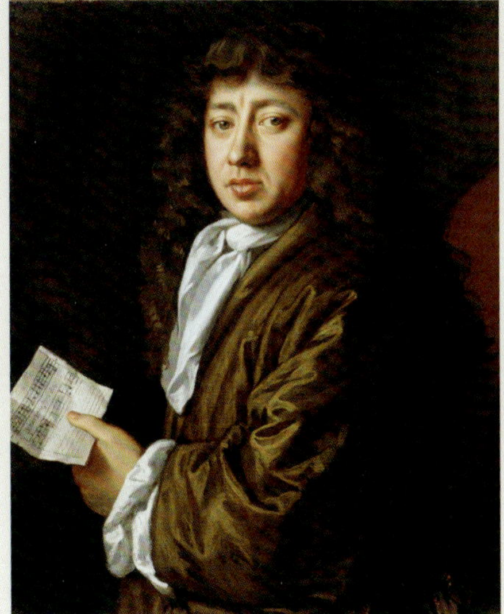

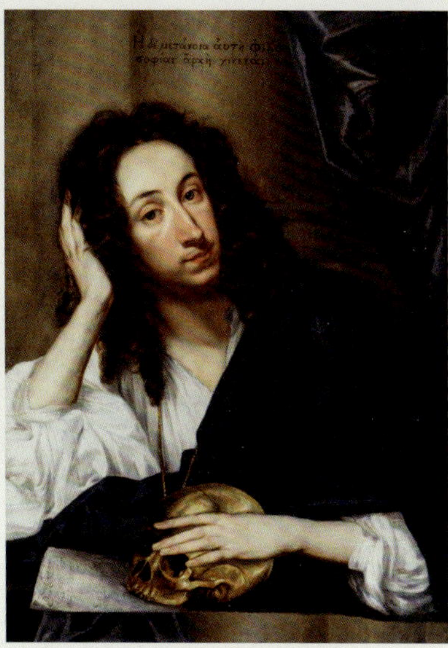

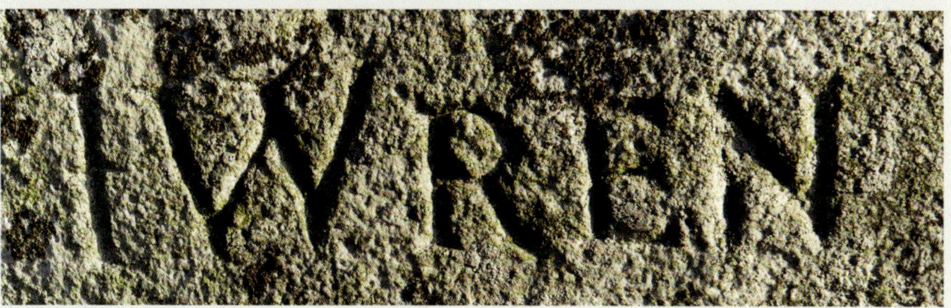

OPPOSITE This watercolour of Stonehenge was painted 'on the spot' in about 1574 by Lucas de Heere, a Flemish resident of England, and was included in a volume describing Great Britain and Ireland.

RIGHT Samuel Pepys, painted by John Halys in 1666 two years before he visited Stonehenge and wrote about it in his famous diary.

FAR RIGHT A portrait of John Evelyn by Robert Walker, 1648. Today Evelyn is best known for his diary which chronicled national and personal events between 1640 and 1706, including a visit to Stonehenge.

BELOW RIGHT The inscription '† Wren' is carved into the stones in two places, most likely by the famous architect Christopher Wren, abbreviating his first name to the form of a cross.

The oldest surviving detailed drawing of Stonehenge was made a short time later, in 1574, by another European, Lucas de Heere, a Flemish refugee who wrote an early guidebook to Britain. Samuel Pepys, the writer of famous diaries, visited in 1668, finding the stones 'as prodigious as any tales I ever heard of them and worth going this journey to see'. The pioneering travel writer Celia Fiennes, who visited Stonehenge in about 1690, described it as one of the 'wonders of England'. These accounts no doubt encouraged other visitors to make their own journeys.

The writer John Evelyn visited Stonehenge in July 1654, and like many others, he attempted to take home a souvenir. He found, however, that the stones were 'so exceedingly hard, that all my strength with a hammer could not break a fragment'. Such activity appears to have been common over a long period; stone removal was recorded in the 1720s by William Stukeley, and a visitor wrote to *The Times* newspaper in 1871 lamenting the damage visible since his last visit, 30 years earlier, and describing how the 'constant chipping of stone broke the solitude of the place'.

As well as removing chunks of the monument, many visitors over the years have carved their names into the stones. The earliest of these appears to be 'IOH : LVD : DEFERRE' on the inner face of Stone 53, an abbreviation of the name John Louis de Ferre, about whom nothing is known, although the style of lettering suggests that he lived in the late 16th or early 17th century. Elsewhere, the name '† WREN' is likely to have been carved by Christopher Wren (1632–1723), architect of St Paul's Cathedral in London, as part of his childhood was spent at East Knoyle, only about 15 miles (24km) from Stonehenge.

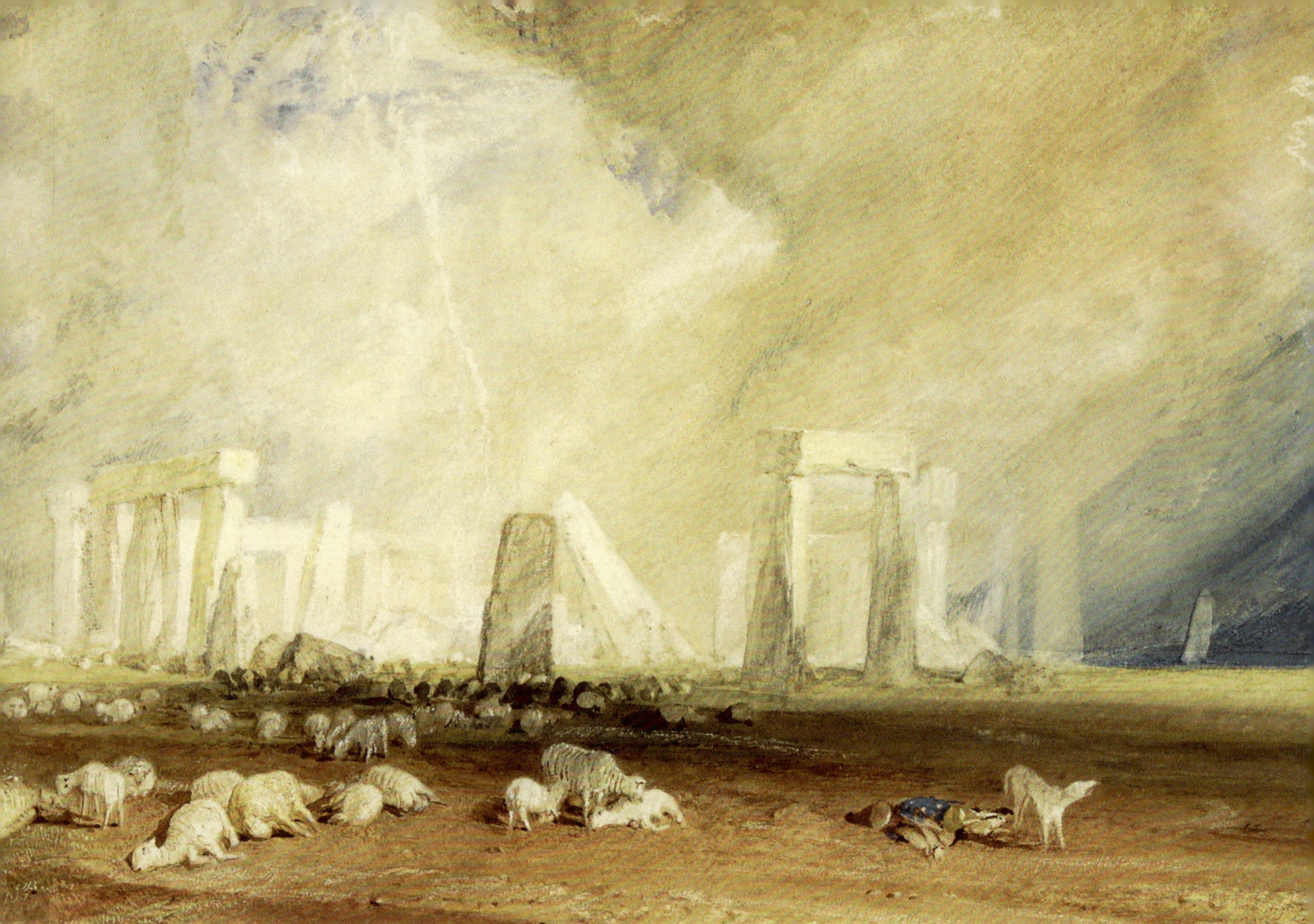

Artistic Responses

The awe-inspiring scale and mysterious origins of Stonehenge attracted late-18th- and early-19th-century artists and writers, including some of the greatest Romantic painters and authors of the time. Their art and writings helped to embed Stonehenge in the popular imagination as an instantly recognisable symbol of both Britain and the deep past.

The Romantic movement of the late 18th to mid 19th century was characterised by an emphasis on personal feeling, often in response to the natural world and the ancient past, and arose partly in reaction to the accelerating pace of the Industrial Revolution. Artists and writers of the Romantic movement were often inspired by 'the Sublime', ruins and landscapes that evoked intense emotions of awe, wonder, horror or mystery. Stonehenge, with its dramatic stones set within a vast open plain and its popular association with the Druids, was the perfect subject for such literary and artistic reflections.

'Pile of Stone-henge! So proud to hint
yet keep
Thy secrets, thou that lov'st to stand
and hear
The Plain resounding to the
whirlwind's sweep
Inmate of lonesome Nature's endless
year.'

WILLIAM WORDSWORTH, *INCIDENTS UPON SALISBURY PLAIN*, c.1793

OPPOSITE In JMW Turner's painting *Stonehenge*, completed in about 1825–8, the enormous stones are shown in the aftermath of a violent storm, with a shepherd and his flock struck down by lightning.

BELOW In this dramatic watercolour from 1835, also entitled *Stonehenge*, John Constable has captured the monument sunlit against storm clouds, with a colourless double rainbow arcing through the sky.

One of the writers who was inspired by Stonehenge was the poet William Wordsworth (1770–1850), who visited in 1793. His experience of the monument and its setting led him to pen his early poem *Salisbury Plain*, which he reworked into further poems at different points throughout his life, including *Guilt and Sorrow; or, Incidents upon Salisbury Plain.*

Landscape painter JMW Turner made several prints and paintings of Stonehenge, many of them based on sketches made in 1811 during a summer tour of south-west England. The most famous of these, created between 1825 and 1828 and simply titled *Stonehenge*, depicts orange-tinged billowing clouds with a bolt of lightning descending from the sky. Around the monument lie a flock of sheep and a fallen shepherd, struck dead by the awesome power of the storm. The painter John Constable toured Stonehenge in July 1820 when he made two sketches of the stones, but it wasn't until 1835 and 1836 that he used these drawings as the basis for more dramatic watercolours and oils. His watercolour *Stonehenge* was created during a time of grief when his wife and a close friend had both recently died, and his mood is perhaps reflected in the stormy skies and two colourless rainbows arcing over the monument. He depicts a running hare in the foreground, providing a temporal contrast to the permanence of the megaliths.

Other landscape artists of the Romantic movement were also inspired to paint Stonehenge, including Richard Tongue (in 1833), John William Inchbold (in 1866 and 1873) and Henry Mark Anthony (in the 1870s). Their paintings usually included dramatic sunrises or sunsets, and the idyllic pastoral scene

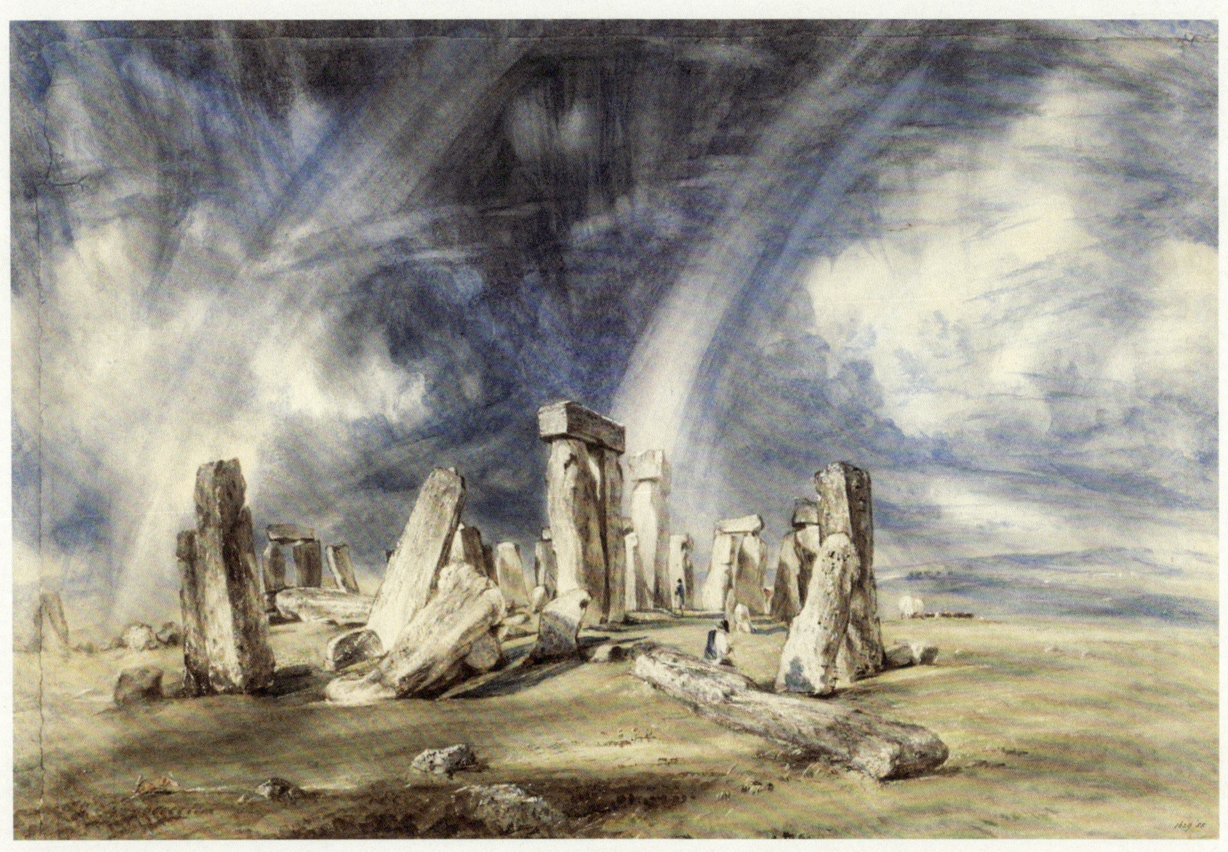

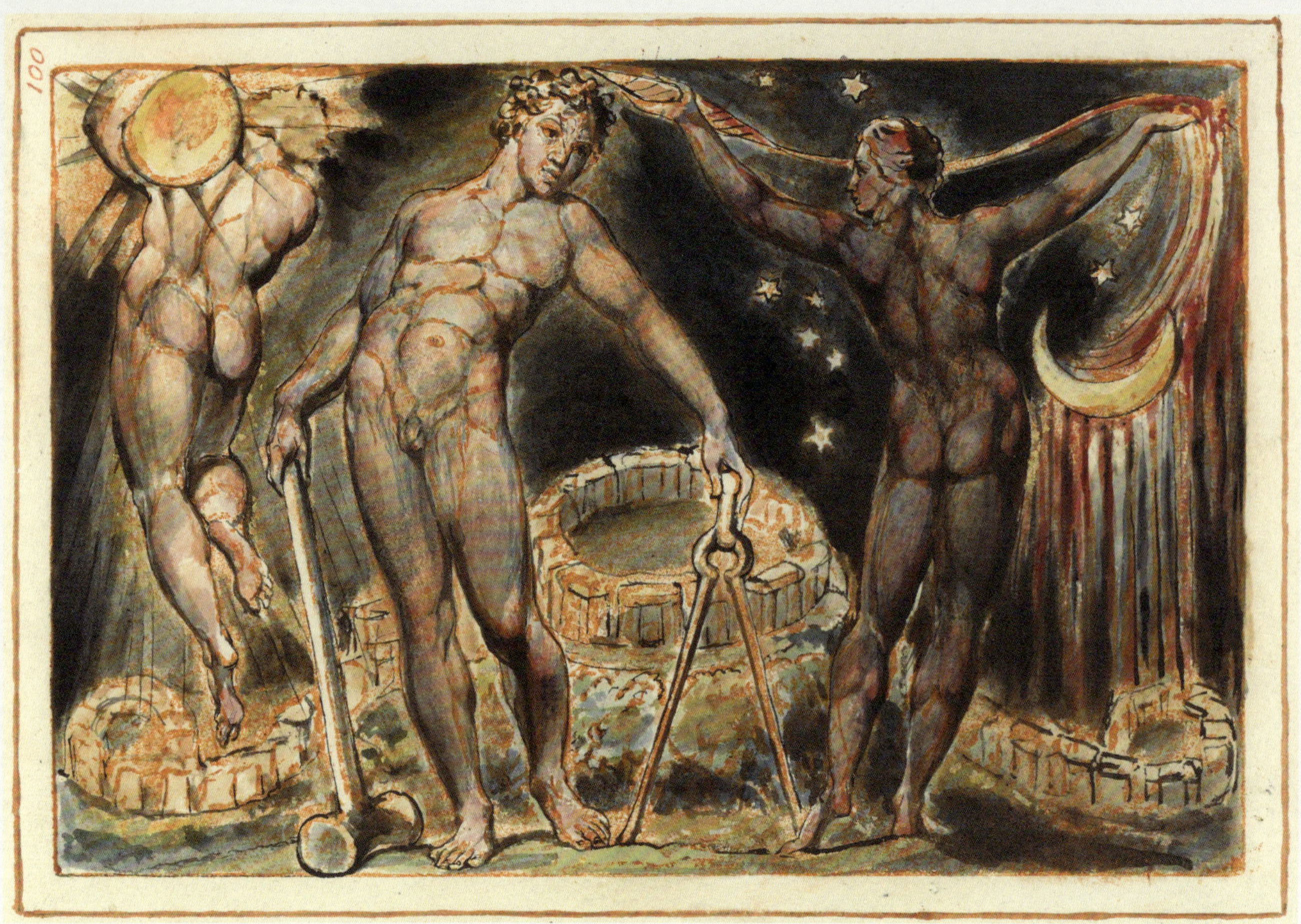

of dotted sheep accompanied by a dutiful shepherd. By this time, however, Stonehenge was far from isolated; a turnpike road had been built near the monument in the 1760s and increasing numbers of visitors had led to the appointment in 1822 of a warden, who helped to guide visitors and protect the stones. Visiting artists were more likely to encounter other tourists than to find a desolate ruin.

Perhaps the most famous appearance of Stonehenge in literature is Thomas Hardy's dramatic finale to his novel *Tess of the D'Urbervilles*, first published in 1891. It was set in his fictional 'Wessex', like many of his books, but features the real monument. The characters Tess and Angel, being forced to flee from the law, arrive at Stonehenge by night, where Tess sleeps on a stone altar, awaiting her fate. The great age and solitude of Stonehenge, as well as the association with pagan sacrifice, are clearly reflected in Hardy's dramatic scene.

Many other artists and writers have been, and continue to be, inspired by the iconic shapes and downland setting of Stonehenge, including William Blake, Henry Moore, Gertrude Hermes, Bernard Cornwell, Jeremy Deller and Kari Kola. It has featured in countless film and television programmes, such as *This is Spinal Tap* (1984), *Doctor Who* (2010) and *Transformers* (2017), and has been adopted by advertisers, for instance in a famous series of 1930s adverts for Shell petrol. Many replicas of Stonehenge, made of a variety of materials including concrete, cars and fridges, have been built across the world, particularly in the United States of America.

ABOVE William Blake's epic poem *Jerusalem: The Emanation of the Giant Albion*, written between 1804 and 1810, features Stonehenge and the Druids, in a story about England's deep mythological past.

OPPOSITE TOP LEFT Artists around the world have been inspired to build replica versions of Stonehenge. Carhenge, near Alliance in Nebraska, USA, for example, was created by Jim Reinders (1927–2021) with vintage American cars, spray-painted grey.

OPPOSITE TOP RIGHT Matt Smith stars as Doctor Who at Stonehenge in *The Pandorica Opens*, an episode in the fifth series, broadcast on the BBC in 2010.

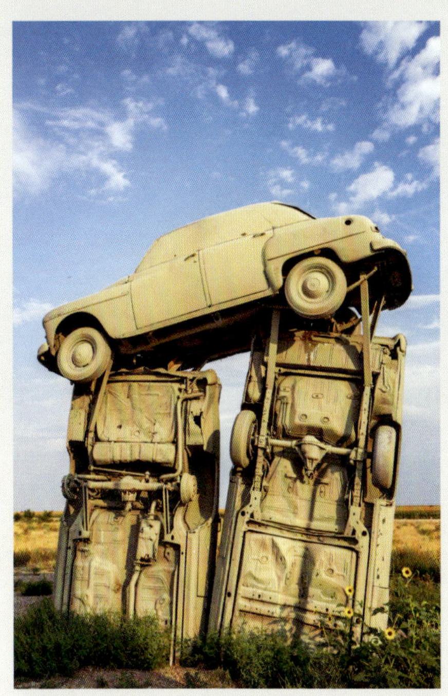

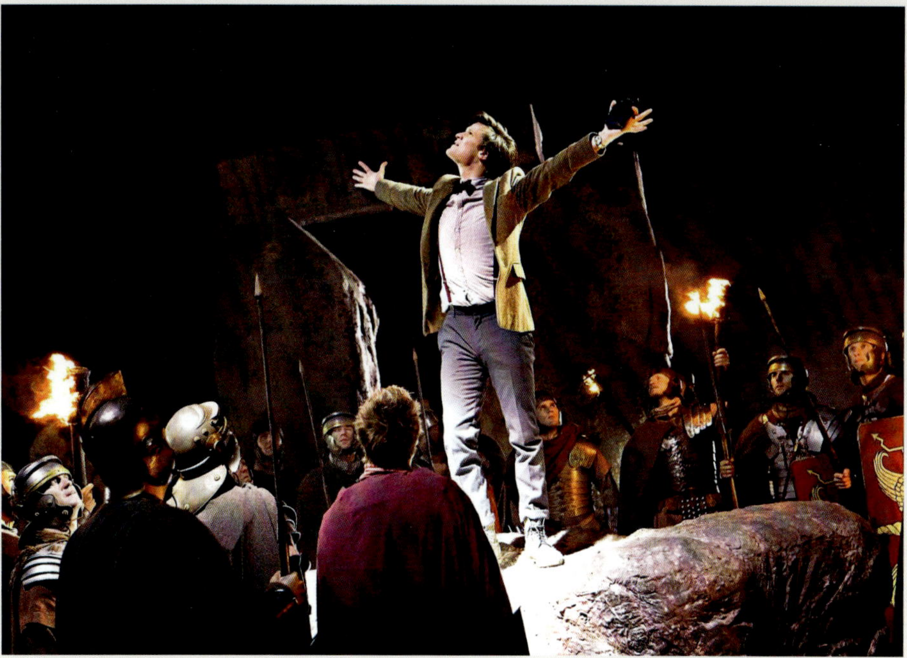

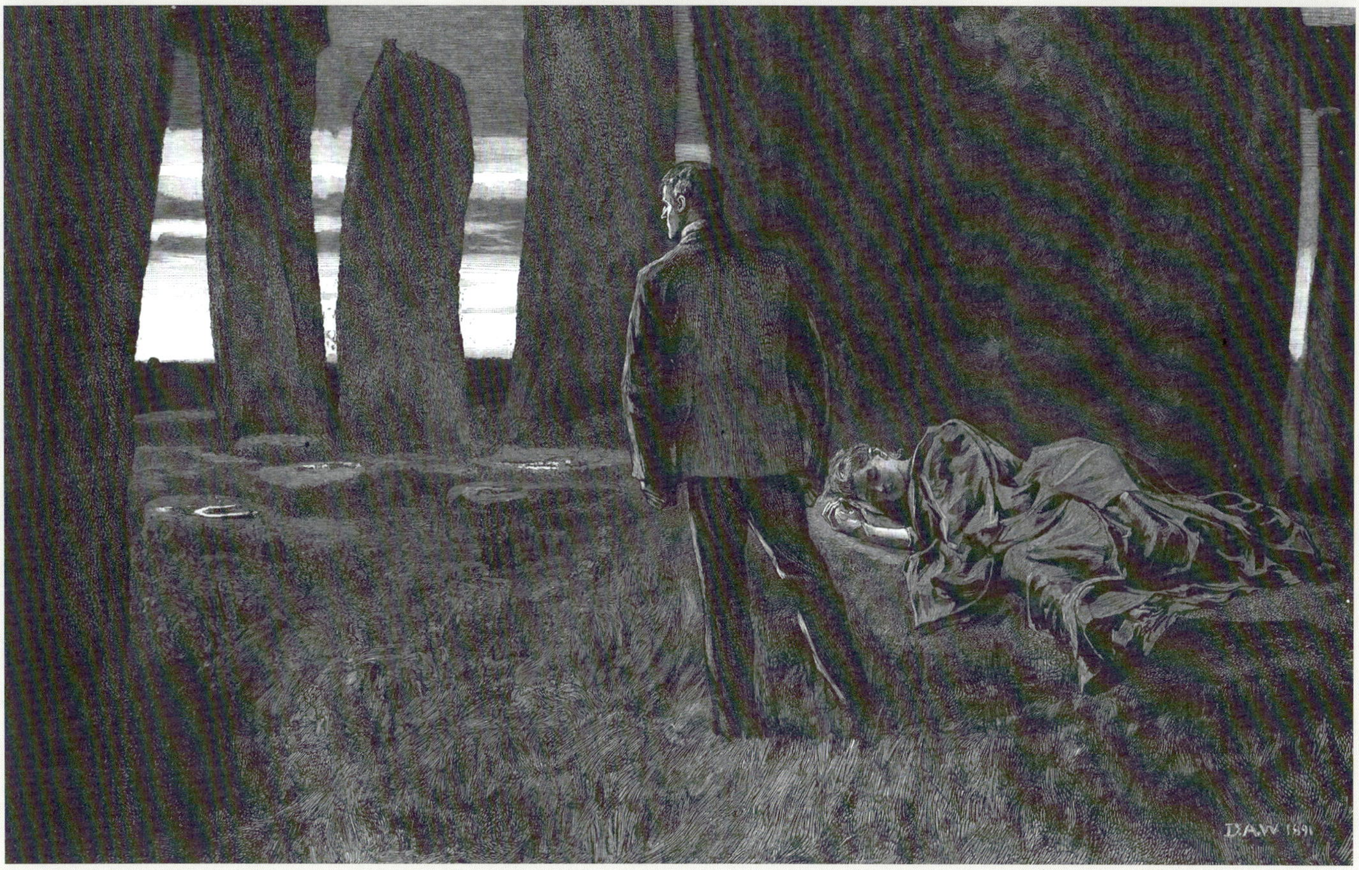

ABOVE Tess and Angel Clare await their fate at Stonehenge in an engraving by Daniel A Wehrschmidt, which illustrated Thomas Hardy's 1891 serialisation of his novel *Tess of the D'Urbervilles* in *The Graphic* magazine.

OVERLEAF In 2013, to mark 100 years of state ownership of Stonehenge, the Finnish artist Kari Kola created a spectacular light installation at Stonehenge.

Many replicas of Stonehenge, made of a variety of materials including concrete, cars and fridges, have been built across the world, particularly in the United States of America.

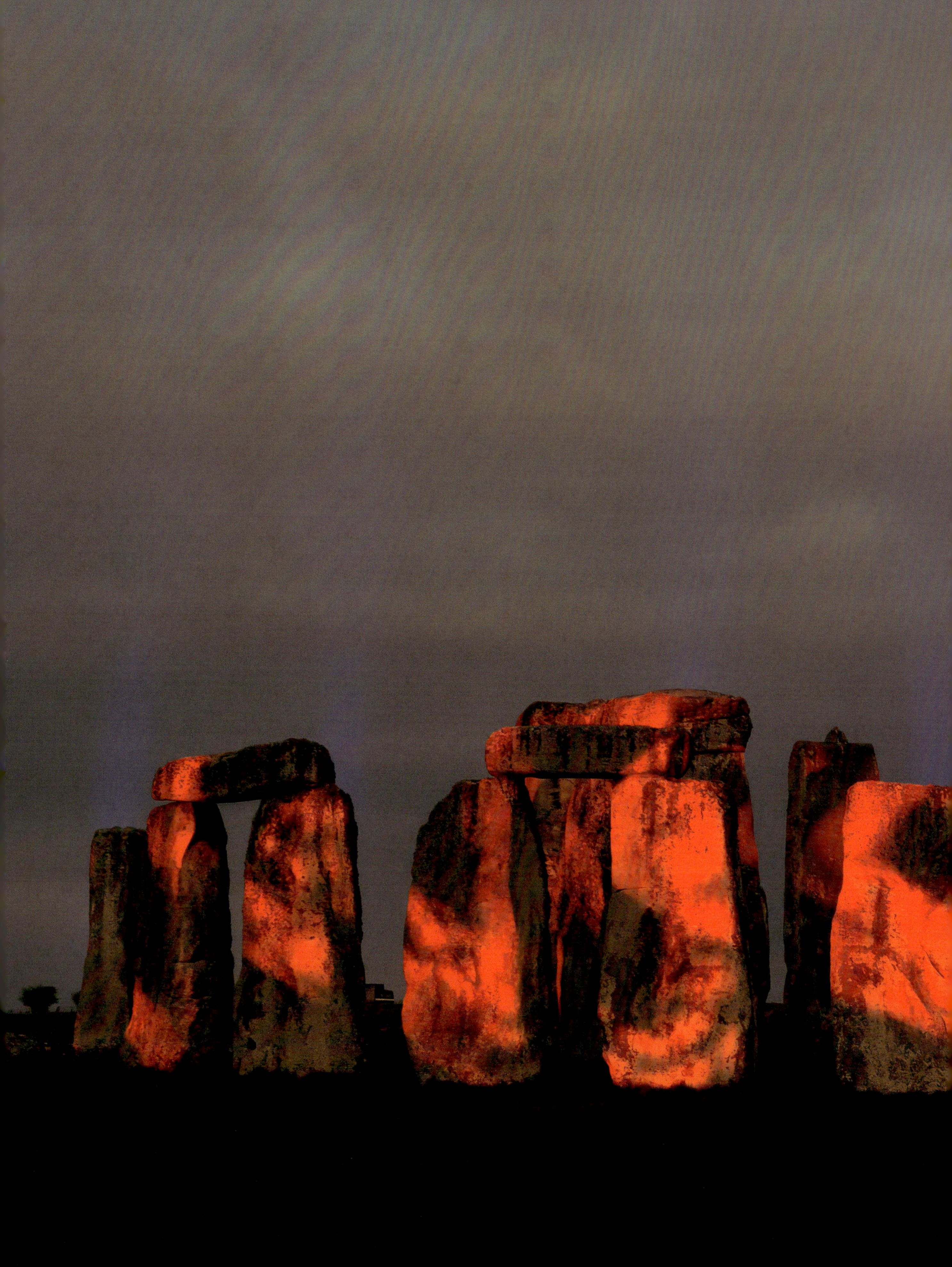

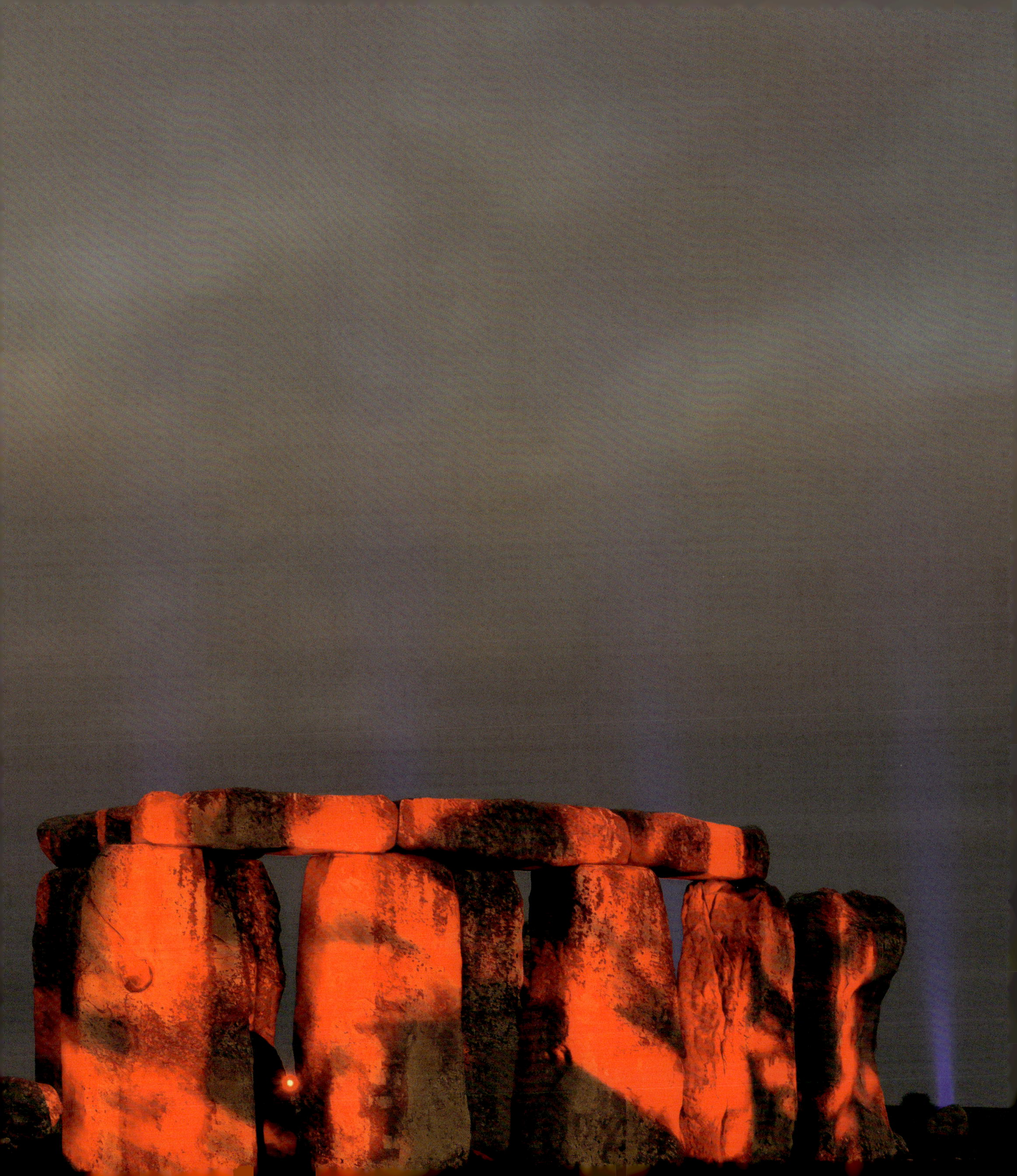

EARLY RESTORATION AND EXCAVATION (1900–1926)

In 1900, at the turn of the 20th century, the fall of a sarsen stone prompted the earliest restoration project, and the first decades of the century saw the site transformed, enclosed and brought into public ownership.

Stonehenge formed part of the large estate owned by the Antrobus family, who lived at nearby Amesbury Abbey, by then a private house. Concerns had been raised by national archaeological institutions that some of the stones were insecure, and were in danger of falling, as an entire trilithon had done in 1797. Sir Edmund Antrobus (1818–99), 3rd Baronet, resisted any requests for restoration or archaeological excavation, however, and declined to place the monument under the protection of the new Ancient Monuments Act of 1882, as he felt government intervention was unnecessary. Antrobus' 'hands-off' approach prevented restoration or excavation projects from taking place; in hindsight this was fortunate, as such interventions at that time were likely to have been damaging rather than helpful. He did erect a substantial timber scaffold under a leaning part of the outer circle, however, to prevent it from falling onto visitors.

Attitudes shifted when, during stormy weather on the last day of 1900, one of the other sarsen stones of the outer circle fell to the ground, its lintel breaking into two. There was an immediate public outcry and considerable discussion as to what should be done. Sir Edmond Antrobus (1848–1915), 4th Baronet, who had inherited the estate in 1899 at his father's death, agreed that some of the more precarious stones could be restored, a trackway that crossed the stone circle diverted and the monument fenced off. A charge to visitors of one shilling was introduced, paying for the services of a full-time policeman to guard against vandalism.

The first part of this project, with the help of architect Detmar Blow (1867–1939), was the re-erection of the perilously leaning sarsen stone at the head of the inner horseshoe. The archaeologist William Gowland (1842–1922) was tasked with overseeing excavations around the base of the stone where scaffolding and concrete supports would be located. He took great care to record the three-dimensional position of every artefact, as well as sieving the soil for anything that had been missed. As no metal objects were recovered, Gowland concluded that Stonehenge had been built in the pre-metal era, identifying it for the first time as a Neolithic monument. Meanwhile, the stone was bolted into a cradle attached to winches and was slowly raised to vertical. None of the other planned restoration works were carried out and, instead, large wooden poles were used to prop up many of the stones of the outer circle.

Sir Edmund Antrobus died in February 1915, aged 66. His only son, also called Edmund, had been killed at Ypres in France only a few months earlier, while serving with the Grenadier Guards in the First World War. The Amesbury

OPPOSITE TOP Stone 56 – the surviving upright of the tallest trilithon – supported by a wooden frame and props, during restoration in 1901, captured by local photographer Clarissa Miles.

OPPOSITE BOTTOM William Gowland (centre, leaning on his knee) conducted excavations around the base of the upright sarsen of the tallest trilithon to record the archaeology before concrete for the foundation was poured. His innovative techniques included using a measuring frame and vertical rod to record the position of every artefact found.

OVERLEAF Major conservation works taking place at Stonehenge in 1920. Here, lintels of the north-east side of the outer sarsen circle are being lowered, so that the uprights could be restored to vertical. Note the tiny black kitten on the sarsen, presumably placed there to contrast with the enormous weight and size of the stone.

Attitudes shifted when, during stormy weather on the last day of 1900, one of the other sarsen stones of the outer circle fell to the ground, its lintel breaking in two.

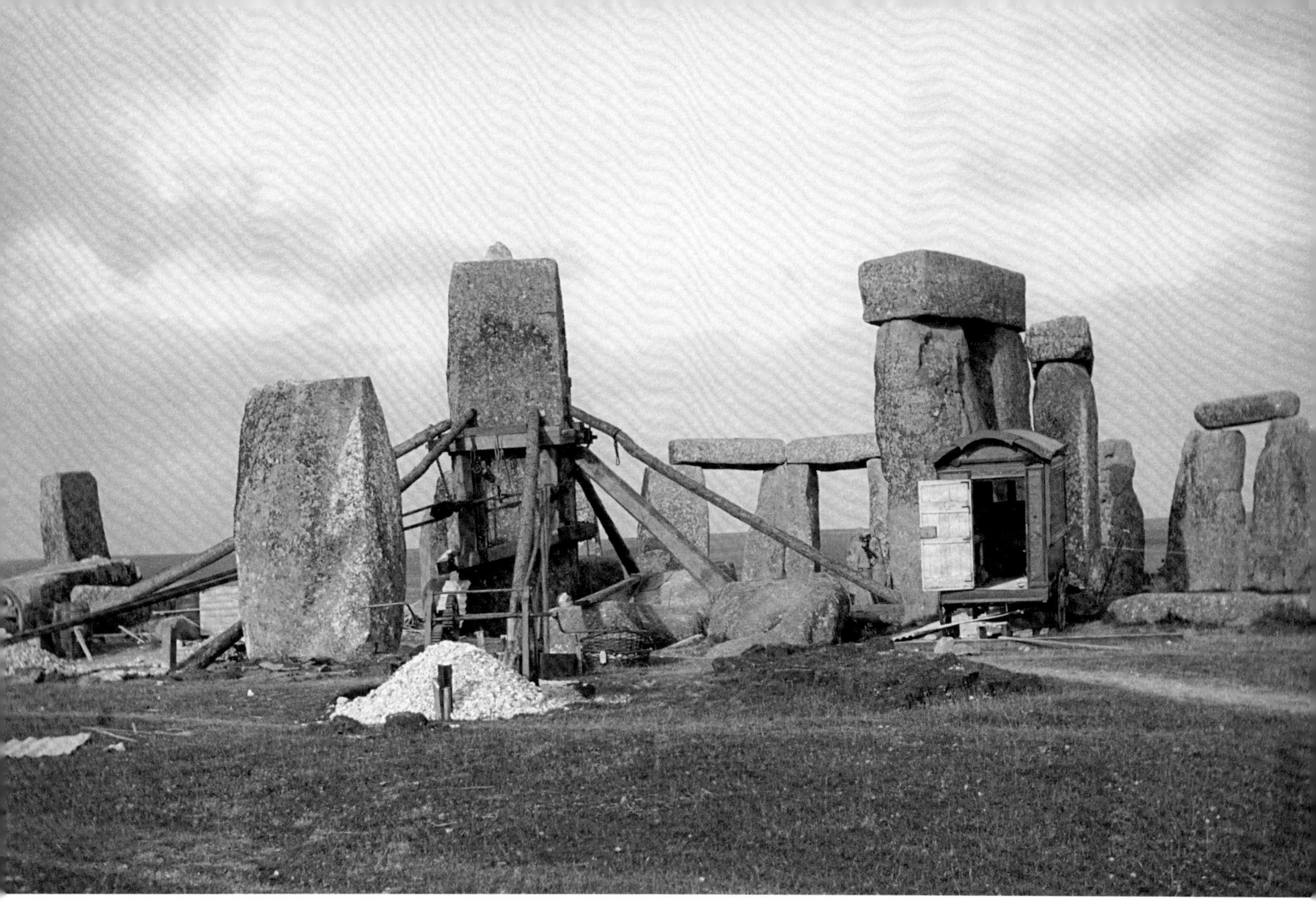

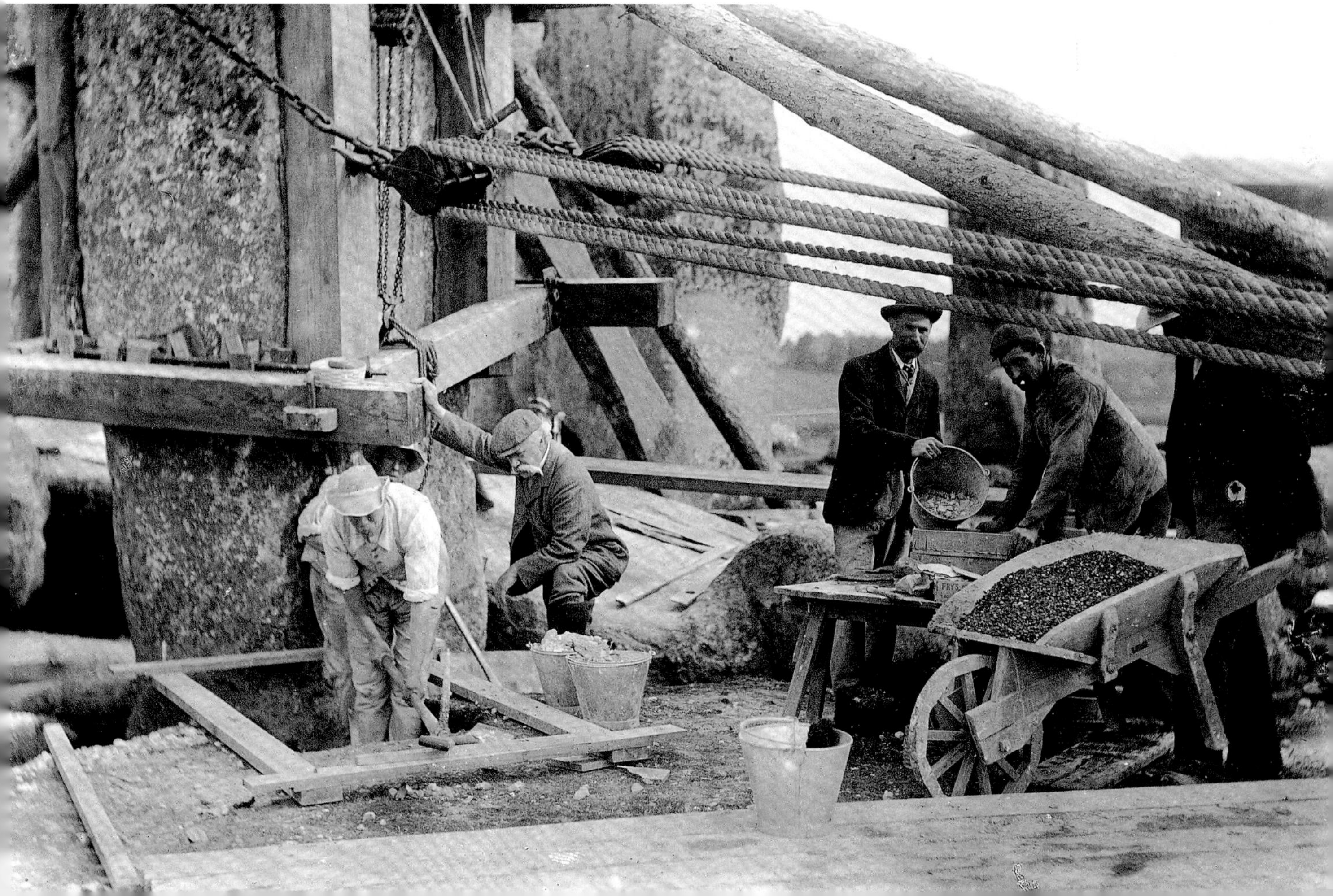

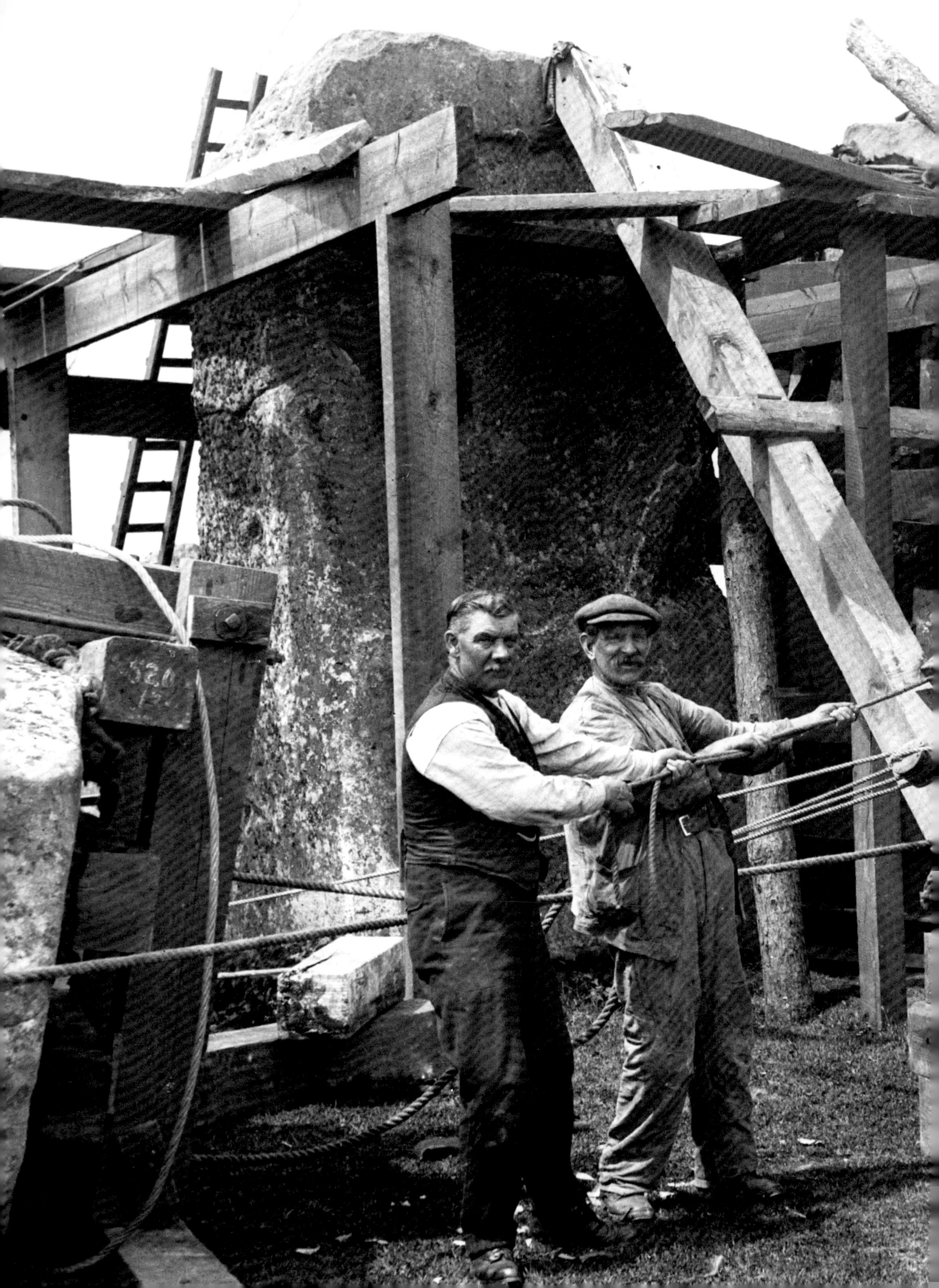

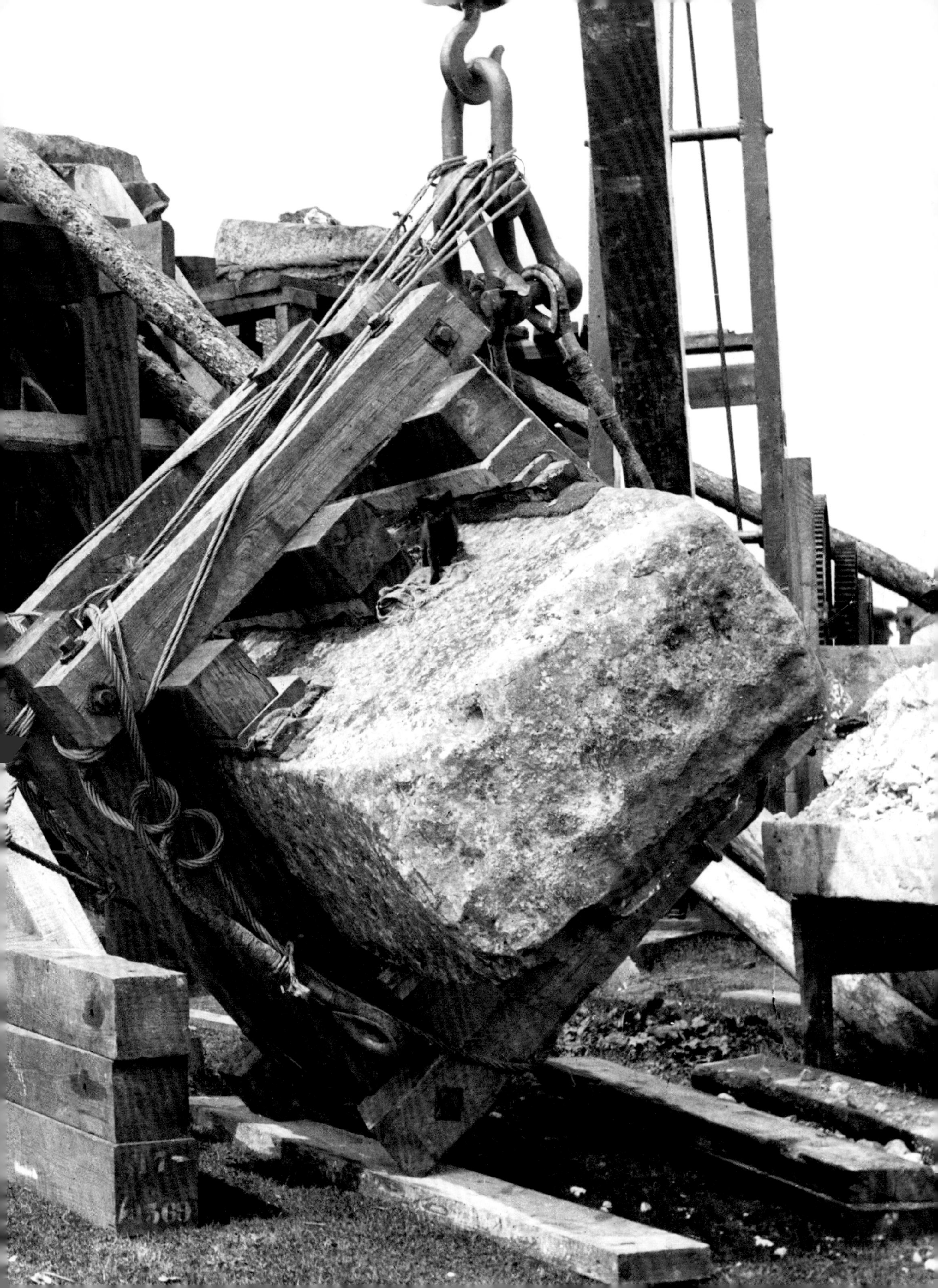

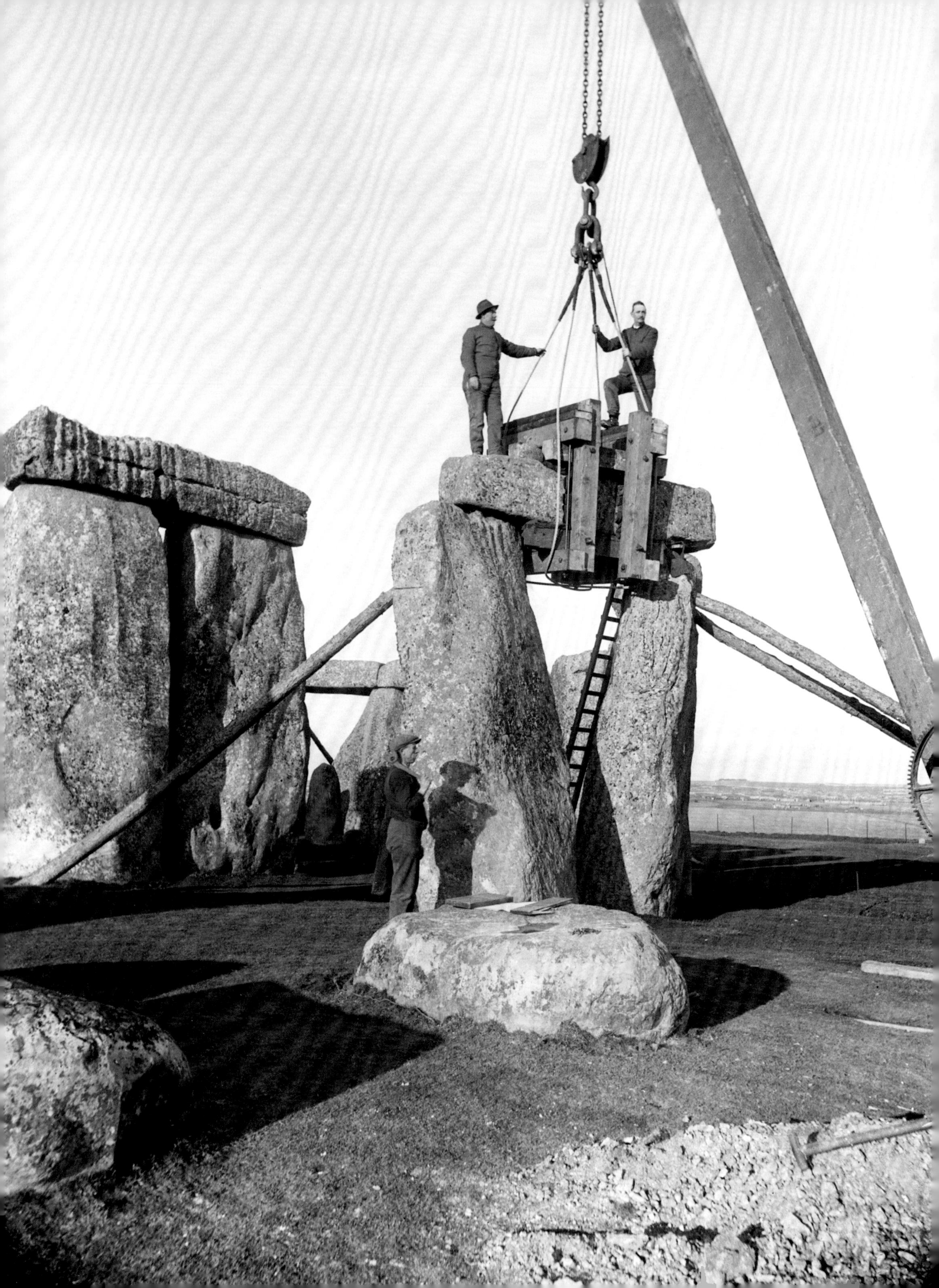

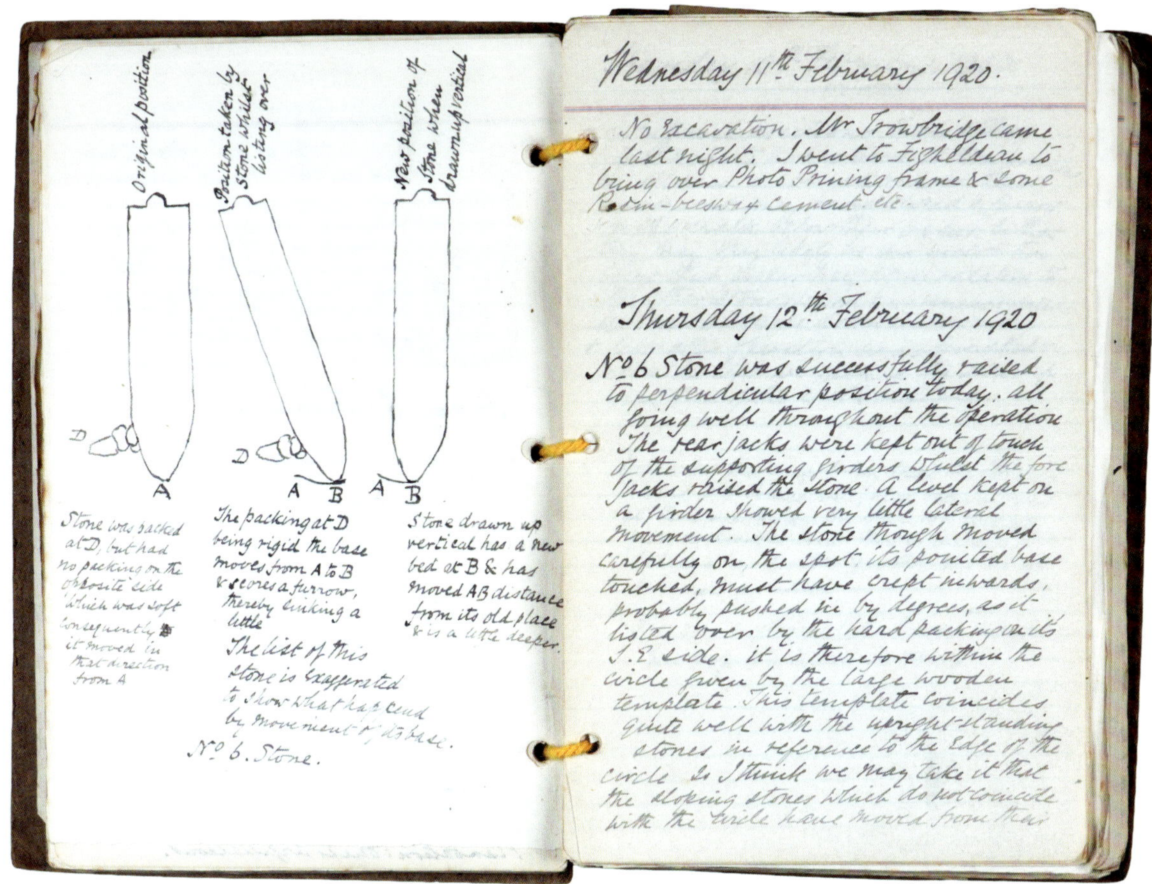

Original position

Position taken by Stone whilst listing over

New position of Stone when drawn up vertical

D A

D A B

A B

Stone was packed at D, but had no packing on the opposite side which was soft consequently it moved in that direction from A

The packing at D being rigid the base moves from A to B & scores a furrow, thereby sinking a little

Stone drawn up vertical has a new bed at B & has moved AB distance from its old place & is a little deeper.

The list of this stone is exaggerated to show what has occurred by movement of its base.

No. 6. Stone.

Wednesday 11th February 1920.

No excavation. Mr Trowbridge came last night. I went to Figheldean to bring over Photo Printing frame & some Rosin-beeswax cement etc.

Thursday 12th February 1920

No 6 Stone was successfully raised to perpendicular position today. all going well throughout the operation. The rear jacks were kept out of touch of the supporting girders whilst the fore jacks raised the stone. A level kept on a girder showed very little lateral movement. The stone though moved carefully on the spot its pointed base touched, must have crept inwards, probably pushed in by degrees, as it listed over by the hard packing on its S.E. side. it is therefore within the circle given by the large wooden template. This template coincides quite well with the upright-standing stones in reference to the edge of the circle so I think we may take it that the sloping stones which do not coincide with the circle have moved from their

OPPOSITE The first stones to be restored in 1919 were stones 6 and 7 on the south-east side of the outer sarsen circle, which were precariously twisted and in danger of collapse.

ABOVE A page from one of William Hawley's field notebooks describing the raising of one of the leaning sarsen stones (stone 6) on 12 February 1920, with diagrams to explain how it had shifted from its original position.

estate passed to Sir Edmund's surviving younger brother Cosmo, who decided to put the entire estate up for auction. Stonehenge was to be sold.

On 21 September 1915, at an auction in the Palace Theatre in Salisbury, local barrister Cecil Chubb bought the monument for £6,600. Chubb had grown up in Shrewton, a village close to Stonehenge, and although he had fond memories of cycling to the site as a boy, he had had no intention of bidding. He later recounted, however, that 'while I was in the room, I thought a Salisbury man ought to buy it and that is how it was done'. Cecil and his wife Mary remained the owners for three years until October 1918, when they formally handed the site to Sir Alfred Mond, the First Commissioner of Works, who received it as a gift on behalf of the nation. To mark Cecil Chubb's generosity, he was made a baronet in 1919.

The Office of Works, the body responsible for maintaining government properties, immediately began major conservation works, restoring leaning stones to upright, placing them into concrete bases and resetting lintels. These repairs were intended to ensure that no further stones fell and that the monument was safe for visitors. The works were accompanied by excavations directed by the archaeologist Lieutenant-Colonel William Hawley (1851–1941).

After the restoration work was completed, Hawley was commissioned by the Society of Antiquaries of London to excavate the whole area within the earthwork enclosure. Until 1926, he worked long seasons at Stonehenge in all weathers, with relatively little assistance. These investigations confirmed the presence of the Aubrey Holes, discovered the Y and Z holes, found the ditch around the Heel Stone and uncovered the cremated remains of many people. Often, however, Hawley found nothing but bare chalk, and in his final report he lamented that 'so very little is known for certain about the place that what I say is mainly conjecture, and it is to be hoped that future excavators will be able to throw more light upon it than I have done.'

Rising Tourism

With transport improvements in the late 19th and early 20th centuries, increasing numbers of people came to Stonehenge to marvel at the famous stones. These tourists required information, refreshments and other facilities, which led to gradual but significant changes to the site.

BELOW Taken in the early 1860s, this is the earliest known family photograph at Stonehenge. It is a stereograph – two nearly identical photographs, which together produce the illusion of a single three-dimensional image when viewed through a stereoscope. It was taken by Henry Brooks and depicts his wife, Caroline, and their children seated on one of the stones.

The arrival of the railway, the rise of bicycle ownership and improved local roads led to increasing numbers of people visiting Stonehenge in the late 19th century. The railway connecting London with Salisbury was opened in 1857, making it far easier for tourists from the capital to reach the historic city, just eight miles (13km) from Stonehenge. An appointed custodian was usually present at Stonehenge to guide visitors and prevent damage, earning their living from the sale of their own guidebooks and drawings, as well as postcards and souvenirs. The custodian from 1870 until 1899 was William Judd, who was also a photographer; his horse-drawn caravan darkroom can often be seen in photographs from this time (see photograph at the top of page 117).

With the rise of car ownership, which enabled families to set out and explore the British countryside for themselves, Stonehenge became a popular destination. In 1927 a café was built nearby to the north-east, and in 1935 the Office of Works acquired land on the north side of the monument to form

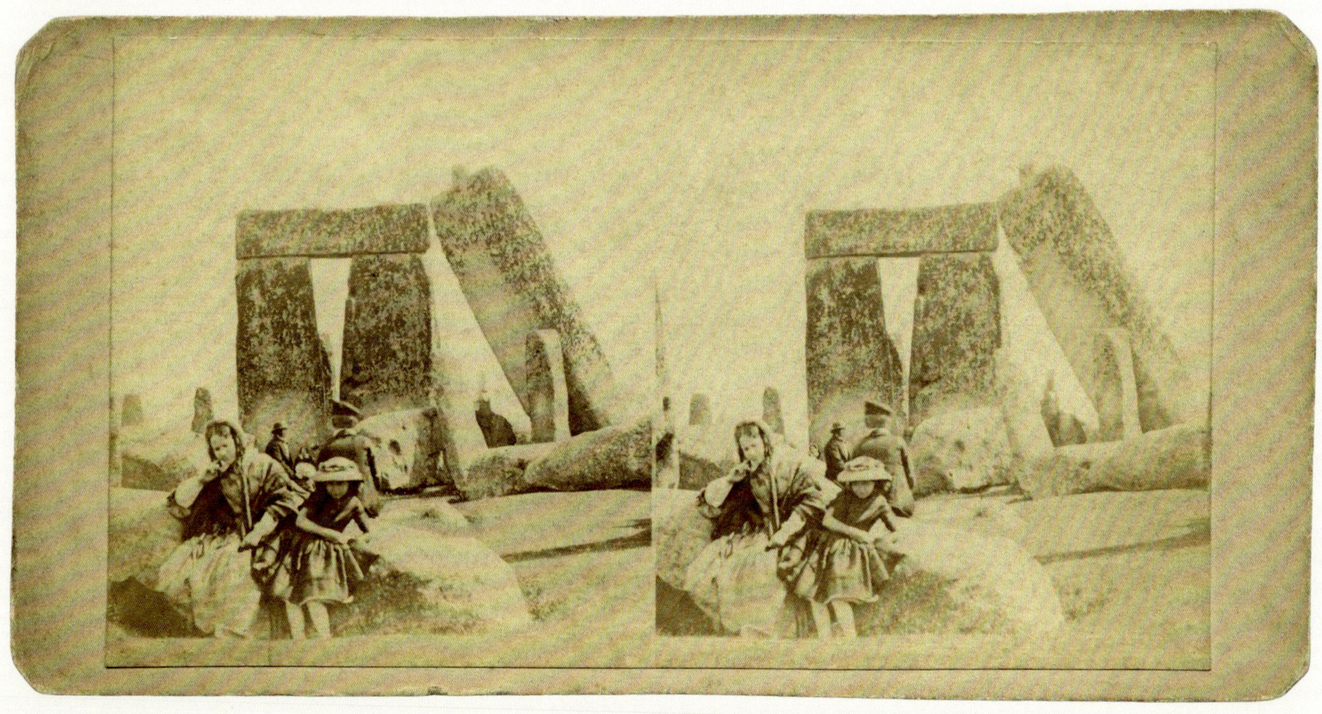

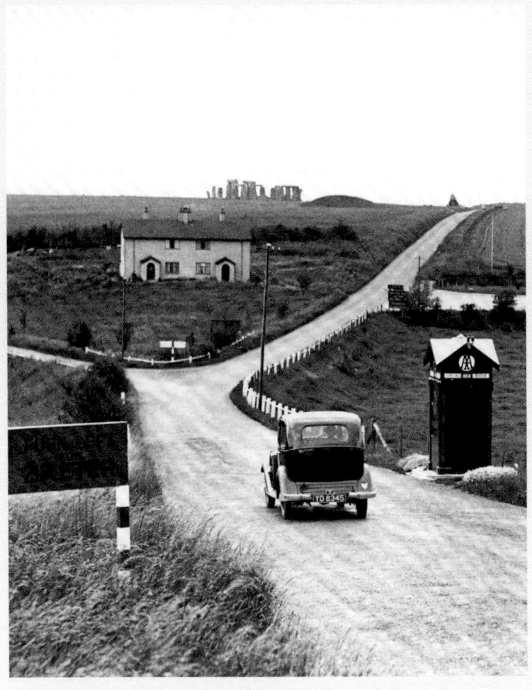

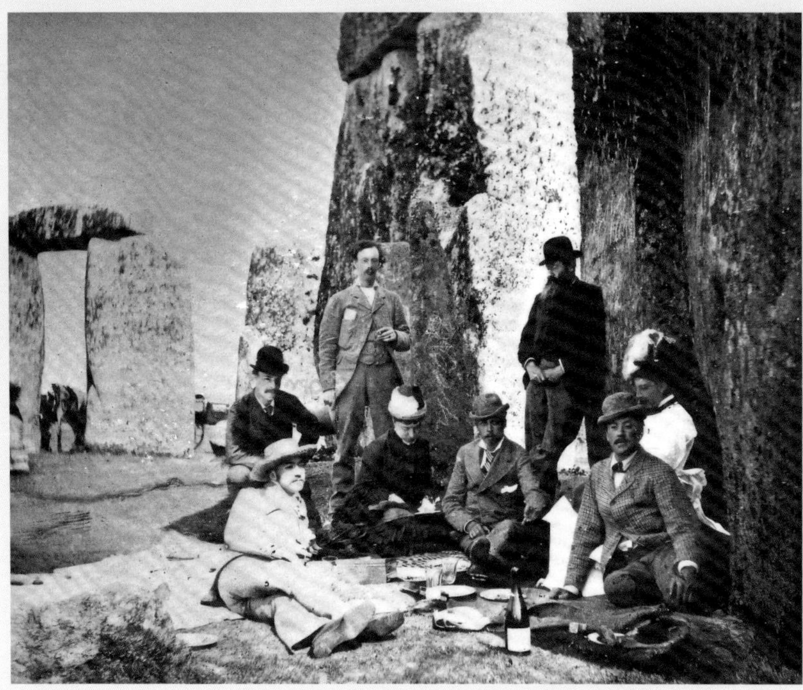

ABOVE LEFT This view has changed dramatically since this photograph was taken, sometime between 1929 and 1933. The lane is now the busy A303 road with the right fork the (now closed) A344. The pair of custodian cottages were demolished in 1938 as their presence was deemed unsightly.

ABOVE RIGHT An elegant party picnicking at Stonehenge in about 1880. Their carriage can just be seen behind the sarsen stones.

a small car park. In 1938 efforts were made to clear modern buildings close to Stonehenge, which led to the demolition of the café and a pair of custodian cottages, which stood in the fork of the nearby A303 and A344 roads. After the Second World War, however, new buildings were required: in 1950 a mobile tea-bar was allowed to operate from the car park; by 1954 underground lavatories had been built; and in 1966 the car park was extended, and a concrete underpass provided safe access to the monument under the busy A344 road.

In 1961 there were 337,000 visitors. Just ten years later, this had increased to over 500,000 annual sightseers. These large numbers of visitors caused problems at the monument itself, where the grass was constantly worn away within the stone circle. The interior was surfaced with gravel in 1964, but this solution only caused further damage to the stones and in 1977 it was decided to fence off the monument completely, returning the site to grass. Since this date, access to the middle of the stone circle has been restricted to managed open access at the solstices and equinoxes and to small groups on pre-booked tours (the Stone Circle Experience).

As the monument is owned by the State, a succession of government organisations has managed the property: the Office of Works; the Ministry of Works, the Department of the Environment and, today, the charity English Heritage.

These large numbers of visitors caused problems at the monument itself, where the grass was constantly worn away within the stone circle.

Military Connections

In 1897, the Army acquired 40,000 acres (16,000 hectares) of land on Salisbury Plain, to the north of Stonehenge, for training purposes. As military flying developed in the early 20th century, the large areas of open grassland closer to Stonehenge were identified as the ideal place for taking off and landing aeroplanes, and it became the location of a First World War training aerodrome.

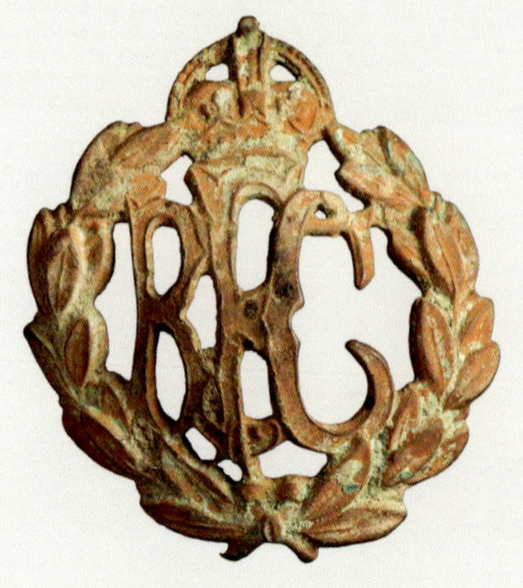

ABOVE A cap badge of the Royal Flying Corps, found not far from Stonehenge. The aerodrome used by the Corps' No.1 School of Aerial Navigation and Bomb Dropping was just 500m from Stonehenge.

The first flying school and airfield was established in 1910 at Larkhill Aerodrome, not far from Stonehenge. The early, flimsy aircraft that were flown there were not always safe. Captain Eustace Loraine and Staff-Sergeant Richard Wilson died when their Nieuport monoplane crashed in 1912, and Major AW Hewetson was killed the following year when his Bristol monoplane came down during his aviator's test. Memorial crosses to commemorate these brave pioneers of flight stand today near the Stonehenge Visitor Centre and on the old road towards Stonehenge. The original aeroplane sheds still stand at Larkhill.

During the First World War there were army camps, hospitals, training trenches and rifle ranges in the wider Stonehenge landscape. Few traces of these remain today, although the track between Woodhenge and the eastern end of the Greater Cursus runs along the line of an old military railway and there are scattered marker stones showing the boundary of the military estate. In 1917, a large aerodrome was built just 500m to the south-west of Stonehenge, the location of the No.1 School of Aerial Navigation and Bomb Dropping. Here pilots were trained in navigation, night flying and bombing raids.

After the aerodrome closed in 1921, the requisitioned land was returned to the land owner and farmer, Isaac Crook. He converted the derelict hangars into a pig farm and leased out some of the structures as dwellings. The presence of these unsightly buildings so close to Stonehenge led to a public appeal to raise money to purchase and clear the land. The campaign caught the public imagination, and enough money was raised to buy several fields around Stonehenge, at a cost of £35,000, the equivalent of about £1.7 million today. This land was donated to the National Trust in 1928 and forms the core of its current landholdings in the area.

OPPOSITE TOP An aerial view of the huts, hangars and storage areas at Stonehenge Camp, February 1919.

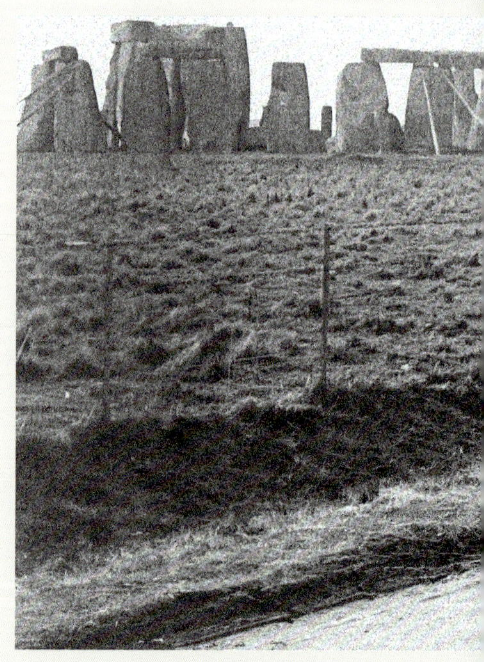

RIGHT Soldiers of the 10th Battalion of the Canadian Expeditionary Force marching past Stonehenge. They trained on Salisbury Plain before departing for the trenches in 1915.

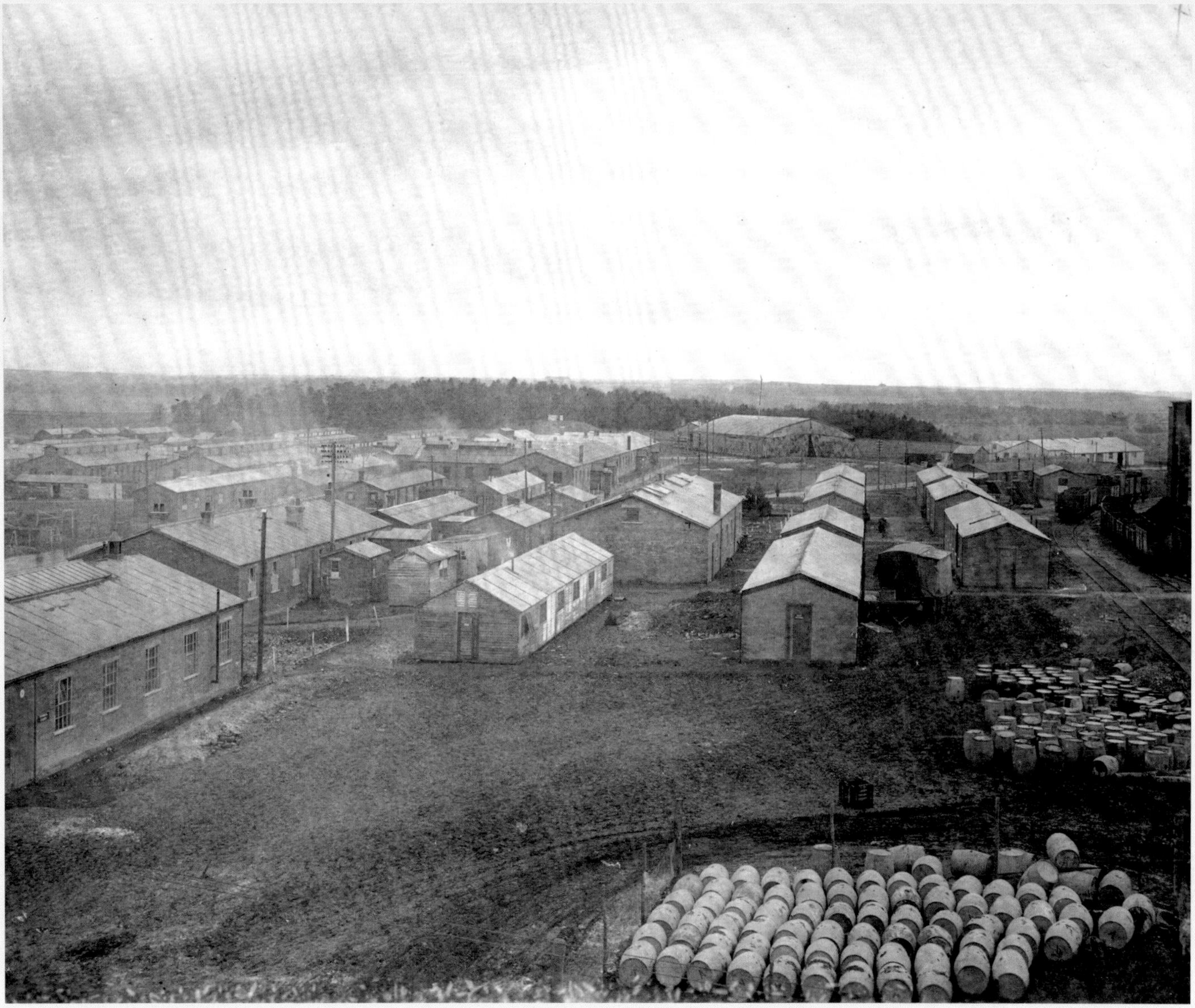

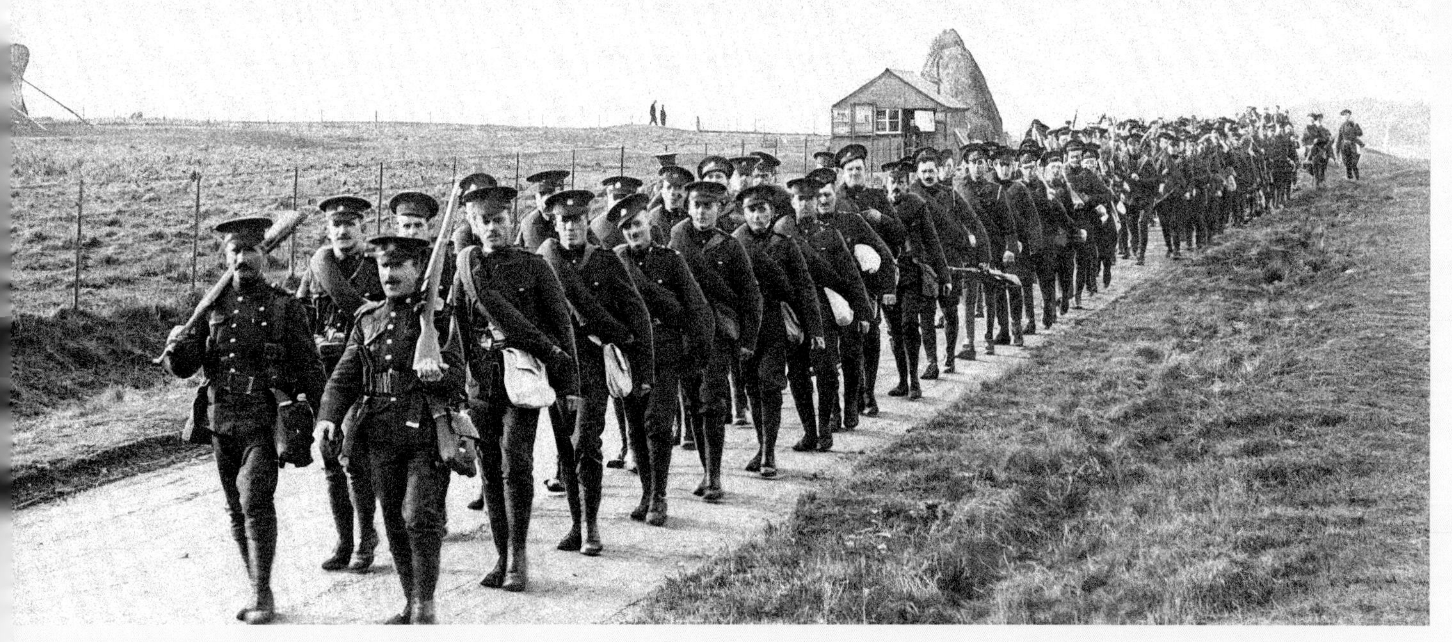

MODERN STONEHENGE (1926–TODAY)

Stonehenge today receives well over one million visitors a year, who come to see the ancient monument for themselves. Many may assume that the site has always appeared as it does now and there is little more to be learned about its history. The appearance of Stonehenge today, has, however, been affected by major conservation works that took place here in the 1950s and 1960s. In addition, excavations both at Stonehenge and in the surrounding landscape in the last few decades have helped to piece together its story.

William Hawley completed his excavations in 1926, although a full report on his discoveries was never published. In 1950 the Society of Antiquaries of London asked a team of three experienced archaeologists – Richard Atkinson, Stuart Piggott and JFS Stone – to rectify the situation by writing up a 'full and definitive' volume on the archaeology of Stonehenge. The trio decided that some limited excavations would help to resolve some questions. In the end they excavated several areas of the site between 1950 and 1956, including two more of the Aubrey Holes, parts of the Avenue, part of the bank and ditch, and a portion of the bluestone circle. The archaeologists wrote a report for the Society of Antiquaries, recommending the restoration of the trilithon that had fallen in 1797, as well as other fallen stones, and securing those in danger of collapse.

The Society supported these proposals and the Ministry of Works, which held responsibility for Stonehenge at that time, eventually agreed on the basis that 'it would enhance the value of the monument for the

BELOW LEFT Excavations at Stonehenge in 1954, led by Richard Atkinson, who can be seen in the trench, smoking with his trademark cigarette holder.

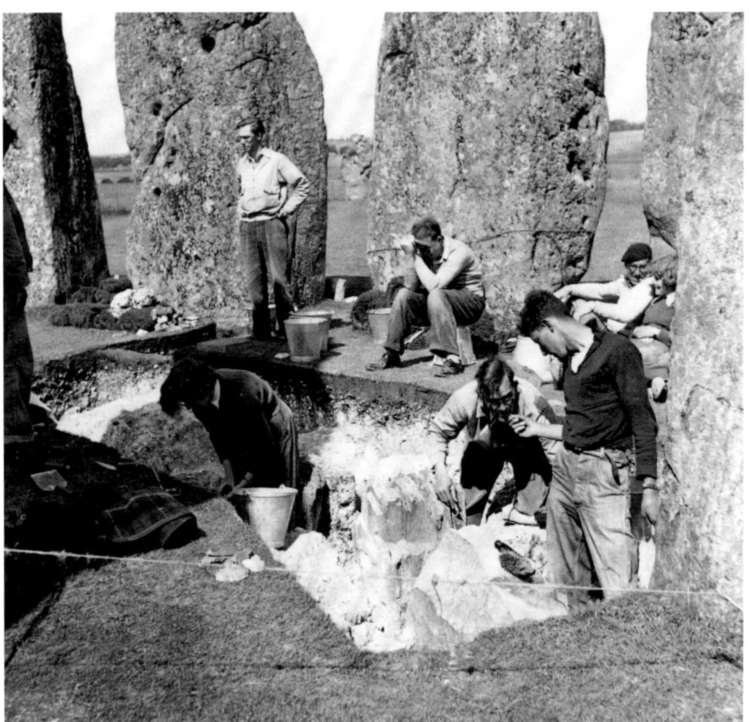

The trilithon was re-erected from where it had lain for 161 years. An upright and a lintel forming part of the outer circle were also put back into position.

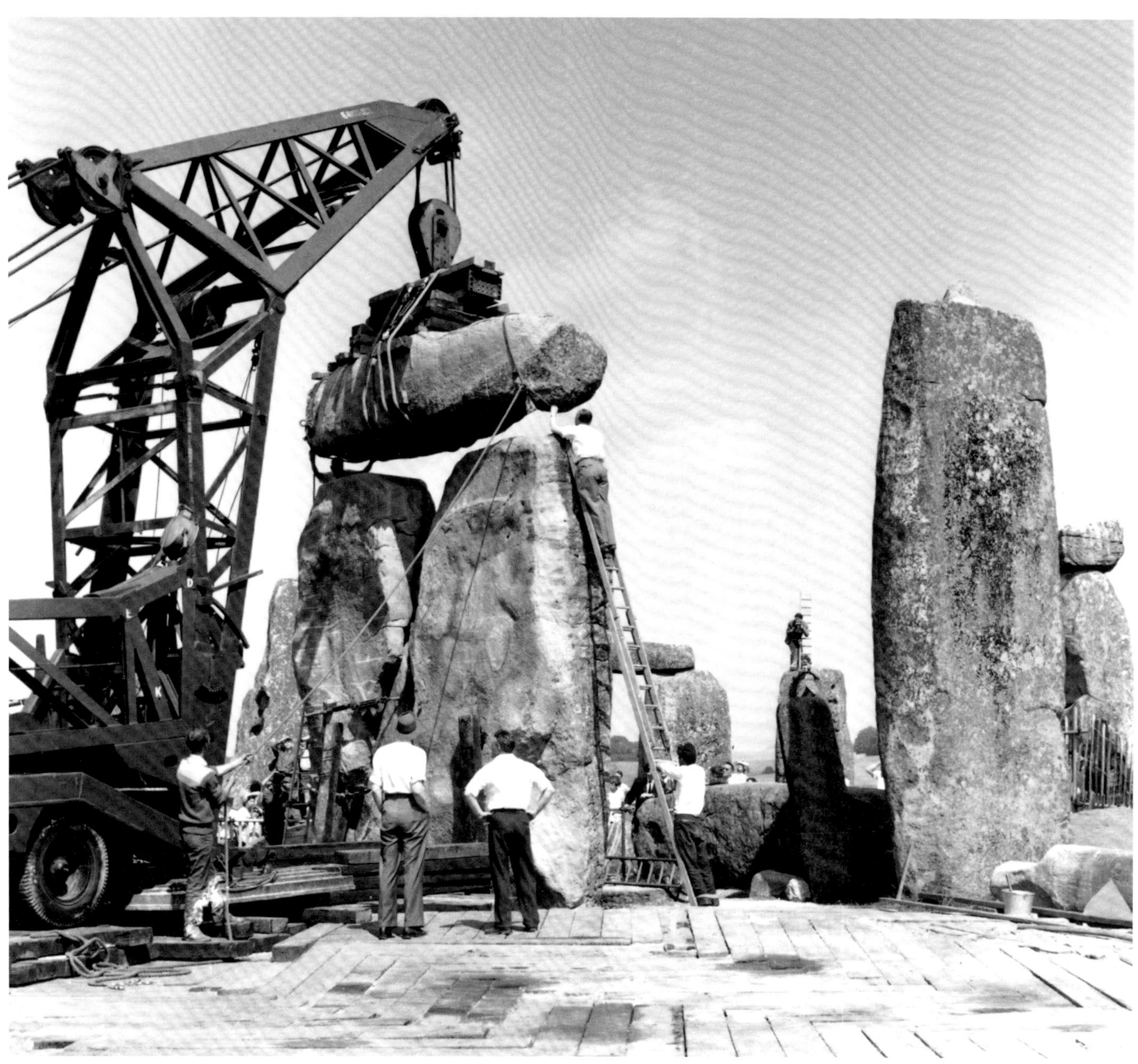

ABOVE During restoration work in 1958, the lintel is lifted into place, restoring the trilithon that had fallen in 1797. On the ladder, guiding the stone into place, is T Aubrey Bailey, the chief architect for the restoration project.

student and make it more intelligent to the ordinary visitor'. Accordingly a major engineering project and associated excavations began in 1958. Atkinson, Piggott and Stone together oversaw the archaeological work. The trilithon was re-erected from where it had lain for 161 years. An upright and a lintel forming part of the outer circle were also put back into position. Several further sarsen bases were set in concrete to prevent future movement, and a large hollow at the base of one of the large sarsens of the inner horseshoe was infilled. Finally, six fallen bluestones were lifted and straightened.

Two seasons of restoration had been successfully completed, but on the morning of 10 March 1963, calamity struck: one of the stones in the outer circle fell during high winds. A long period of frost in the early spring, followed by a rapid thaw and heavy rain, was said to be the cause. This stone had, however, also been given a hefty knock during the works to re-erect the adjacent stone.

Inspectors rapidly surveyed the whole site, amid fears that further stones would fall, perhaps onto unsuspecting visitors. Monthly readings were taken to monitor any movement.

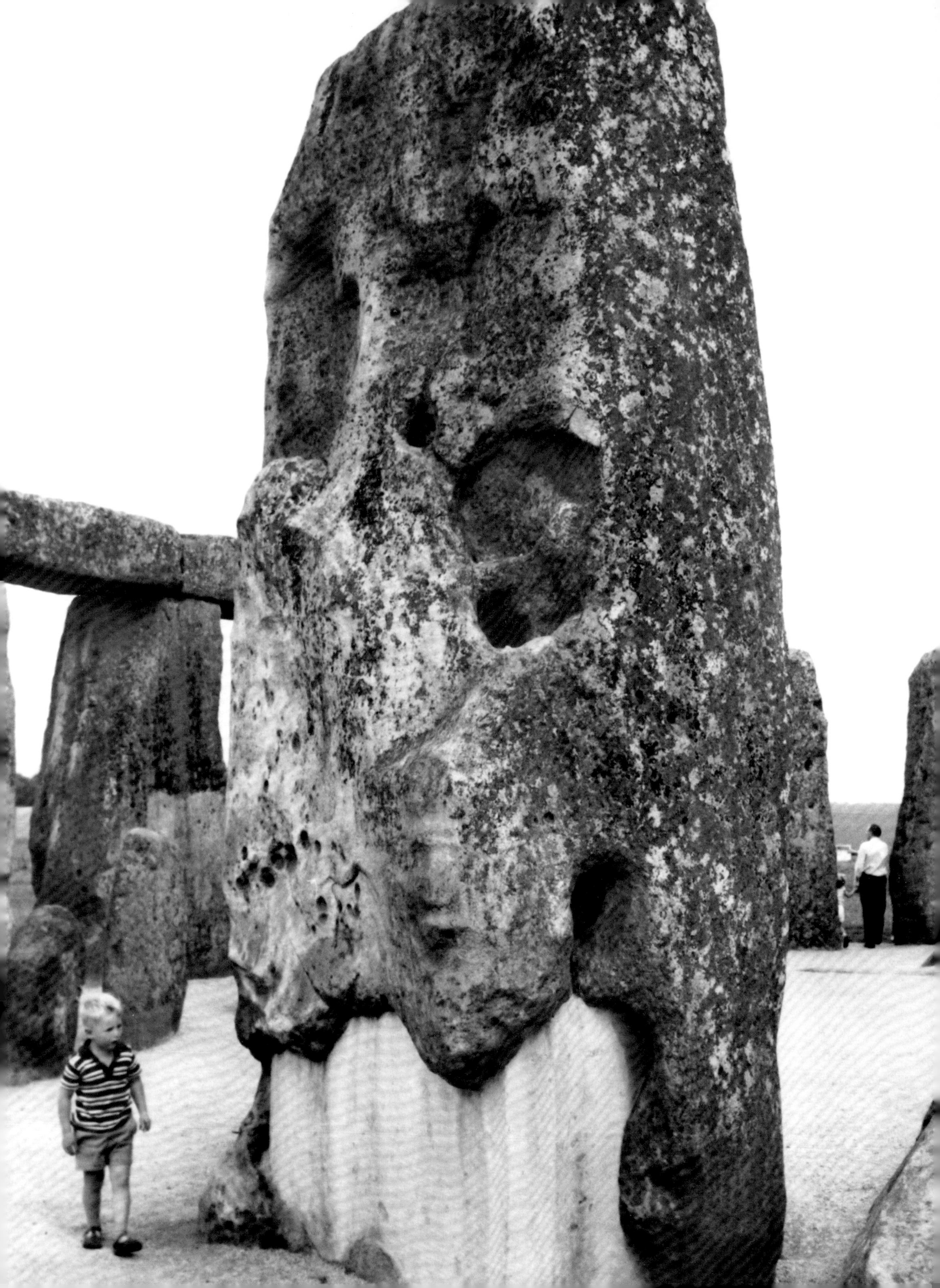

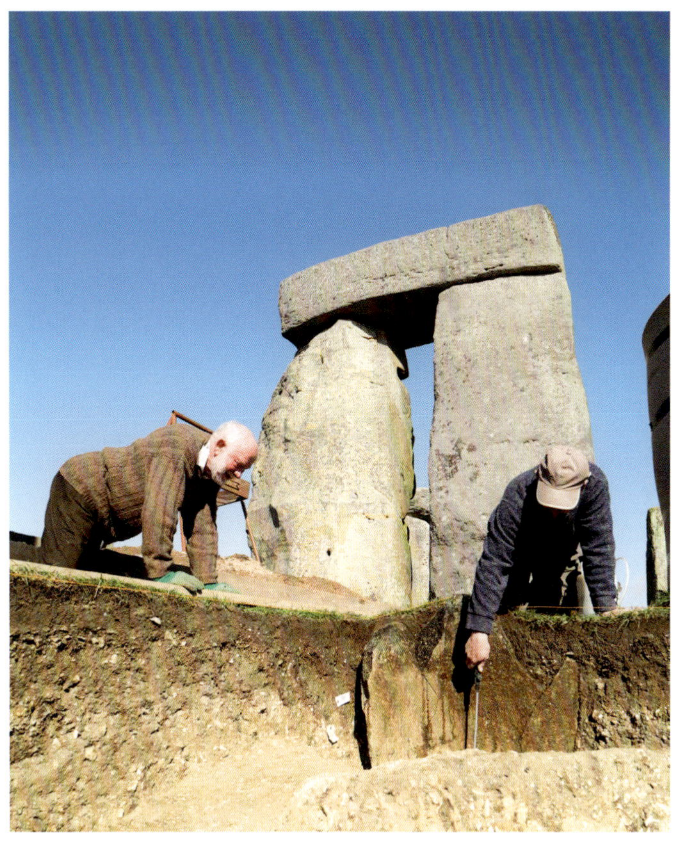

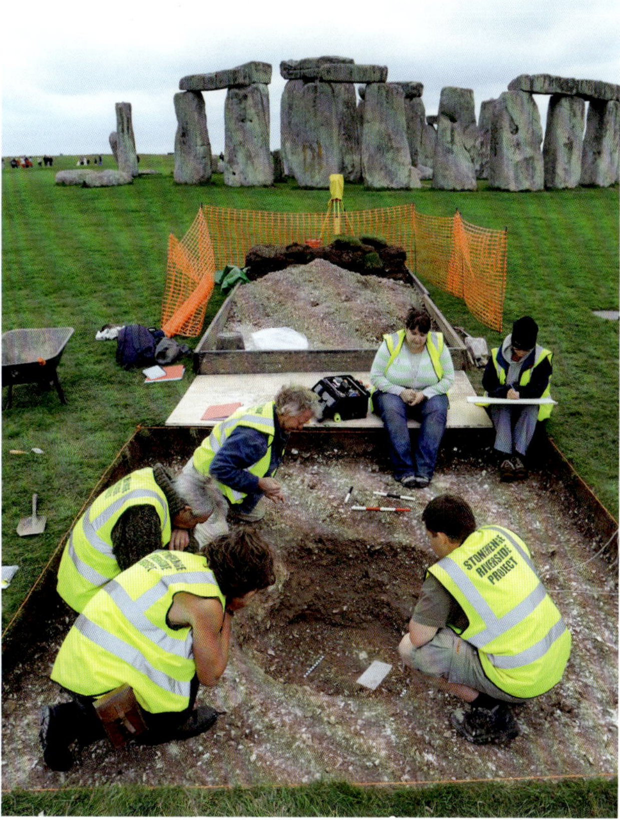

OPPOSITE This sarsen stone – one of the remaining uprights of the horseshoe of sarsen trilithons – was once distinctly hollowed at the base. To prevent further erosion, it was filled with concrete during restoration in the early 1960s. This 1964 photograph also shows the gravel surface laid within the stones at this time.

ABOVE LEFT Geoff Wainwright and Tim Darvill excavating at Stonehenge in 2008, revealing the buried stump of a bluestone.

ABOVE RIGHT Members of the Stonehenge Riverside Project team re-excavating Aubrey Hole 7 in 2008, where many cremation burials from previous excavations had been placed.

This showed that three stones in the outer circle, as well as the so-called Great Trilithon, were indeed slowly leaning and needed to be secured. So, in 1964, in the final phase of restoration at Stonehenge, all these stones were secured in concrete and the fallen sarsen in the outer circle was re-erected.

By now the ruins of Stonehenge were far easier for visitors to understand and the monument had been thoroughly investigated. Yet none of the results of the excavations at the site had been fully published. Perhaps this is one of the reasons that alternative ideas about Stonehenge flourished in the 1960s. Gerald Hawkins' 1965 book *Stonehenge Decoded* argued that the monument was a Neolithic computer for predicting eclipses, an idea endorsed by the astronomer Sir Fred Hoyle. In his 1968 book *Chariots of the Gods*, Erich von Däniken connected Stonehenge with extra-terrestrials.

Further archaeological discoveries took place in 1979, when contractors were spotted digging a trench near the Heel Stone to lay telephone cables. Luckily, the work was halted, and archaeologists were able to record the deposits uncovered, which included a large stone hole, perhaps where the Heel Stone, or another large stone, originally stood. If there had been a pair of stones here it would have framed the sunrise on Midsummer's Day. In the early 1980s excavations and the collection of artefact scatters by systematically walking recently ploughed fields took place in several nearby areas as part of the Stonehenge Environs Project. This led to a better understanding of the wider landscape, including the discovery of the Coneybury Anomaly (see page 17). The results of this project, together with the publication in 1995 of all the results of the 20th-century excavations at Stonehenge, provided a new understanding of both the monument and its surroundings.

Meanwhile, it was clear that facilities at Stonehenge were simply not adequate for the increasing numbers of visitors. Insufficient toilets and space for exhibitions or education, and a

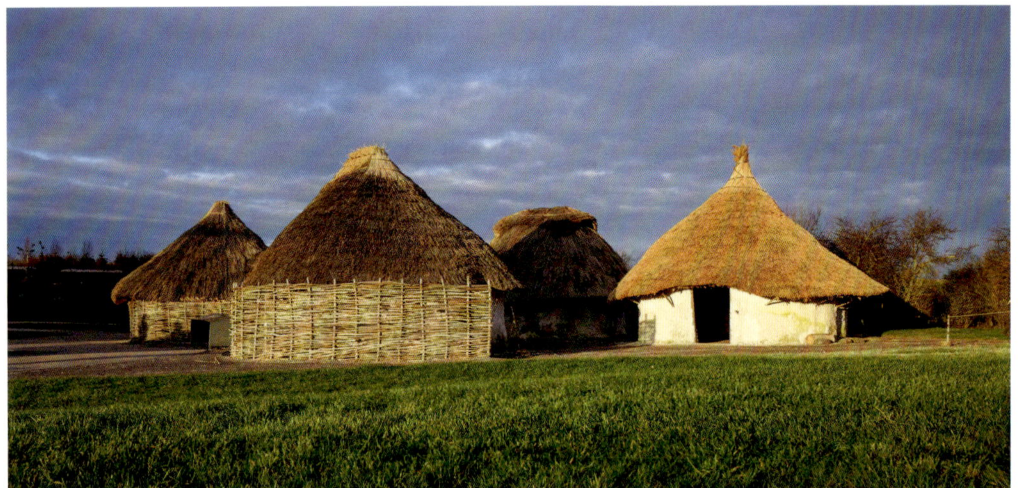

LEFT The replica Neolithic houses at Stonehenge are based on those excavated at Durrington Walls. They provide a sense of what life was like for the people who lived at the time of Stonehenge.

OPPOSITE The current visitor centre at Stonehenge, which opened in 2013, was designed by architectural practice Denton Corker Marshall to sit in the landscape unobtrusively, the many columns evoking a stand of trees.

tiny outdoor café, led the parliamentary Public Accounts Committee to label the facilities 'a national disgrace' in 1993. The roads close to Stonehenge were also becoming busier and noisier, with the A303 road near Stonehenge often forming a traffic bottleneck. In 2013, a new visitor centre was opened and the A344 – the road that passed within 60m of the stone circle – was closed to traffic. The A303 is still an unresolved issue, with a long-awaited tunnel proving an expensive and contentious solution.

In the last 25 years commercial excavations ahead of housing developments or road schemes, and university-led research projects have revealed much new archaeology relating to Stonehenge and its landscape. The Stonehenge Riverside Project (2003–9), led by Professor Mike Parker Pearson, discovered the settlement and avenue at Durrington Walls, the henge and stone circle at the end of the Avenue, and new dating evidence for the Greater Cursus. Excavations by Wessex Archaeology on Amesbury Down led to the discovery of the Amesbury Archer and Boscombe Bowmen burials as well as several monuments. Small excavations at Stonehenge itself in 2008 recovered cremation burials from Aubrey Hole 7 and uncovered part of the bluestone circle. A new causewayed enclosure was found at Larkhill in 2016 during excavations before the building of military housing. Geophysical survey across large parts of the World Heritage Site has uncovered new features, including a timber post monument and a much larger circuit of huge pits, both surrounding Durrington Walls. A laser survey of Stonehenge in 2011 revealed dozens of Bronze Age carvings on the stones. Recent geological work has pinpointed the origins of the different stones used to build the monument: sarsens from the Marlborough Downs, bluestones from specific outcrops (where quarries have been identified) on or near the Preseli Hills, Wales, and most recently the Altar Stone from north-east Scotland.

With each new discovery, our understanding of Stonehenge and its landscape improves, and each fresh piece of evidence provides answers or poses further questions – often both. Stonehenge and its surrounding landscape are a continuing focus for intense archaeological research and the extraordinary story of this place continues to be rewritten.

With each new discovery, our understanding of Stonehenge and its landscape improves, and each fresh piece of evidence provides answers or poses further questions – often both.

OVERLEAF Visitors greet the sunrise at the summer solstice, June 2021. People from around the world are given free access to the stone circle at both the summer and winter solstices.

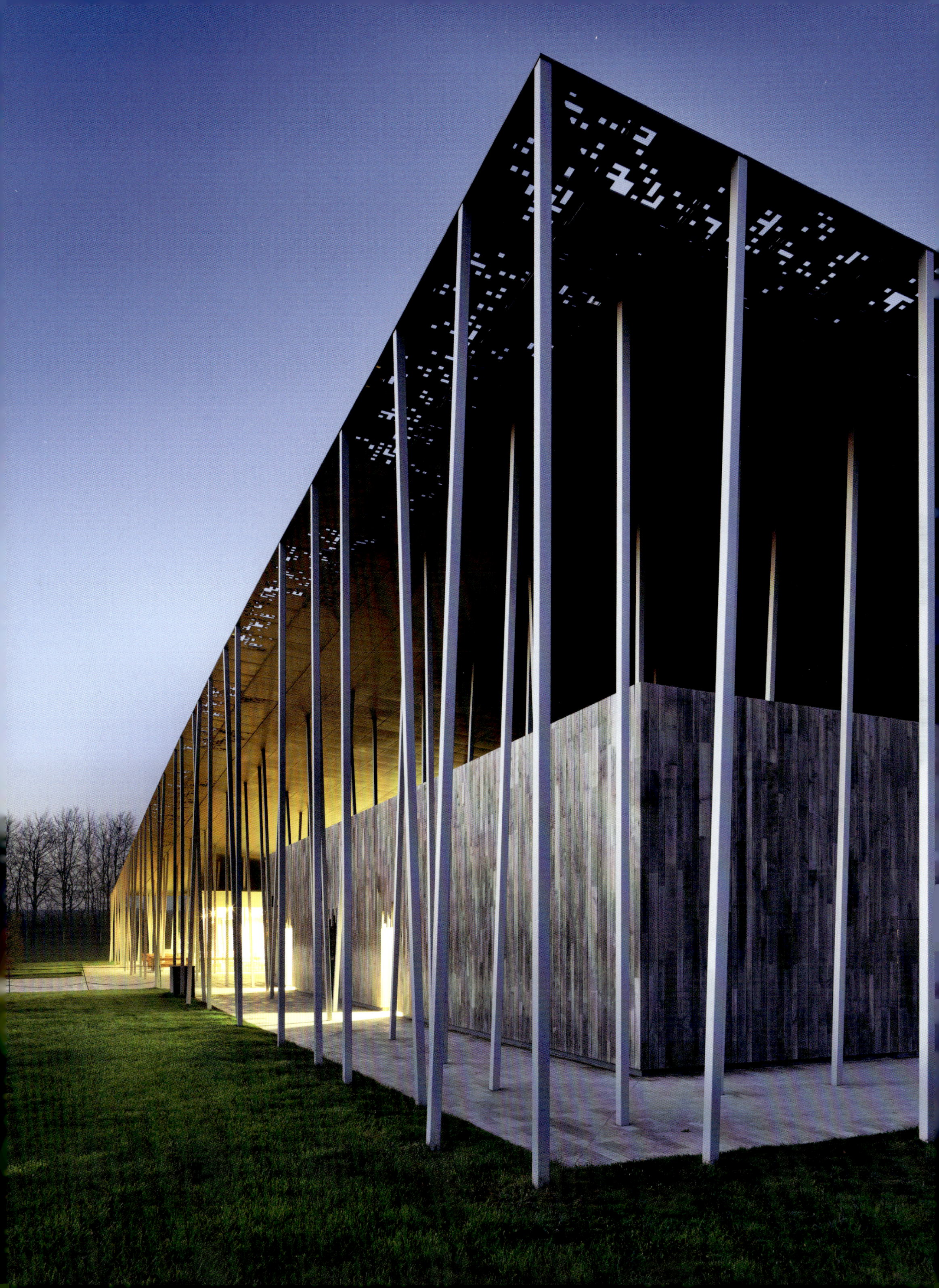

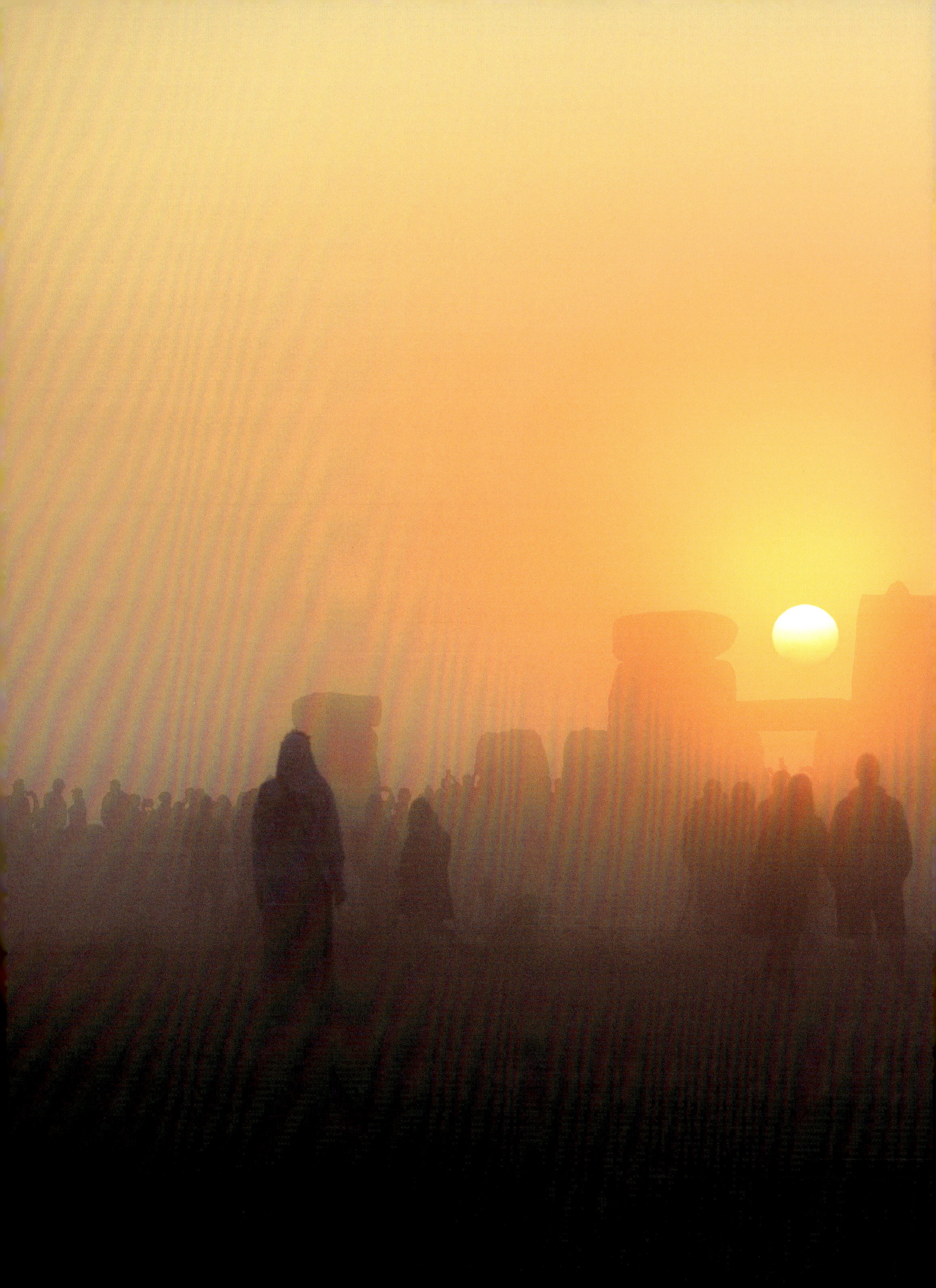

The Stonehenge Free Festival (1974–84)

In the 1970s Stonehenge became a popular gathering place for the countercultural movement, including 'hippie' groups seeking an alternative lifestyle. The Stonehenge Free Festival, an encampment that celebrated music, love, and free thinking, was held over a few weeks every summer between 1974 and 1984.

The festival at Stonehenge was part of the wider Free Festival movement of the 1970s, which sought to create alternative and utopian communal ways of living. The first festival in 1974 was the initiative of 'Wally Hope', an experimental and anarchist philosopher, whose followers called themselves 'the Wallies of Wessex'. With each successive year, the Stonehenge Free Festival grew, until it became a major event, attracting up to 30,000 people in 1984. The festival was a celebration of various alternative cultures and included live music, open drug use and free love. Bands such as Hawkwind, The Damned and Dexys Midnight Runners all performed here, and the event culminated at the summer solstice itself, when the monument was often overrun.

With numbers increasing every year, the police, English Heritage and the National Trust became increasingly concerned about activities such as drug dealing, cars being set alight and extensive damage to the archaeological monuments in the area. In 1985, English Heritage and the National Trust gained a High Court injunction to prevent the festival from taking place at the monument. To enforce it, the police set up an exclusion zone around Stonehenge, with roadblocks on the approach roads.

Tensions that had been building for more than a decade between the police and travellers attending Free Festivals came to a head. On 1 June a large 'peace convoy' of about 600 people and their vehicles heading for Stonehenge were halted at a roadblock seven miles (11km) away. A violent confrontation followed, which became known as the Battle of the Beanfield, with the police smashing vehicle windows, destroying property and hitting people with truncheons. Many people were injured, including some police officers, and 537 people were arrested. The standoff lasted for only a few hours, but still resonates today. The Stonehenge Free Festival was never held again, although open access to Stonehenge for solstice celebrations was restored in 1999.

With each successive year, the Stonehenge Free Festival grew, until it became a major event, attracting up to 30,000 people in 1984.

BELOW On 1 June 1985 a policeman leads a distraught mother and child away from the beanfield where a violent confrontation was taking place between the police and Free Festival attendees. The festival would never take place again.

OPPOSITE TOP People dance to the music of a fiddle near Stonehenge during the summer solstice, 1979.

OPPOSITE BOTTOM Stonehenge Free Festival at the summer solstice, 1979. Beyond the tents can be seen the visitor car park with a temporary toilet block.

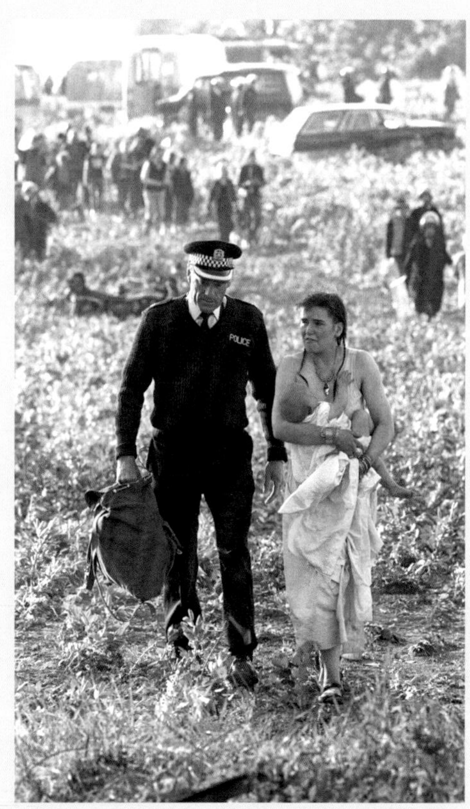

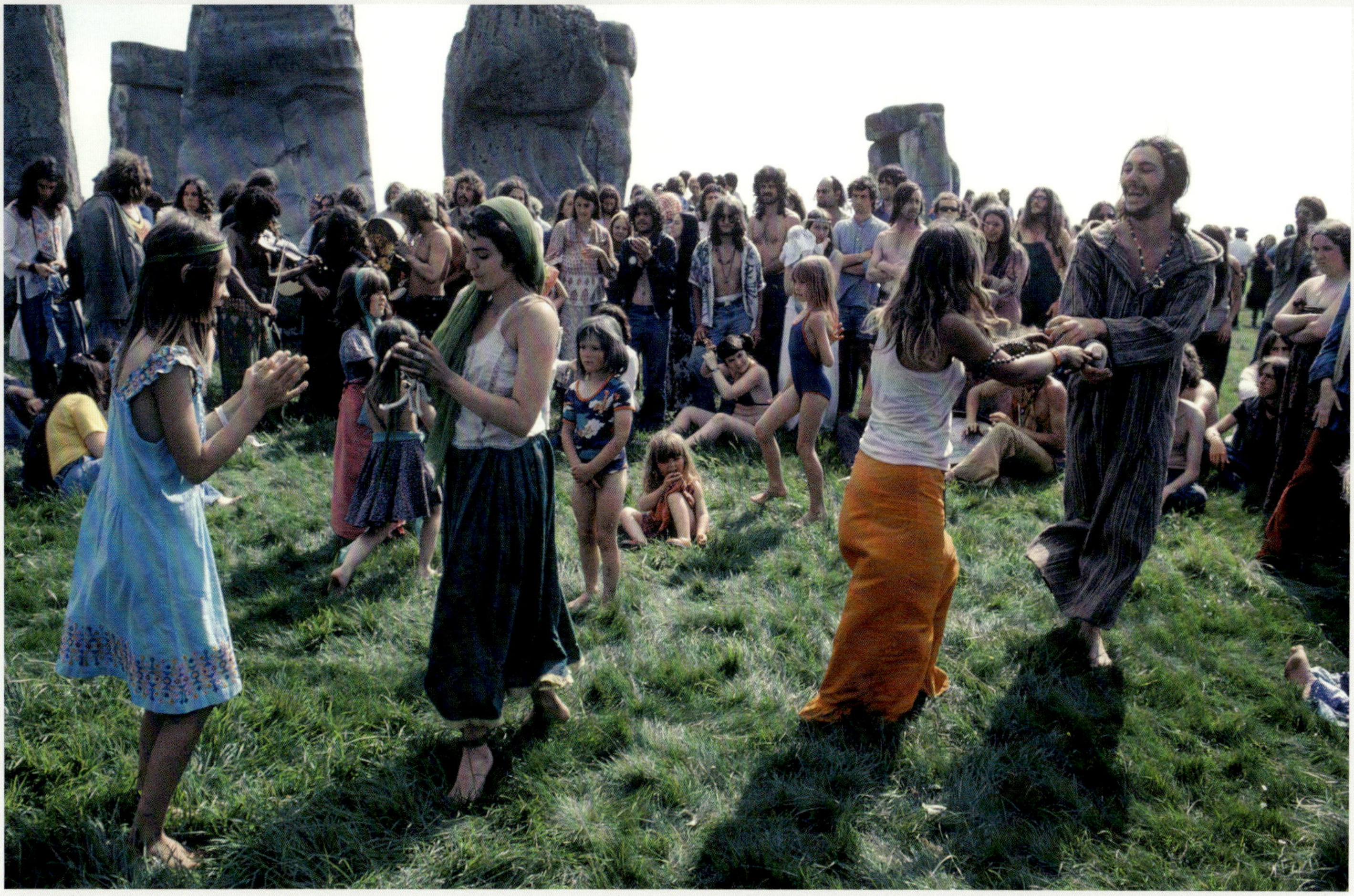

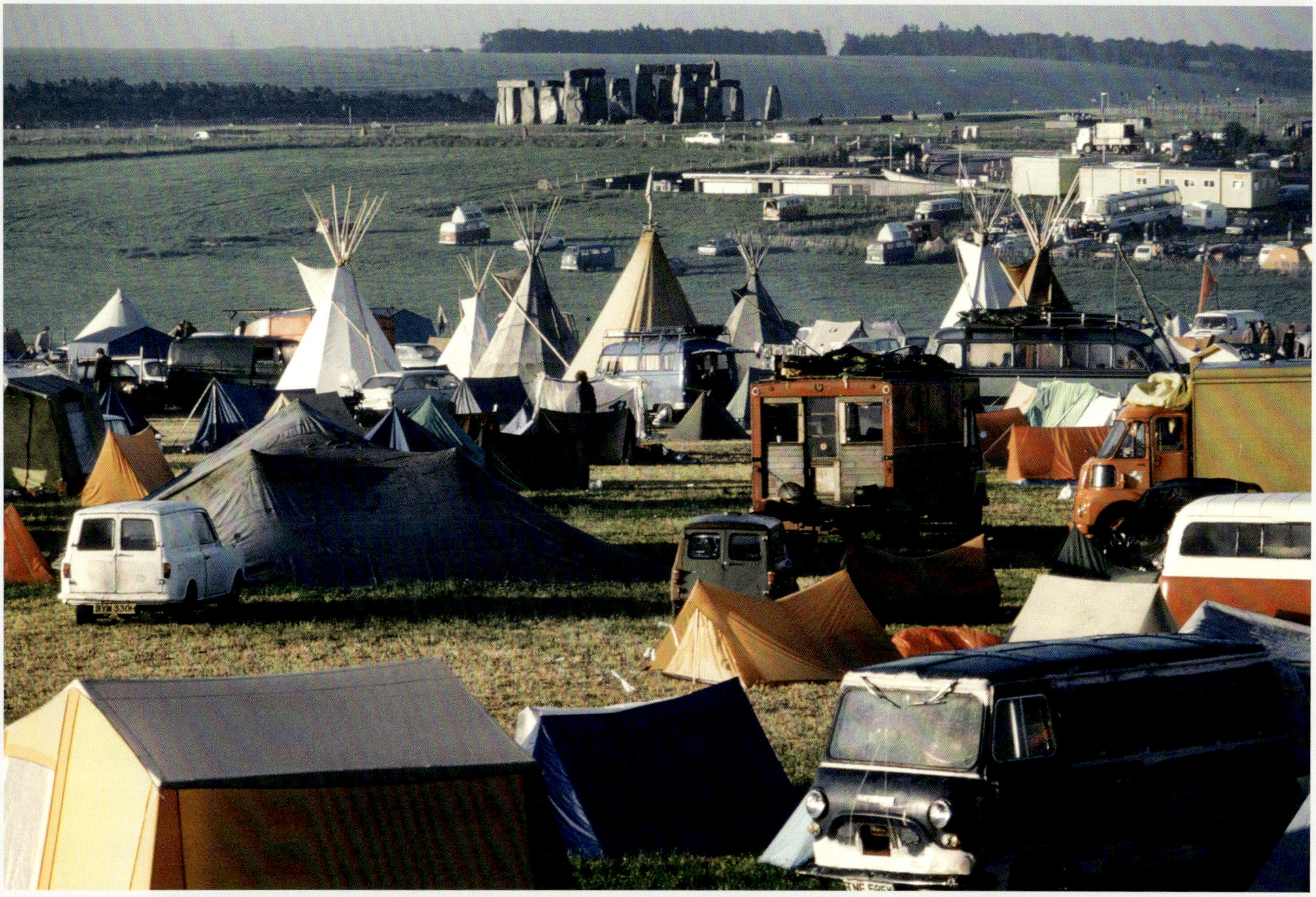

A World Heritage Site

In 1986, Stonehenge was inscribed, together with Avebury, as a World Heritage Site. Stonehenge is the most architecturally sophisticated prehistoric stone circle in the world, while Avebury is the largest. Together with other nearby monuments and their associated landscapes they demonstrate changing ceremonial and funerary practices over some 2,000 years of prehistory.

At Stonehenge the boundary of the World Heritage Site encompasses an area of about ten square miles, and represents one of the richest concentrations of early prehistoric features in the world.

World Heritage Sites are legally protected areas of outstanding value to humanity for their cultural or natural heritage. 'Stonehenge, Avebury and Associated Sites' were inscribed in recognition of their complexes of prehistoric monuments. Inscription as a World Heritage Site means that the British government has committed to protecting and conserving Stonehenge and Avebury for future generations. There are over 1,000 World Heritage Sites worldwide, and 31 in the United Kingdom (excluding overseas territories), including Hadrian's Wall, Ironbridge Gorge and the city of Bath.

The protected area that includes Stonehenge comprises two parts lying about 17 miles (28km) apart – one around the monument of Avebury in north Wiltshire and the other around Stonehenge in south Wiltshire. At Stonehenge the boundary of the World Heritage Site encompasses an area of about ten square miles, and represents one of the richest concentrations of early prehistoric features in the world. It includes over 400 monuments, including Stonehenge and its Avenue, Durrington Walls, Woodhenge, the Greater and Lesser Cursus monuments and many round barrows. The Avebury World Heritage Site covers just under ten square miles and includes the causewayed enclosure at Windmill Hill, West Kennet Avenue and Long Barrow, the henge and stone circles at Avebury, the huge mound of Silbury Hill and the stone and timber circle of the Sanctuary.

Although much of the land within the World Heritage Site at Stonehenge is owned by charities, including English Heritage, the National Trust and the Royal Society for the Protection of Birds (RSPB), much is owned and managed by individual landowners and farmers. This is a dynamic landscape, where people live and work. Its World Heritage Site designation comes with a management plan to guide these landowners and other interested parties in the sustainable conservation and protection of the site for future generations.

The Management Plan for the Stonehenge World Heritage Site, created in 2000, set out a vision to provide a new, high-quality visitor centre, to remove roads from the vicinity of Stonehenge, and to ensure that all farmland at the core of the site would be restored to permanent grassland. Significant progress has been achieved in all these areas, although the busy A303 still runs close to the monument.

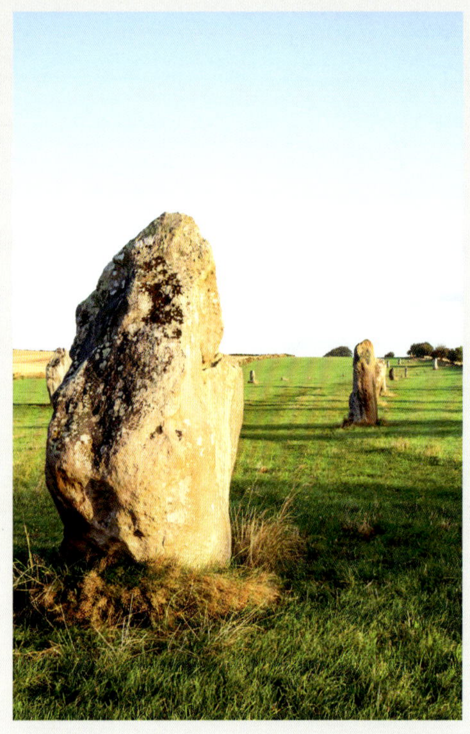

ABOVE The West Kennet Avenue leads south-west from the stone circles and henge at Avebury, linking this monument with the stone and timber circles at the Sanctuary.

OPPOSITE The interior of the West Kennet Long Barrow, where at least 36 men, women and children were buried in the early Neolithic period.

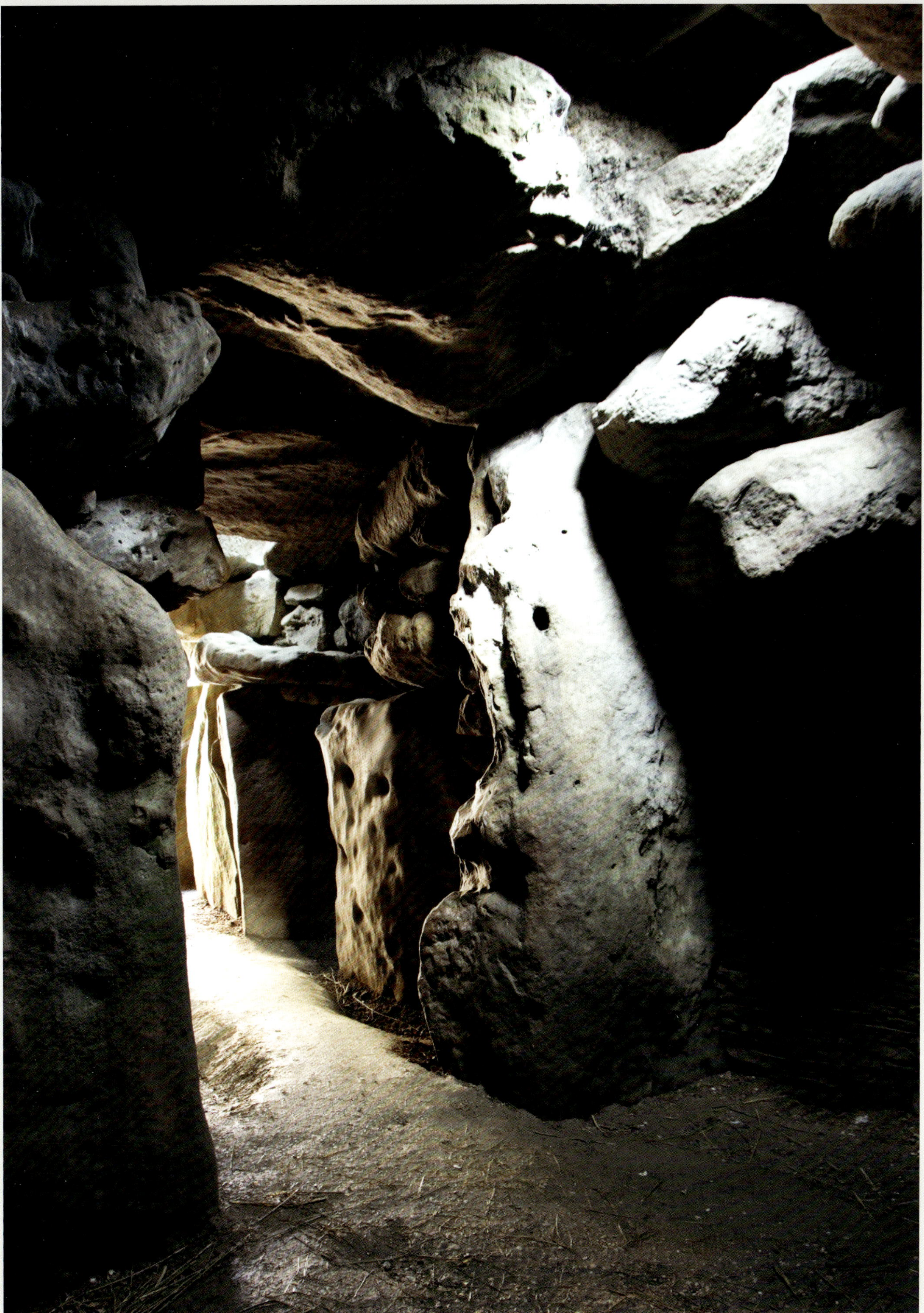

Conservation and Nature

The landscape around Stonehenge is a rich tapestry of chalk grassland and arable fields cut by the wooded valley of the river Avon. Much of this land is owned and cared for by the National Trust which, together with English Heritage, has a long-term vision of returning Stonehenge to a more tranquil and rural setting.

When Stonehenge was built, this area was largely open grazed grassland, not unlike the landscape today. The evidence for this comes from analysing ancient environmental material, such as pollen grains, charred plant remains and the shells of particular species of land snails, collected during excavations. Since 1928, when fields around Stonehenge were first given to the National Trust, the charity has continued to increase its landholdings by buying land in the immediate area to protect it from development and to restore former arable land to chalk pasture. Hundreds of acres have been restored to grassland, protecting vulnerable archaeological earthworks from damage and allowing the landscape to return to a condition closer to its prehistoric state.

THIS PAGE The chalk grassland of the Stonehenge landscape has been carefully restored by the National Trust, to encourage flowers, insects, butterflies and ground-nesting birds.

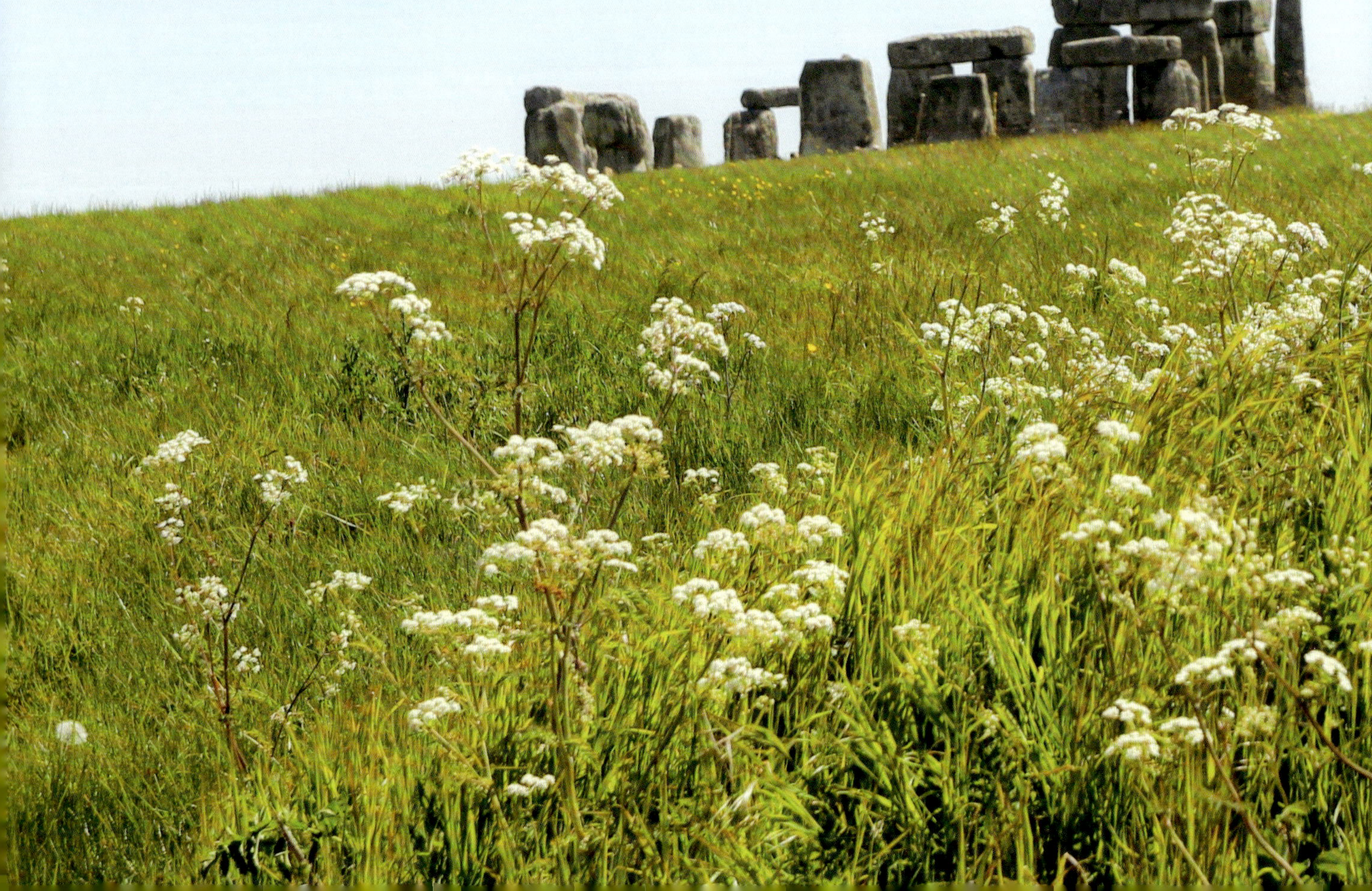

These rare, flower-rich chalk grasslands provide important habitats for a variety of bird, insect and animal species.

These rare, flower-rich chalk grasslands provide important habitats for a variety of bird, insect and animal species. Wildflowers, such as orchids, horseshoe vetch, wild thyme and harebell, can be found here, as well as rare butterflies, including the Adonis blue and marsh fritillary. The melodious song of the skylark pierces the sky above Stonehenge for much of the year and lucky visitors may spot a great bustard, a large bird that was once extinct in Britain, but which has since been reintroduced to Salisbury Plain from Russia and Spain. Other birds, such as quail, stone curlew, lapwing, corn bunting and grey partridge, can all be found in the wider landscape, and the Royal Society for the Protection of Birds (RSPB) manages a reserve on Normanton Down specifically for these species. Mammals such as brown hares and red deer are also frequent visitors.

For English Heritage, the National Trust and other landowners, management of the Stonehenge landscape is a careful balance of protecting the archaeological monuments, maintaining important habitats for nature, and providing access for visitors.

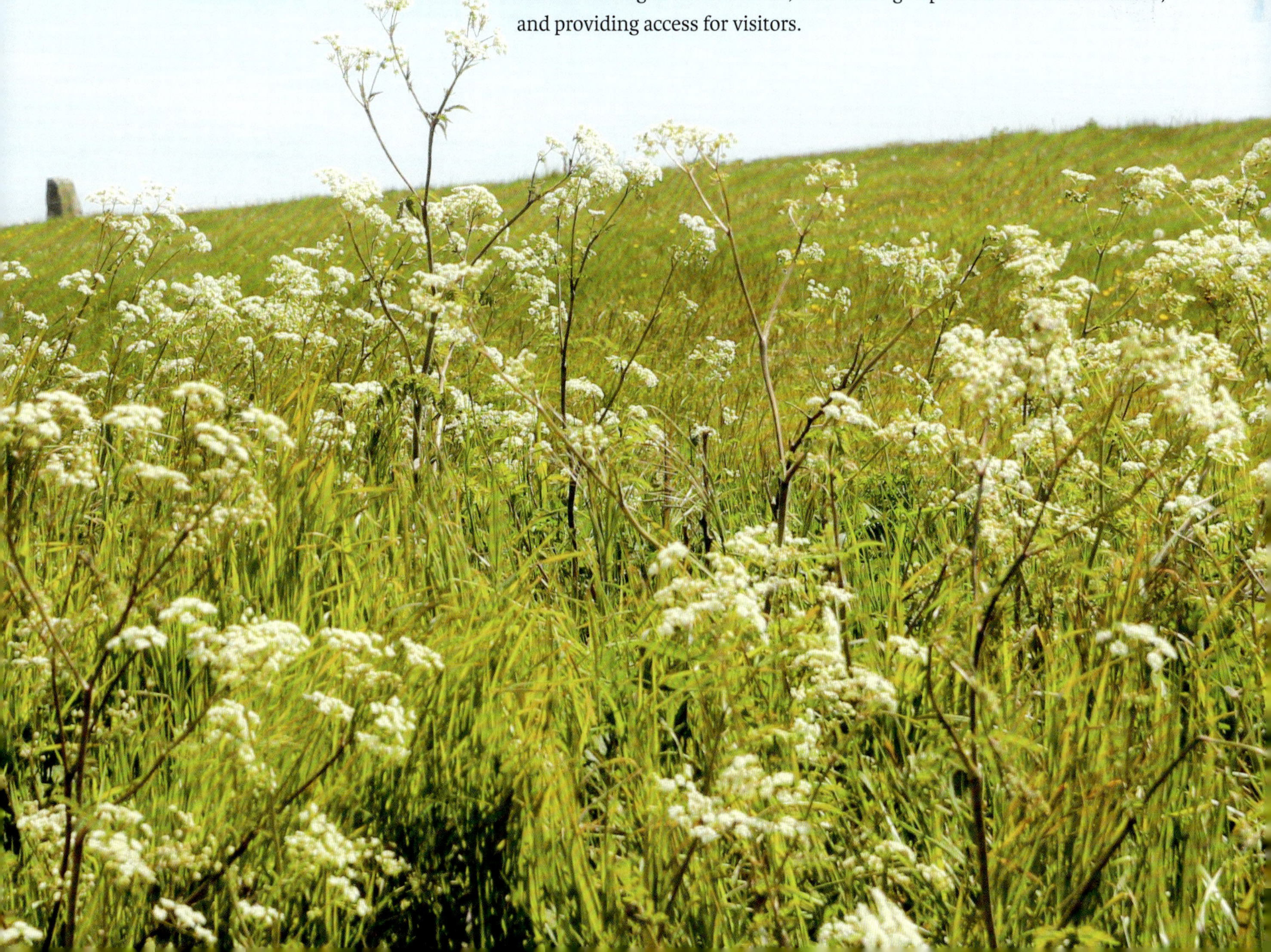

Local Connections

To fully appreciate the archaeology and setting of Stonehenge, it is worth taking the time to explore the local landscape, other nearby prehistoric sites and important local museums.

BELOW Walkers exploring an early Bronze Age burial mound, part of the Cursus Barrow cemetery, within the open access land managed by the National Trust.

Exploring the local landscape is rewarding not only for the spectacular views of Stonehenge set amid rolling chalk downland, but also because many other prehistoric monuments are easily accessible. Much of the land is owned and managed by the National Trust to preserve the archaeology, and is open to visitors on foot. People can see for themselves monuments such as the Stonehenge Avenue, the Greater Cursus and many of the Bronze Age barrows. The enormous earthworks of the henge at Durrington Walls, and the site of Woodhenge, the positions of its timbers now marked by concrete posts, are well worth visiting.

The Salisbury Museum, adjacent to the spectacular Salisbury Cathedral, houses many of the finds from excavations at Stonehenge. The museum's 'Wessex Gallery' includes artefacts from the Coneybury Anomaly, Durrington Walls, and the Amesbury Archer burial. In Devizes, Wiltshire Museum has displays of the spectacular artefacts found by antiquaries in barrows in the area, including from Bush Barrow and many other important Bronze Age sites.

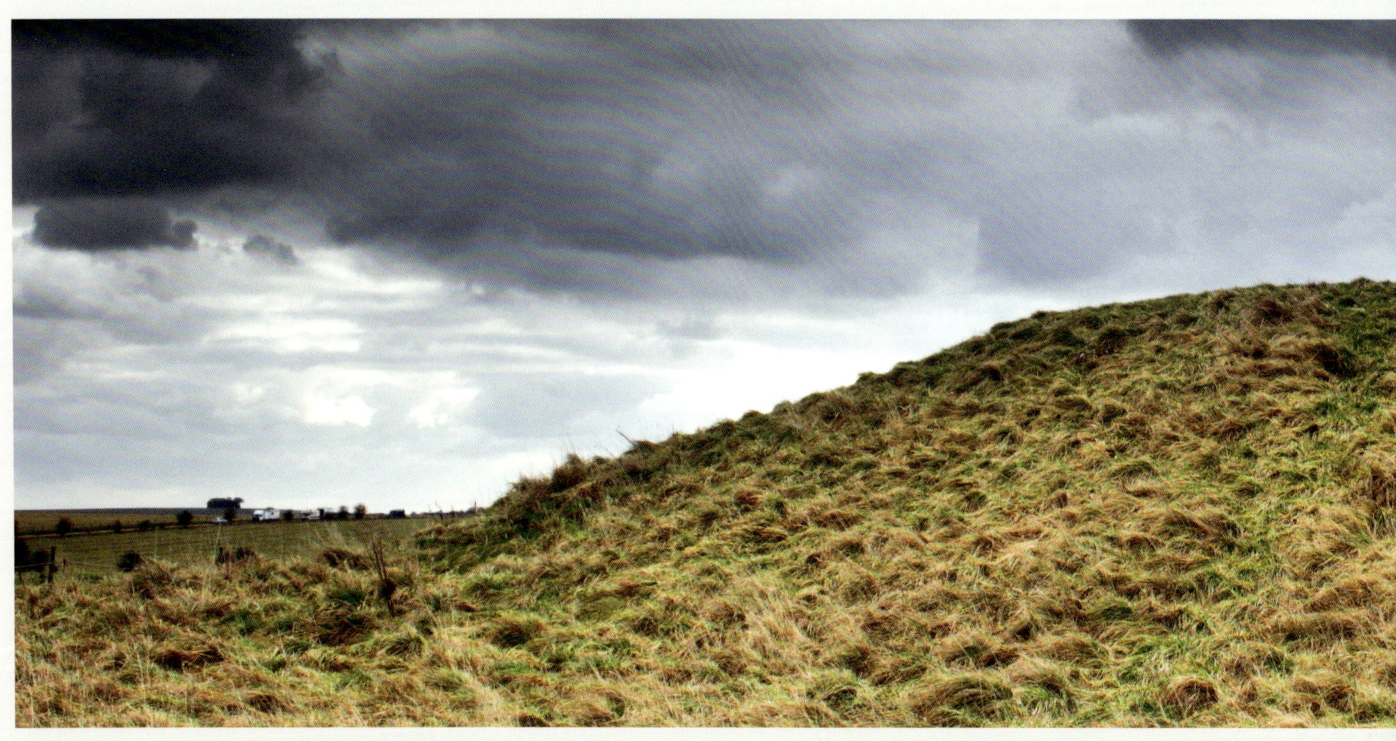

Much of the land is ... open to visitors on foot. People can see for themselves monuments such as the Stonehenge Avenue, the Greater Cursus and many of the Bronze Age barrows.

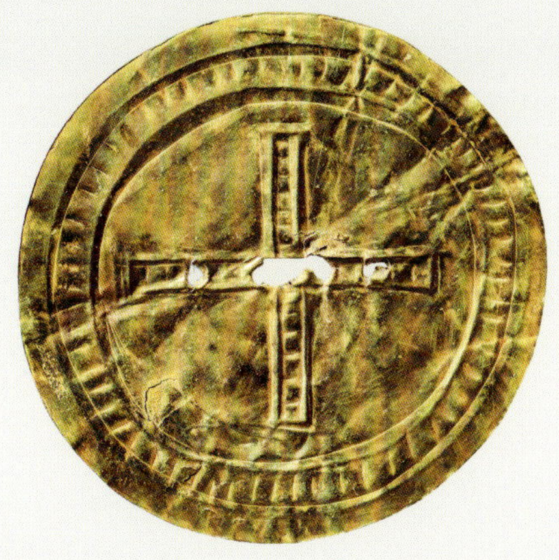

ABOVE This gold sun-disc, dating from the early Bronze Age, was found in a round barrow at Monkton Farleigh, near Bath, in 1947, and is on display at Wiltshire Museum.

The Avebury monument complex, 17 miles (28km) to the north, forms the other part of the World Heritage Site. Here, the henge was built at the same time as Stonehenge but it is much larger (part of a village now lies inside the earthwork enclosure), and contains one large stone circle and two smaller ones. Walking routes in the nearby landscape allow visitors to explore early Neolithic sites such as the causewayed enclosure at Windmill Hill and the chambered long barrow at West Kennet, as well as monuments contemporary with Avebury, including the avenues, the Sanctuary and the enormous artificial mound of Silbury Hill. Finds from these sites are displayed in the Alexander Keiller Museum in Avebury.

Those with an interest in the Neolithic period may want to seek out some of the lesser-known sites in or near the Vale of Pewsey, the low-lying valley between Avebury and Stonehenge. These include the enormous earthwork henge at Marden (Hatfield Earthworks), the causewayed enclosure at Knap Hill with nearby Adam's Grave long barrow, and West Woods, where the sarsen stones of Stonehenge were probably obtained. These earthworks and sites are just the visible remnants of millennia of monument building and other activities that took place in this area during the Neolithic and early Bronze Age, much of the evidence for which remains hidden below ground.

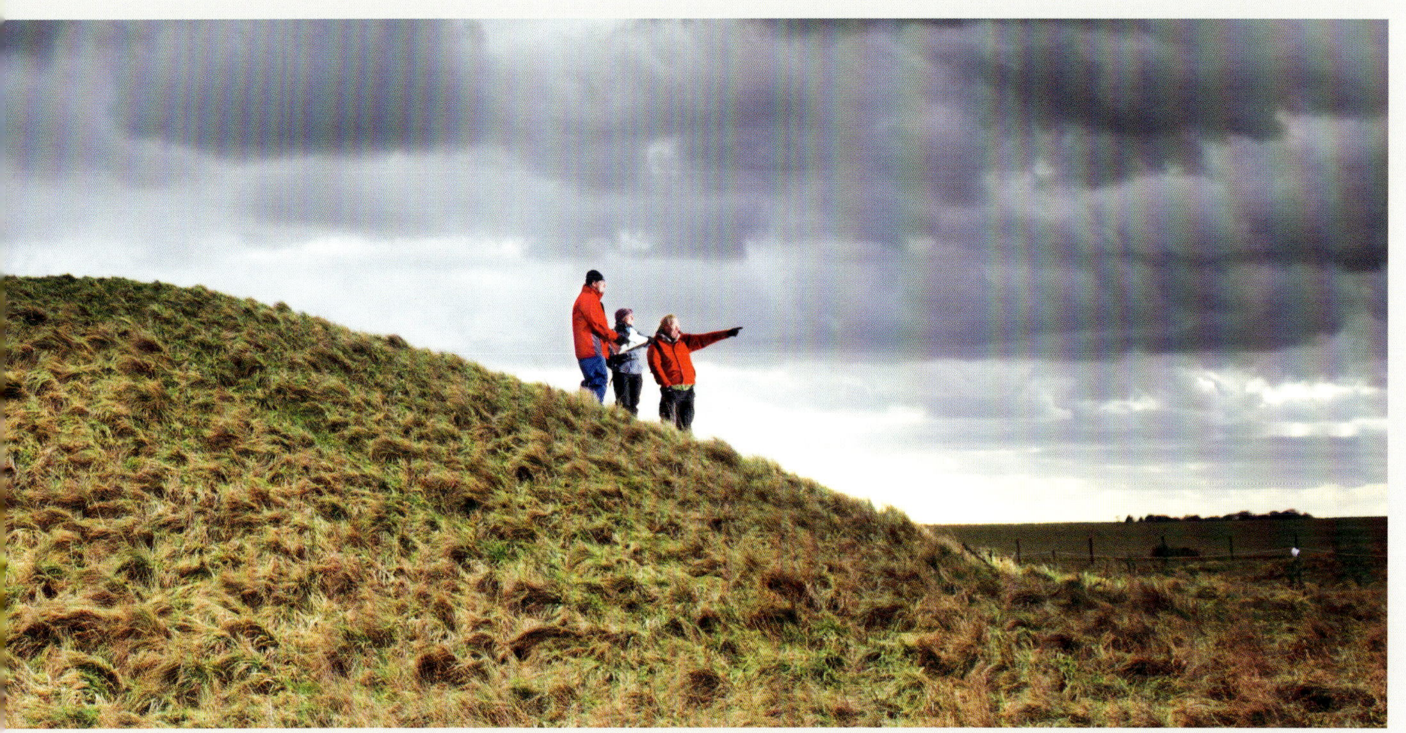

THE STORY CONTINUES

Stonehenge is often thought of as a place so unfathomable and mysterious that it will never be truly understood – somewhere to merely inspire wonder and admiration; a site of unanswerable questions. In recent years, however, archaeology, in the form of traditional excavation and scientific analysis, has provided fascinating new insights about the site. The more we understand about Stonehenge and its surrounding landscape, the more interesting it becomes.

Our understanding of Stonehenge and the people who built it has come a long way in the centuries since early antiquaries first began to study the stones and pose questions about the monument: who built it and how? When was it made and what was it for? Much progress has been made, but this is not a static story – our picture of Stonehenge and its surrounding landscape is constantly evolving. Archaeologists continue to make new discoveries in the field or in the museum store, working alongside geologists, biologists and chemists to apply innovative techniques. Over the last 25 years there have been countless excavations, surveys and research projects that have added to our understanding.

We now know that Stonehenge was adapted, changed and altered over more than 1,000 years during the Neolithic and early Bronze Age, with several different phases of construction and use. We have revealed that its meaning and purpose changed over time, at first being a sacred space for the burial of the dead and later becoming a temple precisely aligned on the movements of the sun. We now understand that the people who built Stonehenge were part of a well-travelled, creative and resourceful community, who were able to dedicate time and energy to coming together, gathering materials, holding great feasts and creating spectacular structures. Their religious beliefs must have been a fundamental part of their lives, closely relating to the sun and the changing seasons of the farming year. The landscape around Stonehenge is full of evidence for other temples and structures that they built and the places where they lived.

More and more evidence is coming to light that the Stonehenge landscape was a place of pilgrimage, an important node in the vibrant social and cultural network of late Neolithic Britain and Ireland. This is shown by the long-distance transport of stones from south-west Wales and north-east Scotland, revealed by new geological analysis, and the herding of cattle and pigs over many miles from across Britain for the great feasts at Durrington Walls, revealed through chemical analysis of their teeth. Stonehenge was clearly a central place within a complex web of connections, around which flowed ideas, artefacts and practices. Close study of the stones at Stonehenge has given us insight into the back-breaking and arduous labour of those who built the monument, far from home but fuelled by feasts and inspired by ceremonies and rituals.

OPPOSITE A pink sunset illuminates two sarsens of the outer stone circle with their lintel. Several species of lichen, some of them rare, grow on the stones.

We have revealed that the meaning and purpose of the monument changed over time, at first being a sacred space for the burial of the dead and later becoming a temple precisely aligned on the movements of the sun.

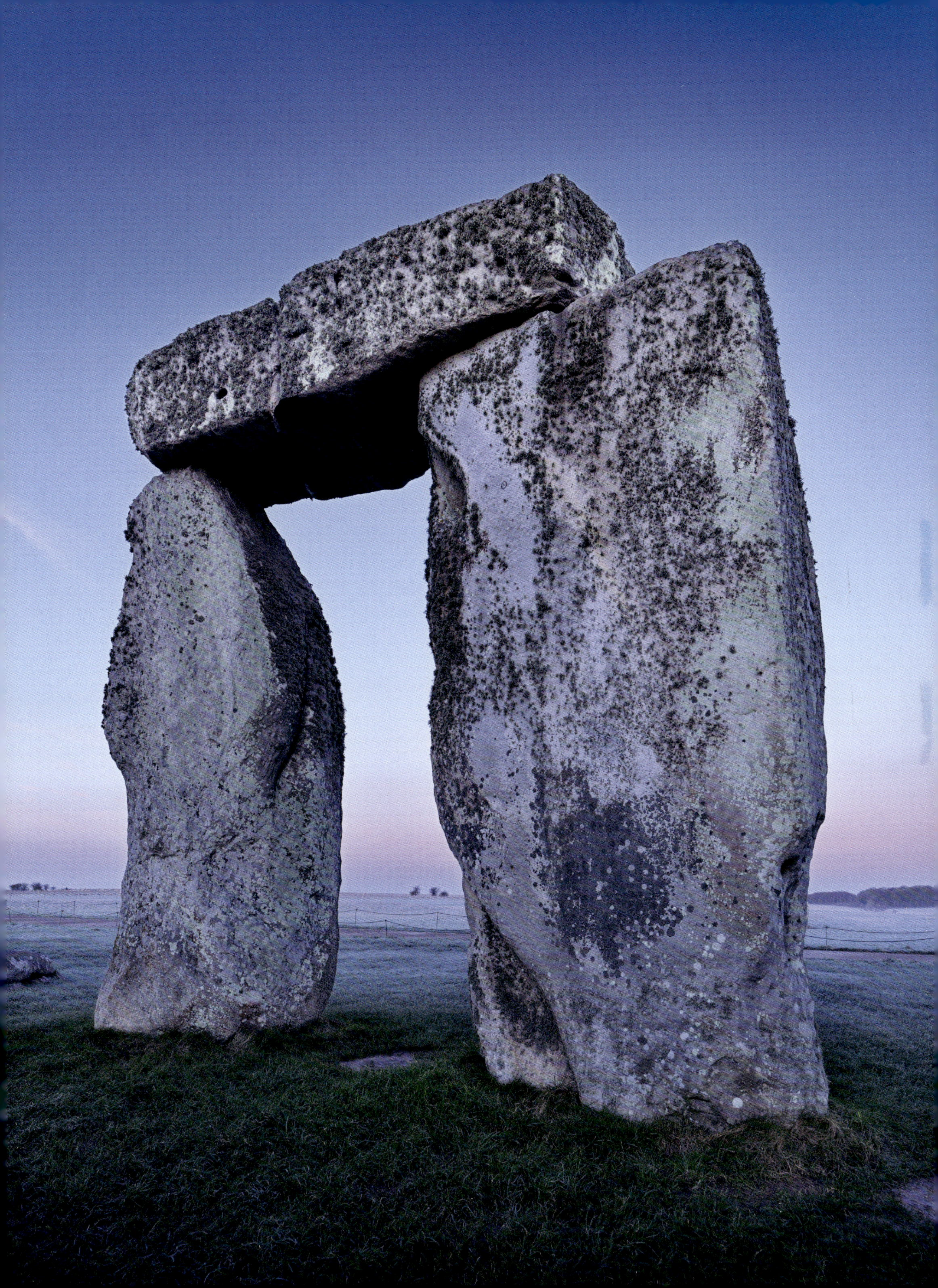

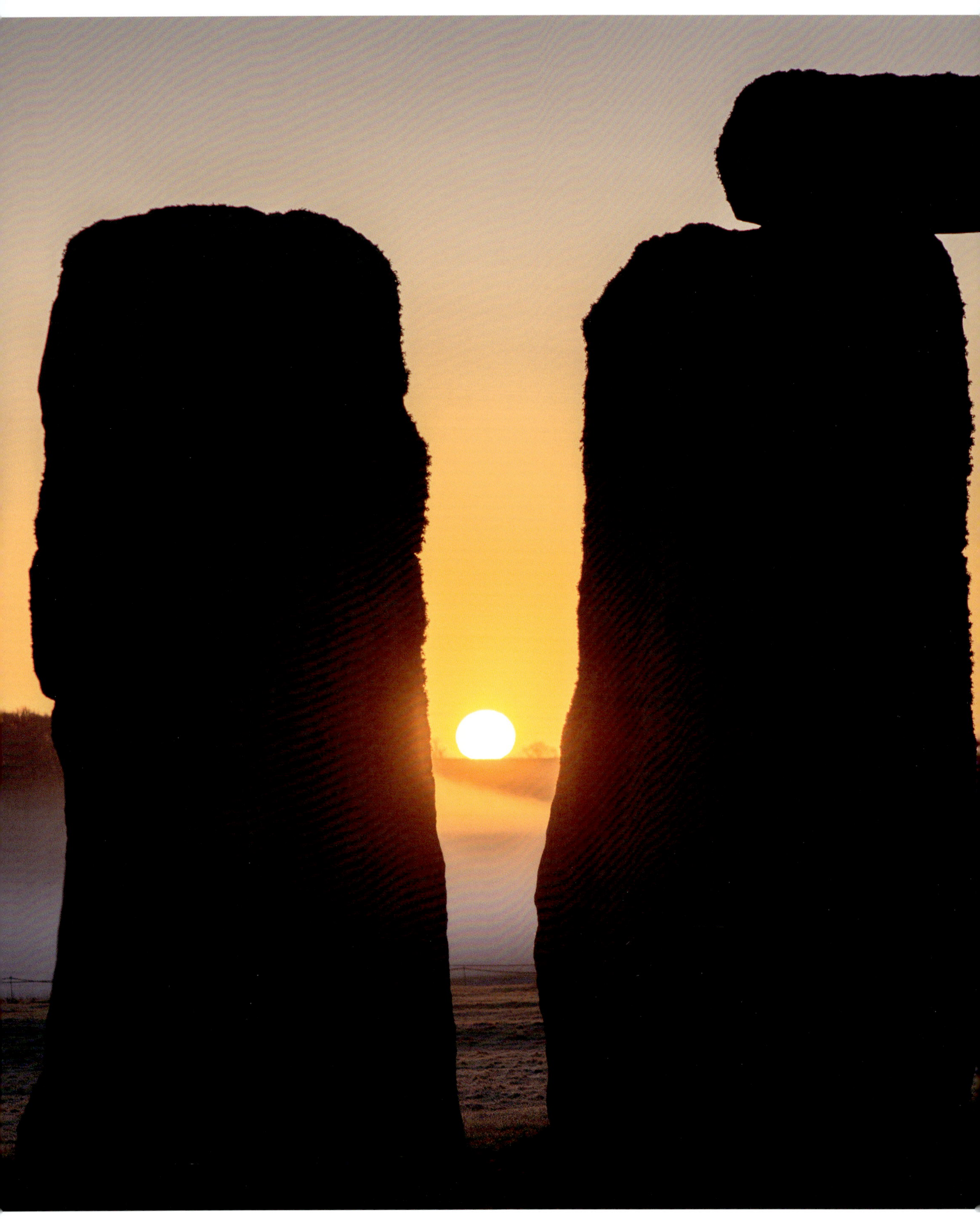

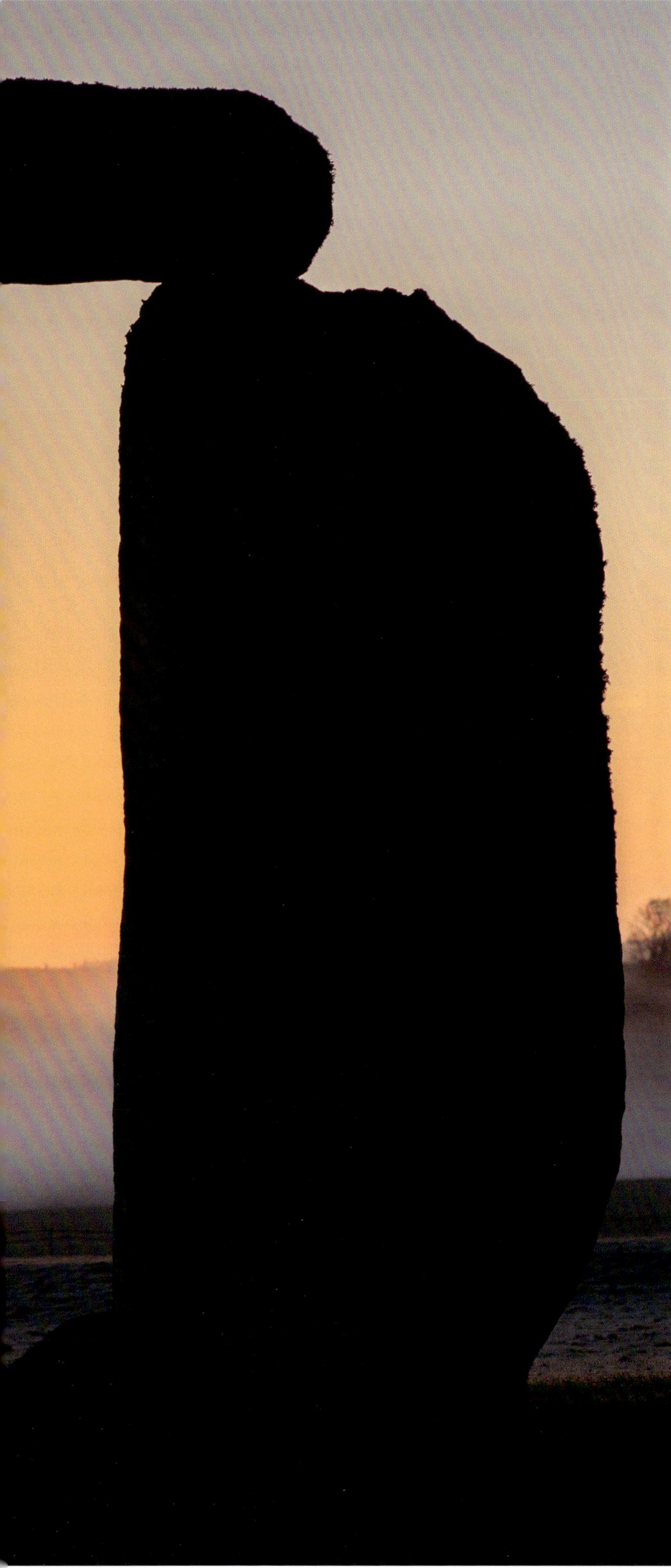

LEFT Stones of the outer sarsen circle silhouetted against the morning sunrise.

We know that the importance of this place continued into the Chalcolithic, with the first arrivals from Continental Europe bringing their Beaker pots and new metals to this area. DNA analysis has shown that, at first, these newcomers lived largely separately from the descendants of those who had built Stonehenge, only truly integrating after 200 years or so. New techniques for analysing metal artefacts show that, in the Bronze Age, gold and tin from the south-west were hugely important in trading networks, which probably involved the individuals who were buried with spectacular objects under the many round barrows that surround Stonehenge.

All these new discoveries mean that no longer is Stonehenge a place of mystery, but a place of discovery, a well-studied and understood landscape. As research continues and scientific techniques are developed and refined, we can look forward to further new understandings and discoveries.

Today, Stonehenge continues to attract travellers, artists and believers who celebrate and marvel at this spectacular monument. Learning about Stonehenge and the people who built it can provide a valuable perspective on our own lives. We can imagine another way of being, when people were more closely connected with the seasons and natural resources and worked together on extraordinary projects. Despite their own societies perhaps being unstable and short-lived, some of the monuments built by these people have endured for thousands of years, witnesses to millennia of human history.

Stonehenge, as a World Heritage Site, is counted among the most important surviving creations in the whole of human history and is a fitting symbol for the extraordinary achievements of these prehistoric people.

A TIMELINE OF STONEHENGE

MESOLITHIC (9700–4000 BC)

Hunter-gatherer communities move through the landscape leaving ephemeral traces of settlement and hunting activities.

c.8000–7500 BC Line of four large pits near Stonehenge

Mesolithic people mark this place by digging pits.

c.7500–4500 BC Settlement and hunting camp at Blick Mead

Mesolithic people repeatedly return to live beside a spring, leaving behind settlement debris including the bones of aurochs. [1]

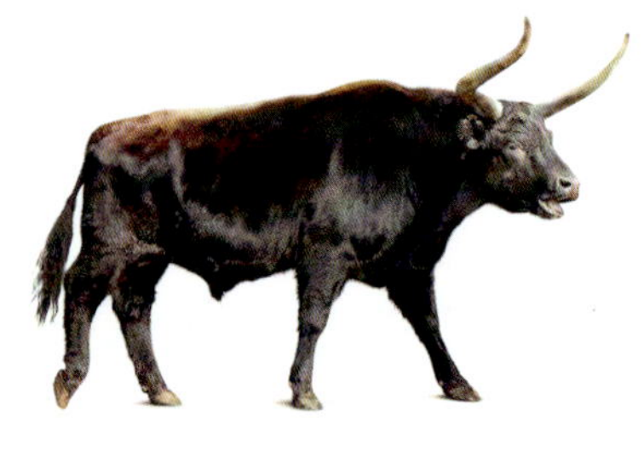

1

EARLY NEOLITHIC (4000–3200 BC)

Communities arrive in Britain bringing with them farming practices. Later, various types of large-scale communal monuments are built in the landscape around Stonehenge.

c.4000 BC Arrival of first farmers in Britain

Domesticated animals, crops and pottery are brought into Britain for the first time.

c.3800–3700 BC Coneybury Anomaly

A group of people, probably both farmers and hunter-gatherers, hold a feast and place the refuse in a pit. [2]

c.3780–3600 BC Causewayed enclosures

Two causewayed enclosures, now known as Robin Hood's Ball and Larkhill, are built within 3 miles (5km) of Stonehenge, probably as communal gathering places. [3]

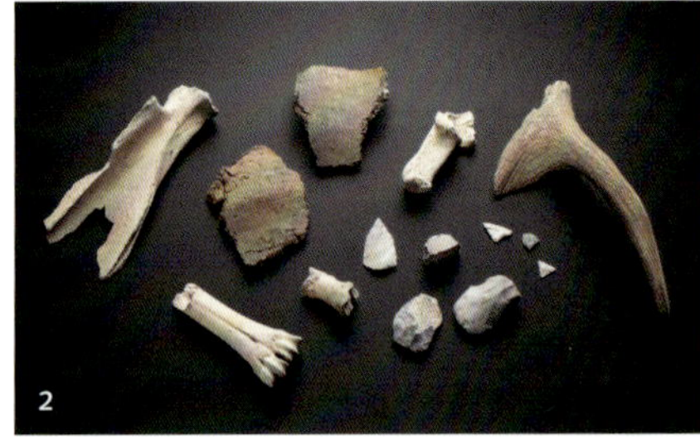

2

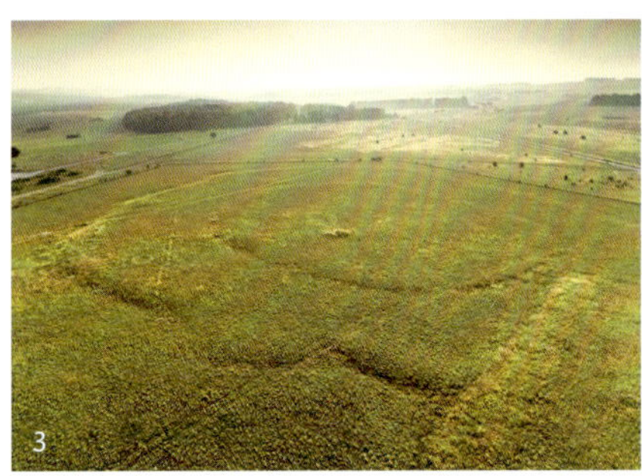

3

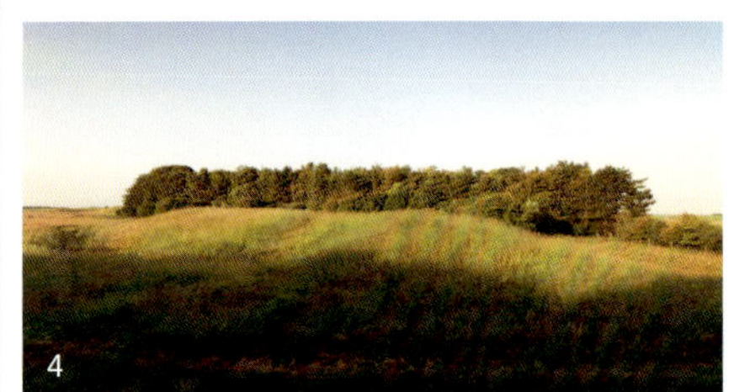

4

c.3700–3300 BC Long barrows

Long barrows, such as Winterbourne Stoke Crossroads Long Barrow, are built. These monuments are usually made to house the dead. [4]

c.3600–3350 BC Cursus monuments

Two huge rectangular enclosures (now known as the Greater and Lesser Cursuses) are built within 1.8 miles (3km) of Stonehenge. Their purpose remains obscure. [5]

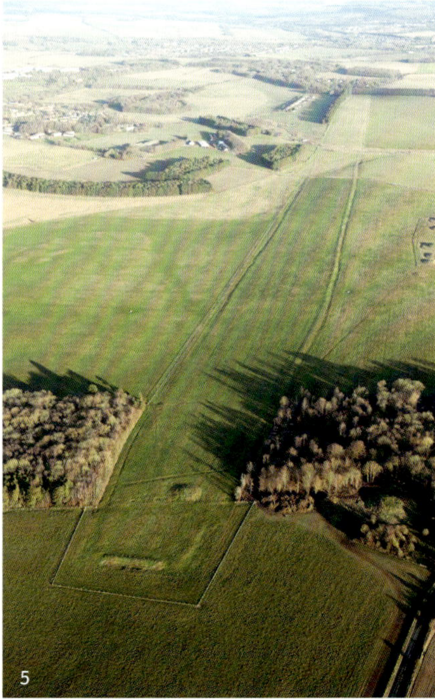

5

MIDDLE NEOLITHIC (3200–2800 BC)

After a long gap when no large monuments were built, but people continued to visit and stay in the area, Stonehenge is constructed – at first probably a simple circular bank and ditch.

c.3300–3000 BC Settlements with pits in Stonehenge landscape

Some pits contain special objects such as chalk plaques.

c.3000–2800 BC Cremations at Stonehenge

The cremated remains of an estimated 150 people are buried within the bank and ditch at Stonehenge, some accompanied by intriguing objects. [6]

c.2950–2800 BC Circular ditch completed at Stonehenge

Within it stands a circle of smaller stones – probably the bluestones – and probably a timber structure. [7]

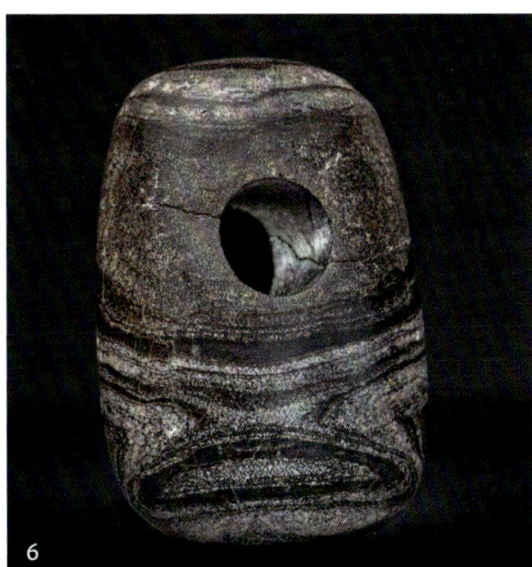
6

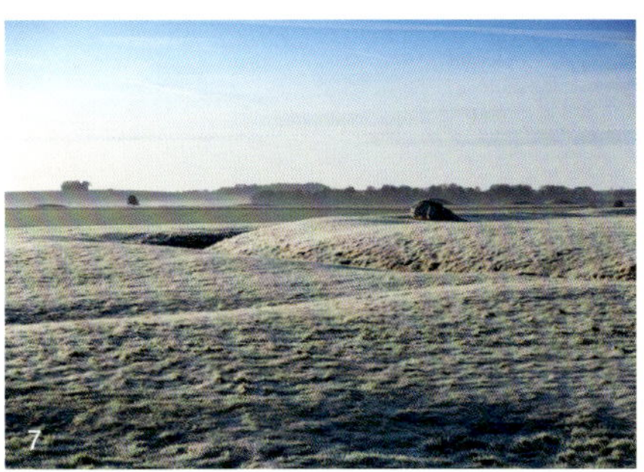
7

LATE NEOLITHIC (2800–2400 BC)

The stone circle at Stonehenge is built, along with a series of other timber and earthwork structures within the wider landscape.

c.2600–2400 BC Large-scale monument building

Across southern Britain, large and complex monuments are built. [8]

c.2500 BC Stone circle built

The huge sarsen stones are brought to Stonehenge and the bluestones are moved into position among them. [9]

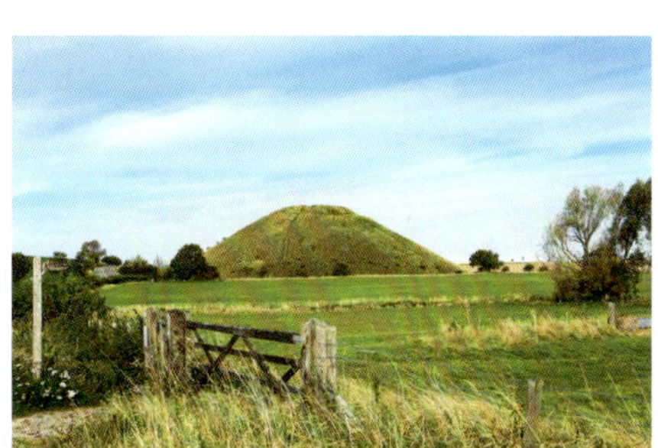
8

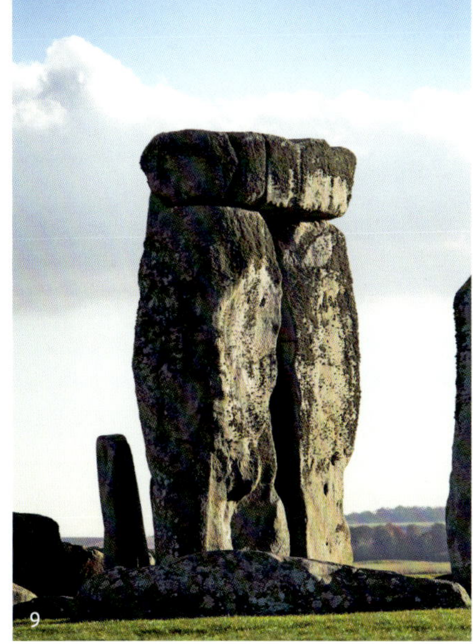
9

c.2500 BC Durrington Walls

Late Neolithic people build small houses and timber structures in a settlement 1.8 miles (3km) north-east of Stonehenge, where feasting takes place. This is later enclosed in a huge henge. [10]

c.2400–2280 BC Avenue built

This feature, a pair of parallel banks and ditches nearly 1.8 miles (3km) long, links Stonehenge to the river Avon. [11]

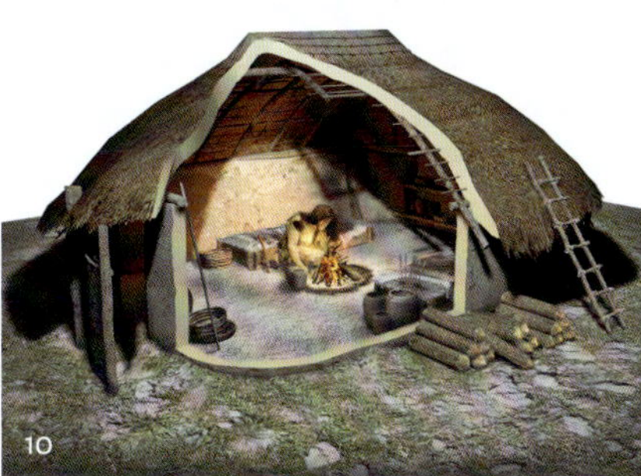
10

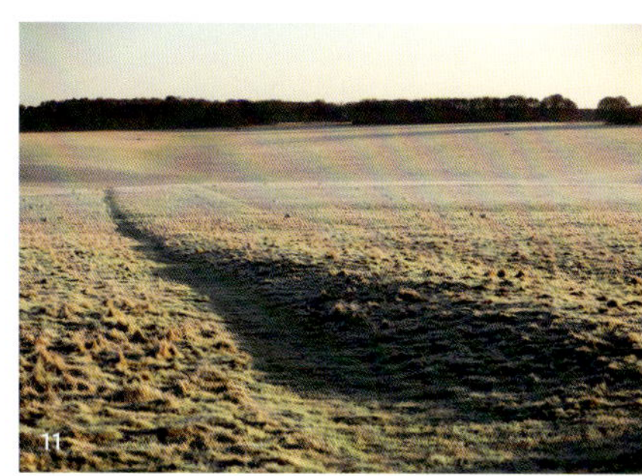
11

CHALCOLITHIC (2400–2200 BC)

People from Continental Europe arrive, bringing new objects, ideas, and artefacts with them, including the first metals and Beaker pots.

c.2400–2200 BC Beaker graves

A type of Continental burial practice, where the body is interred in the ground with Beaker pots and other grave goods, is seen in Britain for the first time. [12]

c.2380–2290 BC The Amesbury Archer

One of the earliest Beaker burials with gold and copper artefacts takes place, just 3 miles (5km) from Stonehenge. [13]

c.2345–2195 BC The Stonehenge Archer

The body of a man who had been killed by being shot with arrows is buried with a number of objects in the ditch at Stonehenge. [14]

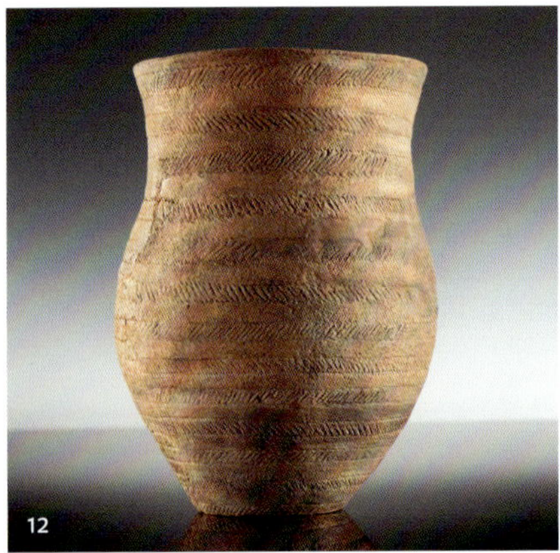
12

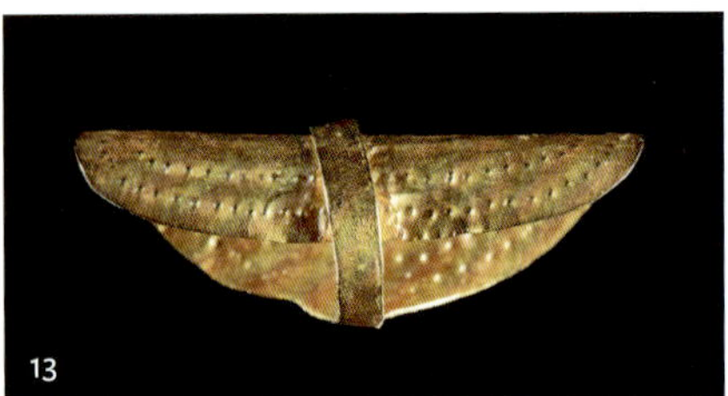
13

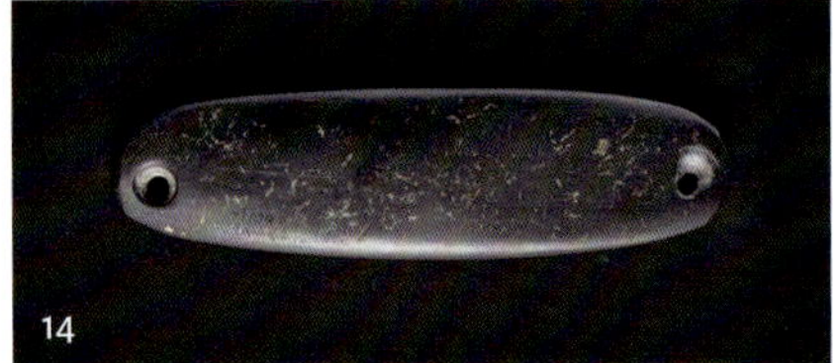
14

EARLY BRONZE AGE (2200–1500 BC)

People rearrange the bluestones at Stonehenge, and begin to build hundreds of barrows in the surrounding landscape.

c.2200–1700 BC Bronze Age barrows

The landscape around Stonehenge is transformed by the construction of hundreds of round burial mounds. [15]

c.2100 BC Bluestones rearranged

The earlier arrangement of the bluestones at Stonehenge – a double bluestone arc – is dismantled, and a circle and oval of bluestones is created. [16]

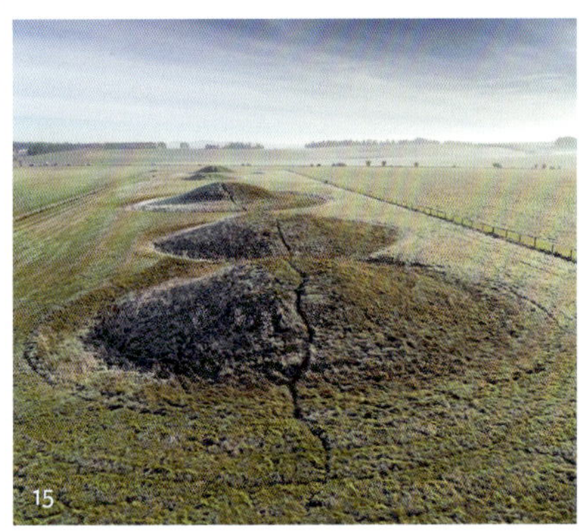
15

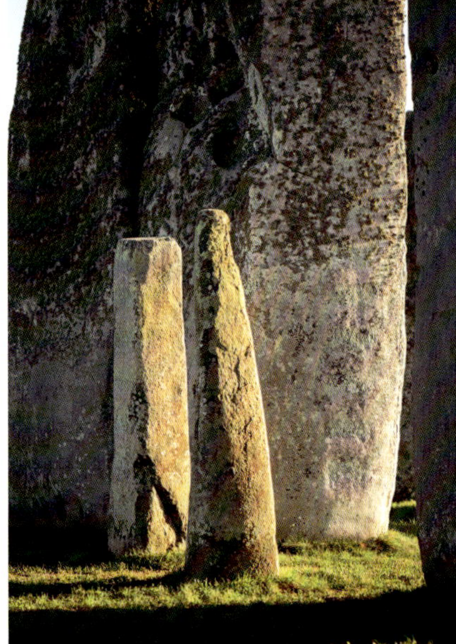
16

c.1800 BC Bush Barrow burial

A man is buried with spectacular gold objects and other artefacts – the richest known burial from prehistoric Britain – in a barrow just 0.6 miles (1km) from Stonehenge. [17]

c.1700 BC Carvings on the Stonehenge stones

Depictions of over 100 axes and a few daggers are carved onto the stones at Stonehenge. [18]

c.1500 BC Field systems and earliest permanent settlements

Field boundaries are laid out and round houses in settlements spring up in the landscape around Stonehenge. [19]

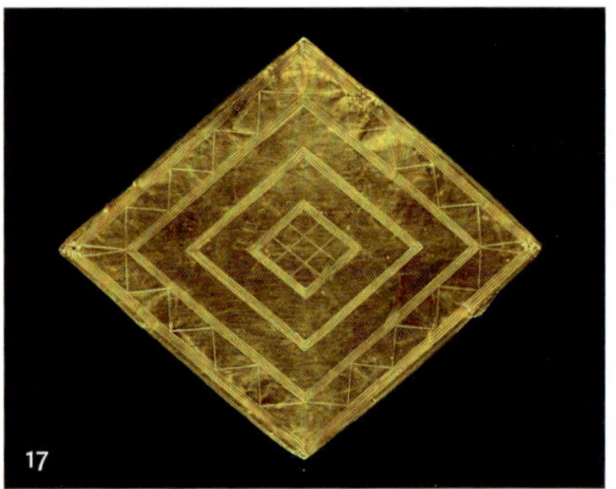
17

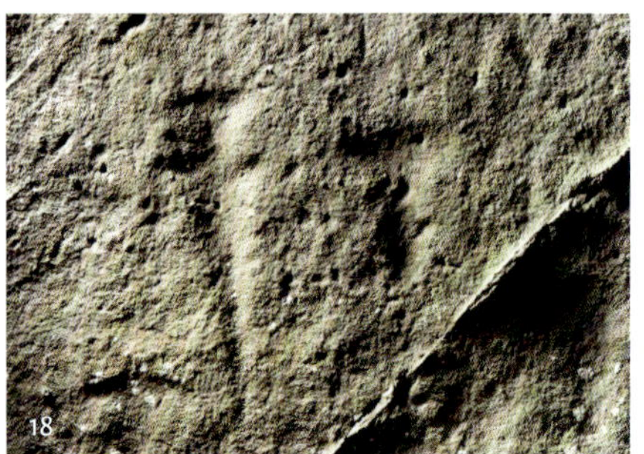
18

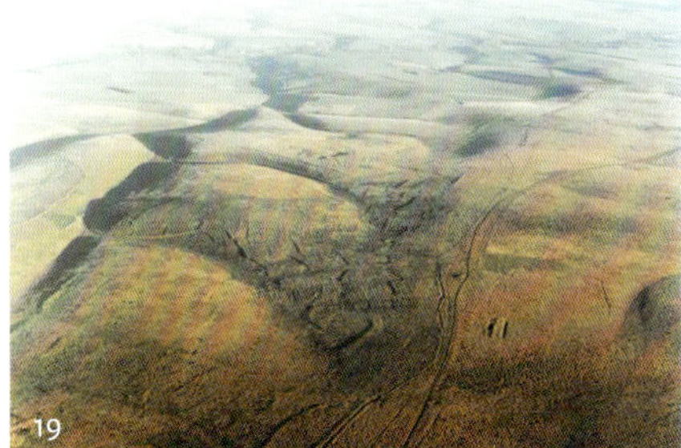
19

LATER PREHISTORY AND ROMAN (1500 BC–AD 400)

Stonehenge is largely abandoned with the wider landscape used for agriculture and small settlements.

c.700 BC Vespasian's Camp

An Iron Age hillfort, now known as Vespasian's Camp, is built just over 1.2 miles (2km) from Stonehenge.

c.AD 200–AD 400 Roman activity at Stonehenge

Roman visitors to Stonehenge leave over 1,500 objects – perhaps offerings – at the site, and dig a deep shaft of unknown purpose within the stone circle. [20]

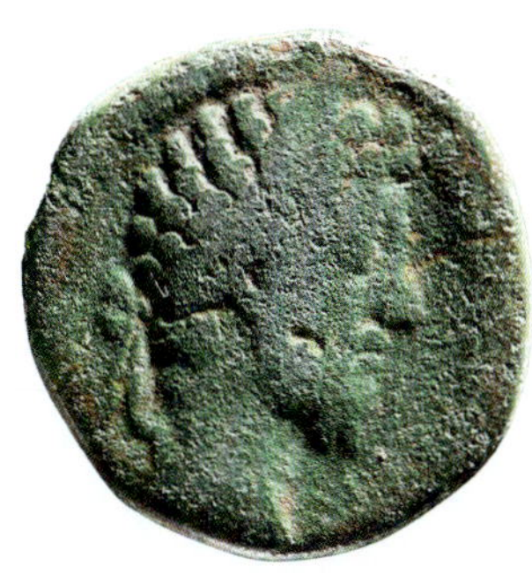

20

EARLY MEDIEVAL AND MEDIEVAL (AD 400–1500)

Stonehenge begins to be associated with myths and tales, and is perhaps used as the burial place for criminals.

c.AD 660–890 Burial of decapitated man

A decapitated man is buried at Stonehenge – perhaps a criminal, or a social outcast?

1136 Origin myths for Stonehenge first recorded

Medieval cleric and chronicler Geoffrey of Monmouth writes the first known origin myth for Stonehenge – a magical tale involving the wizard Merlin. [21]

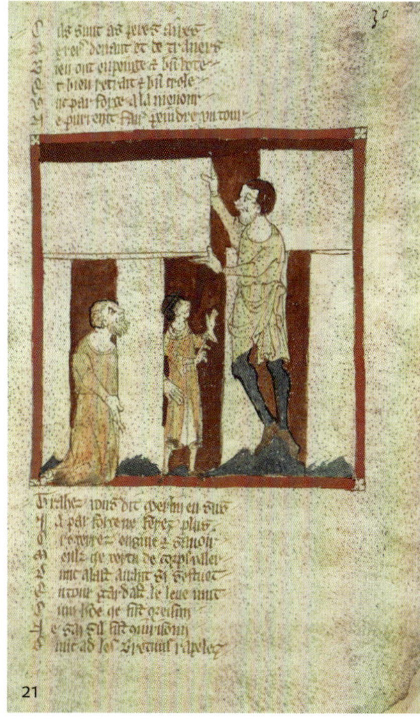

21

1325–1440 Earliest surviving depictions of Stonehenge

All three of the earliest drawings of Stonehenge accompany versions of Geoffrey of Monmouth's mythical story. [22]

c.AD 1200–1600 Sarsens probably broken up for roadstone

Many of the stones at Stonehenge go partly or fully missing, broken up probably for roadstone. [23]

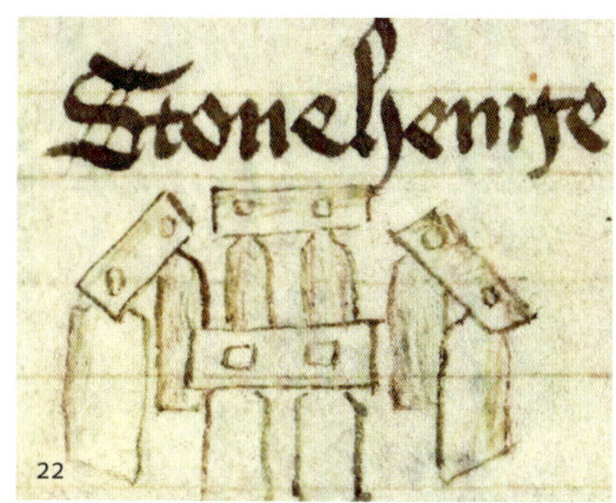

22

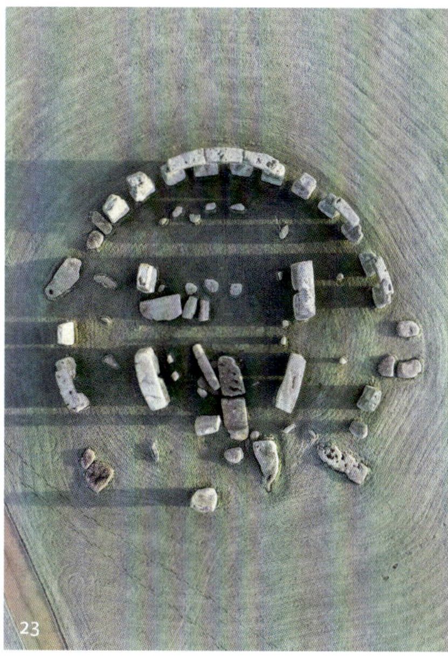

23

EARLY MODERN (1500–1800)

Writers and antiquarians begin to try to explain the origins and purpose of Stonehenge.

c.1560–1850 Early visitors to Stonehenge

People begin to take an interest in Stonehenge, write accounts of their visits and sometimes carve their names into the stones. [24]

1655 Inigo Jones's book published posthumously

The architect Inigo Jones visits Stonehenge and interprets it as a Roman monument. [25]

1666 John Aubrey surveys Stonehenge

The antiquary John Aubrey is one of the first to understand that Stonehenge had been built by prehistoric Britons, and concludes that the Druids were responsible.

c.1720–50 William Stukeley's investigations

The antiquary William Stukeley discovers Stonehenge's solstice alignment, the Avenue and the Greater Cursus. [26]

1780–1850 Friendly societies named after Druids

Friendly societies, inspired by ideas of venerable and ancient Druids, are formed.

1798–1810 William Cunnington and Sir Richard Colt Hoare explore barrows

These antiquaries are fascinated by the barrows in the Stonehenge landscape and together dig more than 450. They discover the famous Bush Barrow burial in 1808. [27]

19TH AND EARLY 20TH CENTURY (1800–1926)

The first restoration works take place at Stonehenge, and tourism increases.

1901 Earliest stone restoration at Stonehenge

The project to stabilise and restore parts of the monument is conceived by architect Detmar Blow, with William Gowland overseeing the excavations. [28]

1905 First Druid ceremony at Stonehenge

Druid groups celebrate for the first time at Stonehenge. Later these societies develop into modern religious Druid groups. [29]

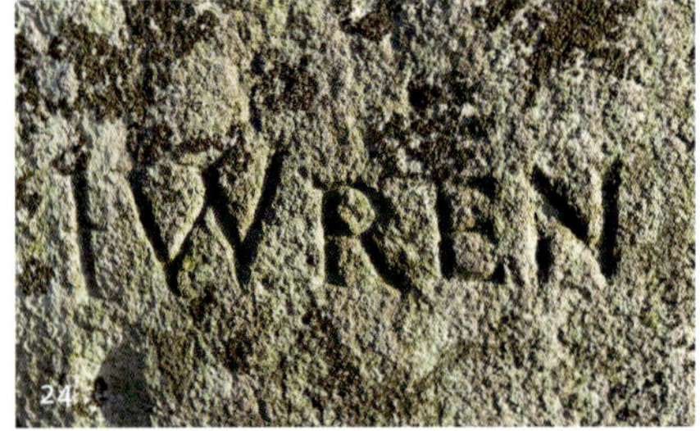

24

25

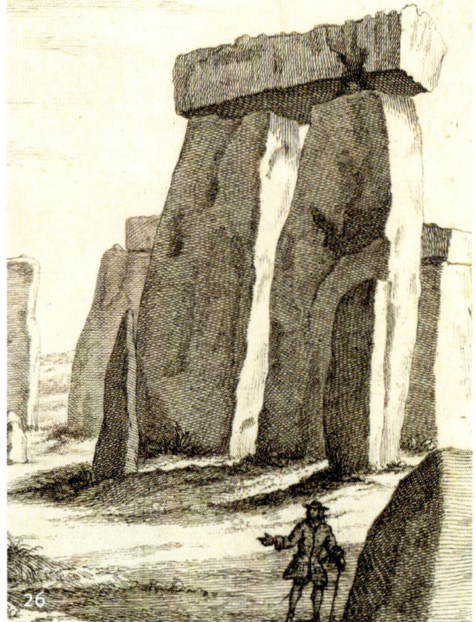
26

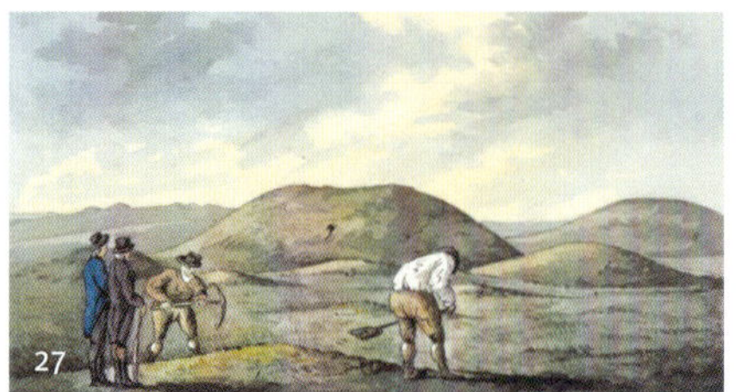
27

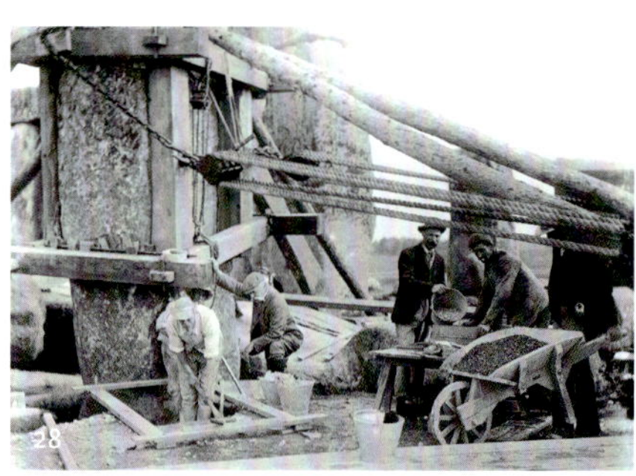
28

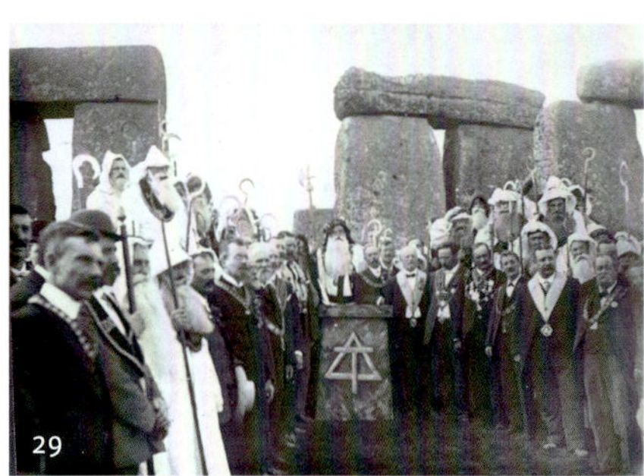
29

1917 Stonehenge aerodrome built

A training school for flying and bombing raids is built just 500m from Stonehenge. [30]

1918 Cecil Chubb gives Stonehenge to the nation

After having purchased it in 1915 for £6,600, Chubb gives Stonehenge to the nation and is awarded a knighthood.

1919–26 Major restoration works and excavations

William Hawley is appointed as archaeologist during major archaeological and stabilising work at Stonehenge. [31]

MODERN (1926–TODAY)

Stonehenge and its landscape have been made more accessible to the public and advances in archaeological and scientific techniques continue to improve our understanding of the monument.

1950–56 Further restoration work by the Ministry of Works

Archaeologists Richard Atkinson, Stuart Piggott and JFS Stone oversee excavations at Stonehenge. [32]

1974–84 Stonehenge Free Festival

The summer solstice becomes a popular time to gather at Stonehenge for live music and alternative living. [33]

1986 Stonehenge becomes a World Heritage Site

Stonehenge is inscribed along with Avebury and their associated sites as a World Heritage Site. [34]

2013 New visitor centre opens

Stonehenge visitor centre is built to provide facilities fit for 1.5 million annual visitors. [35]

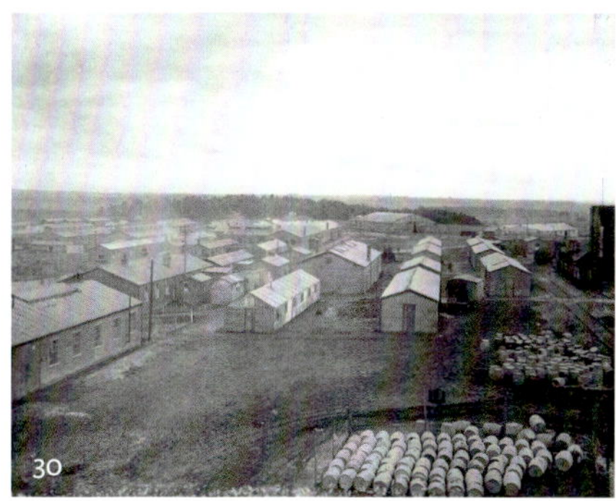
30

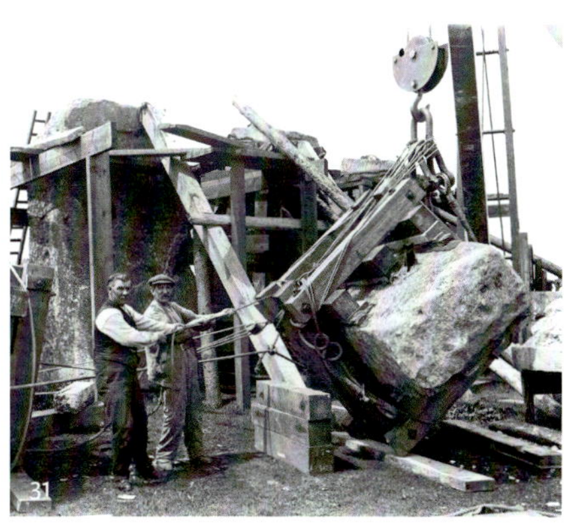
31

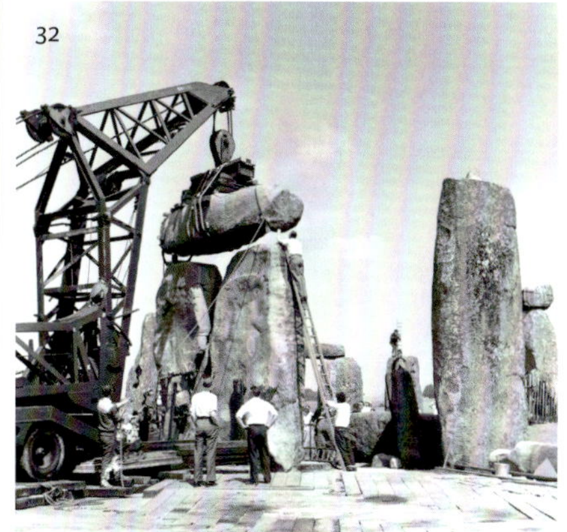
32

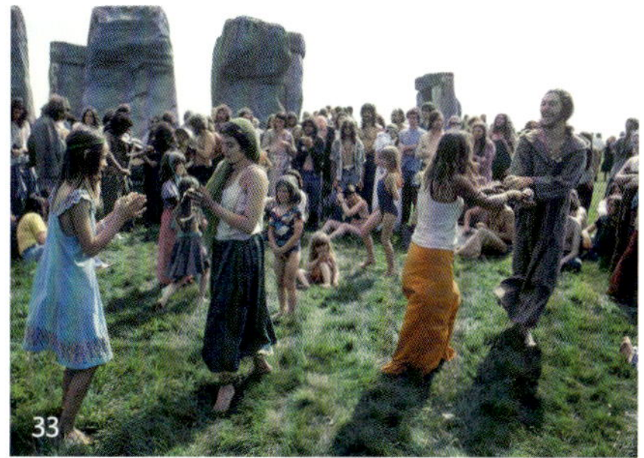
33

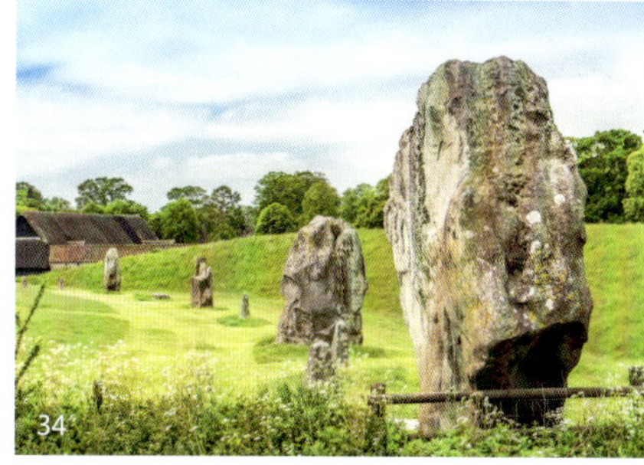
34

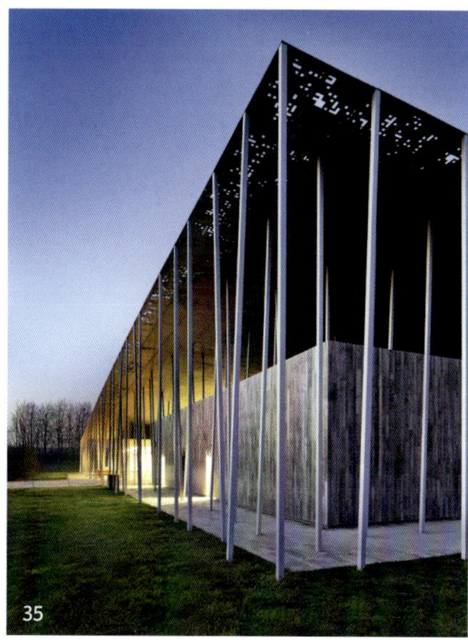
35

SUGGESTED FURTHER READING

B BENDER *Stonehenge: Making Space* (Berg, 1998)

M BOWDEN, S SOUTAR, D FIELD AND M BARBER *The Stonehenge Landscape: Analysing the Stonehenge World Heritage Site* (Historic England, 2015)

R BRADLEY *The Significance of Monuments: On the Shaping of Human Experience in Neolithic and Bronze Age Europe* (Taylor & Francis, 1998)

J BRÜCK *Personifying Prehistory: Relational Ontologies in Bronze Age Britain and Ireland* (Oxford University Press, 2019)

C CHIPPINDALE *Stonehenge Complete* (Thames & Hudson, 2012)

C CONNELLER *The Mesolithic in Britain: Landscape and Society in Times of Change* (Routledge, 2021)

V CUMMINGS *The Neolithic of Britain and Ireland* (Routledge, 2025)

T DARVILL *Stonehenge: The Biography of a Landscape* (History Press, 2006)

D GARROW AND N WILKIN *The World of Stonehenge* (British Museum Press, 2022)

R HILL *Stonehenge* (Profile Books, 2008)

R HUTTON *Blood and Mistletoe: The History of the Druids in Britain* (Yale University Press, 2011)

R HUTTON *Stations of the Sun: A History of the Ritual Year in Britain* (Oxford University Press, 2001)

R JOHNSTON *Bronze Age Worlds: A Social Prehistory of Britain and Ireland* (Routledge, 2021)

AM JONES AND M DÍAZ-GUARDAMINO *Making a Mark: Image and Process in Neolithic Britain and Ireland* (Oxbow Books, 2019)

D MILES *The Tale of the Axe: How the Neolithic Revolution Transformed Britain* (Thames & Hudson, 2021)

M PARKER PEARSON *Stonehenge: Exploring the Greatest Stone Age Mystery* (Simon & Schuster, 2012)

M PITTS *How to Build Stonehenge* (Thames & Hudson, 2022)

F PRYOR *Stonehenge: The Story of a Sacred Landscape* (Bloomsbury, 2016)

K RAY AND J THOMAS *Neolithic Britain: The Transformation of Social Worlds* (Oxford University Press, 2020)

J RICHARDS *Stonehenge: A History in Photographs* (English Heritage, 2014)

J RICHARDS *Stonehenge: The Story so Far* (Historic England, 2017)

C RUGGLES AND A CHADBURN *Stonehenge: Sighting the Sun* (Historic England, 2024)

A WORTHINGTON *Stonehenge: Celebration and Subversion* (Alternative Albion, 2004)

OPPOSITE Stonehenge on a winter's day. The earthworks of the surrounding henge and those of the Avenue, extending into the distance, can still be seen clearly in the low sunlight, more than 4,500 years after they were first made.

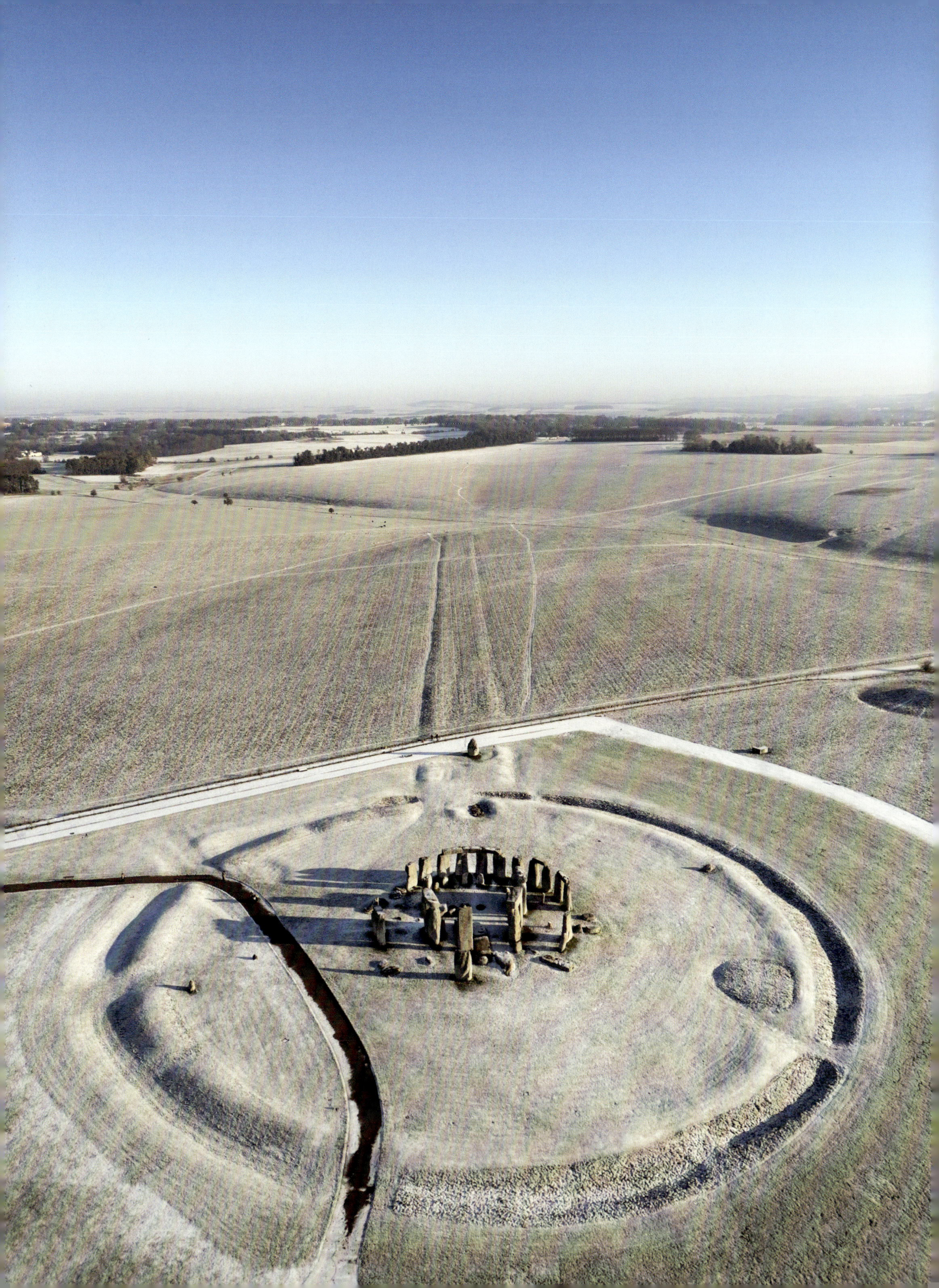

ACKNOWLEDGEMENTS

This book is the culmination of 15 years of researching Stonehenge and its surrounding landscape, a place which constantly reveals itself in new ways. As archaeologist on the team developing the visitor centre (opened 2013), I developed the permanent exhibition and interpretation scheme and later curated a series of temporary exhibitions. During these projects I was ably advised by a panel of experts, including Mike Parker Pearson, Mike Pitts, Ros Cleal, Mike Allen, Clive Ruggles and Julian Richards, as well as the late and much missed John Barrett and Timothy Darvill. Throughout my time at English Heritage, many colleagues individually supported and encouraged my work, but especial thanks go to Paul Pattison, Emma Carver, Amanda Chadburn, Rob Campbell, Melanie Coussens and Heather Sebire.

Following a PhD on Neolithic monument complexes at Cardiff University supervised by Alasdair Whittle and Josh Pollard, within which the Stonehenge landscape formed a major case study, I began as lecturer at University of Exeter in 2022, where I have now had the privilege of teaching the next generation of archaeologists all about Stonehenge.

My editor and friend Jennifer Cryer has shown enormous patience in bringing this book to completion through her careful editing and image research, including noticing the kitten on page 119. Beautiful new photographs gracing many of the pages were taken by the talented Historic England photographer James O Davies and the fold-out reconstruction is the result of many months of work by the brilliant artist Bob Marshall. Thanks are extended to Denis Pellerin for supplying information on the stereoscope image, page 122, and to Mike Pitts for his comments on a draft text; any faults remain firmly my own. Lastly, I'd like to thank my wonderful family who have supported my career since my declaration at the age of seven that I wanted to be an archaeologist.

PICTURE CREDITS

All images are © Historic England Archive unless otherwise stated. Principal photography by James O Davies. Reconstructions by Peter Lorimer: 58–9, 60–61, 79 top, 85; Bob Marshall: 40–41; Drew Smith: 62 top and 147 right top. Other images by kind permission of:

Alamy: 20 (David Lyons), 22 (EVREN KALINBACAK), 23 bottom (serkan senturk), 24 top (Shotshop GmbH), 24 bottom and 25 (Ian Dagnall), 29 right (Susie Kearley), 31 (Will Nichols), 32 bottom (Stephen Shepherd), 43 (Casper Farrell), 53 bottom (Andrew Ray), 63 (National Trust Photolibrary), 69 (Maurice Savage), 104–5 (Walker Art Library), 113 top left (Bryan Mullennix World View), 113 bottom (The Print Collector), 114–15 (PA Images), 134 (PA Images), 135 top and 151 middle bottom (Homer Sykes), 135 bottom (Homer Sykes), 136 (Malcolm Fairman), 138–9 (Mei Choo Teo).

© Ancient Craft/Emma Jones: 44.

Ashmolean Museum: 100 left.

© BBC Archive: 113 top right.

Bibliothèque Municipale Douai: 98 and 149 right top.

The Bodleian Libraries, University of Oxford: 101 (MS Top. gen. c. 24, f.64v).

Brian May Archive of Stereoscopy: 122.

Bridgeman Images: 97 (from the British Library Archive), 99 and 149 middle (from the British Library Archive), 108 (from the British Library Archive), 110 (© Salisbury Museum).

Glenbow Library and Archives Collection, Libraries and Cultural Resources Digital Collections, University of Calgary: 124–5 bottom (asset CU1129561).

Source: Historic England Archive: 7, 39 left, 45 bottom, 105 right and 150 right bottom, 117 top, 118–19 and 151 left bottom, 120, 123 left, 126, 127 and 151 middle top, 128, 159.

© Historic England. English Heritage Trust: 53 top and 151 right top (Mike Lanning), 54–5 and 147 middle top (Tim Rubidge), 56, 130 (Sam Frost), 132–3 (Sam Frost).

© Historic England Archive (from the collection of Martin's Green Museum): 58 left.

© Historic England Archive. Images of objects from the collection of The Salisbury Museum: 17 and 146 middle top, 28, 30, 32 top, 33 left, 33 right and 147 left top, 45 top, 62 all objects, 70 all, 71 all, 72 left, 72 right and 148 left middle, 77 top and 148 left bottom, 77 bottom all, 92 bottom, 94 left and 149 left, 94 right.

© Historic England Archive. Images of objects from the collection of the Wiltshire Museum, Devizes: 57 left, 66 all objects, 68 and 148 left top, 87 all, 88 top and 148 right top, 88 middle and bottom, 89 top, 90 both, 91 all, 92 top, 102–3 and 150 middle top (Source: Historic England Archive), 124 top, 141 top.

Hulton Archive/Stringer/Getty Images: 123 right.

Imperial War Museums: 125 top and 151 left top (MH31416).

Jomon Archives (Kazuno City Board of Education): 23 top.

Lydiard House Museum/Swindon Borough Council: 103 right.

Parker Library, Corpus Christi College Cambridge: 96 (MS 194, f.57r).

Mike Pitts: 15.

© National Maritime Museum, Greenwich, London: 100 right and 150 left bottom.

© National Portrait Gallery, London: 109 top left and top right.

The Salisbury Museum: 76.

Robin Scagell/Science Photo Library: 48–9.

Adam Stanford: 129 right.

Stourhead House © National Trust/David Cousins: 107 bottom right.

Uchytel Studio (Uchytel.com): 14 and 146 left.

Victoria and Albert Museum, London: 111.

Wessex Archaeology: 74, 75 all.

Kelvin Wilson: 89 bottom.

Wiltshire Museum, Devizes: 106–7 and 150 middle bottom, 107 bottom left, 117 bottom and 150 right top.

Yale Center for British Art. Paul Mellon Collection: 112.

Every effort has been made to trace copyright holders and we apologise for any unintentional omission, which we would be pleased to correct in any subsequent edition of the book.

INDEX

Page numbers in *italic* refer to illustrations

OPPOSITE In this photograph of 1894 three visitors lean against the remaining upright of the tallest trilithon, which had tilted to an alarming angle before being restored to vertical at the beginning of the 20th century.

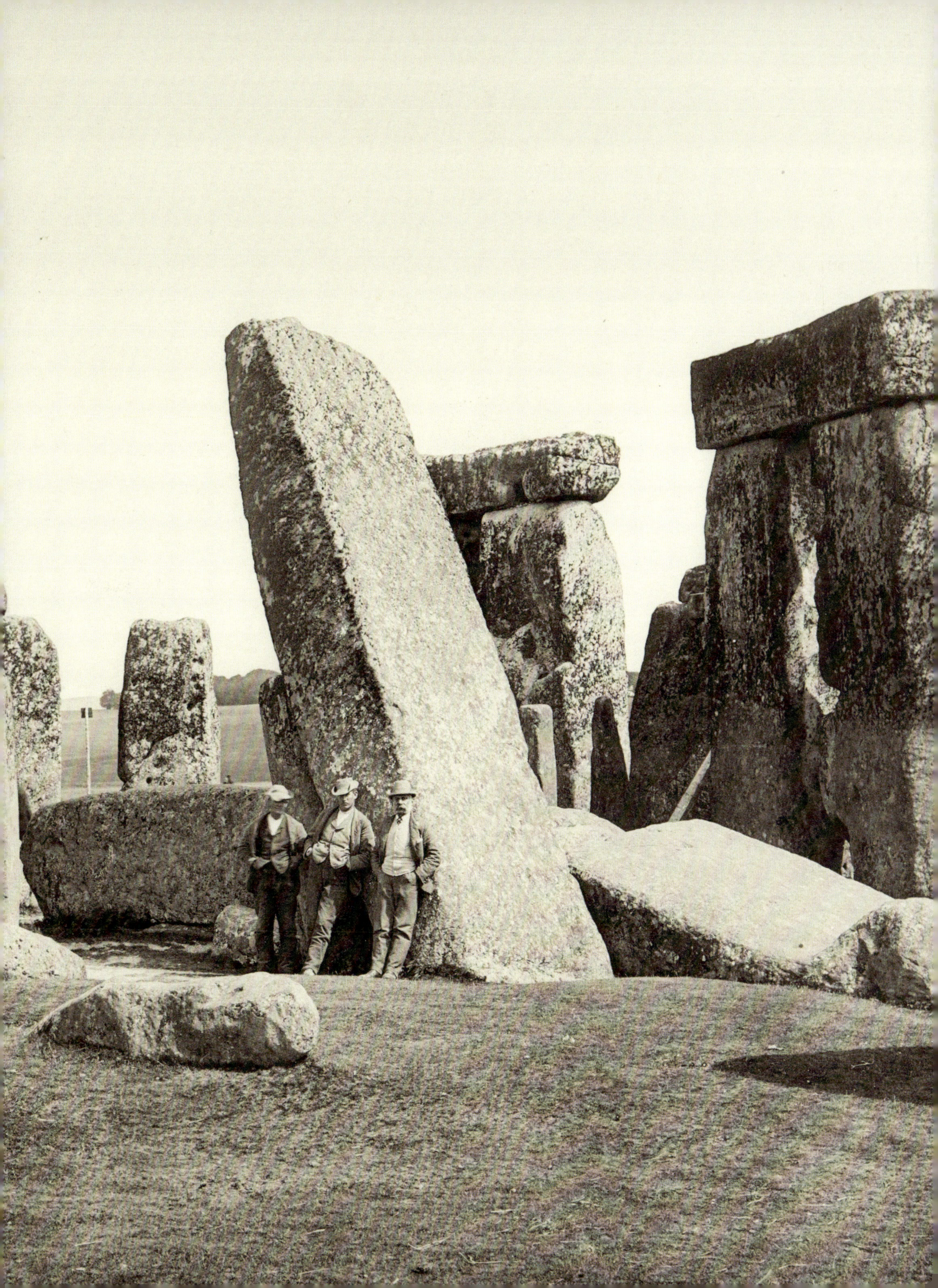

FRONT COVER Stonehenge lit against the night sky. As the earth rotates, the tracks made by the stars across the sky are revealed by the long exposure of the photograph.

INSIDE FRONT COVER Stonehenge at first light on a frosty morning.

FRONTISPIECE A view south-west along the Avenue towards Stonehenge. The parallel banks of this section of the Avenue are aligned perfectly with the summer and winter solstices.

INSIDE BACK COVER The stones silhouetted against the sun.

BACK COVER The uprights and finely carved lintel of one of Stonehenge's surviving trilithons.

100 Wood Street, London, EC2V 7AN
First published by English Heritage 2026

Author: Susan Greaney
Editor: Jennifer Cryer
Designers: Peter Dawson, Ronja Rønning, www.gradedesign.com
Index: Jonathan Eyers

Printed in England by The Pureprint Group

C25 04/26 510323
ISBN 978 1 917564 01 4

The English Heritage Trust is a charity, no.1140351, and a limited company, no.07447221, registered in England and Wales.